Contemporary Readings in
Sociology

THE CONTEMPORARY READINGS SERIES

The new Contemporary Readings Series is unique in undergraduate education. The editors of titles in this series have selected both contemporary journal articles and material from the popular press to create books that are both research focused as well as accessible to introductory students. The journal articles within this series have been carefully edited to ensure that students can easily grasp the concepts discussed while learning from original sources. This, combined with carefully selected magazine and newspaper articles, makes for a practical and informative series of readings.

This new series is inexpensive, interesting, convenient, and stimulating. Each reader offers the latest research tied to the curriculum in an easy-to-use format.

Books in the Contemporary Readings Series to date include:

- Contemporary Readings in Sociology
- Contemporary Readings in Globalization
- Contemporary Readings in Criminology
- Contemporary Readings in Social Problems

Contemporary Readings in
Sociology

Contemporary
CRS
Readings Series

Kathleen Odell Korgen

William Paterson University

Editor

PINE FORGE PRESS
An Imprint of Sage Publications, Inc.
Los Angeles • London • New Delhi • Singapore

For information:

Pine Forge Press
A Sage Publications Company
2455 Teller Road
Thousand Oaks, California 91320
E-mail: order@sagepub.com

Sage Publications Ltd.
1 Oliver's Yard
55 City Road
London EC1Y 1SP
United Kingdom

Sage Publications India Pvt. Ltd.
B 1/I 1 Mohan Cooperative Industrial Area
Mathura Road, New Delhi 110 044
India

Sage Publications Asia-Pacific Pte. Ltd.
33 Pekin Street #02-01
Far East Square
Singapore 048763

Printed in the United States of America.

Library of Congress Cataloging-in-Publication Data

Korgen, Kathleen Odell, 1967-
Contemporary readings in sociology/Kathleen Odell Korgen.
    p. cm.
Includes bibliographical references and index.
ISBN-13: 978-1-4129-4473-1 (pbk.)
    1. Sociology. I. Title.

HM586.K69 2008
301—dc22   2007040186

This book is printed on acid-free paper.

08   09   10   11   12   10   9   8   7   6   5   4   3   2   1

Acquisitions Editor:	Benjamin Penner
Editorial Assistant:	Nancy Scrofano
Production Editor:	Tracy Buyan
Typesetter:	C&M Digitals (P) Ltd.
Proofreader:	Paulette McGee
Indexer:	Joan Shapiro
Cover Designer:	Candice Harman
Marketing Manager:	Jennifer Reed Banando

CONTENTS

TOPICS GUIDE

This topics guide is designed to help instructors easily integrate these excellent and contemporary readings into their courses. This brief guide also helps instructors and students find interrelated articles, which can help support both learning and research.

AGENTS OF SOCIALIZATION

Differences between Actual and Perceived Student Norms: An Examination of Alcohol Use, Drug Use, and Sexual Behavior; The Influence of Friendship Groups on Intellectual Self-Confidence and Educational Aspirations; Student Disengagement and the Socialization Styles of High Schools; Multiple Masculinities? Teenage Boys Talk about Jocks and Gender; William Wants a Doll. Can He Have One?; Feminists, Care Advisors, and Gender-Neutral Child Rearing; Sociology of Terrorism; Making Theological Sense of the Migration Journey From Latin America: Catholic, Protestant, and Interfaith Perspectives; Culture Jamming: A Sociological Perspective

BUREAUCRACY

Circles of Influence and Chains of Command: The Social Process Whereby Ethnic Communities Influence Host Societies; Hate Crime Reporting as a Successful Social Movement Outcome

COUNTERCULTURE

Sociology of Terrorism

CRIME

Reconsidering Peers and Delinquency: How Do Peers Matter?; Exposure to Community Violence and Childhood Delinquency; Mass Imprisonment and the Life Course: Race and Inequality in U.S. Incarceration; Hate Crime Reporting as a Successful Social Movement Outcome

CRIMINAL JUSTICE SYSTEM

Mass Imprisonment and the Life Course: Race and Inequality in U.S. Incarceration; Hate Crime Reporting as a Successful Social Movement Outcome

CULTURE

Elites, Masses, and Media Blacklists: The Dixie Chicks Controversy; Political Culture and the Death Penalty; Reconsidering Peers and Delinquency: How Do Peers Matter?; Talk of Class: The Discursive Repertoires of White Working- and Upper-Middle-Class College Students; A Place in Town: Doing Class in a Coffee Shop; Professorial Capital: Blue-Collar Reflections on Class, Culture, and the Academy; Circles of Influence and Chains of Command: The Social Process Whereby Ethnic Communities Influence Host Societies; Divorce Culture and Marital Gender

Equality; "I'm Not Thinking of It as Sexual Harassment": Understanding Harassment across Race and Citizenship; Multiple Masculinities? Teenage Boys Talk about Jocks and Gender; Feminists, Child Care Advisors, and Gender-Neutral Child Rearing; Glocommodification: How the Global Consumes the Local—McDonald's in Israel; Making Theological Sense of the Migration Journey From Latin America: Catholic, Protestant, and Interfaith Perspectives; Culture Jamming: A Sociological Perspective

CULTURAL DIVERSITY

Elites, Masses, and Media Blacklists: The Dixie Chicks Controversy; Political Culture and the Death Penalty; Talk of Class: The Discursive Repertoires of White Working- and Upper-Middle-Class College Students; Professorial Capital: Blue-Collar Reflections on Class, Culture, and the Academy; College Access, K–12 Concentrated Disadvantage, and the Next 25 Years of Education Research; Circles of Influence and Chains of Command: The Social Process Whereby Ethnic Communities Influence Host Societies; Divorce Culture and Marital Gender Equality; "I'm Not Thinking of It as Sexual Harassment": Understanding Harassment across Race and Citizenship; Glocommodification: How the Global Consumes the Local—McDonald's in Israel; Making Theological Sense of the Migration Journey From Latin America: Catholic, Protestant, and Interfaith Perspectives; Culture Jamming: A Sociological Perspective

DE-INDUSTRIALIZATION

Unmarried with Children; Mass Imprisonment and the Life Course: Race and Inequality in U.S. Incarceration; Corporate Citizenship and Social Responsibility in a Globalized World

DEVIANCE

Authentic Identities: Straightedge Subcultures, Music, and the Internet; Elites, Masses, and Media Blacklists: The Dixie Chicks Controversy; Political Culture and the Death Penalty; Social Capital, Too Much of a Good Thing? American Religious Traditions and Community Crime; Reconsidering Peers and Delinquency: How Do Peers Matter?; Bullies Move Beyond the Schoolyard: A Preliminary Look at Cyberbullying; Professorial Capital: Blue-Collar Reflections on Class, Culture, and the Academy; Multiple Masculinities? Teenage Boys Talk about Jocks and Gender; William Wants a Doll. Can He Have One? Feminists, Child Care Advisors, and Gender-Neutral Child Rearing; Sociology of Terrorism; Hate Crime Reporting as a Successful Social Movement Outcome; Culture Jamming: A Sociological Perspective

DISCRIMINATION

When Fiends Become Friends: The Need to Belong and Perceptions of Personal and Group Discrimination; Unmarried with Children; Mass Imprisonment and the Life Course: Race and Inequality in U.S. Incarceration; Professorial Capital: Blue-Collar Reflections on Class, Culture, and the Academy; Race as Class; A Distorted Nation: Perceptions of Racial/Ethnic Group Sizes and Attitudes Toward Immigrants and Other Minorities; College Access, K–12 Concentrated Disadvantage, and the Next 25 Years of Education Research; I Just Want to Play: Women, Sexism, and Persistence in Golf; "I'm Not Thinking of It as Sexual Harassment": Understanding Harassment across Race and Citizenship; Making Theological Sense of the Migration Journey From Latin America: Catholic, Protestant, and Interfaith Perspectives; Hate Crime Reporting as a Successful Social Movement Outcome

GENDER ROLES

Unmarried with Children; Divorce Culture and Marital Gender Equality; "I'm Not Thinking of It as Sexual Harassment": Understanding Harassment across Race and Citizenship; Multiple Masculinities? Teenage Boys Talk about Jocks and Gender; William Wants a Doll. Can He Have One? Feminists, Child Care Advisors, and Gender-Neutral Child Rearing

GLOBAL INEQUALITY

Sociology of Terrorism; "In the Court of Public Opinion": Transnational Problem Construction in the HIV/AIDS Medicine Access Campaign, 1998–2001; Making Theological Sense of the Migration Journey From Latin America: Catholic, Protestant, and Interfaith Perspectives; Culture Jamming: A Sociological Perspective; Corporate Citizenship and Social Responsibility in a Globalized World

GLOBALIZATION

Sociology of Terrorism; Glocommodification: How the Global Consumes the Local— McDonald's in Israel; "In the Court of Public Opinion": Transnational Problem Construction in the HIV/AIDS Medicine Access Campaign, 1998–2001; Culture Jamming: A Sociological Perspective; Corporate Citizenship and Social Responsibility in a Globalized World

GLOBAL WARMING

Free-Market Ideology and Environmental Degradation: The Case of Belief in Global Climate Change

GROUPS

The Influence of Friendship Groups on Intellectual Self-Confidence and Educational Aspirations; Authentic Identities: Straightedge Subcultures, Music, and the Internet; Elites, Masses, and Media Blacklists: The Dixie Chicks Controversy; Socioeconomic Inequality in the American Religious System; Social Capital, Too Much of a Good Thing? American Religious Traditions and Community Crime; Reconsidering Peers and Delinquency: How Do Peers Matter?; A Place in Town: Doing Class in a Coffee Shop; College Access, K–12 Concentrated Disadvantage, and the Next 25 Years of Education Research; Circles of Influence and Chains of Command: The Social Process Whereby Ethnic Communities Influence Host Societies; Sociology of Terrorism

IDEOLOGY

Elites, Masses, and Media Blacklists: The Dixie Chicks Controversy; Sociology of Terrorism; Free-Market Ideology and Environmental Degradation: The Case of Belief in Global Climate Change; Making Theological Sense of the Migration Journey From Latin America: Catholic, Protestant, and Interfaith Perspectives

ILLEGAL IMMIGRATION

"I'm Not Thinking of It as Sexual Harassment": Understanding Harassment across Race and Citizenship; Making Theological Sense of the Migration Journey From Latin America: Catholic, Protestant, and Interfaith Perspectives

and the Life Course: Race and Inequality in U.S. Incarceration; Talk of Class: The Discursive Repertoires of White Working- and Upper-Middle-Class College Students; A Place in Town: Doing Class in a Coffee Shop; Professorial Capital: Blue-Collar Reflections on Class, Culture, and the Academy; Divorce Culture and Marital Gender Equality; I Just Want to Play: Women, Sexism, and Persistence in Golf; "I'm Not Thinking of It as Sexual Harassment": Understanding Harassment across Race and Citizenship; Multiple Masculinities? Teenage Boys Talk about Jocks and Gender; William Wants a Doll. Can He Have One? Feminists, Child Care Advisors, and Gender-Neutral Child Rearing; Sociology of Terrorism; Culture Jamming: A Sociological Perspective

ORGANIZED PEOPLE

Authentic Identities: Straightedge Subcultures, Music, and the Internet; Elites, Masses, and Media Blacklists: The Dixie Chicks Controversy; Circles of Influence and Chains of Command: The Social Process Whereby Ethnic Communities Influence Host Societies; Sociology of Terrorism; Free-Market Ideology and Environmental Degradation: The Case of Belief in Global Climate Change; "In the Court of Public Opinion": Transnational Problem Construction in the HIV/AIDS Medicine Access Campaign, 1998–2001; Making Theological Sense of the Migration Journey From Latin America: Catholic, Protestant, and Interfaith Perspectives; Hate Crime Reporting as a Successful Social Movement Outcome; Culture Jamming: A Sociological Perspective; Corporate Citizenship and Social Responsibility in a Globalized World

PEER GROUP

Differences between Actual and Perceived Student Norms: An Examination of Alcohol Use, Drug Use, and Sexual Behavior; The Influence of Friendship Groups on Intellectual Self-Confidence and Educational Aspirations; Authentic Identities: Straightedge Subcultures, Music, and the Internet; Reconsidering Peers and Delinquency: How Do Peers Matter?; Bullies Move Beyond the Schoolyard: A Preliminary Look at Cyberbullying; Mass Imprisonment and the Life Course: Race and Inequality in U.S. Incarceration; Talk of Class: The Discursive Repertoires of White Working- and Upper-Middle-Class College Students; A Place in Town: Doing Class in a Coffee Shop; Professorial Capital: Blue-Collar Reflections on Class, Culture, and the Academy; Multiple Masculinities? Teenage Boys Talk about Jocks and Gender

PREJUDICE

When Fiends Become Friends: The Need to Belong and Perceptions of Personal and Group Discrimination; Unmarried with Children; Mass Imprisonment and the Life Course: Race and Inequality in U.S. Incarceration; A Place in Town: Doing Class in a Coffee Shop; Professorial Capital: Blue-Collar Reflections on Class, Culture, and the Academy; Race as Class; A Distorted Nation: Perceptions of Racial/Ethnic Group Sizes and Attitudes toward Immigrants and Other Minorities; College Access, K–12 Concentrated Disadvantage, and the Next 25 Years of Education Research; I Just Want to Play: Women, Sexism, and Persistence in Golf; Multiple Masculinities? Teenage Boys Talk about Jocks and Gender; Sociology of Terrorism; Hate Crime Reporting as a Successful Social Movement Outcome

RACIAL CLASSIFICATIONS

Race as Class; A Distorted Nation: Perceptions of Racial/Ethnic Group Sizes and Attitudes toward Immigrants and Other Minorities; College Access, K–12 Concentrated Disadvantage, and the Next 25 Years of Education Research

Race and Ethnicity

When Fiends Become Friends: The Need to Belong and Perceptions of Personal and Group Discrimination; Unmarried with Children; Mass Imprisonment and the Life Course: Race and Inequality in U.S. Incarceration; Race as Class; A Distorted Nation: Perceptions of Racial/Ethnic Group Sizes and Attitudes toward Immigrants and Other Minorities; College Access, K–12 Concentrated Disadvantage, and the Next 25 Years of Education Research; Circles of Influence and Chains of Command: The Social Process Whereby Ethnic Communities Influence Host Societies; "I'm Not Thinking of It as Sexual Harassment": Understanding Harassment across Race and Citizenship; Hate Crime Reporting as a Successful Social Movement Outcome

Roles

The Influence of Friendship Groups on Intellectual Self-Confidence and Educational Aspirations; Authentic Identities: Straightedge Subcultures, Music, and the Internet; Unmarried with Children; Political Culture and the Death Penalty; Reconsidering Peers and Delinquency: How Do Peers Matter?; Talk of Class: The Discursive Repertoires of White Working- and Upper-Middle-Class College Students; A Place in Town: Doing Class in a Coffee Shop; Professorial Capital: Blue-Collar Reflections on Class, Culture, and the Academy; Divorce Culture and Marital Gender Equality; I Just Want to Play: Women, Sexism, and Persistence in Golf; Multiple Masculinities? Teenage Boys Talk about Jocks and Gender; William Wants a Doll. Can He Have One? Feminists, Child Care Advisors, and Gender-Neutral Child Rearing

Sanctions

Authentic Identities: Straightedge Subcultures, Music, and the Internet; Elites, Masses, and Media Blacklists: The Dixie Chicks Controversy; Political Culture and the Death Penalty; Professorial Capital: Blue-Collar Reflections on Class, Culture, and the Academy; I Just Want to Play: Women, Sexism, and Persistence in Golf; "I'm Not Thinking of It as Sexual Harassment": Understanding Harassment across Race and Citizenship; Multiple Masculinities? Teenage Boys Talk about Jocks and Gender; Sociology of Terrorism; "In the Court of Public Opinion": Transnational Problem Construction in the HIV/AIDS Medicine Access Campaign, 1998–2001; Hate Crime Reporting as a Successful Social Movement Outcome

Schools

Differences between Actual and Perceived Student Norms: An Examination of Alcohol Use, Drug Use, and Sexual Behavior; The Influence of Friendship Groups on Intellectual Self-Confidence and Educational Aspirations; Student Disengagement and the Socialization Styles of High Schools; Bullies Move Beyond the Schoolyard: A Preliminary Look at Cyberbullying; Mass Imprisonment and the Life Course: Race and Inequality in U.S. Incarceration; Talk of Class: The Discursive Repertoires of White Working- and Upper-Middle-Class College Students; Professorial Capital: Blue-Collar Reflections on Class, Culture, and the Academy; College Access, K–12 Concentrated Disadvantage, and the Next 25 Years of Education Research; Multiple Masculinities? Teenage Boys Talk about Jocks and Gender

Self-Identity

When Fiends Become Friends: The Need to Belong and Perceptions of Personal and Group Discrimination; The Influence of Friendship Groups on Intellectual Self-Confidence and Educational Aspirations; Authentic Identities: Straightedge Subcultures, Music, and the Internet; Student Disengagement and the Socialization Styles of High Schools; Reconsidering Peers and

and Educational Aspirations; Unmarried with Children; Student Disengagement and the Socialization Styles of High Schools; Elites, Masses, and Media Blacklists: The Dixie Chicks Controversy; Reconsidering Peers and Delinquency: How Do Peers Matter?; Mass Imprisonment and the Life Course: Race and Inequality in U.S. Incarceration; Talk of Class: The Discursive Repertoires of White Working- and Upper-Middle-Class College Students; A Place in Town: Doing Class in a Coffee Shop; Professorial Capital: Blue-Collar Reflections on Class, Culture, and the Academy; Race as Class; I Just Want to Play: Women, Sexism, and Persistence in Golf; "I'm Not Thinking of It as Sexual Harassment": Understanding Harassment across Race and Citizenship; Multiple Masculinities? Teenage Boys Talk about Jocks and Gender; William Wants a Doll. Can He Have One? Feminists, Child Care Advisors, and Gender-Neutral Child Rearing; Making Theological Sense of the Migration Journey From Latin America: Catholic, Protestant, and Interfaith Perspectives; Culture Jamming: A Sociological Perspective

SOCIAL MOVEMENTS

Elites, Masses, and Media Blacklists: The Dixie Chicks Controversy; William Wants a Doll. Can He Have One? Feminists, Child Care Advisors, and Gender-Neutral Child Rearing; "In the Court of Public Opinion": Transnational Problem Construction in the HIV/AIDS Medicine Access Campaign, 1998–2001; Making Theological Sense of the Migration Journey From Latin America: Catholic, Protestant, and Interfaith Perspectives; Hate Crime Reporting as a Successful Social Movement Outcome; Corporate Citizenship and Social Responsibility in a Globalized World

SOCIAL STRATIFICATION

Unmarried with Children; Student Disengagement and the Socialization Styles of High Schools; Reconsidering Peers and Delinquency: How Do Peers Matter?; Mass Imprisonment and the Life Course: Race and Inequality in U.S. Incarceration; Talk of Class: The Discursive Repertoires of White Working- and Upper-Middle-Class College Students; A Place in Town: Doing Class in a Coffee Shop; Professorial Capital: Blue-Collar Reflections on Class, Culture, and the Academy; Race as Class; College Access, K–12 Concentrated Disadvantage, and the Next 25 Years of Education Research; Circles of Influence and Chains of Command: The Social Process Whereby Ethnic Communities Influence Host Societies; Divorce Culture and Marital Gender Equality; I Just Want to Play: Women, Sexism, and Persistence in Golf; "I'm Not Thinking of It as Sexual Harassment": Understanding Harassment across Race and Citizenship; Sociology of Terrorism; "In the Court of Public Opinion": Transnational Problem Construction in the HIV/AIDS Medicine Access Campaign, 1998–2001; Making Theological Sense of the Migration Journey From Latin America: Catholic, Protestant, and Interfaith Perspectives; Hate Crime Reporting as a Successful Social Movement Outcome; Corporate Citizenship and Social Responsibility in a Globalized World

SOCIAL STRUCTURE

Unmarried with Children; Student Disengagement and the Socialization Styles of High Schools; Elites, Masses, and Media Blacklists: The Dixie Chicks Controversy; Social Capital, Too Much of a Good Thing? American Religious Traditions and Community Crime; Mass Imprisonment and the Life Course: Race and Inequality in U.S. Incarceration; Talk of Class: The Discursive Repertoires of White Working- and Upper-Middle-Class College Students; Professorial Capital: Blue-Collar Reflections on Class, Culture, and the Academy; Race as Class; Circles of Influence and Chains of Command: The Social Process Whereby Ethnic Communities Influence Host Societies; Divorce Culture and Marital Gender Equality; I Just Want to Play: Women, Sexism, and Persistence in Golf; Glocommodification: How the Global Consumes the Local—McDonald's in Israel

STATUS

When Fiends Become Friends: The Need to Belong and Perceptions of Personal and Group Discrimination; The Influence of Friendship Groups on Intellectual Self-Confidence and Educational Aspirations; Authentic Identities: Straightedge Subcultures, Music, and the Internet; Unmarried with Children; Mass Imprisonment and the Life Course: Race and Inequality in U.S. Incarceration; Talk of Class: The Discursive Repertoires of White Working- and Upper-Middle-Class College Students; A Place in Town: Doing Class in a Coffee Shop; Professorial Capital: Blue-Collar Reflections on Class, Culture, and the Academy; Race as Class; College Access, K–12 Concentrated Disadvantage, and the Next 25 Years of Education Research; Circles of Influence and Chains of Command: The Social Process Whereby Ethnic Communities Influence Host Societies; Divorce Culture and Marital Gender Equality; I Just Want to Play: Women, Sexism, and Persistence in Golf; "I'm Not Thinking of It as Sexual Harassment": Understanding Harassment across Race and Citizenship; Multiple Masculinities? Teenage Boys Talk about Jocks and Gender

SUBCULTURE

Differences between Actual and Perceived Student Norms: An Examination of Alcohol Use, Drug Use, and Sexual Behavior; The Influence of Friendship Groups on Intellectual Self-Confidence and Educational Aspirations; Authentic Identities: Straightedge Subcultures, Music, and the Internet; Unmarried with Children; Student Disengagement and the Socialization Styles of High Schools; Elites, Masses, and Media Blacklists: The Dixie Chicks Controversy; Political Culture and the Death Penalty; Social Capital, Too Much of a Good Thing? American Religious Traditions and Community Crime; Reconsidering Peers and Delinquency: How Do Peers Matter?; A Place in Town: Doing Class in a Coffee Shop; Professorial Capital: Blue-Collar Reflections on Class, Culture, and the Academy; Circles of Influence and Chains of Command: The Social Process Whereby Ethnic Communities Influence Host Societies; "I'm Not Thinking of It as Sexual Harassment": Understanding Harassment across Race and Citizenship; Multiple Masculinities? Teenage Boys Talk about Jocks and Gender; Making Theological Sense of the Migration Journey From Latin America: Catholic, Protestant, and Interfaith Perspectives; Hate Crime Reporting as a Successful Social Movement Outcome; Culture Jamming: A Sociological Perspective

TERRORISM

Sociology of Terrorism

ADVISORY BOARD

ABOUT THE EDITOR

Kathleen Odell Korgen, Ph.D., is Professor of Sociology at William Paterson University in Wayne, New Jersey. Her primary areas of specialization are race relations, racial identity, and public sociology. Professor Korgen's published work on race relations and racial identity includes *Crossing the Racial Divide: Close Friendships Between Black and White Americans* (Praeger, 2002) and *From Black to Biracial: Transforming Racial Identity Among Americans* (Praeger, 1998, 1999). Her most recent work on public sociology is *The Engaged Sociologist: Connecting the Classroom to the Community* (with Jonathan White, Pine Forge, 2007). Raised in Massachusetts, Professor Korgen now lives in Montclair, New Jersey, with her husband Jeff, daughters Julie and Jessica, and mother Patricia.

PREFACE

Have you ever wondered why so many college students drink, do drugs, and have sex? Have you ever pondered why inequality is increasing or how social change efforts can be effectively organized? Or, have you ever thought about why professors tend to write in a way only fellow professors can readily understand. If so, you've opened the right book.

These questions and myriad other issues related to how individuals interact with one another and with society are addressed in the following pages. *Contemporary Readings in Sociology* provides a carefully chosen selection of excellent, highly readable articles dealing with the major topics covered in the field of sociology. Once you've finished reading this book, you will have increased your knowledge about key issues in our society and learned how sociology helps us understand and address these issues.

Sociologists recognize that individuals both shape and are shaped by larger social forces. By examining society though a *sociological eye*[1] (looking beneath the surface of social interactions), it is possible to recognize how society really works. By using the sociological eye, sociologists make connections among the patterns in everyday events that the average person might not notice. In doing so, we can understand how different organizations, institutions and societies function.

The sociological eye enables us to recognize how social forces shape individual lives and ideas, and, in turn, how individuals shape organizations and institutions. Using the sociological eye, we can notice when persistent patterns work to create advantages or disadvantages for certain groups in society. For example, by looking beneath the surface of government operations, we can recognize patterns in the types of people to whom office holders are most likely to respond (e.g., those with money, influence over organized groups of voters, or personal connections to the office holders). Recognizing how society operates is essential if we are interested in trying to influence it.

In order to understand how we might shape society, we must also first realize how we are affected by it. Sociology enables us to understand how our individual lives are connected to current and past events in our society. C. Wright Mills described this aspect of sociology as the *sociological imagination.*[2] When we can relate personal troubles to public issues, connecting our individual lives to what's happening in our society, we are using the sociological imagination.

For example, if you are concerned about how you are going to pay for your college education, that's a personal trouble. However, using the sociological imagination, you can relate your personal financial worries to the fact that higher education costs have skyrocketed over the past decade all across the United States. The high cost of higher education is a public issue that has societal ramifications. It must be dealt with at the state and national levels, rather than by individuals, alone.

The authors of the articles in this book show exemplary use of both the sociological eye and the sociological imagination. Through their careful data collection and analyses and use of various theoretical perspectives, they recognize and explain patterns of behavior that others may not notice or be able to make sense of, if they do notice them. Together, the articles in this book provide an overview of the field of sociology and provide examples of the best current research on sociological issues, covering a wide range of theoretical perspectives and methodologies.

After reading *Contemporary Readings in Sociology,* you will have a more focused sociological eye, a broadened sociological imagination, and a greater ability and desire to use them both. You may even want to become a sociologist, yourself! In any event, this reader will help you gain a deeper understanding of contemporary issues in the field of sociology and an increased appreciation for the field itself.

NOTES

1. Collins, Randall. 1998. "The Sociological Eye and Its Blinders." *Contemporary Sociology 27*(1):2–7.
2. Mills, C. Wright. 1967. *The Sociological Imagination*. New York: Oxford University Press.

PART I

CULTURE AND SOCIAL INTERACTION

Whether consciously or not, we rely on culture for our sense of self-identity and in almost everything we do. The articles selected for Part I look at the influence of culture on our society, the groups we belong to, and our individual lives. They also reveal how we construct and change culture. Together, they provide clear examples of the influence of norms, beliefs, subcultures, and some of our primary socializing agents on various aspects of society and on individuals.

Everyone wants to feel they belong and are accepted by other members of society. No one wants to be rejected. In "When Fiends Become Friends: The Need to Belong and Perceptions of Personal and Group Discrimination," Mauricio Carvallo and Brett W. Pelham show that our need to belong impacts our ability to recognize when we are victims of discrimination. While our need to feel socially accepted does not affect our ability to observe general discrimination against a group of which we are a part, being personally discriminated against does harm our sense of belonging. Therefore, we are less likely to notice and report personal discrimination.

Every subculture has its own norms. However, sometimes the perceived norms do not accurately reflect the true behavior of members of the group. In "Differences between Actual and Perceived Student Norms: An Examination of Alcohol Use, Drug Use, and Sexual Behavior" Matthew P. Martens and his co-authors reveal that college students overestimate how much their fellow students drink, use drugs, and engage in sexual activity. Informing students of the real levels of these activities will decrease the likelihood that they will drink, use drugs, or have sex. When such behavior is not seen as the norm, fewer students will engage in it.

In "The Influence of Friendship Groups on Intellectual Self-Confidence and Educational Aspirations in College," Anthony Lising Antonio points out that, if we want to understand the impact of peers on college student development, we need to focus on the influence of the peers with whom college students interact the most (rather than the entire student body). People tend to be most influenced by those they interact with on a regular basis. So, Antonio argues that we should be examining subgroups of college friends, rather than relying on surveys of large populations of college students when we try to understand the impact of college on students' self-concepts and educational success.

Our own identity often comes from our sense of belonging. Subcultures provide a sense of community for their members and shape how members view themselves. While most subculture communities have relied on face-to-face interaction to establish a sense of group identity, the Internet now provides a medium for people who may never meet one another to form and support a sense of subcultural identity. In "Authentic Identities: Straightedge Subcultures, Music, and the Internet," Patrick Williams looks at this phenomenon and the sometimes negative reactions to it in the anti-apathy and anti-drugs straightedge subculture.

As you read the articles in this section, keep in mind the following points:

- Culture is socially constructed and, therefore, varies over time and from society to society.
- Subcultures have generally relied on face-to-face interaction to form communities. However, the Internet offers a new way for subcultures to form and for members to interact with one another.
- We all want to feel as though we are socially accepted. This desire can impact our ability to recognize when we are being discriminated against.
- A society's norms guide behavior in a society.
- Even our moods are guided by the norms for acceptable levels of happiness, unhappiness, optimism, etc.
- Our cultural values and beliefs influence the laws we create.
- What we believe to be true can influence us just as much, or even more, than what is actually occurring.

CHAPTER 1

When Fiends Become Friends

The Need to Belong and Perceptions of Personal and Group Discrimination

Mauricio Carvallo and Brett W. Pelham

Persons who scored above average in the need to belong reported lower levels of personal discrimination but higher levels of group discrimination. The differences were significant, even when controlled for stigma consciousness, gender identify and public collective self-esteem.

An important topic of interest in social psychology is the study of stereotypes, prejudice, and discrimination. Traditionally, research on discrimination attempted to examine how the beliefs and feelings of the members of privileged groups influenced their tendency to discrimination against out-group members (Adorno, Frenkel-Brunswik, Levinson, & Sanford, 1950; Allport, 1954; Dovidio & Gaertner, 1986; Duncan, 1976; Sidanius & Pratto, 1999). More recently, however, social psychologists have become increasingly interested in how the targets of stereotypes, prejudice, and discrimination respond to these negative social experiences. Much of this recent research has focused on (a) how readily the members of stigmatized groups acknowledge that they have been the victims of discrimination (Crosby, 1982; Jost & Branaji, 1994; Major, Quinton, & McCoy, 2002; Stangor, Swim, Van Allen, & Sechrist, 2002; Taylor, Wright, Moghaddam, & Lalonde, 1990) and (b) how the experience of stigma or discrimination influences a person's self-evaluations (Branscombe, Schmitt, & Harvey, 1999; Crocker & Major, 1989; Pelham & Hetts, 1999). In this report, we focus on the first of these two recent questions. Specifically, when and why do stigmatized group members acknowledge their experiences with discrimination, and when and why do they minimize or deny these experiences?

Although research has shown that stigmatized group members frequently experience negative eco nomic and interpersonal outcomes (e.g., Braddock & McPartland, 1987; Crandall, 1995; Crocker & Major, 1989; Dovido & Gaertner, 1986; Sigelman & Welch, 1991), research has also suggested that stigmatized group members may minimize the extent to which they have personally experienced discrimination. Crosby (1982) was one of the first to document this phenomenon. In her study, designed to explore sex discrimination in the work place, Crosby observed that whereas objective indicators of women's experiences suggested that they were victims of discrimination, most women felt extremely positive about their jobs. What puzzled Crosby most was that, when asked to report their personal experiences with discrimination, these women reported experiencing lower levels of discrimination than they reported for women as a group. . . .

Why Does It Matter?

Why should it matter whether the members of stigmatized groups frequently fail to realize the disadvantages they face? Pragmatically, if people are oblivious to the fact that they have often encountered discrimination, they may indirectly communicate to others that discrimination is not an important social problem (e.g., see Taylor, Wright, & Porter, 1994). Moreover, if stigmatized group members fail to realize that discrimination affects them personally, they may not be very motivated to take collective action toward social change (Crosby et al., 1989; Jost, 1995; Major, 1994). That is, if people frequently fail to realize that they have been the victims of discrimination, this increases the likelihood that the status quo will forever remain the status quo. . . .

Why Does It Occur?

Assuming that people do often fail to appreciate the degree to which they are the victims of discrimination, why might this be the case? Research focusing on the personal-group discrimination discrepancy has offered several answers. For example, Crosby (1982) argued that people are motivated to avoid pinpointing the particular villains who might have discriminated against them. Others have argued that admitting that one has been the victim of discrimination would require people to admit that they do not have control over their lives (Ruggiero & Taylor, 1995; but cf. Sechrist, Swim, & Stangor, 2004). People might also be motivated to ignore signs that they have been maltreated because of a need to justify their own inaction in the face of such maltreatment (Taylor & Dube, 1986). Finally, people may wish to distance themselves from the negative attributes stereotypically ascribed to their fellow in-group members (Hodson & Esses, 2002).

. . . [R]esearch has also suggested that stigmatized group members are particularly likely to minimize public reports of personal discrimination in the presence of nonstigmatized group members (Stangor et al., 2002), either out of fear of retaliation (Swim & Hyers, 1999) or to avoid the social cost of appearing to be a complainer (Kaiser & Miller, 2001). Although this research has not assessed people's reports of group discrimination, it suggests the possibility that different social pressures operate at the level of the individual and at the level of the group. At the same time, one of the assumptions underlying much of this research on the social costs of reporting discrimination is that there is often a big difference between what people publicly report and what people personally believe. How can one explain the fact that many people honestly seem to believe that they themselves are rarely the victims of discrimination?

The Need to Belong and Perceptions of Discrimination

In addition to the reasons listed above, we believe that there is another important reason why people might fail to appreciate the degree to which they have been the victims of discrimination. This reason is that acknowledging discrimination represents a threat to people's need to belong. For decades, social and personality psychologists have argued that people have an intrinsic motivation to affiliate and bond with each other (Bowlby, 1969, 1973; Epstein, 1991; Freud, 1915/1963; Maslow, 1968; McClelland, 1951; Murray, 1938). More recently, Baumeister and Leary (1995) have argued that the need to belong lies at the heart of many important social phenomena, ranging from both infant and adult attachment to adult emotional experience and physical well-being (see also Brewer, 2004; Fiske, 2003; Stevens & Fiske, 1995). The need to belong is defined as the desire for frequent, positive, and stable interactions with others (Williams & Sommer, 1997) and is fulfilled primarily through affiliation with and acceptance from others (Gardner, Pickett, & Brewer, 2000). As a result, people show a strong need for social acceptance and an even stronger aversion to social rejection (Leary, 2001). According to this perspective, the need to belong increases following rejection and decreases following social inclusion or acceptance (Leary, Tambor, Terdal, & Downs, 1995; see also Baldwin & Sinclair, 1996). More important, Baumeister and Leary have argued that people strive to fulfill this basic need not only by attempting to maximize their actual acceptance from others but also by structuring their beliefs about the self and others in ways that allow them to feel that most people like and accept them (see also Brewer & Pickett, 1999; Williams & Sommer, 1997).

Consistent with Baumeister and Leary (1995), we use the phrase "need to belong" in this research to refer to a basic human motivation to be accepted or feel accepted by others. However, we realize that there are many ways to conceptualize the basic need for connectedness or acceptance (e.g., Bowlby, 1973; Deci & Ryan, 1985, 2000; Rogers, 1959). Furthermore, we realize that human beings base much of their behavior on specific interpersonal goals rather than general motives (e.g., sexual needs, the desire for power). Nonetheless, our position is that a host of closely related motives that we refer to as "the need to belong" or "the need for acceptance" dominates much of the human interpersonal landscape. Moreover, we agree with Baumeister and Leary that at least some highly specific interpersonal goals (e.g., the desire for fame) may ultimately be rooted in a desire for connectedness or social acceptance. . . .

The need to belong might influence not only how people assess their own personal experiences with discrimination but also how people assess and evaluate the experiences of their fellow in-group members. However, it seems unlikely that the need to belong would motivate people to overlook instances of discrimination directed at the group. On the contrary, the need to belong should probably increase the likelihood that people acknowledge instances of group discrimination. . . . Because of our interest in how the need to belong relates to perceptions of group as well as personal discrimination, and because of the tradition of comparing these two distinct judgments (e.g., Crosby, 1982; Crosby et al., 1989; Taylor et al., 1994), we typically assessed people's beliefs about both personal and group discrimination in this research.

Overview of the Present Research

. . . [W]hereas some researchers have mentioned interpersonal motivations in passing (e.g., Major, Quinton, & McCoy, 2002; Tyler & Lind, 1992), we know of no systematic research that has focused on the hypothesis that the need to belong plays an important role in people's judgments of personal and/or group discrimination (but see Kobrynowicz & Branscombe, 1997). Study 1 was designed as an initial test of this idea. If the need to belong causes people to minimize perceptions of personal discrimination, then people who are higher than average in the need to belong might be particularly likely to report that they typically experience less discrimination than their fellow group members. Furthermore, if the need to belong causes people to acknowledge or accentuate perceptions of group discrimination, then people high in the need to belong might be especially likely to report that the members of their group frequently experience discrimination. Of course, the converse of these two predictions is that people who do not have a very strong need to belong might report (a) relatively high levels of personal discrimination and (b) relatively low levels of group discrimination. Study 2 sought to test these same hypotheses by manipulating rather than measuring the need to belong. Finally, in Study 3, we broadened the scope of this research by (a) using a different approach to activate the need to belong and (b) assessing people's attributions about discrimination rather than perceived levels of discrimination. Specifically, Study 3 tested the idea that participants' desire to be accepted by an attractive interaction partner would influence their judgments of why the partner had evaluated their work negatively.

Study 1

The first study tested our hypotheses by assessing the need to belong before asking male and female participants to report their judgments regarding personal and group discrimination on the basis of their gender. Although most research on how people assess discrimination aimed at themselves and their social groups has focused on stigmatized social groups, recent research has shown that the members of nonstigmatized groups often report judgments of personal and group discrimination that resemble those of stigmatized persons. For example, men often report that they have personally experienced less gender discrimination than has the average man (Moghaddam, Stolkin, & Hutcheson, 1997; Operario & Fiske, 2001; Postmes, Branscombe, Spears, & Young, 1999). Although there is some disagreement about how to interpret this finding, the possibility that men strive to minimize their perceptions of personal gender discrimination is consistent with our motivational framework. After all, the need to belong should apply to all people, not just stigmatized group members.

In addition to assessing the need to belong, Study 1 also examined three other individual difference factors likely to be related to perceptions of perceived discrimination: stigma consciousness, group identification, and the perception that people in general view one's group favorably. Research has shown that stigma consciousness is positively correlated with perceived personal discrimination across a variety of stigmatized groups (e.g., African Americans, Latinos, women; Pinel, 1999). Similarly, studies also show that group identification is positively correlated with perceptions of personal and/or group discrimination among stigmatized group members, including women (Crosby et al., 1989; Operario & Fiske, 2001). Finally, people's judgments of how other people evaluate their gender group (public collective self-esteem) might be expected to predict perceptions of both personal and group discrimination. Specifically, people should perceive less discrimination directed at them or their groups to the extent that they believe that others generally view their groups positively (Luhtanen & Crocker, 1992). In short, we included these three variables in our analyses to control for any potential overlap between the need to belong and stigma consciousness, group identification, or public collective self-esteem.

METHOD

Participants

Participants were 219 undergraduates (74 men and 145 women) from the State University of New York at Buffalo, who ranged from 18 to 43 years old ($M = 21.12$). The ethnic composition of our sample was 77% Caucasian, 9% Asian or Asian American, 4% African American, 5% Latino, and 5% other ethnicities. Participants received credit toward a course requirement.

Measures

Need to belong. Participants' need to belong was assessed using the Need to Belong Scale (Leary, Kelly, Cottrell, & Schreindorfer, 2001). This scale includes 10 items such as "If other people don't seem to accept me, I don't let it bother me," and "My feelings are easily hurt when I feel that others do not accept me." Items were measured on a 9-point scale ranging from 1 (*strongly disagree*) to 9 (*strongly agree*). Items expressing a low need to belong were reverse scored so that higher scores reflected a greater need to belong ($\alpha + .84$).

Stigma consciousness. Stigma consciousness was assessed using Pinel's (1999) Stigma Consciousness Scale. This scale consists of 10 items that were modified to focus on gender (e.g., "I never worry that my behavior will be viewed as stereotypically male (female)" and "Most men (women) do not judge women (men) on the basis of their gender."). Items were measured on a 9-point scale ranging from 1 (*strongly disagree*) to 9 (*strongly agree*) ($\alpha = .76$).

Gender identification. Gender identification was assessed with the four-item Importance to Identity subscale of the Collective Self-Esteem Scale (Luhtanen & Crocker, 1992), rephrased to be gender specific (e.g., "Overall, being a woman (man) has very little to do with how I feel about myself? (reverse coded) and "Being a woman (man) is an important reflection of who I am"). Participants responded to each item on a scale from 1 (*strongly disagree*) to 9 (*strongly agree*). Reliability was acceptable ($\alpha = .70$).

Public (gender) collective self-esteem. Participants' views of how their gender group is seen by others were assessed with the Public subscale of Luhtanen and Crocker's (1992) Collective Self-Esteem Scale. This subscale consists of four items that were slightly modified to focus on gender (e.g., "Overall, women (men) are considered good by others," "In general, others respect women

(men)," and "In general, others think that being a woman (man) is unworthy" (reverse coded)). Reliability was acceptable ($\alpha = .72$).

Perceptions of personal discrimination. Our first dependent measure was a four-item measure of participants' perceptions that they had personally experienced gender discrimination This measure was adapted loosely from past research by Sechrist, Swim, and Mark (2003). The items were as follows: "Prejudice against my gender group has affected me personally," "I have personally experienced gender discrimination," "I have often been treated unfairly because of my gender," and "Because of gender discrimination, I have been deprived of opportunities that are available to women (men)." Items were measured on a 9-point scale ranging from 1 (*strongly disagree*) to 9 (*strongly agree*). Reliability was high ($\alpha = .90$).

Perceptions of group discrimination. To assess group discrimination, we asked participants to respond to four items that closely paralleled the items used in the personal discrimination measure (these items were presented after the personal discrimination measure, preceded by two filler questions about gender discrimination in general). The items were "Prejudice against my gender group has affected the average female (male) college student," "The average female (male) college student has experienced gender discrimination," "The average female (male) college student has often been treated unfairly because of her gender," and "Because of gender discrimination, the average female college student has been deprived of opportunities that are available to men (women)." Participants responded to each item on a 9-point scale ranging from 1 (*strongly disagree*) to 9 (*strongly agree*). Reliability was high ($\alpha = .92$).

RESULTS

Perceptions of Personal Discrimination

We tested the hypotheses that people high on the need to belong would report relatively low levels of personal discrimination by using a simultaneous multiple regression analysis that included five predictors: (a) need to belong, (b) stigma consciousness, (c) gender identity, (d) public collective self-esteem, and (e) perceptions of group discrimination. We controlled for perceptions of group discrimination because we wanted to assess the unique relation between each of our predictors and perceptions of personal versus group discrimination. The analysis showed that the combined effect of the five predictors was significant ($R^2 = .45, p < .001$). Not surprisingly, perceptions of group discrimination were the strongest predictor of perceptions of personal discrimination ($\beta = .51, p < .001, \eta = .45$). Stigma consciousness ($\beta = .18, p < .01, \eta = .16$) and public collective self-esteem ($\beta = -.12, p < .05, \eta = .11$) were also associated with perceptions of personal discrimination (in the expected direction). More important, and consistent with our hypothesis, there was also a significant association for need to belong ($\beta = -.11, p < .05, \eta = .11$). Participants high in the need to belong reported experiencing less personal discrimination than did participants low in the need to belong. Group identity was not significantly associated with personal discrimination ratings ($\beta = .07, ns$).

Perceptions of Group Discrimination

Our analyses for perceptions of group discrimination included exactly the same predictors as our analysis for perceptions of personal discrimination. The only difference was that in this analysis we controlled for perceptions of personal discrimination (so as to look at the unique associations with perceived group discrimination). Together, the five predictors were significant ($R^2 = .43, p < .001$). As expected, perceptions of personal discrimination were the strongest predictor of perceptions of group discrimination ($\beta = .52, p < .001, \eta = .45$). Public collective self-esteem ($\beta = -13, p < .05, \eta = .12$) and gender identity ($\beta = .10, p = .056, \eta = .10$) were also significant or nearly significant predictors. Stigma consciousness was not ($\beta = .09$), though the trend was in the expected direction. Once again, the analysis showed that the need to belong was a significant predictor ($\beta = .12, p < .05, \eta = .11$). In the case of perceptions of group discrimination, however, participants high in the need to belong perceived more group discrimination than did participants low in the need to belong. . . .

Discussion

As we expected, the need to belong was significantly associated with perceptions of both personal and group discrimination. Specifically, even after we controlled for several established predictors of personal and group discrimination (e.g., stigma consciousness and two gender-relevant aspects of collective self-esteem), participants who were high in the need to belong reported lower levels of personal discrimination but higher levels of group discrimination. Although these initial results are supportive of our hypothesis, these findings are correlational.

Thus, the direction of causation is not clear. For example, people may report low levels of the need to belong because they perceive themselves as having been victims of discrimination, rather than vice versa. That is, the belief that one has often been rejected by others could lead a person to decide that connectedness with others is not that important (cf. Gardner et al., 2000). Similarly, past research has shown that perceived discrimination against one's group sometimes leads to increased identification with the group (e.g., Dion & Earn, 1975; Gurin & Townsend, 1986; Tajfel & Turner, 1986).

Although it would still be interesting if perceptions of personal versus group discrimination have opposite effects on the general need to belong, this does not negate this methodological limitation. Accordingly, we conducted a second study in which we manipulated the need to belong. After doing so, we asked participants to report their judgments of personal and group discrimination on the basis of their gender.

Study 2

According to Baumeister and Leary (1995), one criteria for inclusion of the need to belong as a fundamental human motivation is that it should display satiation patterns. That is, the motive should increase when levels of belongingness fall below threshold and should decrease when levels of belongingness are satiated (see also Gardner et al., 2000). In Study 2 we incorporated a manipulation intended to satiate participants' need to belong. We predicted that participants who have been made to feel accepted would report higher than average levels of personal discrimination and lower than average levels of group discrimination.

Method

Participants

Participants were 127 undergraduates (71 men, 56 women) from the State University of New York at Buffalo, who ranged from 18 to 51 years old ($M = 20.28$). The ethnic composition was 56% Caucasian, 18% Asian or Asian American, 15% African American, 9% Latino, and 2% other ethnicities. For their participation, all participants received credit in a psychology course.

Procedure and Measures

Participants completed the same measures of personal and group discrimination as in Study 1. However, the need to belong was manipulated with a priming task intended to create feelings of acceptance. Participants were randomly assigned to an acceptance priming condition or a neutral pleasant word condition. In the acceptance priming condition, participants were asked to complete a word-search task that contained words related to acceptance (e.g., *accepted, included, welcomed, adored, supported, wanted*). In the neutral pleasant-word condition, participants were asked to complete the same word-search task by finding pleasant words that were unrelated to acceptance (e.g., *chuckle, smile, peace, amuse*; Baccus & Baldwin, 2001).

When participants arrived at the study, they were told that the research involved assessing their attitudes and perceptions about gender. Before starting the study, they were asked whether they would be willing to participate in a pilot test that was, ostensibly, unrelated to the present study. All participants agreed to participate. The alleged pilot test consisted of a word-search puzzle. Participants were given 5 min. to complete the word-search puzzles containing either words related to acceptance or words that were neutral. After completing the word-search task, participants were thanked for assisting with the pilot study and then asked to report their judgments regarding personal and group discrimination on the basis of their gender. No participant reported any suspicion that the two tasks were related.

Results

Perceptions of Personal Discrimination

We predicted that people whose need to belong was reduced (because of recent satiation) would report higher than average levels of personal discrimination. We tested this hypothesis by using a one-way analysis of covariance that is conceptually identical to the multiple regression analysis conducted in Study 1. To separate the unique contributions to participants' perceptions of personal discrimination above and beyond any associations for perceptions of group discrimination, we included ratings of group discrimination in the analysis as a covariate. The independent variable was the priming ("accepted") manipulation. The dependent variable was perceptions of personal discrimination. As predicted, the analysis revealed a significant main effect of condition. Participants in the accepted condition (covariate-adjusted $M = 4.26, SE = 0.20$) reported higher levels of personal discrimination than did participants in the control condition (covariate-adjusted $M = 3.69, SE = 0.20$), $F(1, 124) = 3.97$,

$p < .05, \eta = .14$. The covariate was also significant, $F(1, 124) = 75.62, p < .001$.

Perceptions of Group Discrimination

Our analysis of perceptions of group discrimination was patterned directly after our analysis of personal discrimination, the only difference being the obvious change in the covariate. Thus the dependent variable was perceptions of group discrimination, and the covariate was perceptions of personal discrimination. As predicted, the analysis revealed a significant main effect of condition. Participants in the accepted condition (covariate-adjusted $M = 3.94, SE = 1.80$) reported lower levels of group discrimination than did participants in the control condition (covariate-adjusted $M = 4.69, SE = 1.87$), $F(1, 124) = 9.07, p < .01, \eta = .21$. The covariate was also significant, $F(1, 124) = 75.62, p < .001$. . . .

Discussion

Studies 1 and 2 strongly suggest that the need to belong influences the degree to which people perceive that they or their groups are victims of discrimination. Studies 1 and 2 thus identify the need to belong as an important reason why people sometimes fail to appreciate the degree to which they have experienced discrimination. Notice, however, that the need to belong does not simply blind people to all possible instances of discrimination. When it comes to people's judgments that their fellow in-group members have experienced discrimination, the need to belong seems to motivate people to acknowledge instances of discrimination. . . .

If the assumption is made that perceptions of personal and group discrimination are best conceptualized separately, then we believe that our findings regarding personal discrimination may be more important than our findings regarding group discrimination because they suggest a reason why people might fail to appreciate instances of discrimination of the most obvious and self-relevant sort—discrimination aimed at the self. Thus, in Study 3, we decided to focus exclusively on self-relevant rather than group-relevant judgments. In Study 3, we also wanted to broaden the scope of our investigation by assessing attributions about potentially discriminatory behavior rather than judgments of the perceived level of discrimination. As Major, Quinton, and McCoy (2002) noted, the attributions that people make for obviously negative outcomes are at least as important as people's judgments of the nature or level of these outcomes. Finally, self-affirmation theorists might argue that our manipulation of acceptance in Study 2 was actually a subtle self-affirmation manipulation (e.g., see Sherman & Cohen, 2002; Steele & Liu, 1983). In Study 3, we manipulated people's desire for connectedness in a way that was orthogonal to self-affirmation. . . .

People should be most likely to recognize instances of discrimination—and to make self-protective attributions to discrimination—when they are not highly motivated to develop or protect a relationship with a potential perpetrator. On the other hand, in situations in which people are highly motivated to be accepted by potential perpetrators (e.g., when one's romantic partner rather than a stranger is the source of a sexist remark), we believe that they will steer away from making attributions to discrimination. Thus, Study 3 was designed to assess whether the need to belong influences the attributions that people make for the potentially discriminatory evaluations of another person.

In Study 3, we also expanded our approach by manipulating people's desire to be accepted by a particular person (an attractive, opposite-sex stranger), rather than manipulating people's general need to be liked or accepted. At a conceptual level, we think the need to belong (i.e., the need for acceptance or connectedness) may be most likely to manifest itself in the context of established personal relationships. Nonetheless, we believe that the need to belong also influences people's desire to form new relationships or to care about specific short-term interactions, especially when these interactions (a) have the potential to foster long-term relationships or (b) have direct implications for one's general ability to connect to others (see Baumeister & Leary, 1995). Thus, in Study 3 we manipulated the need to belong by manipulating people's desire to be accepted by an attractive stranger. Finally, in contrast to Study 2, in which we experimentally decreased the need to belong for some participants (relative to a control condition), Study 3 experimentally increased the need to belong for some participants.

Study 3

To test the hypothesis that the need to belong influences judgments of the causes of personal discrimination in attributionally ambiguous situations, we conducted a conceptual replication of a study by Crocker et al. (1991, Experiment 1). Crocker et al. showed that women were more likely to attribute negative feedback to discrimination if the feedback came from a seemingly prejudiced as opposed to nonprejudiced (male) evaluator. In the present study, female participants received a negative evaluation of their performance on a creativity task. The evaluator was always a physically attractive man with traditional gender attitudes, and all participants expected to have a meaningful interaction with this man later in the study. We manipulated the need to belong by describing the male evaluator as being either single or married. Past research has shown that the prospect of forming a relationship with a recently met person appears to be sufficient to alter the way in which people process the interaction (Baumeister & Leary, 1995; Clark, 1984). Thus, women should feel more of a desire to be connected to an attractive interaction partner if they believe that he is single than if they believe that he is married.

METHOD

Participants

A total of 41 female students from the State University of New York at Buffalo, who ranged from 18 to 43 years old ($M = 19.97$), participated for course credit. The ethnic composition was 79% Caucasian, 10% African American, 8% Asian or Asian American, and 3% Latino. Two participants were excluded from the analyses because they reported that they did not believe the bogus participant was real.

Laboratory Procedure

Background materials and cover story. When participants arrived at the laboratory they were escorted to a room by the male experimenter and asked to wait for another participant who presumably had not yet arrived. After a few minutes, participants learned that the other participant had arrived and was getting ready for the experiment in a different room. The experimenter then explained that participants were taking part in a study of attitudes, peer evaluation, and problem solving. Participants learned that during the first part of the study they and their partner would each work in separate rooms and would only exchange background information. During the second part of the study, they would presumably meet and work together on a 25-min problem-solving activity. Presumably, this approach would allow us to study how people work individually as well as how people work together in groups.

Next, the experimenter took participants' photos with a digital camera and asked them to write a brief self-descriptive essay and complete an attitude survey. Participants were led to believe that they would exchange this self-descriptive material with the other participant as an initial way for them to get to know each other. After taking the getting-acquainted photo, the experimenter left the room, ostensibly to give the same instructions to the other participant. The self-descriptive essay asked participants to describe who they were and what they were like in 100 words or less (without providing any personally identifying information). The attitude survey consisted of 15 questions, 5 of which assessed participants' attitudes regarding women's role in society. These 5 questions were the same ones used by Crocker et al. (1991, Experiment 1). The other 10 questions assessed attitudes toward affirmative action and social services. The 5-point scale for these 15 attitude items ranged from 1 (strongly disagree) to 5 (strongly agree).

Creativity task and partner evaluation. After participants completed the essay and attitude survey, the experimenter returned to collect their materials and explain the individual performance task. Participants completed a creativity task in which they were given 5 min to list all possible uses for a brick. It is important to note that before listing their responses, all participants were asked to report their gender and age. In addition, participants were told that the other participant had been assigned a different individual task (a problem-solving task). Further, participants learned that they would evaluate the other participant's problem-solving task while he evaluated their creativity task. The experimenter left the room and returned 5 min later to collect the creativity task and to deliver the problem-solving task that ostensibly had been completed by the other participant. From the response sheet provided to them, participants learned that the other participant was a man and 21 years of age. Participants evaluated the problem-solving task on dimensions such as quality and logicality and then provided a summary evaluation. The fact that participants and their bogus partners had completed different tasks made it impossible for participants to compare the quality of their work with that of their partner.

Exchange of background information (need to belong manipulation). After collecting their evaluation of their partner's work, the experimenter gave the self-descriptive essay, attitude survey, and photo of their partner. Participants were left alone to review these materials for 10 min (while their partner presumably did the same).

Participants in all conditions viewed the same photo of an attractive undergraduate man whose essay described him as a friendly, easygoing person who liked to listen to music, play the guitar, read, and spend time outdoors. Participants in the high connectedness condition read that the other participant was new at the university and was looking forward to meeting new people and making friends. Participants in the low connectedness condition read that the other participant was married, that his wife was expecting a baby girl, and that he was very excited about becoming a father. Responses on the bogus partner participant's attitude survey were identical in all conditions. The bogus participant's responses revealed that he had liberal views regarding affirmative action and social services. However, exactly like the bogus male participant in Crocker et al.'s (1991) study, the bogus participant reported highly traditional attitudes when it came to women's role in society. For example, he reported strongly agreeing that "women, who are less serious about their jobs, take jobs away from men with families to support," and he disagreed that "women and men should receive equal pay for work that is similar." Needless to say, there was not a single participant in the study whose own attitudes about gender roles were as traditional as those of the bogus male partner.

Negative evaluation from partner. After participants digested the material regarding their bogus partner, the experimenter returned with their partner's evaluation of their work on the creativity task. The bogus participant was not very impressed. For example, in response to the question, "How would you evaluate the creativity of the responses given?" on a 9-point scale ranging from 1 (not at all creative) to 9 (very creative), he offered a 2. He also gave ratings of 3 on similar scales for both quality and novelty. Finally, in response to an open-ended question about overall creativity, he indicated "In general, the responses given were not very imaginative."

Dependent Measures and Assessment of Stigma Consciousness

Immediately after reading their evaluations, participants were asked to complete a series of questionnaires that included their impressions of the other participant, their attributions for his evaluation of their work on the creativity task, and their memory for his responses on the attitude survey. Next, participants were asked to complete a measure of state self-esteem, a mood measure, the stigma consciousness measure, and some demographic questions. Participants were reminded that all their responses to these questionnaires would remain completely anonymous and that the other participant would not read them. They were also reminded that after completing the questionnaires, they would meet the other participant and begin the final part of the study. After completing these questionnaires, participants were carefully debriefed and completed a final anonymous questionnaire assessing suspicion.

Attributions. Two items assessed the extent to which participants believed that the evaluations they received were due to gender discrimination: "To what extent do you think that the evaluation you received was due to potential gender biases on the part of the evaluator?" and "To what extent do you think that the evaluation you received was due to the evaluator's attitudes toward women?" Items were answered on 9-point scales ranging from 1 (*not at all*) to 9 (*very much*). This measure was highly reliable ($\alpha = .88$). In addition, two items assessed the extent to which participants believed that the evaluations they received were due to the "creativity level of their answers" and to the "strengths and weaknesses of their work" ($\alpha = .47$). Because these two items behaved the same way, we combined them despite their low reliability.

Mood and state self-esteem. Following Crocker et al. (1991), we also assessed mood and state self-esteem. We assessed mood using four items from each of the three subscales of the Multiple Affect Adjective Check List (Zuckerman & Lubin, 1965). We assessed state self-esteem using a modified ("right now") version of Rosenberg's (1965) Self-Esteem Scale.

Impressions of the partner's similarity to self. Using 9-point scales, participants reported their views of their partner on a number of valenced dimensions (e.g., intelligence, sincerity, pleasantness). Embedded among these questions was a single item that assessed how similar participants felt their attitudes were to those of their partner.

Stigma consciousness. As in Study 1, we assessed stigma consciousness using the Stigma Consciousness Scale, modified to be relevant to gender ($\alpha = .73$). We assessed stigma consciousness near the end of the study to avoid sensitizing participants to our interest in stigma prior to the delivery of our experimental manipulation.

Results

Attributions to Discrimination

A one-way analysis of covariance was conducted to test the hypothesis that experimentally created differences

in the need to belong would influence participants' attributions regarding negative feedback from their interaction partner. Thus, the dependent variable was attributions to discrimination for the negative feedback received. The independent variable was the relationship status of the bogus interaction partner (single or married). Stigma consciousness served as a covariate. . . . [T]he analysis revealed a significant main effect of experimental condition. Relative to those who believed that their interaction partner was married, those who believed he was single (i.e., those whose need to belong was strongly activated) were less likely to attribute the same negative evaluation to discrimination. Respective covariate-adjusted means in the married and single conditions were 6.28 ($SE = 0.42$) and 5.08 ($SE = .041$), $F(1, 36) = 4.19$, $p < .05$, $\eta = .29$. The covariate was also significant, $F(1, 36) = 10.86$, $p < .01$. Independent of the experimental manipulation, participants high in stigma consciousness were more likely to attribute their negative evaluation to discrimination. Neither the experimental manipulation, $F(1, 36) = 1.65$, $p > .21$, nor stigma consciousness, $F(1, 36) = 0.03$, $p > .87$, was related to participants' tendency to attribute the feedback to the quality of their work. . . .

General Discussion

The research reported here supports the hypothesis that the need to belong plays an important role in people's judgments of personal and group discrimination. In Study 1, [participants who were high in the need to belong] scored lower levels of personal discrimination but higher levels of group discrimination. Indeed, the need to belong proved to be a significant predictor of personal and group discrimination even when we controlled for participants' stigma consciousness, gender identity, and public collective self-esteem. The results of Study 2 showed a similar pattern. This time, however, the need to belong was manipulated by use of a priming task intended to create feelings of acceptance. As predicted, participants who had been made to feel accepted reported relatively higher levels of personal discrimination and lower levels of group discrimination than participants in a control condition. We find it interesting to note that participants in the accepted condition reported nearly identical levels of personal and group discrimination. Thus, our manipulation eliminated an otherwise robust phenomenon: the tendency to perceive more discrimination aimed at one's group rather than at oneself. In Study 3, we tested the hypothesis that targets of prejudice may be motivated to avoid blaming their negative outcomes on discrimination when doing so would threaten their need for connectedness. Accordingly, we manipulated the desire for connectedness among female participants who believed they would engage in a significant interaction with a sexist but otherwise charming male participant. Consistent with predictions, participants in the high connectedness condition were relatively less likely to attribute a negative evaluation from the male partner to discrimination. Taken together, the results of these studies support the hypothesis that the need to belong influences not only how likely stigmatized group members are to acknowledge or minimize their experiences with discrimination but also how willing they are to attribute negative evaluations to discrimination.

The social psychological literature is replete with references to the ways in which perceivers' motives and goals influence judgments and social perceptions (Fiske & Taylor, 1991; Hilton & Darley, 1991; Kruglanski, 1996; Kunda & Sinclair, 1999; Stevens & Fiske, 1995). Judgments of prejudice and discrimination are no different. In our view, perceptions of potential prejudice and discrimination threaten people's pervasive need to form and maintain relationships with others. Because the need to belong is fulfilled through affiliation with and acceptance from others, the drive to seek social acceptance must be accompanied by mechanisms for enhancing the subjective likelihood that one will, in fact, be accepted rather than rejected by other people (Leary, 2001). Thus, the drive for social acceptance colors people's judgments of others in ways consistent with the belief that one will not be subject to interpersonal rejection. . . .

Likely Role of the Need to Belong in Past Research

Our findings are consistent with past research suggesting that people may be motivated to avoid reporting instances of personal discrimination to others. Thus, past research has shown that blaming negative outcomes on personal discrimination is typically viewed negatively by others, even when it is obvious that discrimination is the cause of these events (Kaiser & Miller, 2001). People who complain about discrimination in public can be seen as impolite, as violators of potent social norms that discourage voicing negative views of others. Thus, even complainers who have much to complain about risk being labeled as hypersensitive, unpleasant people (Crosby, 1984; Kaiser & Miller, 2001; Stangor et al., 2002). From our perspective, the normative influence processes that discourage people from complaining

about maltreatment are likely to be grounded in the basic desire all people have to be part of a group in which social friction is kept to a minimum (Breckler & Greenwald, 1986). In other words, research on how people respond to those they perceive as complainers and how people seek to avoid being perceived as complainers has been highly consistent with our guiding assumption about the need to belong. . . .

The current research has important implications for theories of stigma. Some theorists argue that in most interactions with nonstigmatized individuals, the stigmatized person is likely to expect to experience some degree of prejudice and discrimination (Feldman Barrett & Swim, 1998; Swim, Cohen, & Hyers, 1998). Even if a social interaction with a nonstigmatized person is free of prejudice, the stigmatized person will still be uncertain whether he or she has been treated in a prejudicial manner on the basis of his or her stigma (Crocker & Major, 1989; Crocker et al., 1991). On the basis of this perspective, most research on stigma has focused primarily on the strategies that stigmatized people use to cope with the prejudice and discrimination they inevitably expect to encounter. Although we do not deny that vigilance is an important part of many routine social interactions between stigmatized and nonstigmatized group members, our research suggests that when people are motivated to protect meaningful relationships with their interaction partners, such people will sometimes be motivated to overlook instances of discrimination. Of course, just as extreme vigilance can be maladaptive in situations in which majority group members harbor only good will (Ayduk, Downey, & Kim, 2001; Mendoza-Denton et al., 2002), turning a blind eye to discrimination can be maladaptive when those one wishes to please are likely to act on deep-seated prejudices.

The Need to Belong and Future Research

Whether stigmatized members readily acknowledge that they are victims of discrimination or whether they minimize or downplay such discrimination has recently become the subject of considerable research. The evidence so far supports two seemingly opposing theoretical views. On the one hand, vigilance perspectives suggest that stigmatized group members are highly sensitive to signs of prejudice in their environments and are eager to blame negative outcomes on discrimination. On the other hand, minimization perspectives support the view that stigmatized members fail to perceive that they personally are targets of discrimination or fail to attribute negative outcomes to prejudice even when it is plausible to do so. We agree with Major, Quinton, and McCoy (2002) that there is no use in establishing whether one perspective supersedes the other. The evidence shows that both vigilance and minimization exist. We further agree that future research should focus on finding moderators that explain when and why stigmatized members are more likely to recognize or minimize acts of prejudice and discrimination. Several studies have examined different moderators of perceptions and attributions to discrimination such as group identification and endorsement of status-legitimizing ideologies (Major, Gramzow, et al., 2002; Major et al., 2003; Operario & Fiske, 2001). Our studies extend this research by proposing a basic motivational factor that explains why stigmatized group members might fail to see that they have been the victims of discrimination. By manipulating this motive (e.g., by manipulating people's allegiances to different groups), future research could shed further light on the power of interpersonal motives to shape people's perceptions of discrimination. If the world were full of nothing but distant fiends or devoted friends, there might be a single answer to the question of whether people emphasize or de-emphasize their own personal experiences of discrimination. But in the real world, there are many shades of gray between fiend and friend.

Discussion Questions

1. Why do people tend to recognize group discrimination but minimize personal discrimination?

2. After reading this article, could you see yourself minimizing personal discrimination in certain situations? Why or why not?

Source: "When Fiends Become Friends: The Need to Belong and Perception of Personal and Group Discrimination" by Mauricio Carvallo and Brett W. Pelham, excerpted and notes & references omitted, from *Journal of Personality and Social Psychology*, 2006, Vol. 90, No. 1, pp. 94–108. Reprinted by permission of American Psychological Association via RightsLink and the author.

CHAPTER 2

Differences between Actual and Perceived Student Norms

An Examination of Alcohol Use, Drug Use, and Sexual Behavior

Matthew P. Martens, Jennifer C. Page, Emily S. Mowry,
Krista M. Damann, Kari K. Taylor, and M. Dolores Cimini

Study participants overestimated alcohol use, drug use, and sexual behavior among their peers. There was also a positive relationship between actual behavior and perceived peer norms. This has implications for the health of college students in terms of social norms-based interventions.

Alcohol use, drug use, and safe sexual activity have long been the focuses of intervention efforts on college campuses. Such efforts are warranted given the level of activity and number of negative consequences associated with these behaviors. Traditional prevention methods that consist of educational programs aimed at increasing student awareness of the risks of these behaviors, however, have shown limited effectiveness in reducing harmful drinking. Those interested in reducing high-risk behavior on college campuses have therefore had to address the problems using alternative methods.

One such method that has become increasingly popular is the social norms approach. The National Institute on Alcohol Abuse and Alcoholism (NIAAA) has recently identified, based on strong research evidence with college students, an individual norms clarification approach to be a component of a Tier 1 substance abuse prevention program. The NIAAA has also identified, based on evidence of logical or theoretical promise, broader social norms marketing campaigns as Tier 3 approaches. The theory underlying the social norms approach is based on the notion that individuals generally misperceive the frequency with which their peers engage in unhealthy behaviors (eg, alcohol consumption) and that these

misperceptions have a causal effect on individual behavior. Such misperceptions among college students can result from a number of sources, including attributing another person's behavior to internal dispositions (and thus being more likely to assume that such behavior is typical); vivid affective responses regarding the behaviors of others that are more easily recalled (e.g., seeing someone become intoxicated and make a fool of him- or herself); and cultural perceptions, often perpetrated by various media and entertainment outlets, of what is normal in a collegiate environment. Regardless of the source, the end result is that the individual perceives that a certain behavior is more frequent or typical than it is in reality and is therefore more likely to engage in such behavior him- or herself.

Researchers have conducted a number of studies, primarily involving alcohol consumption, that support the core tenets of social norms theory. Researchers from a wide variety of college campuses have consistently found that college students generally overestimate the amount of alcohol consumed by a typical student. Researchers have also found that this tendency to overestimate peer norm, exists regardless of gender, ethnic group, residential housing type, and fraternity or sorority affiliation. . . .

In contrast to the work that has been done in the area of alcohol use, research testing social norms theory in the areas of drug use (other than alcohol) and sexual behavior is sparse. A need to understand factors that might explain drug use and sexual behavior is evident, as research indicates that drug use among college students is increasing, and a large percentage of college students engage in unsafe sexual practices.

Given (1) the rates of alcohol use, drug use, and risky sexual behaviors on college campuses; (2) the empirical support of social norms theory in the alcohol literature; and (3) the scarcity of information regarding social norms theory and drug consumption and sexual behaviors, the purpose of this study was to assess the relationship between peer norms and individual alcohol use, drug use, and sexual behavior. In addition to replicating prior efforts regarding alcohol use, we tested whether or not social norms theory might also apply to drug use and sexual behavior. It is possible that some of the explanatory mechanisms of social norms theory, especially in terms of cultural acceptance and expression by various media outlets, might not be as strong for the use of various drugs as it is for alcohol use. For example, whereas alcohol use is often glorified and promoted in movies about college life (eg, *Animal House*), use of other drugs may not be shown in a positive light. Sexual behavior, however, if not risky or promiscuous sexual behavior, is often portrayed as a normal part of the college experience. We therefore hypothesized that (1) a positive relationship will exist between perceived peer norms and personal behavior in terms of alcohol consumption, drug consumption, and sexual behavior and (2) such relationships will be stronger for alcohol use and sexual behavior than for drug use.

Methods

Participants and Procedures

This project constituted a secondary analysis of data that we collected from 833 undergraduate students at a large, public university the Northeast region of the United States.

Measure

Participants completed the National College Health Assessment (NCHA). The NCHA has 58 content areas that assess health, risk, and protective behaviors in college students, as well as the consequences of such behavior and various perceptions among the students. . . . For the purposes of this study, the items of interest assessed frequency of substance use in the past 30 days, frequency of sexual behavior in the past 30 days, number of sexual partners in the past 12 months, perceived typical student substance use in the past 30 days, perceived typical student sexual behavior in the past 30 days, and perceived number of sexual partners for the typical student in the past 12 months.

Frequency of Substance Use in the Past 30 Days

The NCHA assesses on how many days in the last 30 days the respondent used a variety of substances, with response options ranging from *never used* and *have used, but not in last 30 days* to *used all 30 days*. To maintain consistency with the perceived typical student use items, we recoded these items into 3 categories: *not used in past 30 days, used between 1 and 29 days in past 30,* and *used all 30 days*. To assess normative perceptions of substance use, we asked respondents how often they think the typical student at their school used a variety of substances in the past 30 days, with response options of *never used, used 1 or more days,* and *used daily*. We assessed the following substances: cigarettes, cigars, smokeless tobacco, alcohol, marijuana, cocaine, amphetamines, and Rohypnol/ GHB/ Liquid X.

Frequency of Sexual Behavior in the Past 30 Days

We assessed these items in a manner similar to the way we assessed the substance use items. We asked respondents how many times in the past 30 days they engaged in oral sex, vaginal intercourse, and anal sex and offered 8 response options, ranging from *never did this sexual activity* and *have not done this during the last 30 days to 11 or more times*. We recoded the response options on a 7-point scale, ranging from 1 (did not engage in the activity in the past 30 days) to 7 (engaged in the activity 11 or more times). We used 3 items that ask how many days within the last 30 days the typical student has had oral sex, vaginal intercourse, and anal sex to assess social norms for sexual behavior in the past 30 days. We coded response options on a 7-point scale ranging from 1(0 times) to 7 (11 or more times).

Number of Sexual Partners

We asked respondents to disclose the number of sexual partners they had in the last 12 months, as well as their beliefs about the number of partners the typical student has had in the past 12 months.

Results

... When we compared perceptions of typical student behavior with actual reported behavior, we found that students overestimated consumption patterns for the typical student. For example whereas 62% of the students reported not smoking cigarettes in the past 30 days, 64% believed that the typical student smoked cigarettes daily. Ninety-six percent and 69% of the students reported not using cocaine and marijuana, respectively, in the past 30 days, but 60% and 94% indicated that the typical student used cocaine and marijuana, respectively, at least once in the past 30 days. For all substances except alcohol and rohypnol/GHB/liquid X the category with the highest percentage in terms of perceived typical student use did not match the category with the highest percentage in terms of actual use, and even within these 2 substances there was strong discordance. For example, whereas 3% of the students reported using alcohol daily in the past 30 days, 43% indicated that the typical student consumed alcohol daily.

... Similar to the alcohol consumption items, results indicated that students overestimated the sexual activity of the typical student. For example, the mean number of sexual partners in the past year was 2.55, but students perceived that the typical student had 4.79 partners. Whereas the average student reported vaginal intercourse around 3 to 4 times in the past 30 days, students perceived that the typical student engaged in intercourse 5 to 6 times.

We were interested in determining if inaccuracies in perceived norms were related to a student's own behavior. That is, do students who engage in the behavior more frequently think that the typical student engages in the behavior more frequently, and vice versa? Researchers have previously attempted to answer this question by correlating estimates of a student's own substance use with estimates of others' substance use. However, in our study, we did not code the data on a ratio or interval scale, making Pearson correlations inappropriate, and the low number of response options (3) made Spearman correlations inappropriate. We therefore treated the substance use items as categorical data and conducted chi-square analyses that compared actual behavior to perceived typical student behavior. ...

A statistically significant chi-square emerged for all analyses, and for all analyses a larger than expected number of people who used the substance reported that the typical student used the substance. ...

Because we coded the sexual activity items on a 7-point scale, we assessed the relationship between actual and perceived normative behavior using Pearson correlations. The correlation between actual and perceived oral sex was .33 ($p < .001$), .25 ($p < .001$) between actual and perceived vaginal intercourse, .10 ($p = .005$) between actual and perceived anal sex, and .06 ($p = .098$) between actual and perceived number of sexual partners. These results suggest a small to moderate relationship between actual and perceived oral sex and vaginal intercourse (r^2 values of .11 and .06, respectively) but a very small relationship between actual and perceived anal sex and number of sexual partners (r^2 values of .01 and .004, respectively).

Discussion

The purposes of this study were to (1) compare perceptions of normative behavior in terms of alcohol use, drug use, and sexual behavior with actual behavioral norms in a large sample of college students and (2) determine the relationship between perception of such normative behaviors and students' own actual behaviors. Results from the study indicated that students had considerable misperceptions of the social norms for all behaviors, and the majority of students overestimated normative behaviors for alcohol use, drug use, and sexual behavior. Results also indicated a significant relationship between students' own behaviors and the perceptions of the behavior norms (eg, those who frequently engaged in a behavior were more likely to see the behavior as normative), although the effect sizes for most of the behaviors were fairly small. These findings are consistent with prior research that has found that, in general, college students overestimate peer norms for alcohol use, drug use, and sexual behavior, and that a relationship exists between personal behaviors and perceived normative behaviors. However, results from our study were unique in that they (1) documented a relationship between personal drug use (other than alcohol) and perceived normative use and (2) provided effect sizes that allowed for comparisons to be made regarding the strength of such relationships across a variety of substances and sexual behaviors.

Only a few previous studies have attempted to examine the relationship between personal drug use (other than alcohol) or sexual behavior and perceived norms for such behaviors, and these prior studies suffered from important limitations. For example, Perkins and colleagues found inflated perceived norms for drug use regardless of actual campus norms, but the reported data were on a campus-wide level. Thus, it was impossible to determine if any relationship existed between personal drug consumption and personal perceptions of normative behavior. The design of our study allowed us to make such comparisons. In one of the only studies assessing the relationship between personal and perceived normative sexual behavior, Page and colleagues found that such a relationship did exist. However, this study only included 3 yes or no questions that assessed whether or not the person had engaged in sexual intercourse in the past month, if he or she had had 4 or more lifetime sexual partners, and if he or she had decided to wait until marriage to engage in intercourse, as well as assessing the perceptions regarding the percentage of students who engaged in such behaviors. Our study provided more detailed information than did this study by assessing several different sexual behaviors and providing more specific frequency information for such behaviors. Our study has implications for the overall health of college students, primarily in terms of its implications for social norms-based interventions. Although some researchers have suggested that social norms interventions are not effective in reducing harmful behaviors among students, well-designed studies continue to show that they can in fact be effective prevention tools. Because a precursor for social norm intervention effectiveness is that perceptions of normative behavior are related to personal behavior, our results suggest that the scope of social norms interventions could be expanded. Most researchers who have tested specific social norms interventions have focused primarily on alcohol use, leaving interventions focusing on other drug use or sexual behavior absent from the literature. If such interventions were in fact effective at reducing drug use and unsafe sexual behavior, as has been shown with high-risk alcohol use, then the health of college students engaging in such behaviors could be improved.

We also suggest, based on results from our study, that social norms interventions should be applied to both the general student body and to specific high-risk groups (eg., heavy drinkers) in an effort to improve the health of all students. Our results clearly showed misperceptions in terms of alcohol use, drug use, and sexual behavior. If our study also found that a very strong relationship existed between personal and perceived normative behaviors, then an argument could be made that social norms interventions should be primarily focused on those who frequently engage in the target behavior. Given the small to moderate effect sizes from all of our results, we conclude that general misperceptions exist across the overall student body, although greater misperceptions exist among those who frequently engage in a particular behavior. Thus, social norms interventions might not only provide a remedial effect by reducing the frequency with such individuals who already engage in a behavior choose to do so, but they might also provide a preventative effect by correcting misperceptions among those who are not yet frequently engaging in the behavior.

Discussion Questions

1. According to the Social Norm literature, how do perceived student norms relate to alcohol use among college students?

2. How might college administrators use these research findings in efforts to curb drinking, drug use, and sexual behavior on your campus?

Source: "Differences between Actual and Perceived Student Norms: An Examination of Alcohol Use, Drug Use and Sexual Behavior" by Matthew P. Martens, Jennifer C. Page, Emily S. Mowry, Krista M. Damann, Kari K. Taylor and M. Dolores Cimini, excerpted and with notes & references omitted, from *Journal of American College Health*, Vol. 54, No. 5, 2006. Reprinted with permission of the Helen Dwight Reid Educational Foundation. Published by Heldref Publications, 1319 Eighteenth St., NW, Washington, DC 20036–1802. Copyright © 2006.

CHAPTER 3

The Influence of Friendship Groups on Intellectual Self-Confidence and Educational Aspirations in College

Anthony Lising Antonio

Variation of peer effects at the interpersonal level may be different from, or even cancel out, overall peer effect at the institutional level. Also, reliance on a single aspect of the peer environment may neglect the effects of other peer characteristics; the processes are often interrelated. Positive effects of school-average SES were found to be due to group identification processes while negative effects of school-average ability were the result of social comparison processes, for White students only.

Introduction

Over the past 30 years, research on how college impacts student development has continually pointed to the peer group as perhaps the dominant change agent during the college years (Feldman & Newcomb, 1969; Pascarella & Terenzini, 1991). A college student's peers act as a reference group, or an environmental source of sociocultural norms in the midst of which a student grows and develops (Clark & Trow, 1966). A large body of empirical evidence has been collected over the years to support this conclusion (Astin, 1977, 1993a; Feldman & Newcomb, 1969; Pascarella & Terenzini, 1991).

A review of the research on the impact of college peer groups reveals an interesting trend. The earliest work on peer groups (primarily in the 1950s and early 1960s) focused on peer associations that were structured organizationally by either residential circumstances or formal group affiliations (Feldman & Newcomb, 1969). Most of this work was conducted at single institutions. Furthermore, there was recognition that while the student body characteristics of individual colleges may accentuate initial differences between students attending different institutions, student subcultures and friendship groups within institutions probably mediate the developmental impact

of the student body (Feldman & Newcornb, 1969). . . . Given concurrent research underscoring the importance of student interaction and engagement on campus for development and retention (Astin, 1984; Pascarella, 1985; Tinto, 1975; Weidman, 1989), it is surprising that little current work on peer group influence in college focuses on interpersonal environments such as friendship groups and cliques.

The campus environment itself has changed greatly since the 1950s and 1960s. Colleges and universities are rapidly becoming ethnically and racially diverse student communities (Justiz, 1994), and increasing campus diversity has been accompanied by a rise in racial tension on campus, battles over free speech and the curriculum fought across racial lines, and social self-segregation by race (Altbach, 1991). These troubling patterns are forceful reminders that issues of racial and ethnic difference pervade many corners of the university, and questions regarding student experiences and student development on today's campuses must include the role of racial diversity in their formulation. The general purpose of this study is to conduct a contemporary examination of peer group influence in college that focuses on interpersonal environments and also addresses the role of racial diversity in those environments.

Peer Groups and Peer Group Influence

Researchers in the fields of sociology and social psychology have tended to view student peers as a determinant of school context, which acts as a referent against which students evaluate themselves (Alwin & Otto, 1977). The vast majority of the work that has drawn conclusions on the influence of college peer groups reflects this view, if not explicitly so, in the manner in which the peer group is operationalized methodologically. In these studies, the peer group was thought of as a *reference group* encompassing the entire student body. Early work, for example, likened the campus to a frog pond within which students formed judgments of their abilities and aspirations. Such studies typically measured the relationship between an individual characteristic and the aggregate characteristics of a sample of a school's student body to infer peer group effects (e.g., Bassis, 1977; Davis, 1966; Drew & Astin, 1972; Pascarella, Smart, Ethington, & Nettles, 1987; Thistlethwaite & Wheeler, 1966; Werts & Watley, 1969). The most recent research on college peer group effects continues to follow this conceptual and methodological model. For example, a number of studies continue to use the average freshman class SAT scores of an institution to characterize the peer academic context (e.g., Astin, 1993a; Hurtado & Carter, 1997) and institutional aggregates of individual-level variables such as social attitudes and political views to characterize the peer social context (e.g., Astin, 1993a; Dey, 1996, 1997; Milem, 1998)....

As Feldman and Newcomb (1969) have noted, peer groups can also be thought of as *membership groups.* Within such social groups, shared and consensual sets of norms are developed through interpersonal interaction. Individuals then change under the pressure of direct approval (or disapproval) of valued, trusted peers. This process of peer influence is theoretically distinct from that occurring via reference groups. Reference group peers influence students through school-level, macrosocial processes. Researchers assert, however, that microsocial processes, particularly interpersonal interactions within membership groups, mediate these institutional-level influences (Alexander & Eckland, 1975; Alwin & Otto, 1977). A separate line of research focusing on the effects of Student involvement on development has, in fact, shown that interpersonal interactions are a primary contributor to overall development in college (Astin, 1977, 1993a; Pascarella & Terenzini, 1991)....

Wallace's book, *Student Culture,* clearly illustrated the importance of the college student's interpersonal peer group in influencing members' attitudes towards the attainment of high grades, academic achievement, and aspirations for graduate study (Wallace, 1966). To show these effects, he measured the relationship between the student's interpersonal environment (Rossi, 1966) and changes in views and aspirations during the first year of college. The interpersonal environment for each student was determined not by the researcher, but by each individual respondent. That is, each student responding to a questionnaire examined a list of names of all students at the college, and beside the name of each student recognized, indicated a degree of like or dislike for that person and the number of hours per week he/she spent time with them. Clearly, Wallace's method allows the researcher to access the most proximal of students' social environments in college and provides a model in which to study *interpersonal* peer groups. The downside to this method is that it is methodologically difficult to carry out given the size and complexity of many postsecondary institutions, and correspondingly, may realistically be limited to the study of single institutions. Perhaps it is because of the greater efficiency of gathering institutionally based peer data and the increasing interest in between-institution effects that little research along this vein has followed Wallace. The result, however, is that we know much more about the influence of reference groups on campus and tend to rely on that knowledge to understand the role played by interpersonal peer groups in student learning and development. . . .

Racial Diversity and Peer Group Research

Recently, a handful of studies have investigated the role of racial diversity in the student body on development in college. A primary objective of these studies has been to understand the effects of interacting with someone of another race or ethnicity. Astin (1993a, 1993b) included interracial interaction among a number of student involvement activities in his multi-institutional studies of student development and found cross-race socialization to be associated with increases in cultural awareness, commitment to racial understanding, and commitment to the environment, as well as higher levels of academic development and satisfaction with college. Villalpando (1996) and Tanaka (1996) reported similar findings for Chicanos and white students. In another multi-institutional quantitative study, Chang (1999) found that interracial interaction in college is associated with discussing racial issues, taking ethnic studies courses, and attending racial/cultural awareness workshops. Furthermore, he demonstrated that these behaviors associated with interracial interaction also enhance student retention, college satisfaction, intellectual self-concept, and social self-concept.

Scant attention, on the other hand, has been given to racial diversity in peer groups. . . .

Given the importance of understanding interpersonal peer environments in the context of racial diversity in student development, this study focuses on the college friendship group[1]—a student's best friends on campus—and its effect on students over time. The specific questions addressed in this study are:

(1) To what extent does the interpersonal environment created by the academic abilities and aspirations of the friendship group affect intellectual self-confidence and degree aspirations in college?

(2) What role, if any, does the racial diversity of students' best friends affect the development of intellectual self-confidence and degree aspirations?

Conceptual Framework

Weidman's (1989) model of socialization in college is perhaps the most appropriate theoretical model with which to investigate and interpret peer group effects. My use of Weidman's model follows similar studies of peer effects by Dey (1996, 1997) and Milem (1998). Weidman conceptualizes the major influences on student change in college to be precollege or student background characteristics, the academic and social normative context of an institution, and the impact of parental and non-college reference groups. Normative contexts are particularly important in Weidman's model for influencing change in personal orientations during college. However, Weidman also makes three points about the role of the interpersonal environment and interpersonal processes in socialization. First, he cites Homans (1950, 1961) and argues that the socialization process is quite dependent on interpersonal interaction and the sentimental intensity of the relationship associated with interaction. Second, he notes that frequency of interaction is also critical. Lastly, he underscores a conclusion made by a number of researchers, that the long-term academic impacts of college are not the result of classroom experiences, but of informal forms of social interaction with students and faculty.

By focusing on friendship groups, this study concentrates on two parts of Weidman's model, the normative context of informal peer groups and implicitly, the socialization process of interpersonal interaction. To isolate these elements of the socialization process in college, I borrow from the conceptual and methodological models of college impact of Astin (1984, 1993a), models that are also implicit in Weidman's (1989) framework. Astin's (1993a) model of college impact emphasizes the intercorrelated nature of student precollege characteristics (inputs) and environmental elements of the college experience. . . .

Data and Methodology

Data for this longitudinal, quantitative study were collected during the 1996–1997 academic year at the University of California, Los Angeles (UCLA), a racially and ethnically diverse, public research university.[2] A sample of 2222 third-year students who were previously surveyed as freshmen in 1994 (using a general freshman survey) were surveyed again in the 1996–97 school year with an instrument specifically designed for the study. . . .

The follow-up instrument collected demographic data, measures of behavior and involvement in activities in college, and data on various outcome measures including self-rated abilities and highest level of degree aspirations. Most significant to this study, the names of fellow students whom students identified as members of their friendship group were also collected. Respondents were asked to name up to seven UCLA students with whom they spent most of their time and who they considered to be their "best friends" on campus. They also identified the racial/ethnic composition of their friendship group. The written names were used to retrieve data on friendship-group members collected by the annual freshman surveys. Aggregates of the friends' freshman survey data for each identified friendship group were computed and operationalized as measures of actual friendship-group characteristics. Because it was not possible to obtain freshman data for all friendship-group members, only respondents with sufficient friendship-group data were retained for analyses involving friendship-group measures. In these analyses, the sample size was reduced to 426 students.

The two dependent variables are single item measures taken from the follow-up survey. Academic self-concept was measured with a traditional self-rated ability question that asked the student to rate her "self-confidence (intellectual)" as compared to "the average person your age." The rating was made on a five-point scale ("lowest 10%" to "highest 10%"). A separate question on the survey asked students to report the highest academic degree they intend to obtain and was scored on a four-point scale ("none" to "Ph.D/Ed.D, M.D., J.D"). Both variables were pretested prior to college entry in 1994 with similar measures.

The independent variables derived from the surveys are listed in the Appendix in Table A. The precollege data were collected by the freshman survey in 1994. These measures include the relevant pretest measure for each analysis, gender (female), race/ethnicity, socioeconomic status, and a measure of academic ability, the student's SAT score. . . .

Five friendship group measures were chosen for the model. Three variables are aggregate measures and include group averages of intellectual self-confidence in 1994, SAT composite scores, and degree aspirations in 1994. . . .

The racial composition of each student's friendship group was collected with the follow-up survey and used to calculate a measure of the racial diversity of the friendship group. Racial diversity of the friendship group was measured on a four-point scale. The degree of racial diversity was defined by the percentage of the largest racial or ethnic group represented in the friendship group:

(1) Homogeneous—the largest racial/ethnic group makes up 100% of the friendship group;

(2) Predominantly one race/ethnicity—the largest racial/ethnic group makes up 75–99% of the friendship group;

(3) Majority one race/ethnicity—the largest racial/ethnic group makes up 51–74% of the friendship group;

(4) No majority—the largest racial/ethnic group makes up 50% or less of the friendship group.

These definitions were applied only to friendship groups consisting of two or more students. . . .

The final three variables in the model incorporate one of Weidman's primary mechanisms of socialization, interaction among students. A composite variable of three "time diary" items (studying, partying, and talking with students) provides a general measure of student interaction. Two additional variables measure the frequency of one specific type of interaction hypothesized to be related to both intellectual self confidence and educational aspirations, having conversations about homework or classwork (with best friends and with other students).

The primary set of analyses featured blocked multiple regression procedures to estimate the relationship between the outcome measures and the five friendship-group characteristics while holding constant precollege characteristics and 1994 pretests of intellectual self-confidence and degree aspirations. Independent variables were entered in three discrete blocks for all equations, in accordance with the college impact and socialization models of Astin (1984, l993a) and Weidman (1989). Precollege characteristics were entered into the regression equation first, followed by the block of friendship-group measures and subsequently, the measures of college involvement. Since preliminary analyses indicated a strong, statistically significant

interaction between friendship-group diversity and race, separate analyses were conducted for white students ($n = 151$) and students of color[3] ($n = 285$). . . .

Results

Before reporting the results of the multivariate analyses, it is instructive to examine a number of bivariate relationships between the dependent variables and key independent variables. . . . Statistically significant differences were found for intellectual self-confidence. While a large majority of men (81%) rate themselves highly in intellectual self confidence, a smaller proportion of women (64%) rate themselves similarly. At the lower end of the scale, women are more than twice as likely as men to report themselves among the lowest in terms of intellectual ability, though this difference is not significant at the 0.05 level. Similarly, white students are much more likely than are students of color to rate themselves highly on intellectual self-confidence. No significant race or gender differences were found with respect to student's highest degree aspirations.

The major premise of this study is that elements of the interpersonal environment are important influences on socialization in college. . . . For the purposes of comparison, three dichotomous friendship-group variables were created. For both intellectual self-confidence and degree aspirations, friendship groups were classified as "high" or "low," based upon whether the score for each group measure was above or below the sample mean for each respective variable. . . . Students who have best friends with relatively high levels of intellectual self-confidence tend to be more self-confident intellectually after two years of college compared to students with less confident friendship groups. A similar relationship between individual and group characteristics is evident with respect to degree aspirations. Interpersonal environments that are high or strong in a particular quality, characteristic, or trait, appear to enhance that same quality among students over time. . . .

Comparing students with a low level of diversity in their friendship group ("homogeneous" groups) to their counterparts with relatively higher levels ("no majority" groups), we find no statistically significant differences in intellectual self-confidence or degree aspirations. Some relationship is implied, however, with degree aspirations. While about 11% of students who have diverse friendship groups restrict their educational aspirations to the baccalaureate degree, a larger proportion (18%) have similarly low aspirations among students with homogeneous friendship groups.

As noted above, preliminary regression analyses of the two outcome measures indicated an interaction between race and diversity of the friendship group. . . .

For white students, those who have a higher degree of diversity in their friendship group tend to be less self-confident and have lower educational aspirations than do those with homogeneous groups. For students of color, diversity is associated with enhanced self-confidence and aspirations. . . .

Elements of the interpersonal environment of the friendship group exhibit significant relationships with intellectual self-confidence for both white students and students of color. The effects, however, are quite distinct between the two groups of students. Among students of color, the group level of intellectual self-confidence has the positive effect consistent with the notion of environmental press; they appear to benefit psychologically from interaction within a highly confident set of best friends. For white students, a positive influence on intellectual self-confidence appears to emanate more from high group levels of educational aspirations than with high group self-confidence. The simple correlations indicate that group levels of both intellectual self-confidence and degree aspirations are associated with intellectual self-confidence midway through college. Controlling for individual-level variables diminishes the association with group intellectual self-confidence . . . , leaving group degree aspirations as the only positive group effect. Unlike the case of students of color, white students' friendship groups also exhibit negative effects. The depressive effect of group SAT score is indicative of the Davis (1966) classic relative-deprivation interpretation, in which students are likely depressing their self-evaluations in the presence of high-achieving friends.

. . . . [R]acial and ethnic diversity in the friendship group has a positive effect on intellectual self-confidence for students of color. Among white students, friendship-group diversity is negatively correlated with intellectual self-confidence (partial correlation = $-.21$, p < .05, after controlling for the pretest only) but fails to gain significance in any of the regression models. For students of color, a diverse interpersonal environment of friends appears to enhance intellectual self-confidence regardless of the academic ability, educational trajectories, or degree of self-confidence possessed by themselves or by their closest friends. For white students, friendship-group diversity, at best, has no bearing on their intellectual self-confidence.

It is worth noting that the role of SAT scores as a predictive characteristic is markedly different as well for the two groups of students. At both the individual and group levels, SAT scores are closely associated with white students' sense of their intellectual abilities. High scores at the individual level enhance self-confidence, and as we have seen, group level scores appear to have a relative-deprivation type

of effect. The same variables show no effects, positive or negative, among students of color.

Lastly, measures of involvement have no significant effect on intellectual self-confidence for either group of students, holding constant precollege variables and friendship-group characteristics.

. . . Among white students, high aspirations are associated with initially high aspirations as freshmen and by having a highly self-confident friendship group. Despite a negative value for the bivariate correlation (r = -0.17, p < 0.05), racial diversity in the friendship group again appears to be unrelated to the outcome for white students. Again, a slightly different pattern of effects is suggested by the data for students of color. No relationships were found between any of the three academically oriented friendship-group characteristics and educational aspirations among students of color. Diverse interpersonal environments also appear to have beneficial effects on aspirations. . . .

Discussion

In studying the interpersonal environment of the friendship group, this study serves as a meaningful call to refocus empirical and theoretical treatments of college peer group influence. The peer group effects found in this study are convincing evidence that the microlevel interpersonal environments of a college campus are important sites of influence on socialization and student development. The supposition by researchers that interpersonal environments mediate institutional-level peer group effects is strongly supported by this research, and further, the complexity of the findings underscore a need for researchers and administrators to better understand the role of microenvironments in socialization in college.

With regard to theory, evidence of both relative deprivation and environmental press was found to operate *simultaneously* at the interpersonal level. However, different aspects of the interpersonal environment accounted for each type of influence. In the analysis of intellectual self-confidence, group SAT scores had a depressive effect while educational aspirations had an enhancing effect. The inclusion of multiple measures of the interpersonal environment reveals that different but related aspects of the peer environment can have opposite effects. . . . Finally, while the current study does not make an attempt to compare the relative influence of membership groups (best friends) to reference groups (the campus peer group), the variation of effects found within the white student sample and between white students and students of color suggests that membership groups may not merely mediate campus peer influence, they may serve to isolate members from more distal institutional influences as well.

These findings, coupled with the positive effects of racial diversity evident for students of color only, suggest that the peer factors that influence students' intellectual self-confidence and degree aspirations operate differentially by race.... The variations found between white students and students of color in this study suggest that the factors which produce differential patterns of effects on self-concept may originate in the frequently unmeasured interpersonal environment of students....

The results also raise interesting questions with regard to diversity. The assessment of the influence of racial diversity in the interpersonal environment showed that diversity is an important peer characteristic to consider along with traditional measures of peer ability and self-concept. A previous study showed that racial diversity in the friendship group is important for increasing a student's commitment to racial understanding and is associated with interracial interaction outside of the friendship group (Antonio, 2001). The present study indicates that racial diversity is also important when examining academically related cognitive outcomes. While it is important to recognize that diversity does have an effect on academically oriented outcomes, what is missing from this discussion is a theory of *how* diversity operates in the context of academics. In the case of interracial interaction and racial understanding, the mechanism appears to be the exposure and dealing with issues of racism, discrimination, and cultural difference (Antonio, 2001). The connection that interracial interaction and friendships have to academic outcomes is less clear.

The positive effect of friendship-group diversity on intellectual self-confidence and (more tentatively) educational aspirations was found for students of color only, and the absence of a similar effect among white students can help us think about the relationship between diverse friendships and academic outcomes. In the realm of self-concept and aspirations, diversity may simply provide students—students of color—a normative context which contains more varied reference points from which to evaluate themselves. Under this interpretation, diversity in the friendship group presents students with multiple referents with respect to academic ability, and the presence and tacit acceptance of cultural diversity supports the legitimacy of adhering to multiple norms while remaining a cohesive group. The standard deviation in SAT scores among best friends who are members of the more

homogenous friendship groups (s = 121), for example, is smaller than among best friends in the more diverse groups (s = 131) in this sample. Alternatively, a racially diverse comparative context may reduce a devaluation of ability among students of color due to "stereotype threat" (Steele, 1995) that may be triggered in predominantly white settings and in this manner, function to enhance self-esteem. In this interpretation, racially diverse friendship groups act as enclaves of safety against threats to self-esteem in the greater environment. Finally, perhaps there is simply an environmental press effect for students of color because they are validated by interacting closely with nonwhite students with high (relative to stereotypical assumptions) aspirations and competencies. The combination of this validation with the reframing of their psyche in a nonwhite frame may make group diversity as influential, and in some cases, more influential than academic competencies or self-esteem in the group, as the findings indicate.

The results for white students also raise questions and suggest directions for future study. Are white students' academic self-beliefs and aspirations unaffected by racial diversity? Results of the current study imply that racial diversity is not a salient environmental characteristic in academic domains for white students. In fact, the data suggest a negative effect for diversity on intellectual self-confidence. This result contradicts the findings of Chang (1999) who found interracial interaction among white students to enhance intellectual self-concept. These discrepant findings indicate a need to probe deeper into the friendship groups of white students and understand the differences in interaction within racially diverse groups compared to more homogeneous ones....

Finally, why do white students appear more susceptible to the effects of relative deprivation on intellectual self-confidence than do students of color? The differential effects of SAT scores at both the individual and group levels suggest that SAT scores may carry heavier psychological weight for constructing self-concept among white students as corn pared to students of color. At the group level, it is difficult to exactly determine what group average SAT scores represent. For white students, higher group SAT scores may be a measure of academic ability, competitiveness, or perhaps, academic stress. Future research that "unpacks" the operational meaning of this classic peer measure in the context of the friendship group will help us to further understand the mechanism of relative deprivation and the differential effects observed in this study.

Appendix Table A   Variable in the regression model

Precollege characteristics

Intellectual self-confidence pretest	5-point scale, "lowest 10%" to highest 10%
Highest degree aspirations pretest	6-point scale, "none" to "Ph.D/Ed.D., M.D., J.D."
Gender-female	1-male, 2-female
SES	3-item composite ($\alpha = .803$) composed of:
Mother's education (self-report)	8-point scale, "grammar school or less" to "graduate degree"
Father's education (self-report)	8-point scale, "grammar school or less" to "graduate degree"
Family income (self-report)	14-point scale, "less than $6,000" to "over $200,000"
SAT composite score (self-report)	Continuous
Friendship-group measures Group intellectual self-confidence in 1994	Continuous (group average)
Group degree aspiration in 1994	Continuous (group average)
Group SAT composite score	Continuous (group average)
Racial diversity of friendship group	4-point scale, "homogeneous:" to "no majority/mixed"

College-involvement measures

Student-student Interaction	3 item composite ($\alpha = .660$ composed of:
Studying with other students	8-point scale, "None" to ">20" hours per week
Partying with other students	8-point scale, "None" to ">20" hours per week
Talking with students outside of class	8-point scale, "None" to ">20" hours per week
Conversations about classwork:	
w/students in friendship group	3-point scale, "Not at all" to "Frequently"
w/students outside of friendship group	3-point scale, "Not at all" to "Frequently"

NOTES

1. The term "friendship group" is used here to mean the interpersonal environment composed of a student's best friends on campus. With this definition, best friends may form a singular, cohesive group or a more diffuse friendship network. The term is used in lieu of the somewhat more cumbersome, "interpersonal environment of best friends."

2. The undergraduate student body at the time of the study was approximately 40% white, 35% Asian American, 16% Latino, and 6% African American.

3. In this study, students of color were defined as students not self-identifying as "white/Caucasian."

Discussion Questions

1. According to Antonio, why is it important to study the influence of friendship groups, as well as the overall campus-wide peer experience, on students?

2. How do you think your friends have influenced your intellectual self-confidence and educational goals?

Source: "The Influence of Friendship Groups on Intellectual Self-Confidence and Educational Aspirations in College" by Anthony L. Antonio, excerpted and with references and some notes omitted from *The Journal of Higher Education,* Vol. 75, No. 4, July/August 2004. Reprinted by permission of The Ohio State University Press.

CHAPTER 4

Authentic Identities

Straightedge Subculture, Music, and the Internet

J. Patrick Williams

The author shows that a new type of music-based subculture is emerging whose participation is limited to the Internet. Participants in a straight-edge internet forum negotiate their affiliations with the subculture and some members attempt to halt others' claims to a straightedge identity. The study suggests that the Internet is emerging as a new, but highly contested, subcultural scene.

Since the publication of Dick Hebdige's (1979) highly influential book, *Subculture: The Meaning of Style,* youth culture researchers have used the subculture concept primarily to study music- and style-based cultural phenomena. Participation in youth subcultures has therefore typically been characterized by the consumption of specific types of music and clothing and participation in local, face-to-face music scenes. What has emerged over the past 25 years of research utilizing the subculture concept is a tacit assumption that music is *the* nexus of subcultural phenomena. I offer a corrective to this trajectory in subculture studies by exploring the emerging importance of the internet in subcultural experience and participation. . . .

However important music might he for the study of youth subcultures, there are changes occurring in contemporary societies that require we reassess music's central status in facilitating subcultural participation and identification. Through a multiyear ethnography in an internet forum dedicated to the straightedge youth subculture. I have explored various ways in which youth online affiliate with subcultures. What I have found challenges the thesis that youth cultural phenomena—whether subcultures or scenes—rotate on a primary axis of music production and consumption. In particular, I study the interaction that occurs among self-identifying members of the straight-edge youth subculture in an internet forum. A rift between

two different types of straightedge participants has emerged as more people outside of traditional straightedge music scenes learn about straightedge on the internet and begin interacting within online subcultural spaces.[1]

In this article, I focus specifically on claims for "authentic" straightedge identity that participants made online. I then relate such claims to the larger issue of the symbolic meanings participants attach to music and the internet, respectively. The central issue I address revolves around the fact that there were at least two types of straightedgers present in the internet forum: those who used the forum as a *supplement* to participation in a face-to-face music scene and those whose internet use was a *primary* or *sole* source of subcultural participation. By unpacking the debate among forum participants over the authenticity of various participants and the symbolic value attached to music and the internet, I highlight how the internet functions as a new social space for subcultural identification and change.

The Straightedge Subculture Offline and Online

Straightedge emerged in the United States in the early 1980s from within the music-driven punk subculture as a sort of subcultural reaction to the uncritical and apathetic attitudes and behaviors of many mainstream American youth as well as to the emphasis placed on alcohol consumption by adult culture. Straightedgers, especially in the early to mid-1980s, subscribed to a punk ideology of resistance to mainstream cultural values and norms, which they articulated most often through music (Wood 1999). Two songs released in 1981 by Washington, D.C., band Minor Threat are especially noteworthy in the creation of straightedge. In the first song, titled "Straight Edge," lyricist Ian MacKaye wrote about how he differed from other youth in his disdain for recreational drug use (alcohol, cigarettes) and promiscuous sexual activity. In another song by Minor Threat, titled "Out of Step," MacKaye claimed. "I don't smoke, I don't drink, I don't fuck, at least I can fucking think! I can't keep up, can't keep up, can't keep up! Out of step with the world." These lyrics were almost immediately appropriated by many punks as a set of subcultural norms or "rules:"

The band's new "rules" of resistance were not exceptional among punk bands as Minor Threat existed within a larger North American network of "positive youth" punk bands. However, the term "straightedge" seemed to strike a chord with some punks around the United States, and within a year of its release, youth around the country had begun claiming to *be* straightedge. Unlike many youth subcultural identities, which are grounded in sets of shared practices, the straightedge identity is based on a combination of shared practices and "not doings" (Mullaney 2001). On the one hand, straightedgers gather in local idiocultural scenes, producing and consuming straightedge music and contributing to an international D.I.Y. punk ethic (Haenfler 2004a; Mattson 2001). Such communal interaction is crucial in the construction of a straightedge social identity. At the same time, straightedgers develop personal identities grounded in an ascetic lifestyle of *not* doing drugs and *not* engaging in promiscuous sex.

Since the late l990s, the straightedge subculture has been diffused around the globe through the internet. This diffusion has taken many forms. Individual straightedgers have posted information about the subculture, such as song lyrics and band biographies on personal and official band web sites. They have started internet listservs and developed FAQs. They have traded straightedge music via peer-to-peer networks, and they have started interactive forums that thousands of people have joined. As a result of this subcultural diffusion, individuals have discovered straightedge in a dislocated form, fractured from its musical roots. Many of these people learn about straightedge online and decide to claim a personal straightedge identity. Many of them subsequently join face-to-face straightedge scenes and develop a social straightedge identity, but many others do not. Those who join face-to-face scenes come to agree that music is a tie that binds, and participation in a face-to-face scene is an essential component of *being* straightedge. Many of these straightedgers argue that the diffusion of straightedge through the internet is leading to a "defusion" of the subculture, a stripping away of its resistant and countercultural heritage as "drug-free kids" appropriate the straightedge label. This perspective is resisted by many of these so-called drug free kids who identify as straightedge and who rely on the internet as their sole subcultural resource and means of subcultural interaction. At stake are young people's subcultural identities and their social-psychological functions (e.g., self-esteem, self-efficacy), as well as membership in an extensive, global subcultural network.

Social and Personal Dimensions of the Authentic Self

Developing a symbolic interactionist conception of authentic identity helps us understand how straightedgers affiliate with the subculture as they write about the relative importance of music and the internet in their subcultural lives. In exploring how straightedgers write about music, the internet, and subcultural authenticity online, I want to emphasize the socially constructed nature of authenticity as well as its social-psychological functions in terms of social and personal identity. Many researchers assume the objectivity of authenticity, assigning labels such as "insider" and "outsider" or describing logics of subcultural capital as if they were essential qualities of people's selves (see, e.g., Fox 1987). This is problematic because it concretizes "dominant" definitions that may arise through interaction among members of subcultural networks or from outside actors (e.g., the mass media) without adequately addressing the sociological implications of authenticity discourses. Authentic characteristics do "not inhere in the object. person or performance said to be authentic. Rather, authenticity is a claim made by or for someone, thing or performance and either accepted or rejected by relevant others" (Peterson 2005, 1086). What have been traditionally ignored in subculture research are the voices of marginal actors that exist on the peripheries of the subculture under investigation.[2]

In everyday life, subcultural youth often talk about themselves in essentialist terms. For example, they regularly claim to *be* real while charging others with simply *doing* subcultural things, such as dressing, speaking, or acting in certain ways in order to be cool or fit in (Widdicombe and Wooffitt 1990; Williams 2006). This is *social* identification: "[S]ocial identity . . . goes beyond any particular [context], for it places the individual as a member of a social category that differs from other categories. Membership in [a] category accompanies the person even when he or she is not [interacting with other subculturalists]—hence, the social identity of [e.g., a straightedger] is larger in scope and longer in duration than the particular situated activities on which it is based" (Hewitt 2003, 107). Of course, it is only in interaction that we can observe the articulation of a social self. Successful identification rests upon expressing a similarity of self to one's peers as well as distinction from members of mainstream society. Subcultural participants may, for example, construct narratives that emphasize their allegiance to a group ethos or to subcultural values and norms (Williams and Copes 2005; Copes and Williams forthcoming). Such narratives build in-group cohesion and highlight how subculture differs from mainstream culture. The resulting subcultural boundaries situate some people on the "inside" and others on the "outside." Such identifications are an affective as well as a cognitive experience, invoking positive feelings and emotions as people identify as members of a group. Because straightedgers identify themselves in contrast to mainstream culture, many of them construct rigid subcultural boundaries to control who successfully claims a straightedge identity. In short, the social dimension of authenticity refers to how individuals claim insider status in a social category.

At the same time, however, authenticity "is partly dependent on warranting claims not to have been influenced by others, subject to peer pressure and conformity" (Widdicombe and Wooffitt 1995, 212). The personal dimension of authenticity therefore represents "the valorization of individualism and the demonization of conformity" (McLeod 1999, 14). From this perspective, the authentic self is one that commits to a personal life project and is not controlled by outside influence. Subculturalists may identify in terms of a lifelong commitment to a subcultural lifestyle, for example, even if that lifestyle commitment precedes or follows subcultural affiliation. Williams (2003) and Wood (2003), for example, independently found that some straightecigers talked about *being* straightedge even before they learned about the subculture; straightedge was something inside of themselves

that they discovered. Similarly, Mullaney (2001) found that discourses of virginity were grounded in personal narratives of resistance to temptation, and McLeod (1999) explored how members of hip-hop subculture constructed authentic personal identities vis-à-vis sellouts and tagalongs. In short, the personal dimension of authenticity refers to how individuals articulate a personal commitment to a subcultural value structure or lifestyle.

Community and Identity Online

The expression of authentic selves occurs in the face-to-face world as well as online. I investigated a computer-mediated social space, one in which subcultural participants came and went over weeks, months, and years. Participants gathered from around the globe—from the United States and Canada, the United Kingdom and Europe, to Australia and New Zealand to discuss their everyday lives within the frame of the straightedge subculture. As individuals interact in internet-based cultural sites, they construct and affirm meaningful collective identities based on norms and beliefs that are personally important and that are supported by others (see Rheingold 2000; Kollock and Smith 1999). . . .

Researchers have for some time studied how internet users express aspects of self in computer-mediated contexts. Turkle (1995), for example, studied how individuals develop, through online personae, new understandings of their personal identities. Viewing cyberspace as sites of psychological moratoria, Turkle described cyberspaces as social spaces where individuals can try out different roles, identities, and ways of acting. Most people are concerned with how others perceive them, as Goffman (1959, 1963) so thoroughly demonstrated in his studies of the presentation of self. Of course, people are not necessarily concerned with what everybody thinks about them, but rather with the reflected appraisals of significant others (Shibutani 1955). This concern exists in both face-to-face situations and computer-mediated contexts. The anonymous qualities of the internet may empower many people to play with how they present themselves online, yet many studies suggest that users are interested in building and expressing stable, continuous selves grounded in meaningful interaction with significant others (Baym 1995; Bromberg 1996; Coate 1997; Schleef 1996).

More recently, researchers have begun to study the relationship between the internet and subcultures. Williams (2003, 67) explored how straightedgers strategically created usernames and signature files to use as "subcultural identifier[s] online that marked participants as in-group members," while Hodkinson (2004) found that the internet played a key role in facilitating the construction of a translocal British identity among members of the goth subculture. In their comparison of rave and straightedge subcultures online, Wilson and Atkinson (2005) argued that straightedgers tended to use the internet "in more countercultural ways than the more apolitical and incorporated raver/clubber subculturalists" and that straightedgers were concerned with the expression of "true" subcultural identity in online as well as offline contexts. Lastly, Williams and Copes (2005) studied the variety of participants on a straightedge internet site and how subcultural boundaries were constructed to distinguish "real" straightedgers from "sellouts." With the exception of the last study, most recent research on subcultural internet usage has not adequately explored the diversity of voices within subcultural sites. Instead, online identities are often represented by researchers as mirrors or extensions of subculturalists' offline identities. Thus, it is time to give more attention to the conflicts that are emerging between types of subcultural internet users—those whose use supplements their offline lives and those whose use substitutes for offline, face-to-face participation in subcultural scenes.

Research Site and Method

The internet forum I studied was dedicated to the straightedge subculture. This forum fit previous definitions of an online community as it had its own "norms, its rules (netiquette), its own emotional vocabulary—guidelines for posting, acceptable subjects, regular users, leaders, oldtimers, and a constant circulation of newcomers" (Denzin 1998, 99–100). The web site utilized an asynchronous bulletin board service, wherein individuals posted messages in forums that anyone with an internet connection and a web browser could access. Participants could interact with one another by clicking on "threads" in each forum. Once they chose a thread, participants could read statements or questions posted by other participants and add their own voice to the conversation it they wanted by posting a message of their own. . . .

I approached the Internet forum from an ethnographic standpoint. My initial interest was in answering the question "What is going on here?" However, after only a day or two casually reading posts, I realized that the internet functioned as a key source of conflict among

various participants in the forum. At that moment, my focus became more analytic (Snow, Morrill, and Anderson 2003) as my interest in exploring the role that the internet played in subcultural interaction and identification developed. I collected data using two methodological strategies that Bainbridge (2000, 57) calls "observation ethnography" and "informant ethnography." The former was an unobtrusive research role in which I conducted content analysis of forum threads without focused interaction with participants. During the observation ethnographic phase, I analyzed the first message of every thread posted in the forum between February 2001 and September 2001 (n 285) using interpretive and ethnographic content analysis methods (Altheide 1996) and the QSR NVivo software package.

It was during my analysis of these early posts that I noticed that straightedgers were arguing among themselves about who was and was not "really" straightedge. Therefore, using individual posts as the unit of analysis, I began coding posts using a grounded theory method (Charmaz 2000). Informed by an initial set of topical codes, I began to develop coding schema to categorize my initial understandings of what was theoretically and empirically significant.

My second strategy, informant ethnography, was more interactive. Here, I used the themes that emerged during my initial coding phase (for example, patterns of affiliation, authenticity claims, and mechanisms of boundary maintenance) to start "focused discussions"—new thread topics for the participants to respond to. I started threads that asked participants about their affiliation with straightedge, their understandings of subcultural rules, their opinions about mainstream culture, and so on. By monitoring the threads daily, I could guide conversations, bring them back on track when participants strayed off topic, and ask follow-up questions based on initial responses. The focused discussions I developed over two years—from 2001 to 2003—resulted in nearly 1,000 posts, which I analyzed in the same way as previous, nonsolicited posts. that is, further developing my coding schema through constant comparison of forum data. In addition, I continued to monitor other threads in the forum. My analysis below includes data from my focused discussions and from several other threads that were relevant to my research interests.

During the informant ethnographic phase, I also interviewed nine key informants in order to gain clarification on the meaning of subcultural forms and activities. I selected key informants according to their level of participation (measured by total number of posts), the extent to which I noticed their participation in specific threads, or the opinions they expressed. I interviewed the web site's owner/administrator, individuals who posted regularly over a long period, as well as some people who posted frequently for a short time before quitting. I made sure to include participants who identified themselves as members of face-to-face music straightedge scenes and members who identified themselves as being totally reliant on the internet for straightedge-related interactions. Interviews lasted between 90 and 180 minutes, and all took place online using either an instant-messaging or internet-relay-chat program, both of which are popular among young internet users. I developed the interview schedule from the themes that emerged from earlier analysis but left it semistructured so that I could develop and change questions as the research progressed and new areas of interest emerged. . . .

Throughout the research project, several significant codes emerged, including *affiliation* (how individuals affiliated with the subculture), *authenticity* (instances where "real" or "fake" straightedge identity was discussed), *rules* (the normative structure of the subculture), and *boundaries* (the cleavages and distinctions between the so-called mainstream and the subculture). In the remainder of this article, I focus in particular on the first two codes—affiliation and authenticity—and how they function together to illuminate the internet's role in subcultural change.

Authenticity Claims and the Importance of the Scene

With few exceptions, the discussions I observed in my research focused on the practice and experience of straightedge subculture and identity. Participants in the forum seemed generally invested in expressing a social self that was in line with their own personal sense of self. In other words, participants strived to present a straightedge self comprised of congruous social and personal identities. The internet forum provided a meaningful subcultural space within which participants could do discursive identity work. This identity work tended to ground itself in the articulation of either a self that resisted mainstream culture or a self that was locatable within the straightedge community (offline or online). However, social and personal identities expressed in the forum were not necessarily accepted by other forum participants. On the contrary, I observed a significant amount of debate and contestation over what it meant to *be* straightedge.

The debates, disagreements, and verbal fistfights online reflect the fluid and contextual characteristics of subcultural identity. While different participants took different positions on the matter of subcultural authenticity, I distilled them into a continuum with two poles. At one pole were those forum participants who utilized the internet forum as a supplement to their participation in face-to-face straightedge music scenes. I refer to these participants as *music-straightedgers* because they tended to support the idea that only participants of a face-to-face straightedge music scene could claim a straightedge identity. At the other pole were those users for whom the internet was a primary or exclusive subcultural resource and medium for subcultural participation. I refer to these individuals as *net-straightedgers*. Users in this analytic category tended to express the belief that anyone who lived a straightedge lifestyle following straightedge "rules" against drug uses and promiscuous sex—could be straightedge. All along the continuum, participants were concerned with expressing authentic straightedge identities.[3]

There were several threads in the forums that clearly contextualized the debate surrounding authenticity. One thread in particular clearly represents the heterogeneous perspectives of participants. Below, I have extracted posts from several participants to highlight some of these perspectives:

Confederate: Does punk rock, hardcore or whatever it is called nowadays still have a role in the straightedge movement? I guess what I'm asking is, can you separate the music from the scene or are they intertwined? I think the music and the "punk rock" culture is what makes straightedge unique so the two cannot and should not be separated.

XzeroX: I too believe that straightedge and hardcore/punk should forever be intertwined. I wouldn't, however, tell someone that they can't be sXe unless they listen to punk. This will be a touchy subject, so heads up.[4]

Amalek: I don't believe so at all. Music may have 'spawned' straightedge, but I believe straightedge is fully independent from any musical 'scene,' besides, I don't listen to punk rock.

XantagX: Straightedge can't he independent of the music. It's a subculture centered around a style of music. You take away the music, you take away the sub culture, and all you have left is a bunch of drug free kids.

Amalek:　So you're saying I'm not straightedge? I find that extremely funny, because that's bullshit. I don't listen to hardcore, and I'm straightedge.

In the opening post, Confederate stated his belief that music was a fundamental aspect of straightedge culture and asked others for their opinions. Some participants such as XantagX supported Confederate and stated explicitly that straightedge derived from the punk and hardcore music subcultures. Amalek and others who did not identify as straightedge music scene members typically disagreed, claiming a straightedge identity while disavowing any connection with a music scene. Still other participants, such as Xerox, stated that the issue was more complicated than a simple "agree" or "disagree" answer. The heat of the debate can be understood by what was at stake the perceived authenticity of participants' straightedge identities. Authenticity claims link directly to the larger issue of music's, versus the internet's, role in the straightedge subculture. Some music-straightedgers sought to establish a rigid subcultural boundary online, while other participants argued in favor of a broader definition of straightedge that included anyone who lived the straightedge lifestyle. . . .

For music-straightedgers, the face-to-face music scene represented the embodiment of collective resistance. Early on in my research, I realized that "the scene" was an important resource for articulating resistance because a significant amount of everyday interaction online was about local scenes. The scene was not only a site of resistance but also the source of a resistance based straightedge identity. For example, in another post from the above focused discussion, a participant authoritatively stated that "without the scene, without the music, there is straight but no edge." In response, Amalek asked. "Where do you get the idea that if you don't listen to a certain style of music you're not edge? Or if you don't 'go to shows' or aren't 'in the scene' you're not edge? Straightedge is a commitment till death of being drug free. [It] is a bond." Participants framed their authenticity as subculturalists in terms of resistance to the mainstream. In the first post, being straightedge was different than simply being straight; participating in the scene made one uniquely straightedge, while not participating in the scene made one "straight." . . . In the second post, Amalek constructed straightedge as an individual commitment "till death" against society's accepted practices, rather than as a collective form of resistance. . . .

Mapping a Geography of "the Scene"

Music-straightedgers repeatedly wrote about the scene as a necessary element in constructing a straightedge identity, while net-straightedgers regularly contested such claims. Because of this conflict, we need to understand how straightedgers in the forum constructed the concept of "scene" and what currency it had within the subculture.

Subcultural theorists and subculturalists alike use the term *scene* "to signify some kind of . . . located and subcultural space" (Bennett and Kahn-Harris 2004, 13). According to Straw (1991, 379), scenes "actualize a particular state of relations between various populations and social groups, as these coalesce around specific coalitions of musical style." People who regularly come together to consume music—in clubs, at parties, even through sharing purchased CDs—constitute a local scene. . . .

For the music-straightedgers in the forum, the scene had to do with their relationship to the production, distribution, and consumption of straightedge music. Belonging to the scene involved listening to straightedge music and actively helping to keep the music scene alive. One participant explicitly stated that the scene was "more than just kids sitting around not doing drugs." Only those who participated in local subcultural events such as concerts, straightedge parties, and so on represented the scene. The apparent reverence that music-straightedgers held for local scenes cannot be explained by some external locus of control. Rather, participants expressed the relationship in dialectic, even symbiotic terms. The scene depended on people who were willing to make sacrifices in everyday life to ensure its survival. At the same time, the scene helped ensure the survival—sometimes in a very real sense—of its members.

SubPush:　My life revolves around supporting the scene because I know that I owe [it] my life. Without it I would be dead or alone with no self-confidence. It wasn't until I was exposed to the hardcore scene that I felt like I could stand up for myself and use my own voice. Because of the support of some older members of the scene I learned how to stand up for myself and I learned that I could have joy in my life and not be absolutely anti-social. I cannot say that I would still be alive today if I was not exposed to [the scene] as I constantly considered suicide during my early adolescence due to feelings of alienation, loneliness, and disillusionment. I felt like there was no one who I could relate to. I owe it to the scene to give back as much as I can because it has given me everything.

This music straightedger emphasized the scene's embeddness in the larger punk and hardcore cultures and claimed that it was senseless to think of straightedge any other way. More important, he created a vivid picture of the importance that the scene held for some of its members. The scene was symbolically constructed in sincere and reverent terms. Net-straightedgers were consequently constructed as outsiders who could not understand the "true" meaning of the scene.

In interviews, I specifically asked music-straightedgers to define the straightedge scene. Most definitions placed explicit emphasis on attending straightedge music shows and being part of an active face-to-face community.

XXXwah: Yeah going to shows would be the base [definition of the scene] I guess, but not just that. I think it's a lot in helping out to fuel that scene in any way you can, whether it he posting flyers, helping setup gear at a show, working the door, doing favors for bands etc. Being in a band is all good, too.

The scene had many aspects, foremost of which was music. Participants saw concerts as the nexus from which straightedgers constructed their subcultural selves. Playing in a band and working with/for straightedge bands were important activities. Another straightedge music fan, xHCgrrrlx similarly pointed to music's importance when she described the scene as "a group of kids in a city that are all edge and go to edge shows and listen to edge hands." Yet another music-straightedger conceived of the scene in terms of whom he associated with.

xTxTx: Well I hang out with a lot of kids that share my anti-drug beliefs within the hardcore community. . . . [T]t's generally the same kids hanging out together almost every weekend and exchanging ideas. I'd say it is a scene, because it's at least some hat based on the fact that we have mutual interests and goals.

Besides the cultural dimensions of the scene (e.g., the music), additional dimensions became apparent. including social (a *group* of kids, kids hanging out *together*), geographical (a group of kids in a city), as well as participatory (going to edge shows, *helping* out, *exchanging* ideas, *doing* favors, *listening* to music). These dimensions of the scene

represented criteria for subcultural authenticity from a music-straightedge perspective.

In an interview, xTxTx went on to explain how forum members who did not belong to face-to-face straightedge scenes were "not really edge." When I asked other music-straightedgers about forum participants who self identified as straightedge but did not participate in the hardcore music scene, one replied, "a lot of those kids I think are becoming straight but not edge." For xTxTx, they were "straight" because they did not use drugs, but he (and others) expressed a belief that net-straightedgers lacked the rebellious "edge" that characterized participants in the hardcore music scene. He did not challenge the positive choices these kids were making, but he was clear in his conviction that they were not authentic straightedgers. . . .

In sum, music-straightedgers who participated in the forums conceived the scene as an essential component of the subculture and a straightedge identity. The scene symbolized the centrality of music and the close-knit, face-to face tradition of straightedge subculture. Music-straightedgers expressed the belief that participation in the scene made them qualitatively different from people who did not participate in a scene. Thus, music-straightedgers constructed symbolic boundaries and worked to convince net-straightedgers to give up their claims to a straightedge identity. This did not always happen. As Peterson and Bennett (2004, 3) point out, there are almost always those "few at the core of the scene [who] may live that life entirely, but, in keeping with a late-modern context in which identities are increasingly fluid and interchangeable, most participants regularly put on and take off the scene identity." For many participants, the straightedge identity was not salient all the time, although it remained very central.[5] Equally important is the idea that some participants had little or no access to scenes at all in the face-to-face world. Finally, we can look at xTxTx's definition of scene above and ask, Is this not just what forum participants were doing online—hanging out with other kids who shared similar beliefs, similar experiences, and similar strategies for resisting mainstream culture? . . .

The Internet as a Straightedge Scene

Regardless of their orientation toward straightedge music, many of the forum participants agreed that straightedge was about a scene, yet were not certain whether the scene was *only* about music. Some participants, who at one point argued against the authenticity of net-straightedgers, came to change their opinions over time and subsequently claimed in the forum that at some level the definition of *scene* was vague and open to multiple interpretations.

Confederate: What is important is participation in the punk/indie subculture. Participation includes listening to the music, interacting with others in the scene, going to shows, even popping up on the internet. Scene includes everything from listening to music, to going to shows to the internet.

In this and similar cases, forum users acknowledged that internet participation counted for something, though music preference appeared to remain a key criterion for inclusion. In another example, XdoitdoitX wrote that the internet functioned primarily as a source of information to individuals outside of the punk/hardcore music scene. "Since most people who are straightedge come from the hardcore scene, everyone assumes one has to listen to hardcore to be straightedge. Sure that's where it came from, but people make the decision all the time to be drug free without ever hearing of *Chain of Strength* [a straightedge band]. They just happen to start claiming edge because of the education through the internet and other media." Importantly, XdoitdoitX recognized that, in addition to information, the internet served as a source from which identities were constructed. . . .

In the public forums and in a private interview, the web site's owner/administrator and I discussed the idea of the internet as a new type of straightedge scene. During the interview, he wrote about how he learned about straightedge.

The Man: I think I was wasting time in some chat room and someone was asking me all this stuff, "Do you drink" "Do you, etc., etc." And they pretty much just said, "You're straightedge, are you?" And having no idea what the hell they were talking about . . . I looked up some info on it that day and sort of took the name on at the same time.

Like him, other net-straightedgers reported learning about straightedge from the internet. PunkRockBob, for example, said that he researched the term *straightedge* after he heard about it from a schoolmate: "My main source of info was the internet because no one else I know knows anything about it really." Similarly, Non related to me how, although she knew some punk straightedgers in the face-to-face world, most of her information and communication about straightedge came from the forum. Yet another participant wrote, "I was told about sXe by a cyber goth friend." Most of the participants I interviewed—even music-straightedgers—shared similar stories of first hearing the word "straightedge" through friends, TV, or magazines but gaining most of their early information directly from internet sites.

The usefulness of the internet in facilitating the diffusion of straightedge subculture is clear in these comments, just as it is clear in the discussions about authenticity. As one participant wrote, a scene is "just about creating a positive space that's drug free and supporting it. That's all. I guess it's about making a difference. Small as it may be, its something, you know?" Added to this growing awareness of the power of the internet, there were many net-straightedgers who openly questioned the relative roles of music and the internet in spreading straightedge culture. In the following post, Listen made clear a cultural truth: all cultures change as people come to attach new sets of meaning to their own practices and to the social objects involved in those practices.

Listen: Music is transient. Hardcore will eventually warp into other forms of music and fade from existence, whether you like to believe it or not. Once the music is gone, does that mean you hardcore scenesters want sXe and all of its ideals gone with it? sXe is a positive movement that could influence SO many people for the better, It has helped so many people change their lives for the better. That, to me, is a LOT more important than your stupid scene. Maybe you think "that's great" but you still don't think they should call themselves sXe. Well I say who gives a damn? Obviously the sXe label helped them Out, so for fuck's sake . . . let them have it! If the internet can provide that, then I think that's great. I know I found out about sXe one way and someone else found out about it another way, etc. and this is just yet another way of doing it. It opens up the harrier a little bit. If you don't like how it does that, then I don't know why you would sign up here and support its occurrence.

Conclusion

The diffusion of subculture through the internet is indicative of how subcultures spread globally as well as the extent to which information and communication technologies now inundate everyday life (Wellman and

Haythornthwaite 2001). Sherry Turkle argues that "as people spend more and more time in virtual places, there is a push, a kind of expression of human desire, to make the boundaries between the physical and the virtual more permeable. To have communities on the screen and to bring them into the physical surrounds, to have communities in the physical and bring them into the virtual, and in so doing, to enhance their possibilities for action and communication, and political power" (Turkle and Salamensky 2001, 236). Certainly, we can see such desire in the discourse of net-straightedgers as they transgressed boundaries not only between the online and face-to-face worlds but between mainstream cultures and subcultures.

The quality and quantity of threads that emphasized the differences among music- and net-straightedgers represent the extent to which computer-mediated communication is affecting the straightedge subculture. The continuingly assumed predominance of music in the straightedge subculture is evident in even the most recent social-scientific research (Helton and Staudenmeier 2002; Wood 2003; Haenfler 2004b). Among straightedgers who participate in online scenes, however, the centrality of music is repeatedly contested. Appropriating prior researchers claims about music, I have explored how *the internet* "is not simply a static cultural object . . . but . . . is used for the formation of new forms of individual and collective identity" (Cushman 1995, 91). Similarly, Frith's (1996, 91) words help us conceptualize how "the issue is not how [*the internet*] reflects the people, but how it produces them, how it creates an experience." Much like straightedge music has created an experience for members of music scenes over the past 25 years, internet forums simultaneously function as a subcultural resource, a form of subcultural expression, and a medium for subcultural existence for young people outside music scenes.

Following Thornton (1995), we can see that media, including the internet, "are integral to the formation of subcultures, playing a significant role in both their origin as well as prolonging their lifecycle. The media exist as systems of communication critical to the circulation of ideas, images, sounds and ideologies that bind culture(s) together Some media legitimate while others popularize, some preserve the esoteric while others are seen to sell out" (Stahl 2004, 3 I). Understanding how the internet functions within youth subcultural formations therefore depends on how we conceptualize it. In symbolic interactionist terms, it is a social object to which different people attribute different (sets of) meanings. For participants of face-to-face subcultural scenes, the internet may be an information and communication medium in the strictest sense it gets used primarily to communicate information about the face-to-face world (Hodkinson 2002). For individuals who do not participate in face-to-face scenes, however, the internet is more than a medium; it is a social space through which personal and social identities are constructed, given meaning, and shared through the ritual of computer-mediated interaction. From this perspective, "communication becomes a powerful tool that organizes individual desires and dreams of belonging by representing a certain range of experiences, thereby offering the possibility for deep, affective investment" (Stahl 2004, 36).

I have linked the conflict between music and the internet to such affective investment via the struggle for authentic subcultural identity. By constructing alternate paths to authentic selfhood, individuals who do not meet preexisting subcultural criteria still have the opportunity to construct a subcultural identity and to reap the social psychological benefits that come with it (Rosenberg and Kaplan 1982). . . .

The struggle for authenticity occurs through the active appropriation of new communication media. Young people appropriate and rework communication media, constructing new narratives of personal and social experience. The traditional measurement of authenticity within straightedge appears to be through *doing* straightedge community in local punk/hardcore music scenes and earning respect through what one net-straightedger facetiously called "the scenester point system." The growth of internet scenes confounds the idea that a face-to-face scene is necessary because the internet allows individuals who are disconnected from local punk/hardcore music scenes to interact within the subculture. New members, disconnected (often by choice) from hardcore music scenes, consider themselves authentic and utilize computer-mediated spaces to articulate their identities and experiences *as* straightedgers.

. . . The internet provides sources of information and new social spaces within which youth from outside punk cultures come to learn about, and self-identify as, straightedge. These youth evaluate their own positions within youth (drug) cultures and decide to claim a resistant, abstinent identity. But the influx of youth from outside the punk/hardcore music subculture does not go unchallenged. Net-straightedgers' personal commitments to straightedge norms do not convince all music-straightedgers that they are more similar to each other than net-straightedgers are to drug-free grandparents, Mormons, or DARE, participants. Nevertheless, net-straightedgers continue to build their own forms of authenticity online as internet sites emerge as new subcultural scenes. These scenes are built with the understanding of the fluid and contingent nature of subculture.

Notes

1. To date, *all* social scientific research on straightedge has assumed the centrality of music within the subculture Examples are Haenfler (2004a, 200db). Helton and Staudenmeier (2002), O'Hara (1999), Wilson and Atkinson (2005), and Wood (1999, 2003).

2. This is a problem not simply of subculture studies but of mainstream sociology as well. See Fraser, Kick, and Williams (2002) for a discussion of taking a margin perspective in sociological research

3. I do not mean to imply that any person who claims to be straightedge is *more* or *less* straightedge than anyone else The two "types" of straightedge participant are analytic categories that I employ to contextualize my discussion of authenticity, music, and the internet. These analytic categories are not merely ideal types in the Weberian sense. Rather, the categories emerged from my analysis of participants' naturally occurring interaction that is the categories represent how many of the forum participants construct straightedge boundaries.

4. I edited the posts for grammar and spelling mistakes but was careful not to edit out subculturally relevant argot For example, forum participants regularly use the acronym *sXe* as shorthand for "straightedge." It compromises the S and E from *straightedge* surrounding an *X*, which is a straightedge symbol. The *X* can also be seen incorporated into many usernames. In many cases, participants chose usernames that represented some aspect of their personal or subcultural selves. I changed the participants' usernames for confidentiality purposes but created user pseudonyms that maintained some sense of these expressed identities.

5. Fine and Kleinman (1979) described two axes of subcultural identification, salience and centrality. Salience refers to the frequency with which a person activates a subcultural identity in a situation Centrality refers to the level of commitment a person feels toward that identity. As one example: an inmate in a penitentiary is likely to have a very salient "prisoner" identity at alt times because of the situations in which s/he finds her/himself (e.g., interacting with other "prisoners" and "guards," being confined, and so on). However, s/he may he ashamed of that identity or very uncommitted to it, hoping to shed it as soon as possible: therefore, the identity would not be very central to her/her self concept. Similarly, net straightedgers expressed high levels of commitment to the straightedge identity without necessarily making it highly salient in their offline lives, such as through a tack of music consumption or regular interaction in a music scene.

Discussion Questions

1. What is straightedge? After reading this article, do you think net-straightedgers are really straightedge? Why or why not?

2. Name a subculture to which you belong. What distinguishes this subculture from mainstream culture?

Author's Note: The author thanks the regular participants of the Georgia Workshop on Culture. Power and History: the anonymous reviewers at *JCE;* and the members of the 2005 Young People and New Technologies conference in Northampton, United Kingdom, for their helpful feedback on an earlier draft of this article.

Source: "Authentic Identities: Straightedge Subculture, Music, and the Internet" by J. Patrick Williams from *Journal of Contemporary Ethnography*, Vol. 35, No. 2, April 2006, pp. 173–200. Reprinted by permission of Sage Publications.

—————— \\\\ ——————

PART II

SOCIAL STRUCTURE, SOCIAL INSTITUTIONS, AND THE MEDIA

While Part I provided examples of the influence of culture and social interaction, Part II focuses on how social structure and social institutions influence our individual lives and our society. Regularized patterns of behavior form the social structure of society. The major social institutions in a society are social structures that direct how the society will carry out its basic needs. These institutions socialize us, provide us with information, unify members of society, and establish a sense of order, purpose, and stability.

In order to survive, every society must establish family, economic, educational, governmental, and religious institutions. In the United States, the mass media perform many of the functions of a social institution (they socialize us, give us information, provide us with a sense of order and stability, etc.). However, the mass media in the United States are dominated by for-profit companies, whose key goal is to make money, rather than to strengthen society.

The articles in this section illustrate the impact of social institutions and the mass media on our society. We all have the freedom to make our own decisions but not in situations of our own choosing. Our position in the social structure plays a major role in our lives. How our society is structured and our position in the social structures of our society influence our aspirations, how we make sense of the world, how we conduct our lives, and what we can accomplish. Often, our position in one social institution (like education) influences our position in other institutions (like economic and family).

In "Unmarried with Children," Kathryn Edin and Maria Kefalas reveal that poor, unmarried women have the same aspirations for a stable marriage and family as do middle class members of society but their place in the social class structure makes it difficult for them to realize these desires. Edin and Kefalas find that because poor women, like most people, believe that marriage should last a lifetime, they are unwilling to enter into it without first finding a trusted partner and establishing a firm financial grounding. Poor women's positions in our economic and educational social structures make both of these goals largely elusive. The low income of their families decreases their chances of going to a good school, while their low level of education makes it difficult for them to find a good, high-paying job. Their low levels of education and pay make it highly unlikely that they will interact with potential mates who have decent education and good jobs. Therefore, while many are eager to have children, they often opt to do so outside of marriage.

The structure of the schools young people attend can also influence their aspirations and achievements. In "Student Disengagement and the Socialization Styles of High Schools," Lisa A. Pellerin shows that schools structured around an authoritative socialization style have students with the lowest levels of disengagement. Her findings indicate that, just as authoritative parents who both demand much from their children *and* provide them with plenty of attention have successful offspring, authoritative schools, which set high standards and give children the attention and training they need to meet them, are those most likely to foster student engagement and educational achievement.

Finally, in "Elites, Masses, and Media Blacklists: The Dixie Chicks Controversy," Gabriel Rossman looks at the role of the media in a crisis. He shows that opposition to the Dixie Chicks after the lead singer's anti-war statements deriding President George W. Bush came not from big media chains but from independent stations influenced by grassroots conservative sentiment. In doing so, he challenges the ideas of the political economy tradition of media sociology and the notion that independent ownership of the media always leads to greater freedom of speech.

As you read the articles in this section, keep in mind the following points:

- Our position in the social structure influences our aspirations and our opportunities for success.
- Schools that both challenge and support have the most engaged students.
- Media have a tremendous influence on how we view the world but grassroots sentiments can also influence the media.
- Institutions are interdependent. For example, if schools fail to educate the workforce, the economy will falter.
- One's position in one social institution influences one's position in another. For example, in order to support a family, one needs a good job. In order to attain a good job, one needs a solid education.

CHAPTER 5

Unmarried with Children

Kathryn Edin and Maria Kefalas

> Poor, unmarried mothers have not given up on marriage, as middle-class observers often conclude. To the contrary, many of them take marriage very seriously and are simply waiting for the right partner and situation to make it work.

Jen Burke, a white tenth-grade dropout who is 17 years old, lives with her stepmother, her sister, and her 16-month-old son in a cramped but tidy row home in Philadelphia's beleaguered Kensington neighborhood. She is broke, on welfare, and struggling to complete her GED. Wouldn't she and her son have been better off if she had finished high school, found a job, and married her son's father first?

In 1950, when Jen's grandmother came of age, only 1 in 20 American children was born to an unmarried mother. Today, that rate is 1 in 3—and they are usually born to those least likely to be able to support a child on their own. In our book, *Promises I Can Keep: Why Poor Women Put Motherhood Before Marriage*, we discuss the lives of 162 white, African American, and Puerto Rican low-income single mothers living in eight destitute neighborhoods across Philadelphia and its poorest industrial suburb, Camden. We spent five years chatting over kitchen tables and on front stoops, giving mothers like Jen the opportunity to speak to the question so many affluent Americans ask about them: Why do they have children while still young and unmarried when they will face such an uphill struggle to support them?

Romance at Lightning Speed

Jen started having sex with her 20-year-old boyfriend Rick just before her 15th birthday. A month and a half later, she

was pregnant. "I didn't want to get pregnant," she claims. "He wanted me to get pregnant." "As soon as he met me, he wanted to have a kid with me," she explains. . . .

In inner-city neighborhoods like Kensington, where childbearing within marriage has become rare, romantic relationships like Jen and Rick's proceed at lightning speed. A young man's avowal, "I want to have a baby by you," is often part of the courtship ritual from the beginning. This is more than idle talk, as their first child is typically conceived within a year from the time a couple begins "kicking it." Yet while poor couples' pillow talk often revolves around dreams of shared children, the news of a pregnancy—the first indelible sign of the huge changes to come—puts these still-new relationships into overdrive. Suddenly, the would-be mother begins to scrutinize her mate as never before, wondering whether he can "get himself together"— find a job, settle down, and become a family man—in time. Jen began pestering Rick to get a real job instead of picking up day-labor jobs at nearby construction sites. She also wanted him to stop hanging out with his ne'er-do-well friends, who had been getting him into serious trouble for more than a decade. Most of all, she wanted Rick to shed what she calls his "kiddie mentality"—his habit of spending money on alcohol and drugs rather than recognizing his growing financial obligations at home.

Rick did not try to deny paternity, as many would-be fathers do. Nor did he abandon or mistreat Jen, at least intentionally. But Rick, who had been in and out of juvenile detention since he was 8 years old for everything from stealing cars to selling drugs, proved unable to stay away from his unsavory friends. At the beginning of her seventh month of pregnancy, an escapade that began as a drunken lark landed Rick in jail on a carjacking charge. Jen moved back home with her stepmother, applied for welfare, and spent the last two-and-a-half months of her pregnancy without Rick.

Rick sent penitent letters from jail. "I thought he changed by the letters he wrote me. I thought he changed a lot," she says. "He used to tell me that he loved me when he was in jail. . . . It was always gonna I be me and him and the baby when he got out." Thus, when Rick's alleged victim failed to appear to testify and he was released just days before Cohn's birth, the couple's reunion was a happy one. Often, the magic moment of childbirth calms the troubled waters of such relationships. New parents typically make amends and resolve to stay together for the sake of their child. When surveyed just after a child's birth, eight in ten unmarried parents say they are still together, and most plan to stay together and raise the child. . . .

Most poor, unmarried mothers and fathers readily admit that bearing children while poor and unmarried is not the ideal way to do things. Jen believes the best time to become a mother is "after you're out of school and you got a job, at least, when you're like 21. When you're ready to have kids, you should have everything ready, have your house, have a job, so when that baby comes, the baby can have its own room." Yet given their already limited economic prospects, the poor have little motivation to time their births as precisely as their middle-class counterparts do. The dreams of young people like Jen and Rick center on children at a time of life when their more affluent peers plan for college and careers. Poor girls coming of age in the inner city value children highly, anticipate them eagerly, and believe strongly that they are up to the job of mothering—even in difficult circumstances. . . .

When I Became a Mom

When we asked mothers like Jen what their lives would be like if they had not had children, we expected them to express regret over foregone opportunities for school and careers. Instead, most believe their children "saved" them. They describe their lives as spinning out of control before becoming pregnant—struggles with parents and peers, "wild," risky behavior, depression, and school failure. . . .

Children offer poor youth like Jen a compelling sense of purpose. Jen paints a before-and-after picture of her life that was common among the mothers we interviewed. "Before, I didn't have nobody to take care of. I didn't have nothing left to go home for. . . . Now I have my son to take care of. I have him to go home for. . . . I don't have to go buy weed or drugs with my money. I could buy my son stuff with my money! . . . I have something to look up to now." Children also are a crucial source of relational intimacy, a self-made community of care. After a nasty fight with Rick, Jen recalls, "I was crying. My son came in the room. He was hugging me. He's 16 months and he was hugging me with his little arms. He was really cute and happy, so I got happy. That's one of the good things. When you're sad, the baby's always gonna be there for you no matter what." . . .

I'd Like to Get Married, but . . .

The sharp decline in marriage in impoverished urban areas has led some to charge that the poor have abandoned the marriage norm. Yet we found few who had given up on the idea of marriage. But like their elite counterparts, disadvantaged women set a high financial bar for marriage. For the poor, marriage has become an elusive goal—one they feel ought to be reserved for those who can support a "white picket fence" lifestyle: a mortgage on a modest row home, a car and some furniture, some savings in the bank, and enough money left over to pay for a "decent" wedding. . . .

Unlike the women of their mothers' and grandmothers' generations, young women like Jen are not merely content to rely on a man's earnings. Instead, they insist on being economically "set" in their own right before taking marriage vows. This is partly because they want a partnership of equals, and they believe money buys say-so in a relationship. . . .

Economic independence is also insurance against a marriage gone bad. Jen explains, "I want to have everything ready, in case something goes wrong. . . . If we got a divorce, that would be my house. I bought that house, he can't kick me out or he can't take my kids from me." "That's what I want in case that ever happens. I know a lot of people that happened to. I don't want it to happen to me." These statements reveal that despite her desire to marry, Rick's role in the family's future is provisional at best. "We get along, but we fight a lot. If he's there, he's there, but if he's not, that's why I want a job . . . a job with computers . . . so I could afford my kids, could afford the house. . . . I don't want to be living off him. I want my kids to be living off me."

Why is Jen, who describes Rick as "the love of my life," so insistent on planning an exit strategy before she is willing to take the vows she firmly believes ought to last "forever?" If love is so sure, why does mistrust seem so palpable and strong? In relationships among poor couples like Jen and Rick, mistrust is often spawned by chronic violence and infidelity, drug and alcohol abuse, criminal activity, and the threat of imprisonment. In these tarnished corners of urban America, the stigma of a failed marriage is far worse than an out-of-wedlock birth. New mothers like Jen feel they must test the relationship over three, four, even five years' time. This is the only way, they believe, to insure that their marriages will last. . . .

Given the economic challenges and often perilously low quality of the romantic relationships among unmarried parents, poor women may be right to be cautious about marriage. Five years after we first spoke with her, we met with Jen again. We learned that Jen's second pregnancy ended in a miscarriage. We also learned that Rick was out of the picture—apparently for good. "You know that bar [down the street?] It happened in that bar. . . . They were in the bar, and this guy was like badmouthing [Rick's friend] Mikey, talking stuff to him or whatever. So Rick had to go get involved in it and start with this guy. . . . Then he goes outside and fights the guy [and] the guy dies of head trauma. They were all on drugs, they were all drinking, and things just got out of control, and that's what happened. He got fourteen to thirty years."

These Are Cards I Dealt Myself

Jen stuck with Rick for the first two and a half years of his prison sentence, but when another girl's name replaced her own on the visitors' list, Jen decided she was finished with him once and for all. Readers might be asking what Jen ever saw in a man like Rick. But Jen and Rick operate in a partner market where the better-off men go to the better-off women. The only way for someone like Jen to forge a satisfying relationship with a man is to find a diamond in the rough or improve her own economic position so that she can realistically compete for more upwardly mobile partners. . . .

These days, there is a new air of determination, even pride, about Jen. The aimless high school dropout pulls ten-hour shifts entering data at a warehouse distribution center Monday through Thursday. She has held the job for three years, and her aptitude and hard work have earned her a series of raises. Her current salary is higher than anyone in her household commands—$10.25 per hour, and she now gets two weeks of paid vacation, four personal days, 60 hours of sick time, and medical benefits. She has saved up the necessary $400 in tuition for a high school completion program that offers evening and weekend classes. Now all that stands between her and a diploma is a passing grade in mathematics, her least favorite subject. "My plan is to start college in January. [This month] I take my math test . . . so I can get my diploma," she confides.

Jen clearly sees how her life has improved since Rick's dramatic exit from the scene. "That's when I really started [to get better] because I didn't have to worry about what he was doing, didn't have to worry about him cheating on me, all this stuff. [it was] then I realized that I had to do what I had to do to take care of my son. . . . When he was there, I think that my whole life revolved around him, you know, so I always messed up somehow because I was so busy worrying about what he was doing. Like I would leave the [GED] programs I was in just to go home and see what he was doing. My mind was never concentrating." Now, she says, "a lot of people in my family look up to me now, because all my sisters dropped out from school, you know, nobody went back to school. I went back to school, you know? . . . I went back to school, and I plan to go to college, and a lot of people look up to me for that, you know? So that makes me happy. because five years ago nobody looked up to me. I was just like everybody else." . . .

Becoming a mother transformed Jen's point of view on just about everything. She says, "I thought hanging on the corner drinking, getting high—I thought that was a good life, and I thought I could live that way for eternity, like sitting out with my friends. But it's not as fun once you have your own kid. . . . I think it changes [you]. I think, 'Would I want Cohn to do that? Would I want my son to be like that . . . ?' It was fun to me but it's not fun anymore. Half the people I hung with are either . . . Some have died from drug overdoses, some are in jail, and some people are just out there living the same life that they always lived, and they don't look really good. They look really bad." In the end, Jen believes, Cohn's birth has brought far more good into her life than bad. "I know I could have waited [to have a child, but in a way I think Cohn's the best thing that could have happened to me. . . . So I think I had my son for a purpose because I think Cohn changed my life. He saved my life, really. My whole life revolves around Cohn!"

Promises I Can Keep

There are unique themes in Jen's story—most fathers are only one or two, not five years older than the mothers of their children, and few fathers have as many glaring problems as Rick—but we heard most of these themes repeatedly in the stories of the 161 other poor, single mothers we came to know. Notably, poor women do not reject marriage; they revere it. Indeed, it is the conviction that marriage is forever that makes them think that divorce is worse than having a baby outside of marriage. Their children, far from being liabilities, provide crucial social-psychological resources—a strong sense of purpose and a profound source of intimacy. Jen and the other mothers we came to know are coming of age in an America that is profoundly unequal—where the gap between rich and poor continues to grow. This economic reality has convinced them that they have little to lose and, perhaps, something to gain by a seemingly "ill-timed" birth.

The lesson one draws from stories like Jen's is quite simple: Until poor young women have more access to jobs that lead to financial independence—until there is reason to hope for the rewarding life pathways that their privileged peers pursue—the poor will continue to have children far sooner than most Americans think they should, while still deferring marriage. Marital standards have risen for all Americans, and the poor want the same things that everyone now wants out of marriage. The poor want to marry too, but they insist on marrying well. This, in their view, is the only way to avoid an almost certain divorce. Like Jen, they are simply not willing to make promises they are not sure they can keep.

Discussion Questions

1. According to Edin and Kefalas, why are increasing numbers of poor women having children out of wedlock? Would this decision make sense for you? Why or why not?

2. If you were a policy maker, what policies would you enact to address the dramatic rise in poor, unmarried women having children?

CHAPTER 6

Student Disengagement and the Socialization Styles of High Schools

Lisa A. Pellerin

School socialization style is differentially associated with student disengagement. Authoritative schools have the lowest levels of disengagement and indifferent schools the highest, while authoritarian and permissive schools have moderate levels of disengagement.

Student disengagement has been described as the "most immediate and persistent issue" facing students and educators because disengaged students lack the psychological investment necessary to master academic knowledge and skills (Newmann et al. 1992). One of the strongest indicators of disengagement is physical withdrawal from schooling, which includes such behaviors as tardiness, cutting classes, chronic truancy and dropping out (Carnegie Council on Adolescent Development 1989; Connell et al. 1995; Fordham and Ogbu 1986; Kindermann, McCollam and Gibson 1996; Lamborn et al. 1992; McCall 1994).

In the substantial literature on risk factors for truancy and dropout, few studies explicitly evaluate the impact of school climate (e.g., Bryk and Thum 1989; Gamoran and Mare 1989; Pittman 1991; Wehlage and Rutter 1987; for a review see Wang et al. 1997). Most consider only family and individual factors such as parents' education and students' test scores. Yet many students, regardless of background, become disengaged when they encounter the impersonal context of secondary schools (Bowers 1985; Eccles et al. 1991; Newmann 1981). Intolerably high truancy rates and violent events in schools have led to a political climate favoring stricter discipline in schools, but stricter policies may have the unintended consequence of increasing student disengagement

(Gullatt and LeMoine 1997; Meece and McColskey 1997). There has been little empirical research in this area; however, a few studies suggest that strict policies may be ineffective (Quinn 1995) or even counterproductive (Mount Diablo Unified School District 1990). There is clearly a need for empirical research on factors in the schools that foster or erode students' investment in their schooling.

Both qualitative (Cusick 1973, 1983) and quantitative researchers (Bryk and Thum 1989; Wehlage and Rutter 1987) have described characteristics of schools that contribute significantly to student alienation and disengagement such as bureaucratization and low academic standards. In contrast, schools in which students remain engaged combine high standards for academics and behavior with responsive adult concern (Coleman, Hoffer and Kilgore 1981; Rutter et al. 1979; Shouse 1996; Wehlage 1983). These descriptions of positive school climate echo descriptions of authoritative parenting. In numerous studies, parenting style researchers have found that children have the most positive outcomes when their parents are authoritative—both responsive and demanding—and do worst when their parents are indifferent—neither responsive nor demanding (Baumrind 1967, 1978, 1991; Cohen and Rice 1997; Dawson 1996; Dornbusch et al. 1987; Lamborn et al. 1991; Radziszewska et al. 1996; Shucksmith, Hendry and Glendenning 1995; Slicker 1998).

Family researchers and school climate researchers have separately come to the same conclusion—authoritative socialization promotes the most positive outcomes. My goal, in a series of analyses, is to build a bridge connecting the parenting style and school climate literatures. Mindful of Merton's (1968) exhortation to develop middle-range theory, I aim to transcend context-specific findings with a context-bridging exploration of authoritative socialization. In a prior study (Pellerin 2005), I classified high schools by socialization style and modeled the effect of style on mean disengagement levels, while controlling for school characteristics. As the socialization style literature would predict, I found that authoritative schools had the lowest mean disengagement, and indifferent schools the highest. In this study, I use multilevel modeling to test the effect of high school socialization style on student disengagement from 10th to 12th grades, controlling for both the sociodemographic context of schools and student characteristics including gender, race/ethnicity, socioeconomic status and academic achievement.

Socialization Styles

Family researchers have identified four main parental socialization styles—authoritative, authoritarian, permissive and indifferent (Baumrind 1967, 1978, 1991; Maccoby and Martin 1983). Researchers have consistently found, on a variety of outcomes and at a range of ages, that children with authoritative parents have the most positive outcomes, and children with indifferent parents the worst (Baumrind 1991; Cohen and Rice 1997; Dawson 1996; Dornbusch et al. 1987; Lamborn et al. 1991; Radziszewska et al. 1996; Shucksmith, Hendry and Glendenning 1995; Slicker 1998).

Authoritative socialization is characterized by high demandingness (high standards for behavior and maturity, and firm enforcement of rules) and high responsiveness (warmth, open communication and respect for the developmental needs of the child). . . . Adolescents with authoritative parents have been shown to have higher social and cognitive competence, higher aspirations, better grades, better psychological well-being and better behavior compared to others (Cohen and Rice 1997; Dawson 1996; Dornbusch et al. 1987; Lamborn et al. 1991; Radziszewska et al. 1996; Shucksmith et al. 1995; Slicker 1998).

Authoritarian socialization is also characterized by high demandingness, but coupled with low responsiveness—these parents emphasize obedience

to themselves as authority figures and resist granting autonomy to their growing children. Because the discipline of authoritarian parents is imposed on their children and not negotiated, these children tend to rely on external controls rather than self-regulation (Hoffman 1970, 1976). This external imposition of authority can increase the likelihood that adolescents will rebel (Baumrind 1978). In general, however, adolescent children of authoritarian parents have relatively low rates of problem behaviors and drug use, along with low social competence and self-esteem (Baumrind 1991; Lamborn et al. 1991; Slicker 1998). Their aspirations and grades are close to, but lower than, those of authoritatively-reared adolescents (Radziszewska et al. 1996; Slicker 1998).

Permissive socialization is characterized by low demandingness (minimal discipline, self regulation by the child, few maturity demands) and high responsiveness (warmth, attention and acceptance). Permissive parents may want to be perceived by their adolescent children more as friends than as authority figures, and they attempt to exercise influence through friendship. Adolescents with permissive parents have been shown to have relatively high social competence and self-esteem, but relatively low achievement and school engagement, and high rates of problem behaviors and drug use (Baumrind 1991; Lamborn et al. 1991; Slicker 1998).

Indifferent socialization is characterized primarily by minimal effort—low responsiveness and low demands. Affection may be provided inconsistently or not at all. Similarly, discipline may be completely absent or used sporadically. Not surprisingly, adolescents with indifferent parents have the worst outcomes of any style group on virtually any measure of well-being, competence, academic achievement or behavior (Baumrind 1991; Lamborn et al. 1991; Radziszewska et al. 1996: Shucksmith et al. 1995; Slicker 1998).

The outcome of interest in this study is disengagement, operationalized using behavioral indicators such as lateness and cutting class. To summarize the findings presented above regarding problem behaviors, adolescents who are authoritatively-reared have the lowest levels of problem behavior followed closely by those who are reared by authoritarian parents. Permissively reared adolescents have relatively high rates of problem behaviors, while the indifferently reared have the highest rates of any group. My hypothesis is that the same pattern will emerge when comparing student groups based on the socialization styles of their schools.

Schools as Agents of Socialization

Adolescents have the task of integrating themselves into their community as members in their own right (Newmann 1981). To do this, they seek socialization experiences beyond their parents, with peers and with other adults, such as teachers, school administrators and coaches (Csikszentmihalyi and Larson 1984). It is a more straightforward conceptual leap to extend the typology of socialization styles to individual non-parental adults than it is to extend it to schools. Schools are, after all, complex organizations whose personnel are not uniform in their attitudes or behavior. Yet the school climate literature is testament to a widely-accepted understanding that schools as institutions differ in the degree to which they are engaging or alienating, are strict or lax, have high standards or low. These differences result from the attitudes and behaviors of past and current school personnel, and shape the attitudes and behaviors of new personnel. Although individual teachers and administrators vary in their interactions with students, the organizational structure and formal rules of a school constrain its personnel to a narrower range of interactions with students than they might otherwise have. Informal culture, organizational structure and formal policies of schools form the social context within which the socialization of students takes place. Though school climate researchers have conceptualized schools as agents of socialization, they have not linked their work to the research on family socialization.

Indeed, the only researcher to make such a linkage has been Hetherington (1993), a child psychologist. In a study of the effects of divorce on children, she classified the schools attended by her sample children into "parenting" style groups and tested whether authoritative schooling compensates for the lack of authoritative parenting in many divorcing families. Her results are illuminating. She found that children in authoritative schools had the best outcomes in achievement, social competence and behavior, while children in chaotic-neglecting (defined similarly to indifferent) schools had the worst outcomes. . . . In this study, I hypothesize that students attending authoritative high schools are least disengaged by 12th grade, that students attending indifferent high schools are most disengaged, and that students attending authoritarian or permissive schools have intermediate levels of disengagement. I test this hypothesis using multilevel modeling, controlling for gender, race/ethnicity, socioeconomic status and academic achievement at the student level, and sociodemographic characteristics of the student body at the school level.

Data and Methods

Data are from the High School Effectiveness Study (HSES), a component of the National Educational Longitudinal Study of 1988 (NELS: 88). From the high schools attended by NELS:88 sample members in 10th grade (1990), a sample of 247 schools in the central city and suburbs of the 30 largest metropolitan areas was selected for HSES. For each school, the NELS sample was augmented with additional randomly-selected students to achieve representative within-school samples of approximately 30 students (NCES 1996). The 1990 (10th grade) HSES sample includes approximately 9,000 students: 3,000 NELS sample members and 6,000 augmented students. Of these, 7,339 completed a student questionnaire and a cognitive achievement test. School administrators were also surveyed in 1990, and both groups were re-surveyed in 1992 when most students were in 12th grade. . . .

Several data filters are used at the student level. Students with missing data for race/ethnicity ($n = 85$) are removed. Native American students are also removed, because they represent only 1.5 percent of the total student sample ($n = 80$), and are present in less than one-third of the school samples. For consistency in school effects, students who transferred to other schools or programs after 10th grade ($n = 268$) are removed from the sample.

Of the 172 public schools, eight are lost due to closure, administrator non-response or inadequate student response (fewer than five in the within-school sample). Thus, the final school sample size is 164, and the student sample sizes are 4,743 for 10th grade disengagement analyses, and 3,927 for 12th grade disengagement analyses. Exactly half of the schools are urban, and half are suburban. The student sample is 49 percent female, 10 percent Asian, 19 percent black, 21.5 percent Hispanic and 49.4 percent white. These proportions are nearly identical to those reported above for the full public school sample, suggesting that selection bias has not occurred as a result of the data filters or school attrition. . . .

Dependent Variables and Student-Level Controls

Disengagement is measured in this study using both transcript data and student questionnaire items. The transcript items are the number of absences recorded for the 1989–90 and 1991–92 school years. The student items are self-reports of being late for school or cutting class in the previous term, and their frequency of going to class without their homework, measured in 1990 (10th grade) and 1992 (12th grade for most). Responses for the lateness and cutting variables are ordinal categories: in 1990, five categories ranging from "never" to "over 10 times;" in 1992, six categories ranging from "never" to "over 15 times." For this study, values are recoded to category midpoints (with "over 10 times" recoded as 10, and "over 15 times" recoded as 17. These maximum values were chosen to minimize skewness). The "no homework" variable has four ordinal categories, from "never" to "usually" (recoded to 0–3 for analysis). Students may be expected to under-report undesirable behavior, while absence records may include excused as well as unexcused absences. As a group, the four variables minimize bias created by under- or over-reporting disengaged behavior. The four measures for each grade are combined using principle components analysis. . . .

Both 10th grade disengagement and 12th grade disengagement are standardized variables (mean 0, s.d. 1). Thus the models predict change in relative disengagement across the sample, rather than in absolute disengagement. On average, students follow a trajectory of increasingly disengaged behavior as they approach the end of high school (e.g., the mean frequency for cutting class is 1.8 in the 10th grade, and 3.0 in the 12th). . . .

Achievement is a composite of reading and math achievement tests administered to 10th graders. Scores were standardized over all completed tests with a mean of 50 and standard deviation of 10. It is included in models estimating student-level effects on 10th grade disengagement, since academic performance is expected to be associated with disengagement. Poorly-performing students may disengage as a result of discouragement (Rumberger et al. 1990). This is likely to initiate a vicious cycle, in which disengagement leads to further performance declines.

School Styles

Schools are classified into socialization-style groups in a three-step process. In the first step, I created factor scores for each school measuring responsiveness and demandingness. Indicator variables are from the 1990 student and administrator files.

Responsiveness is the degree to which the school climate is characterized by warmth expressed toward students, two-way communication and perceived fairness. Administrator measures of responsiveness are five items that address teacher attitudes toward students and the degree to which student input is sought and used. Student measures of responsiveness are five items that address warmth and nurturance from teachers, teacher interest, teacher listening and the fairness of disciplinary practices.

Demandingness is the degree to which the school climate is characterized by high standards for performance and behavior, and by enforcement of rules to meet those standards. Four items from the administrator questionnaire address what is often referred to as "academic press," the degree to which students are expected to work hard and challenge themselves academically (McDill, Natriello and Pallas 1986). Student measures of demandingness are two items that measure students' perception of the strictness and enforcement of behavior rules.

In the second step, student and administrator measures were analyzed separately using principal components analysis. . . . Factor scores for each school were calculated using a regression method. (Each factor score variable is standardized with a mean of 1, s.d. 0.) Then, a responsiveness score and a demandingness score were created for each school by adding the student and administrator scores on each dimension.

In the third step, schools were classified as Authoritative, Authoritarian, Permissive or Indifferent based on their responsiveness and demandingness scores. For example, schools that are above the mean on both responsiveness and demandingness are classified "Authoritative."

Results and Discussion

. . . The student-level model for 10th grade disengagement includes female, Hispanic, black, Asian, locus of control, SES [Socioeconomic status] and achievement as independent variables. This model explains 17.7 percent of within-school variance in disengagement. Net of other effects, female students are similar to male students on average, but the female slope does vary significantly among schools. Hispanic and black students are no different from whites in their average level of disengagement, nor do these effects vary significantly; while Asian students are significantly less disengaged, on average, than the other groups, with significant variance in the slope among schools. Both SES and locus of control (higher SES and internal control, respectively) are associated with lower levels of disengagement; neither effect varies significantly. Achievement has a similar negative effect on disengagement, but the effect of achievement does vary significantly among schools. Based on these results, in the level two model for 10th grade disengagement, female, Asian, SES and locus of control are entered as fixed effects. Achievement, which varies, is entered as a random effect. In the interest of parsimony, both Hispanic and black are omitted from the level two model, because, net of other effects, Hispanic and black students do not differ from whites.

The student-level model for 12th grade disengagement includes female, the race/ethnicity variables, locus of control and l0th grade disengagement as independent variables. This model explains 32.9 percent of within-school variance in disengagement. SES and achievement are omitted because test models demonstrated that, with 10th grade disengagement controlled, SES and achievement have no further effects. In other words, whatever effects SES and achievement have on disengagement are fully realized by 10th grade. Looking at the results, net of other effects, only female and Asian effects are significant. Of the two, only the female slopes vary significantly among schools. Hispanic and locus of control, on average, do not have significant average effects, but both vary significantly. As in the 10th grade model, black is neither significant nor variable. Tenth grade disengagement, as one would expect, is a strong predictor of 12th grade disengagement, with significant variation among schools. Based on these results, in the level two model for 12th grade disengagement, Asian is entered as a fixed effect, female, Hispanic, locus of control and 10th grade disengagement are entered as random effects, and black is omitted. . . .

Looking first at the model for 10th grade disengagement, the model for the level one intercepts (β_0) includes the school styles (with Authoritative as the reference category), and proportion Asian, proportion black, proportion Hispanic, mean SES and mean achievement as controls (all controls are standardized). Grade 10 enrollment is omitted, having been non significant in test models. The intercept represents the mean disengagement of non-Asian males with grand mean levels of SES, locus of control and achievement, who attend Authoritative schools with mean (zero) values for the control variables ("average" non-Asian boys attending "average" Authoritative schools). The intercept is negative and significant, indicating that Authoritative schools have the lowest mean disengagement of the four groups, as predicted, net of school and student characteristics. The coefficients for Permissive and Indifferent are significant and positive. The coefficient for Authoritarian is not

significantly different from zero, indicating that levels of disengagement in Authoritarian schools are between the two extremes, and significantly different from both. School socialization style is already differentially associated with student disengagement by 10th grade, controlling for the socio-economic and achievement distributions of student populations. As hypothesized, the pattern of effects is the same as that found in studies of family socialization.

Looking next at the control variables, the coefficients for the race/ethnic proportions variables are all significant and positive, indicating that schools with higher minority enrollments have higher mean disengagement. From the student level model for 10th grade disengagement presented above, however, we know that this result is not due to higher disengagement, net of other effects, among the minority students in these schools. Since SES and achievement are controlled at both the student and school levels, these effects must be related to other, unmeasured characteristics of inner-city schools such as inadequate school facilities, crowded classrooms or less-experienced faculty. The effect of school mean SES is also contrary to the student-level effect. Higher *school mean* SES is associated with higher disengagement, whereas higher family SES is associated with lower disengagement at the individual level. A possible explanation may be that higher SES schools have more open campuses (and more students with cars), giving students more opportunities to leave campus during the school day.

Turning now to the fixed and random effects, the fixed slopes for female, Asian and locus of control are similar to their mean effects in the level one 10th grade model, as expected. The effect of SES remains negative and insignificant, but the magnitude of the effect is substantially reduced. Achievement is the only level one slope entered as a random effect. Of the variables tested for their effects on the achievement slope (mean achievement and the school styles) only mean achievement is significant. The negative effect of mean achievement on the achievement slope indicates a contextual effect of achievement. The predicted achievement slope in a high-achieving school (+1 s.d. on mean achievement) is –.196. Thus in high-achieving schools, the difference in disengagement scores between low-achieving and high-achieving students is larger, with low-achieving students much more disengaged than high-achievers. The results also suggest that the reverse occurs in low-achieving schools. In these schools (–1 s.d. on mean achievement), the predicted achievement slope is .082, suggesting that, in this context, high-achieving students may actually be more disengaged than low-achieving students. A possible interpretation is that high-achieving students feel unchallenged and are discouraged by attending classes with low-performing peers.

In the model for 12th grade disengagement, the model for the level one intercepts (β_0) is identical to that for the 10th grade. The intercept represents the mean disengagement of white and black males with grand mean locus of control and 9th grade disengagement, attending "average" authoritative schools. It is negative but just fails significance at the .10 level. The coefficients for Authoritarian, Permissive and Indifferent are all positive and significant, with Indifferent having the largest effect. Keep in mind that, since 10th grade disengagement is controlled, this model reports additional effects on disengagement after 10th grade. Net of other effects, students in authoritarian, permissive and indifferent schools become more disengaged over the course of their high school years than students in authoritative schools. Once again, the pattern of effects is the same as that found in studies of family socialization.

The effects of the control variables in this model are somewhat muted compared to the 10th grade model. Looking at the race/ethnic proportions variables, the effect of proportion black is no longer significant, and that of proportion Hispanic is reduced. Only proportion Asian retains its magnitude and significance. This may reflect the higher likelihood of dropping out between 10th and 12th grades among disengaged black and Hispanic students. An analysis of race/ethnic group means on the dependent variables indicates that black and Hispanic students, on average, are more disengaged in 10th grade than white and Asian students, and also more likely to drop out between 10th and 12th grade. In 12th grade, the remaining Hispanic students are still more disengaged than the other groups, but the remaining black students are no more disengaged than whites and Asians. This selection effect may also explain, in part, the continued positive effect of mean SES. Students in higher-SES schools may be more likely to remain enrolled even if disengaged.

Turning, finally, to the fixed and random effects, recall that Asian is entered as a fixed effect in this model, female, locus of control, Hispanic and 10th grade disengagement are entered as random effects, and SES, achievement and black are omitted. The average slopes for female and 10th grade disengagement are similar to those reported in the student-level model. None of the

level two variables tested in these slopes models (female mean and styles for female, 10th grade mean disengagement mean and styles for 9th grade disengagement) proved significant, and were omitted in the final model. The fixed effect of Asian is somewhat smaller than its mean effect in the student-level model and insignificant.

Looking at locus of control, the average slope is zero, but locus has a positive slope in permissive schools. In these schools, students who are internally controlled (positive locus of control) are at least as disengaged in 12th grade as students who are externally controlled. It is important to interpret this result in conjunction with the effect of locus of control on 10th grade disengagement. Internally-controlled 10th graders are significantly less disengaged than those who are externally-controlled. Controlling for 10th grade disengagement, locus of control has further effects only in permissive schools where internally controlled students lose their advantage. The results indicate that in permissive schools, internally-controlled students *initially* remain engaged while their externally-controlled peers become disengaged. Over time, however, these students may see that there is no benefit to their engaged behavior, and no penalty for disengaged behavior. It is important to note that disengaged behaviors (lateness, cutting class and the like) are against the rules in all public schools. But adults in permissive schools remain warm and responsive while presiding over low standards, in a sense reassuring students that breaking the rules is actually acceptable. In that context, internally-controlled students apparently adjust over time to the lower standards. After all, internal locus of control refers to doing *what is expected* without external coercion; it does not refer to making up one's own set of expectations. In this vein, it is interesting that internally-controlled students maintain their advantage over their externally-controlled schoolmates in *indifferent* schools, although the mean level of disengagement in these schools is high. While *indifferent* schools share low behavioral standards with permissive schools, as non-responsive settings they do not provide reassurance that it is acceptable to ignore or bend the rules. In the absence of this positive feedback, internally-controlled students may be more likely to simply follow the rules.

Variance in the Hispanic slope is also partly explained by at least one school style. The average Hispanic slope is positive and significant, indicating that, net of other effects, Hispanic 12th graders are more disengaged than members of other ethnic groups. However, this is not the case in indifferent schools. The negative coefficient for Indifferent in the slope model indicates that in indifferent schools, Hispanic students are no more disengaged than others. One possible interpretation is that, whatever advantages are provided by authoritative, authoritarian or permissive schools, Hispanic students are not benefiting from them to the same degree as other students. In indifferent schools that offer neither responsiveness nor demands, all students are equally disadvantaged.

To summarize the multilevel results, controlling for the socio-economic and achievement distributions of students, school socialization style is differentially associated with student disengagement by 10th grade; and controlling for 10th grade disengagement, school styles have further effects on disengagement by 12th grade. As hypothesized, the pattern of effects is the same as that found in studies of family socialization authoritative schools have the lowest levels of disengagement and indifferent schools the highest, while authoritarian and permissive schools have moderate levels of disengagement.

Conclusion

Not unlike the parable of the three blind men and the elephant, family researchers and school climate researchers have been studying the same phenomenon—authoritative socialization—without recognizing it, because it presents itself differently in different contexts. My goal is to link the contexts, family and school, to move toward a middle-range theory of authoritative socialization. This is worth doing because a cross-contextual understanding of socialization can promote collaborative partnerships between families and schools, promoting consistent authoritative socialization in both settings. In this study, I advanced this project by measuring the effects of school socialization on student disengagement. My hypothesis that, as in family socialization, the authoritative style promotes the best outcomes while the indifferent style allows the worst, was supported by my analyses.

This study, like any other, has its limitations. The most significant, I believe, is the sparseness of variables in the HSES data set to measure school responsiveness and demandingness, and student disengagement. It is particularly unfortunate that students were not asked about the academic demands of their schools, and administrators were not asked about behavioral demands. The disengagement measures rely heavily on measures of physical withdrawal, in part because little else was available. I chose not to use time spent on homework in and out of school, as Smerdon (1999) did, because the amount of time students spend on homework in school is usually not under their control and may reflect a poor use of instructional time by teachers rather than the engagement of individual students (Cusick 1973). Time spent on homework outside of school depends, in part, on the amount of homework assigned and on the student's proficiency. (Less proficient students will take longer to complete assignments, but this is not an indication of greater engagement.) Ideal measures of engagement would include a student's level of interest and effort when in class, but these are not available in this data set. HSES has many strengths nonetheless, including its unique multilevel structure, high response rate and rich data at both the student and administrator levels.

Another limitation is the lack of pre-high school baseline data. Eighth-grade data are available for only a third of the current sample. Their use would have required more extensive use of multiple imputation and a larger number of imputed data sets, which was prohibitive given the complexity of nested, multi-level models. As Lee and Bryk (1989) point out, some of the school effects I hope to capture are likely to have already occurred by the 10th grade. My solution was to test for the *association* of disengagement with school style while controlling for the socio-economic and achievement intake of the school. The results of this analysis suggest that school socialization style has already had a significant effect on student disengagement by 10th grade. My models also demonstrate further effects of school style from 10th to 12th grade, making a stronger argument for the importance of socialization style.

In the current school reform climate mandated by No Child Left Behind, reforms have taken a decidedly authoritarian tone. Schools are punished for not meeting improvement goals, and students are retained in grade for failing end-of-grade exams. The threat of negative consequences is assumed to improve teaching and learning. But engagement in learning cannot be forced, especially among adolescents. My findings support an authoritative, rather than an authoritarian, approach—high standards for behavior and academic performance met through responsive adult-adolescent partnership.

Discussion Questions

1. What are the characteristics of authoritative socialization? Imagine you are a school superintendent. How would you try to create authoritative schools?

2. What was the socialization style of your high school? Do you think it influenced your level of engagement? Why or why not?

CHAPTER 7

Elites, Masses, and Media Blacklists

The Dixie Chicks Controversy

Gabriel Rossman

Independent country music stations were more likely than large media chains to blacklist the Dixie Chicks after the lead singer's anti-war statements deriding President George W. Bush. This challenges the ideas of the political economy tradition of media sociology and the notion that independent ownership of the media always leads to greater freedom of speech.

The Dixie Chicks controversy has its roots on March 10, 2003, when the group performed at the London nightclub, Shepherd's Bush Empire. On March 12 the British newspaper *The Guardian* published a brief, three-star review of the concert, approvingly noting that in a "profoundly punk rock" moment, lead singer Natalie Maines told the audience, "Just so you know, we're ashamed the president of the United States is from Texas." The remark reached American country music fans a few hours later with a post to the small Web site, countrynation.com, which had been following the European press coverage of the Dixie Chicks tour. That evening the article was copied in a post entitled "Dixie Chick Tea Party—dump Lipton tea for sponsoring anti-American Chicks!" to the Internet discussion group rec.music.country.western.

On March 13, the day after the *Guardian* article and Internet discussion, the Associated Press published the first story in the major American media on the controversy, noting that "angry phone calls flooded Nashville radio station WKDF-FM on Thursday, some calling for a boycott of the Texas trio's music." After the wire story, several newspapers carried stories on the subject and Internet discussion bloomed, spreading to alt.fan.dixiechicks and numerous political discussion groups. Much of the Internet discussion referred to the Dixie Chicks as

"sluts" and associated them with other antiwar celebrities, evident in the insult "hillbilly Jane Fondas." Some posters said they agreed with Maines or discussed the nature of dissent and rebuttals to it in a democracy at war, but many of the posts simply expressed contempt for the musicians. . . .

On March 14 the Associated Press reported that radio stations had begun dropping the Dixie Chicks from their playlists and engaging in such publicity stunts as providing "trash cans outside the radio station for people to throw their Dixie Chicks CDs away." The week before the controversy began their songs were number one on the adult contemporary and country airplay charts as published in the trade journal, *Radio and Records*. During the week that the story broke, their numbers began to slip on the country chart but held steady for adult contemporary. Maines rapidly apologized for the disrespectful tone of her remarks, but maintained her right to oppose the war, to no avail. Within two weeks they had dropped from both charts entirely. As will be shown below, however, the drop was not spread evenly among radio stations, but varied by locale, format, and owner in both surprising and predictable ways.

In a *New York Times* essay that was widely circulated and quoted on the Internet and alternative print media,

Princeton economist Paul Krugman accused the massive radio conglomerate Clear Channel of conspiring against the Dixie Chicks as a favor to the Bush administration because, among other reasons, "the Federal Communications Commission is considering further deregulation that would allow Clear Channel to expand even further, particularly into television" (March 25). Clear Channel is widely reviled because it is the largest radio chain and allegedly abuses its market power. The notion that Clear Channel is out to punish the Dixie Chicks for their political statement has become a small bit of received wisdom in some circles. This fits into the familiar frame of the "corporate media" serving to legitimate conservative interests.

Ironically, were Krugman correct about the chains' actions and motives, these actions would nonetheless be counter-productive. Although in the following months the Federal Communications Commission (FCC) continued with its long anticipated deregulation agenda, the Dixie Chicks blacklist was the subject of a Senate Commerce Committee hearing which contributed to a backlash against media concentration in Congress.

This article uses radio airplay data from *Radio and Records* to determine the source of the Dixie Chicks' blacklisting. I assess competing hypotheses of conglomerate media ownership and local sentiment.

Theory

This article draws on three distinct literatures: the political economy of the mass media tradition, the social movements literature, and the sociology of culture. To the extent that cultural industry organizations shape cultural discourse, and to the extent that cultural discourse shapes our thoughts and actions, these organizations have a tremendous amount of power. Both assumptions of this syllogism are disputable, and the inquiry is the object of the political economy of the mass media.

Political economy theorists assume that cultural organizations derive their primary interests and political influences from ownership. . . .

Political economists have noted a large increase in the concentration of media ownership since World War II. Particularly of note is the shift of media properties from wealthy families to publicly traded firms, the latter often called "the corporate media." The managerial capitalism of corporations is theoretically and empirically distinct from heroic capitalism in its approach to media properties.

For decades radio largely escaped the trend of conglomeration thanks to FCC regulations that limited firms to owning just a few dozen stations. The Telecommunications Act of 1996 effectively eliminated ownership restrictions, and within a few years the industry reached its current level of conglomeration, with Infinity/Viacom, Cumulus, and Citadel owning over one hundred stations each and Clear Channel with over one thousand.

Its large size has not made Clear Channel popular with political economists, activists, recording artists, record labels, or its radio rivals. . . . Indeed, Clear Channel is sometimes portrayed as the source of all evil, strife, and upheaval in the music industry. It was in this context of academic and political discourse about corporate media in general and Clear Channel in particular that Krugman and numerous other commentators accused the company of initiating the Dixie Chicks' blacklisting. This provides the first hypothesis:

Hypothesis 1: Large chains, especially the industry leader, Clear Channel, reduced Dixie Chicks airplay more than independent stations and small chains.

It is useful, however, to appreciate how songs are actually chosen for radio airplay, as several trade publications and production of culture studies explain. Most commercial radio stations do not operate according to the romantic notion of a connoisseur disc jockey sharing his favorite records with the audience. Rather, at nearly all commercial radio stations there is a division of labor between the disc jockey, who plays the records and makes patter, and the program director, who chooses which records to play and when. The typical program director is a skilled professional who creates a "music schedule," which is essentially a script for DJs to follow. At smaller stations the program director may also be a disc jockey or the general manager, but at large stations it is a distinct position, and at especially large stations there is a further division of labor between the program director and the music director. It is also common for a program director to program two or more radio stations owned by the same chain. To create the schedule, the program director uses trade magazines, other radio stations' playlists, airplay and sales charts, systematic audience telephone surveys, audience phone calls and letters, information from record companies and their promoters, and the database software, Selector. Intuition and taste play some role, but it is a highly technical profession. Chain-owned radio stations are especially likely to employ this technical, research-driven method, which has the consequence of promoting homogeneity in their playlists. This production of culture literature on the bureaucratic nature of large radio chains provides a counter-hypothesis to that provided by political economy:

Hypothesis 1a: Large chains will reduce Dixie Chicks airplay more slowly than independent stations and small chains.

The political economists Herman and Chomsky list flak from social movements and other aggrieved parties as a major source of media distortion, but their tradition largely abstains from systematic study of where flak comes from and what effect it has. Some media scholars have described the role of social movements in shaping the media and the political sociology of social movements provides a useful framework for studying the phenomenon.

Social movement organizations actively seek to influence the mass media and some, such as the American Family Association and Fairness and Accuracy In Reporting, have this as their sole purpose. . . .

The Dixie Chicks situation has parallels to the Hollywood blacklist, which is commonly, but inaccurately, imagined to have been a conspiracy between the studio owners and the House Committee on Un-American Activities (HUAC). In fact, the blacklist is a striking example of the power that social movements can exert on the mass media. The 1952 *Miracle* decision put the studios in a very strong legal position from which to face Congress, but competition from television and the 1948 *Paramount* decision ending vertical integration put them in a very weak economic position from which to face a boycott.

Contemporary leftist accounts of the blacklist did not claim that the moguls acted from class interest, personal animus for Communists, or even fear of unfavorable legislation. Rather the leftist critique of the studios was that they were too "cowardly" to stand up to American Legion pickets. Management and the unions together formed the Motion Picture Industry Council (MPIC) to fight the blacklist, although MPIC eventually adopted a strategy of appeasement. The blacklist and the related "clearance" system were effectively run by the American Legion and other right-wing social movement organizations that published lists of those who had been named by informers or were tied to front organizations. The Legion promised to mobilize their four million members and auxiliaries to picket any film involving these suspected Communists. Likewise, once exposed as a Communist, folk singer Pete Seeger was "banned from many mainstream venues either because there were outspoken anti-Communists to oppose him or because venues wished to avoid *potential* controversy."

Even if social movement organizations have no proximate involvement in a political event, they can have an indirect effect through socializing their members to address a certain set of concerns with a certain repertoire of political tactics. Therefore, a collection of proximately spontaneous acts can meaningfully be considered a form of collective action and part of a social movement. Movements have taught their members that boycotts are an appropriate response to offensive cultural content. This tactic is so practiced that it no longer necessarily requires central coordination.

Gamson found that in small-group discussions of political issues, Americans almost reflexively invoke the potential for grass-roots political action, particularly if they view themselves, or those with whom they sympathize, as having suffered an injustice. The links among public opinion, social movements, and spontaneous political action motivate the second major hypothesis:

Hypothesis 2: Stations in states and regions with conservative politics more greatly reduced Dixie Chicks airplay than stations in liberal areas.

Disagreement and distaste need not necessarily lead to protest. Even if one is offended by speech, a commitment to political tolerance may allow one to let the offense pass without censure. Evidence from survey experiments, ethnographic interviews, and focus groups shows that framing issues in terms of free speech makes people more willing to tolerate offensive speech. This should translate to the macro level. Areas where free speech is a popular value may see free speech invoked more often—and resonate more often—in cultural conflicts.

Hypothesis 2a: Expressed tolerance for critical speech suppresses the negative impact of conservative politics on Dixie Chicks airplay.

The sociology of culture literature on country music provides further perspective on the Dixie Chicks. The country music form originated with the folk music of Anglo-Saxons, Celts, and African Americans in the American South. In the 1920s a burgeoning commercial recording and broadcasting industry sought out new music beyond New York to feed a ravenous and diverse market. Anthropologists such as Alan Lomax and Tin Pan Alley A & R men such as Ralph Peer recorded "hillbilly" and "race" records, and in the process split a fairly integrated roots music tradition into genres that would eventually become white "country" music and black "blues." In the mid 1920s Henry Ford sponsored "old timey" musicians, such as Fiddlin' John Carson as a way to promote a whole-some nationalism grounded in pastoralism and the identity of old white ethnic stocks. This music stood in contrast to the commercial jazz music of Tin Pan Alley, which was associated with blacks, Jews, sex, alcohol, and big cities. Beginning in the 1930s, the Communist Party used folk music in meetings and labor organizing. In 1953, Congressional redhunters attacked the Communist folk group, the Weavers, splitting the genre further—not by race but by politics. Thenceforth, "folk" music was identified with the political left, whereas "country" music was identified with the political right. . . . As its various historical names ("hillbilly," "country," "country-western," "folk," and "old timey") imply, country music has always been associated with pastoral white America and its values, such as independence, patriotism, and religion.

Like country music, the related concepts of "Texas" and "cowboy" have strong connotations. Shively found that uneducated, rural, white, and Indian men adore Western movies and consider "cowboy" a high compliment. This perspective is not universally shared; "cowboy" is a favorite epithet used by the left, both in America and abroad. . . .

Conservatives [embrace] the image of the cowboy. For instance, they frequently use the 1952 western film, *High Noon,* as a metaphor for current events, with the cowardly townspeople representing the Europeans and the town marshal—who alone has the strength of character to fight the bandits—as the Americans and British. This is merely a colorful metaphor for the neoconservatives' general principle that a Hobbesian world can only be faced by a strong and hard-headed Anglo-American alliance, with most of Europe being too weak and naïve to defend the West from barbarism. Thus one can see that the iconography of "cowboys" and "Texas" resonates with both sides of the debate as to whether world problems are best resolved by a forceful hegemon or through a balance of power and negotiations in international institutions—a debate that is at the core of the dispute over the second Gulf War.

The ideological connotations of country music and its related iconography provide my final hypothesis:

Hypothesis 3: Country stations reduced Dixie Chicks airplay more than adult contemporary stations.

Data

The primary dataset is composed of all country and adult contemporary playlists posted to *Radio and*

Records' Web site for the week ending March 22, 2002—the first full week after Maines' remarks. *Radio and Records* is the premier trade magazine for the radio industry and largely consists of airplay charts and other data tables. The print edition used to publish playlists, but now these are only found on the Web site. These lists report what songs were played by specific stations in several different "formats," or music genres.

For each of the 224 country and 136 adult contemporary (AC) playlists, I measured how often the appropriate Dixie Chicks single was played from March 16 through March 22. Although Natalie Maines made her controversial remark about the President on March 10, this was not reported by any major American news organization until March 13, and few newspapers took note until March 15. Therefore the week ending on March 22 captures the initial reaction to her remark, a considerable drop in airplay. Comparing the two weeks will, if anything, underestimate the consequent drop in airplay, since for half of the earlier week, rumors had been circulating at a low level, and as the first two AP stories tell, some stations had already received phone calls.

In the previous week the Dixie Chicks had two singles on the charts from their quintuple-platinum album, *Home.* "Landslide," written by Stevie Nicks . . . , was largely played on adult contemporary (soft rock) stations. Country stations played "Travelin' Soldier," which tells the story of a young girl's love letters to and from a soldier who ultimately dies in Vietnam. Both songs are ballads . . . that were written by other songwriters. Aside from being on different charts and "Landslide" being released first, the principal difference between the two songs is that the lyrics of "Travelin' Soldier" deal with military themes whereas "Landslide" is more abstract. Neither song is overtly critical of the U.S.

I am interested in the change in airplay the Dixie Chicks received. If a song is currently on a station's playlist, the playlist provides the previous week's figures alongside the current information for that song, but if a song has dropped off a station's playlist, then the previous week's information is not reproduced. Unfortunately the website is not archived. Therefore, I only observe how many times a given station played the Dixie Chicks from March 9 to March 15 if that station continued to play them from March 16 to March 22. However, in the earlier week "Landslide" was number one on the adult contemporary chart, and "Travelin' Soldier" was number nine on the country chart. Checking against data on other singles shows that such preeminence ensures that nearly all stations will play a given song. To further test the validity of this assumption, I randomly drew a subsample of twenty-five AC and twenty-five country stations that did not play the Dixie Chicks from March 16 through March 22. By e-mail or telephone I asked their program directors, when available, and other personnel otherwise, if they had been playing the Dixie Chicks in early March, before the controversy. Thirty-four out of thirty six respondents acknowledged that they had been playing the Chicks then. One even told me "[t]hey had a top charting record. I anticipate all country stations were playing the Chicks at or near the top of their playlists." Therefore, the most reasonable operational assumption is to impute that stations unobserved for the earlier week were in fact playing the Dixie Chicks then.

I summarize this change in airplay with airplay ratio: the number of plays in the week after the comment divided by the number of plays in the week of the comment. For my dependent variable, I log this ratio, first adding a small constant to allow values of zero to be transformed. A high score indicates that the Dixie Chicks were kept on at about the same rate as before Maines' comment. A low score indicates that they either were greatly reduced or dropped entirely. . . .

My independent variables fall into two categories: ownership and local political climate. To code ownership, I create a dummy set with flags for all eight chains that own at least five stations in the sample or subsample. The omitted category consists of small chains and independent stations.

I measure the local political climate through two variables at the state level and two variables at the regional level. For those radio stations in markets defined by Arbitron as being evenly split between two states, I averaged the two states' traits, weighted by their population sizes. The first variable is the percentage of the state's 2000 popular vote going to George W. Bush. This is a fine-grained measure of support for Bush among the state's politically active population, which is relevant because Maines not only denigrated the war but also insulted him personally. The second state-level measure is the percentage of the state population composed of active duty military personnel. This figure proxies not only the servicemen and women themselves, but their relatives and those who depend economically on local military bases. All three groups could be expected to be especially supportive of troops in the field and defensive of policies that put them there.

To measure public opinion towards the war per se, I pool two consecutive ABC News polls from August and September of 2002, with a joint sample size of 1,264.

Both polls asked, "Would you favor or oppose having U.S. forces take military action against Iraq to force Saddam Hussein from power?" I measure this variable at the level of the 9-category census division and attach it to each radio station within the appropriate division.

Because the notions of free speech and tolerance for dissent figure prominently in popular debate over the Dixie Chicks, I tested the effect of regional levels of tolerance using a 2000 General Social Survey question: "Now, I should like to ask you some questions about a man who admits he is a Communist. Suppose this admitted Communist wanted to make a speech in your community. Should he be allowed to speak, or not?" The GSS question does not directly address the Dixie Chicks' situation both because they were not espousing Communism and because they are being repressed by private firms, not the state. Nonetheless, the question is a reasonable proxy for attitudes towards repression of this kind. First, pacifism and disrespect for a Republican president, like Communism, are disliked by people on the right. Second, although in principle it is completely consistent to oppose state repression of nonviolent political deviants while simultaneously favoring private boycotts against them, many people, both for and against private punishment of speech, lump it in with state repression under the rubric of "censorship." Like the ABC data, I measure tolerance at the census division level. Since tolerance should not have an effect in and of itself, but rather should suppress the effects of conservative politics, I specify both tolerance itself and the interaction of the region's tolerance with the state's vote for Bush. So it will be on the same zero to 100 scale as the other opinion variables. I divide the interaction term by one hundred. The interaction is meaningful since at the state level, tolerance for leftist speech and Bush's share of the vote have only a moderate correlation.

Analysis

The analyses consist of OLS regressions of logged airplay ratio for stations on ownership, format, and local political climate. I specified the model in several different ways: OLS of the logged variable with several different constants, OLS of the untransformed variable, logistic regression of zero plays versus else, and logit event history analysis of mortality over the four weeks following the AP story. In each case the results were similar. . . . I model the equation for country stations only, adult contemporary stations only, and all stations pooled together. . . .

The analyses show that most of the major chains either do not differ from independent firms or differ in the Dixie Chicks' favor. Directly contrary to Krugman's accusation and hypothesis 1, Clear Channel is actually the chain that most maintained the Chicks' airplay. This may be because in addition to its radio interests, Clear Channel is a major concert promoter and promoted the Dixie Chicks' then pending American tour. Clear Channel may face a conflict of interest—whether it skews its playlists to buy political favors or does so to cross-promote its concert interests. In this case it appears that direct financial interest won decisively over enforcing hegemony.

Krueger, however, found no relationship between the firm's concert and radio interests, so one should be cautious about assuming conflict-of-interest effects. . . . Infinity and Citadel country stations were also relatively forgiving of the Chicks. In general, the dummy set follows a trend that the larger the chain, the more it retains the Chicks on its stations' playlists. This is confirmed by replacing the dummy set with the log number of sister stations, which maintains the pattern, even if one excludes Clear Channel stations from the analysis. . . . This is congruent with the chains' greater dependence on research, which, whatever its merits, may be less effective at responding to unpredictable shocks (such as a scandal) than are less rationalized approaches to programming. Thus, we have tentative support for hypothesis 1A as the organizational inertia of large media firms may make it difficult for them to respond to political crises in the ways that the black-boxed assumptions of interest and outcome found in political economy theories would predict.

Hypothesis 2 is also supported, although the effects are weak for the adult contemporary sample. The greater proportion of the state population in military service, the greater the decline in Dixie Chicks airplay. But the effect is only marginally significant when the sample is split by format. This interpretation is supported by one program director who told me that his station's proximity to a military base factored into his decision to stop playing the Dixie Chicks. The magnitude of George W. Bush's showing in the 2000 presidential election strongly predicts a decline in Dixie Chicks airplay on country stations and the pooled sample. The percentage of the region favoring war with Iraq strongly predicts a decline, but only for country stations and the pooled sample. Although Bush's 2000 vote is statistically stronger than pro-war sentiment, the latter has a larger coefficient but more measurement error, being measured at the regional rather

than state level and being a sample rather than census. Likewise, the tolerance interaction allows the main Bush effect to come through more clearly. Therefore, it may be that support for the war actually has a slightly stronger relationship with decline in the Dixie Chicks' airplay, but this is concealed by different levels of measurement error and the particulars of my interaction specification.

These variables were all intended to measure the level of disagreement with Maines' statement, but disagreement does not automatically yield censure. The interaction of tolerance for deviant leftist speech and the state's vote for Bush is large and positive, consistent with hypothesis 2A. This is partially cancelled by a negative effect of tolerance, which must be considered net of the interaction term and not by itself. Nonetheless, the overall impact shows that at the macro level the expression of tolerance for leftist dissent translates to the practice of tolerance for it. As with the other public opinion variables, adult contemporary results are the same direction but of much less magnitude and significance than the country results.

Adult contemporary stations continued playing the Dixie Chicks at a much greater rate than country stations, supporting hypothesis 3. This may be, in part, because adult contemporary stations have slightly different audiences than country stations. For instance, both formats skew female, but country does less so. More likely, though, is that listeners found the sentiment "we're ashamed the president of the United States is from Texas" conflicted with the values expressed by country music, but not those in the less ideologically loaded genre of adult contemporary. It is noteworthy that contemporaneously with the Dixie Chicks controversy, the top single on the country charts was Darryl Worley's "Have You Forgotten?" and several other staunchly prowar songs graced the country charts, whereas the adult contemporary charts largely avoided the issue, except for Fleetwood Mac's antiwar song, "Peacekeeper."

Not only does the pooled model show that country format stations more greatly reduce the Chicks' airplay than adult contemporary stations, but comparing the two separate samples also shows that all public opinion variables have a stronger effect on country stations. Mathematically stated, country format not only has a significant negative additive effect on airplay, but also a significant negative interaction effect with measures of conservative public opinion. This is not a mere artifact of the fact that the adult contemporary subsample is two-thirds the size of my country subsample, since mathematically adjusting the standard error of the adult contemporary (AC) equation's effects to levels commensurate with the size of the country sample fails to make the AC public opinion results nearly as significant as are the public opinion effects in the country equation. Thus, it seems that conservative public opinion affects both formats in similar ways, but the ideology of country music magnifies its impact.

Predicting and exponentiating the results, the three regression equations suggest that an independently owned adult contemporary station or a Clear Channel country station in liberal Massachusetts would likely maintain the Dixie Chicks' airplay at about the same rate as before Maines' comments, perhaps with a slight drop. The same station in moderate Florida would cut their airplay severely. In conservative Texas they would be dropped from play entirely. If the station were both adult contemporary format and owned by Clear Channel, the prediction does not change for Massachusetts or Texas, but the expected cut in Florida becomes less severe. Independently owned country stations are predicted to drop or severely cut the Dixie Chicks no matter how liberal the local political climate. . . .

Discussion

Many fans see country music as an oasis of tradition in a world where tradition is besieged by liberal elites. Many country songs "show that it is impossible to 'go home' because the old ways are being destroyed *everywhere*. Often, the federal government is seen as the agent of undesired change." Thus, when country musicians express the same values in the same patronizing tones as those liberal elites, it is not merely disagreeable, but a betrayal of their essential identity. The *Guardian* was right. The "Texas" incident was a punk rock moment, but unfortunately for the Dixie Chicks, they are not punk rock musicians with a punk rock audience. Pearl Jam, a punk-influenced rock band, made similar statements without serious consequences.

Much of the public was offended by statements against the war by Michael Moore, Martin Sheen, or Susan Sarandon. And some institutions, such as the Baseball Hall of Fame, the United Way, and the Motion Picture Academy, have sought to distance themselves from these antiwar celebrities. However, none of them suffered anything like the material consequences or vitriol leveled at the Dixie Chicks. About the same number of Americans bought the Dixie Chicks' album *Home* as saw the theatrical release of Moore's film *Bowling for Columbine*, but in all probability a majority, if not most, of the former favored war with Iraq, whereas almost certainly most of the latter opposed it.

My analysis has shown no evidence that corporate elites have taken vengeance against disloyalty. Boycotts and conflict are a source of instability that business seeks to avoid. The recording and radio industries thrive on star power and have no desire to destroy the viability of any of those relatively few acts who resonate with the public as powerfully as the Dixie Chicks did until March 2003.

Rather the data suggest that country music has a vengeful audience to whose wishes corporations responded with varying degrees of haste. Thus, the most important consequence of my analysis is that it turns the notions of "false consciousness" and "hegemony" on their heads. Rather than corporate interests punishing dissent and imposing conservative values on the citizenry, in this instance citizens imposed conservatism and punitiveness on corporations.

My findings suggest that, to use Herman and Chomsky's theoretical framework, it is not ownership, but flak that was responsible for the hostile response to Maines' insult. In fact, corporate ownership delayed censure. This may be disturbing to political economists, who tend to believe that if "corporate control" were only balanced by "democracy," then the media would have been purged of any conservative bias. To the extent that the demos is to the right, then responsiveness to its voiced demands brings media content there as well.

Discussion Questions

1. Why do you think corporations might be reluctant to refuse airplay to a star who criticizes the actions of the President?

2. What does Rossman's conclusion suggest about how the power of democracy might be used to quench free speech?

Source: Rossman, G. (2004). Elites, masses, and media blacklists: The Dixie Chicks controversy. *Social Forces*, Vol. *83*(1): pp. 61–79. Copyright © The University of North Carolina Press.

PART III

DEVIANCE AND CRIME

Part III shows how deviance and crime are social constructions. The articles in this section illustrate how deviant and criminal behaviors are defined. They also show how such behavior affects and can be influenced by individuals and societies, that social capital is not always the solution to crime, and that exposure to violence, rather than delinquent peers, is a predictor of violent behavior.

Beliefs in the appropriate punishment for deviant behavior also vary from culture to culture. Even within the same society, regions with different subcultures can vary in how they pass or enact laws. In "Political Culture and the Death Penalty," Patrick Fisher and Travis Pratt reveal how our cultural norms and beliefs lead to varying support for the death penalty in different areas of the United States.

Just as different areas of the nation have different subcultures with their own influence on crime and punishments, different organizations can create social capital that affects crime rates for the better or the worse. While it may seem hard to believe that people socializing with fellow believers could have negative societal repercussions, in "Social Capital, Too Much of a Good Thing? American Religious Traditions and Community Crime," Kraig Beyerlein and John R. Hipp point out that not all social capital is good for society. When members of religious organizations are very active in their own religious circles but do not socialize with those outside their own faith, crime in the area actually goes up! So, not all types of religious civic participation are beneficial for the greater society. Only when members of society relate to people in groups beyond their own circle of believers does crime diminish.

Two articles take a closer look at causes of violent behavior among youth. In "Reconsidering Peers and Delinquency: How Do Peers Matter?" Dana L. Haynie and D. Wayne Osgood reveal that the influence of peers on delinquent behavior may have been overstated in the past. They find that, while delinquent peers can have a negative influence, unsupervised time seems to have more of an influence on delinquent behavior. Justin W. Patchin and his co-authors also provide good data for those interested in establishing policies to curb criminal behavior with their article, "Exposure to Community Violence and Childhood Delinquency." They show that youth who witnessed more violence in their neighborhoods were more likely to self-report assaulting people and weapon carrying.

In the last article, "Bullies Move Beyond the Schoolyard: A Preliminary Look at Cyberbullying," Patchin and Sameer Hinduja look at how bullying has migrated to the Internet, with damaging consequences to both victims and perpetrators. With the Internet, bullying can take place at all times of the day or night. However, many Internet bullies fail to realize that they can be traced, caught, and exposed when they bully online.

As you read the articles in this section, keep in mind the following points:

- Not all forms of social capital curb community crime.
- Unsupervised time seems to be a more powerful influence than peers on delinquent behavior.
- Death penalty legislation and implementation of existing death penalty laws vary according to the subcultures of different regions of the United States.
- Exposure to violence is related to rates of violent delinquency.
- Cyberspace provides the means for bullies to harass their victims at all times of the day and night.

CHAPTER 8

Political Culture and the Death Penalty

Patrick Fisher and Travis Pratt

Political culture is an important determinant of the adoption of death penalty statutes and the frequency of executions. States that are characterized by a more traditionalistic political culture are more likely to have adopted a death penalty statute and to execute inmates more frequently, even when controlling for other factors previously linked to the death penalty.

Introduction: The Variation in the Usage of the Death Penalty Among the 50 States

In 1972, the Supreme Court struck down all existing state death penalty laws in *Furman v. Georgia*. This halt in the usage of the death penalty, however, was short lived. Since the Supreme Court ruled in 1976 in *Gregg* v. *Georgia* that the death penalty was not inherently unconstitutional, most states have adopted new capital punishment statutes that have passed constitutional muster. Yet 14 states do not have the death penalty on the books. And in those states that do have the death penalty, execution rates vary considerably. The mean execution rate per state between 1990 and 1995 was 3.68, but this was highly skewed; the median execution rate was 0.50. Whereas Texas executed 71 people between 1990 and 1995, one half of the states (25) executed no one.

Why does the usage of the death penalty vary so considerably among the 50 states? The objective of this work is to analyze the degree to which political culture is a determinant of states' implementation of capital punishment. We find that political culture, as measured by Daniel Elazar's (1984) prototype classifications of American political subcultures, is an excellent determinant of whether states implement the death penalty and the degree to which they do so.

Daniel Elazar's Political Subcultures

Political culture consists of a shared set of ideas about the role of government and about who should influence public policy. Politics cannot be understood apart from culture and ideology (Kincaid, 1982). It is a common mistake to try to explain the diversity of everyday behavior in the United States on the grounds of uniformity in shared national values. As Aaron Wildavsky (1998) states, "though the United States is a single nation, Americans do not constitute a single culture" (p. 49).

A significant departure for the conception of a consensual national political culture is proposed by Daniel Elazar (1984). . . . According to Elazar, the national political culture is the synthesis of three major political subcultures that are dominant in varying parts of the country. Elazar terms these subcultures individualistic, moralistic, and traditionalistic.

The individualistic political culture is based on the utilitarian conception that politics should work like a marketplace. Government should handle only those functions demanded by the people it is created to serve. This businesslike conception of politics places a premium on limiting community intervention on private activities and restricts government action to only those areas that encourage private initiative. Ideological concerns are eschewed, as both politicians and citizens look on politics as a specialized activity for professionals, with only a small role to be played by the general public.

The moralistic political culture, on the other hand, stresses the conception of the commonwealth as the basis for democratic government. Politics is viewed as being a positive activity in which citizens have an obligation to participate. Good government is measured by the degree to which it promotes the public good. Individualism is abated by a commitment to communal power to intervene in private activities when it is considered necessary for the public good. Communitarian principles dictate that government has the responsibility to promote the public welfare. Moralistic political cultures are also more likely to produce political systems that are more responsive to the demands of reformers than are individualistic and traditionalistic political cultures (Ritt, 1982).

The traditionalistic political culture views the proper role of government in a much different light: Politics is viewed as a privilege, not an obligation. It has an ambivalent attitude toward the marketplace and an elitist conception of the commonwealth. The traditionalistic political culture reflects a precommercial attitude that accepts the inevitability of a hierarchical society. It accepts government as an actor with a positive role in the community, but unlike the moralistic political culture, it tries to limit that role to securing the continued maintenance of the existing social order. Those who do not have a definite role to play in politics are not expected, nor encouraged, to be politically active.

Each of the three political cultures is dominant in varying areas of the country. . . . [T]he individualistic political culture tends to be dominant in the middle-Atlantic states, the Midwest, and the mountain states; the moralistic political culture dominant in New England, the Great Lakes region, and the West Coast; and the traditionalistic political culture is relatively isolated to the South and Southwest.

The Relationship Between Political Culture and the Death Penalty

Political culture is relevant to capital punishment practices in a variety of ways. Maintaining law and order, for example, is one of the acceptable roles for the more limited government favored in the traditionalistic states. The death penalty, therefore, may be seen as a way in which the elites in a traditionalistic culture can control the masses. On the other hand, the belief that all should

participate in the betterment of the commonwealth may lead a moralistic political culture to value all citizens, even those convicted of the most hideous crimes. Thus, moralistic states may be less likely to support capital punishment. Individualistic states may be supportive of the death penalty on the "eye-for-an-eye" belief that capital punishment is an appropriate sanction for those convicted of murder, but the individualistic political culture's fear of intrusive government may also create an environment fearful of the death penalty, on the basis of individual rights being forsaken. An individualistic political culture, therefore, seems to be more likely to be divided on the death penalty than would the traditionalistic or moralistic political cultures.

Elazar's (1984) political subcultures have been found to predict public policy variations among the states. Though research on the relationships between political cultures, process, and policies has produced mixed findings (Kincaid, 1982), Erikson, Wright, and McIver (1993) find strong support for Elazar's typology of political subcultures among the American states—the politics of the states do vary somewhat along these lines. In terms of ideological direction, the authors found that state policies tend to reflect the ideological sentiment of the state electorates. The most liberal states enact the most liberal policies, whereas the most conservative states enact the most conservative policies. This suggests a potential relationship between political culture and implementation of the death penalty.

Using path analysis, Barbara Norrander (2000) finds that state public opinion, the number of years the state has had the death penalty on the books, how urban the state population is, the percentage of African Americans in the state, and the proportion of Catholics in the state shaped the rate at which states applied capital punishment. Norrander also tests what she terms an institutional lag model, which suggests that state policy will fall behind current public opinion because state institutions are structured according to a political culture shaped in an earlier era. Her hypothesis is that political culture may have *a* greater impact on the implementation of the death penalty than contemporary public opinion does, because politicians are more likely to be long-term residents and thus more likely to reflect the historical values of a state. She found that political culture has an effect on a state's current public policy on the death penalty, but she argues that past policy (how long the state has had the death penalty) and political culture share some of the same explanatory variance in capital punishment practices.

In another study of implementation of the death penalty among the states, David Nice (1992) found that proportionally large death row populations are more likely in states with ideologically conservative populations, high rates of murder, and higher levels of urbanization. His multivariate analysis found that ideological forces in particular are significant influences in shaping state responses to capital punishment. The conservative belief that severe penalties are needed to deter crime, Nice argues, enhances the appeal of the death penalty . . . .

The South has long been considered the most violent region of the United States. A history of previous violence is the single best known predictor of future violence. From the end of the Civil War until the 1930s, the South's subculture of violence can be seen in its preponderance of lynchings, which accounted for more than 1,000 deaths in the 1890s alone (Clarke, 1998). Lynchings began to decline after the turn of the century as court-ordered execution supplanted lynching in the South. The increase of executions in the South can thus be considered to be the result of a movement away from ad hoc mob lynchings to so-called legal lynchings. The result is that by "the end of the 1930s, the death penalty, like lynching, already had a peculiarly Southern stamp" (Clarke, 1998, p. 287). Because the traditionalistic subculture is found almost solely in the South, this would seem to support the argument that political culture influences state implementation of capital punishment.

Deterrence and the Death Penalty

. . . Perhaps the most methodologically rigorous study of the impact of the death penalty was Cochran, Chamlin, and Seth's (1994) interrupted time-series analysis of Oklahoma's return to the death penalty. Their study is considered to be the most methodologically sound analysis of the effect of the death penalty on homicide rates for three reasons. First, Oklahoma's adopting of the death penalty was geographically isolated (i.e., no surrounding states conducted a similar execution at the same time to produce a "history effect"). Second, the researchers were able to gather weekly estimates of state-level homicides from the FBI's Supplemental Homicide Reports (SHRs) to avoid temporal aggregation bias. Finally, the SHRs allowed for separate analyses of felony murder and stranger homicides to avoid potential offense aggregation bias. In a time series analysis of the "naturally occurring experiment" of Oklahoma's return to the death penalty, Cochran et al.'s (1994) models found

no evidence of a deterrent effect, even after disaggregating the homicide time series into felony murder and stranger homicides. In fact, their analyses revealed a mild but statistically significant "brutalization effect," where the public execution in Oklahoma actually produced a corresponding increase in stranger homicides.

The fact that the death penalty has been found not to be related to deterrence suggests that something else is at work in states that adopt the death penalty—something other than a simple calculation of enacting policy that is perceived to work for the benefit of the public good. States that adopt the death penalty are not doing so because it will reduce homicides. A possible ulterior explanation is that states that adopt capital punishment do so because it maintains an elitist social order of a hierarchical society. In other words, the death penalty can be seen as a means by which governing elites keep the general populace in check. If so, this suggests that capital punishment will be more likely to be used in states with the elitist inclinations of a traditionalistic political subculture.

Method

To test the influence of political culture on the death penalty, two measurements of Elazar's (1984) typology are used. The conventional measure of Elazar's political culture is a 3-point scale, with 1 representing a state that is classified by Elazar as a moralistic political culture, 2 indicating a state that has an individualistic political culture, and 3 denoting that the state has a traditionalistic political culture. Another means of measuring political culture is Ira Sharkansky's (1969) operationalization of Elazar's typology, which rates states on a scale from 1 to 9, with low scores given to moralistic states and high scores given to traditionalistic states, with individualistic states in between. This is the measurement that Norrander (2000) uses to test the institutional lag model, which predicts that a state's political institutions are structured according to a political culture dominant in the state.

To measure capital punishment rates in the states, two variables related to the death penalty are employed, the information for both of which was obtained from Death Penalty USA (http://www.agitator.com/dp). The first variable is a dummy variable representing whether a state has a death penalty statute (values coded as 0 = no, 1 = yes). Because it has been argued that sentencing rates are more important in explaining capital punishment policy in the states than enactment dates are

(Norrander, 2000), the second death penalty variable measures the frequency of executions during the period from 1990 to 1995....

Given the relatively weak empirical support for the effect of the death penalty (or specifically the effect of executions) on crime, assessing the factors underlying why states keep such laws on the books—and at times, actually enforce them—takes on added importance. To that end, ... consistent with the discussion above, we [first] determine whether a state's political culture is significantly related to whether a state will sanction legal executions (i.e., whether the law is on the books). Second, because not all states that may have enacted death penalty legislation enforce it in the same way, we then assess whether a state's political culture significantly predicts the extent to which a state actually carries out executions....

Results

The first step in the analysis examines whether the two measures of political culture are significantly related to the death penalty variables we have specified. Accordingly, [we found] that both measures of political culture are significantly related to whether a state has adopted a death penalty statute and to the frequency of executions....

On controlling for whether a state has a death penalty statute, for the murder rate, and for the structural disadvantage index, ... Elazar's (1984) typology (in this model, it is treated as a dummy variable reflecting the traditionalistic culture) is a strong and significant predictor of the frequency of executions ($\beta = .54$, $p < .01$). The same can also be said of the model that includes Sharkansky's (1969) typology of political culture, which is also a rather robust predictor of the frequency of executions ($\beta = .45$, $p < .05$). Taken together, these models indicate that, net of statistical controls, political culture is an important determinant of states' frequency of executions.

Discussion

... [T]he broad purpose of this article was to explain why states vary with regard to two facets of the death penalty; whether the state has the law on the books and, if so, the frequency with which states actually carry out our nation's most severe punishment. Our more particular concern centered on the degree to which this variation in death penalty laws and the frequency of executions may be attributable to variation in states' political culture. Accordingly, the analyses we conducted to examine these issues leads us to three major conclusions.

First, our results indicate that political culture is an important determinant of the adoption of death penalty statutes and of the frequency of executions. To be sure, states that are characterized by a more traditionalistic political culture are more likely to have adopted a death penalty statute in the wake of the *Gregg* case and to execute inmates more frequently. Second, the link between political culture and the death penalty remains strong and stable even when controlling for a host of other factors that have been linked to the death penalty in prior research. Indeed, the effect of political culture on the death penalty is robust enough that it does not "wash out" in the presence of additional covariates.

Finally, our results indicate that the relationship between political culture and the death penalty revealed in our analysis is not contingent on one particular method of measuring political culture. Although Elazar's (1984) typology of political culture was a stronger predictor of the frequency of executions, Sharkansky's (1969) typology was also significantly related to states' use of the death penalty. The strength of the political culture–death penalty link across these two measures gives us added confidence that this relationship is not a methodological artifact. Rather, it reflects an ongoing phenomenon where the political culture of a state is a substantively important determinant of the degree to which states employ this severe sanction.

On a final note, the work presented here also has important implications for continued research into cultural perspectives in the social ecology of crime. In particular, the Southern subculture of violence thesis, which sets forth a cultural explanation for the relatively high rates of violent crime in the South, has been the subject of considerable debate, and empirical support for this contention is, at best, rather weak (Gastil, 1971; Hackney, 1969; Huff-Corzine, Corzine, & Moore, 1986). Even so, Pratt and Cullen (in press) note that the measures typically employed by researchers as indicators of Southern culture rarely extend beyond the single dummy variable for whether the unit of analysis is located in the former confederate South. Pratt and Cullen go on to note that with such weak proxies for Southern culture, it is perhaps unsurprising that the theory has received such limited empirical support. Thus, before sweeping the Southern subculture of violence thesis into the criminological dustbin, it would be wise to first develop alternative macrolevel measures of culture, such as those presented in the present analysis, when testing this perspective.

Discussion Questions

1. According to Fisher and Pratt, why is a state with a traditional political culture more likely to support the death penalty than one with a moralistic or an individualistic political culture?

2. According to Fisher and Pratt, what type of political culture is dominant in your part of the country? Do you agree with it? Why or why not?

Source: "Political Culture and the Death Penalty" by Patrick Fisher and Travis Pratt, excerpted and with notes and references omitted from *Criminal Justice Policy Review,* Vol. 17, No. 1, March 2006, pp. 48–60. Reprinted by permission of Sage Publications.

CHAPTER 9

Social Capital, Too Much of a Good Thing?

American Religious Traditions and Community Crime

Kraig Beyerlein and John R. Hipp

This study uses American religious traditions as measures of bonding and bridging social capital in communities. It suggests that the bonding networks evangelical Protestants promote in communities explain why counties with a greater percentage of residents so affiliated have higher-than-expected crime rates. Conversely, the bridging networks that mainline Protestants and Catholics foster in communities explain why counties where a greater percentage of residents are so affiliated generally have lower crime rates.

Few concepts in the social sciences have received more scholarly attention and public notoriety over the past decade than social capital. When conceptualized as networks that link individuals and the resources embedded in those linkages, social capital has substantially enhanced our understanding of various social processes and outcomes. The majority of research on social capital has focused on its positive benefits. Among other things, this research has shown that social capital promotes social support, boosts physical health, improves academic performance and increases job contacts (Granovetter 1985; Hurlbert, Haines and Beggs 2000; Pong 1998). However, the tendency to focus on social capital's positive effects has recently drawn a chorus of criticism from scholars who point out that social capital need not necessarily produce positive consequences, and that it may even produce negative results (Fiorina 1999; Paxton 1999, 2002; Portes 1998; Putnam 2000:350–363).

Social capital by definition benefits those who possess it. Yet there is good reason to expect that the advantages individuals accrue from social capital often come at the expense of others. For example, while strongly knit groups provide various benefits to members, their general exclusivity restricts entry to others and denies benefits to nonmembers (Portes 1998). Strongly knit groups can also have deleterious consequences for the wider community in which they reside. Consider militia groups that have strong internal ties but few or no external ties in communities. Their intense within-group solidarity provides numerous benefits to members, such as emotional support and a sense of belonging. However, because militia groups do not forge connections with other residents, they truncate the wider network structure of the community and thus decrease its overall cohesiveness (Paxton 1999).

This problematizes viewing social capital as a homogenous concept at one level of aggregation, and points to the importance of distinguishing *types* of social capital and the differing effects they can have at different levels of aggregation. We differentiate bonding social capital in which linkages are mainly or exclusively among members of the same group from bridging social capital in which linkages exist among members of different groups in communities (Paxton 1999, 2002; Putnam 2000). Although bonding groups increase social capital within their group, they can reduce social capital at the community level, as the above example of militia groups illustrates. On the other hand, bridging groups that establish connections with others outside their group increase social capital at the community level by expanding the overall network structures of the communities in which they are embedded.

To the extent that community cohesion and connectedness influence the incidence of crime (Lee 2000; Sampson, Raudenbush and Earls 1997), the *type* of social capital that groups foster in communities should be of considerable importance for explaining differences in crime rates across communities. We do not assume, however, that members of bonding and bridging groups are committing crimes in communities or that they are doing so at different rates. We argue rather that groups exhibiting bonding social capital will be less effective in generating network structures that help the larger community deal with the threat of crime, while groups exhibiting bridging social capital will be more effective in creating these network structures. Importantly, by providing an empirical test of this hypothesis, we substantially advance the literature on social capital.

Providing an empirical test of the differing effects of bonding and bridging groups on community-level outcomes is a challenge due to the difficulty of measuring these types of social capital. Adequately measuring bonding and bridging social capital requires capturing entire network structures of communities, a daunting task for researchers. An alternative strategy utilizes measures that serve as proxies for these concepts, and recent scholarship in the sociology of religion generally demonstrates the division of American major religious traditions into bonding and bridging camps (Ammerman 2002; Beyerlein and Hipp 2006; Chaves, Giesel and Tsitsos 2002; Iannaccone 1994; Putnam 2000:63–79; Wilson and Janoski 1995; Wuthnow 1999, 2002). Consequently, religious traditions are one way to operationalize bonding and bridging groups in communities, and to test whether these types of social capital have differing effects on communities" crime rates.

Linking Bonding and Bridging Social Capital to Community Crime

Although scholars have defined social capital in various ways, we conceptualize social capital as network structures linking individuals in communities (Coleman 1988; Paxton 1999; Putnam 2000). Because network structures vary in the extent to which they narrowly or broadly link residents in communities, it is important to differentiate *bonding* social capital from *bridging* social capital. Bonding social capital consists of network structures in which connections are primarily or entirely among members of the same group, while bridging social capital consists of network structures in which connections crosscut members of different groups (Putnam 2000).

Ties comprising bonding social capital tend to be stronger in nature, while ties comprising bridging social capital tend to be weaker in nature (Granovetter 1973).

While not using the language of bonding and bridging social capital, scholars working within the social disorganization tradition have suggested that such differences in network structures are important for explaining variation in crime rates across communities. Bellair (1997) focused on the degree of interaction among neighbors, theorizing that because infrequent interaction is more likely to occur among a greater percentage of residents than frequent interaction, it plausibly reflects a wider constellation of ties within the larger community and thus a more disperse overall network structure. He observed that even with frequent interaction ("strong ties") among residents, without infrequent interaction ("weak ties") as well, communities will be partitioned and disorganized because a large portion of residents will be unknown to each other (c.f. Granovetter 1973). Because broad-based network structures increase the degree of interconnectedness among residents in communities, they should facilitate the diffusion of information and collective social control efforts. As Bellair (1997:683) states, "communities with extensive networks are assumed to be more integrated and cohesive, and the residents more likely to engage in informal surveillance, to develop movement-governing rules, and to intervene in disturbances." Empirically, Bellair (1997) identified that progressively less frequent interaction among neighbors generally had strong negative effects on various types of crime. Other empirical evidence also suggests that broader network linkages may help depress the incidence of crime in communities. For example, Taylor, Gottfredson and Brower (1984) showed that those communities with a greater proportion of residents who shared organization memberships had lower rates of violent crime, and Sampson and Groves (1989) observed that the combination of friendship networks and acquaintanceship networks resulted in consistently lower rates of various types of community crimes than friendship networks alone.

Conversely, in communities where residents are not broadly linked, supervision, guardianship and informal efforts to promote community goals are likely to be weak (Freudenburg 1986; Jacobs 1961). Importantly, bonding groups should hinder the formation of broad network structures that allow communities to mobilize effectively to protect collective interests. As Sampson and Raudenbush (1999:612) articulate, "personal ties and friendship are not sufficient; the private world of strong kinship ties may actually interfere with public trust and expectation of collective responsibility for getting things done."

Bonding network structures are thus likely to increase crime rates in communities by reducing collective efficacy or the sense that others will participate and respond to problems (Sampson, Morenoff and Earls 1999; Sampson and Raudenbush 1999; Sampson et al. 1997). Sampson and colleagues have consistently shown that *collective efficacy* has a significant inverse effect on disorder and crime. (See also Lee 2000.) Where bonding network Structures are pervasive, the lack of linkages among groups in communities should weaken collective efficacy, making communities more vulnerable to crime. . . .

Religious Traditions as Measures of Bonding and Bridging Social Capital

An ideal test of our theoretical model would collect and analyze data on the entire network structure of a large number of communities. Given that this is an impractical task, we employed a measure that approximates the entire network structure of communities. Considerable literature in the sociology of religion documents that American religious traditions are such a measure. Because of contrasting theological orientations, adherents of the major U.S. religious traditions behave in ways that give rise to very different network structures in communities. As Putnam (2000:77–78) summarizes " . . . [today's] evangelicals are more likely to be involved in activities within their own religious community but are less likely to be involved in the broader community . . . [while] today's mainline Protestants and Catholics are more likely to be involved in volunteering and service in the wider community."

A large body of research has shown that because of their emphasis on otherworldly pursuits, evangelical/conservative Protestants tend to participate exclusively in activities and groups in their own congregations or other religious organizations consisting of fellow believers (Hoge et al. 1998; Wuthnow 2002). For example, using the General Social Surveys (GSS) from 1984 to 1990, Iannacone (1994) found considerable differences among Protestants in belonging to church-affiliated groups. Splitting Protestant traditions into four categories of varying conservatism/liberalism, he found that members of the most conservative traditions were 31 percent more likely than were members of the most liberal traditions to belong to church- affiliated groups. Using the Giving and Volunteering Surveys from the Independent Sector, Wuthnow (1999) reported that the majority of volunteer work in which evangelical Protestants engage is focused on the religious life of their congregations, such as teaching Sunday school or assisting pastors. Based on similar evidence, Wilson and Janoski (1995:149–50) concluded that "conservative Protestants do volunteer work more if they are integrated into the church, but what they volunteer for is church maintenance work."

On the other hand, mainline/liberal Protestant and Catholic traditions stress that believers should engage the broader community and help those outside of their religious groups." Numerous studies have shown that mainline Protestants and Catholics participate in various activities and organizations that serve the needs of and establish connections with others in the wider community (Beyerlein and Hipp 2006; Wilson and Janoski 1995; Wuthnow 2002, 2004). In his analysis of the Giving and Volunteering Surveys, Wuthnow (1999) demonstrated that the more frequently mainline Protestants and Catholics participated in congregations, the more likely they were to volunteer not only for religious organizations, but also for organizations focused on improving communities, such as those providing medical assistance to the needy or helping struggling students. Wuthnow (1999), however, found no such effects for evangelical Protestants. In his study using GSS data from 1984 to 1990, Iannacone (1994) found that members of the most liberal Protestant traditions belonged to 50 percent more nonreligious organizations than members of moderately conservative traditions, and *twice* as many as members of the most conservative traditions.

Given these religious tradition differences in bonding and bridging activity, we expect that a greater percentage of mainline Protestants and Catholics will decrease crime rates in communities, while a greater percentage of evangelical Protestants will increase these rates. By participating in activities and organizations that link them to others in their broader environment, mainline Protestants and Catholics foster bridging network structures and thus their greater presence in communities should reduce crime for communities as a whole. Conversely, by generally participating in activities and organizations that consist exclusively of their own people, evangelical Protestants promote bonding network structures and thus their greater presence in communities should increase crime for communities as a whole. . . .

Religious Congregations and Community Crime

The social disorganization perspective has long emphasized the importance of organizations in combating crime in communities. Organizations increase awareness of various community problems, and they have formal resources that facilitate solving community problems, such as the direct provision of services to people who are in need (Kornhauser 1978; Shaw and McKay 1942). Some have speculated that to the extent that various organizations coordinate and pool their resources, they will be even more effective in reducing disorder and crime in communities (Mesch and Schwirian 1996; Morenoff and Sampson 1997). Prior research has shown that the congregations of all the major American religious traditions engage in various social service programs in communities, though mainline Protestant and Catholic congregations tend to be more engaged in these programs than evangelical Protestant congregations (Ammerman 2002; Chaves 2004; Chaves et al. 2002; Chaves and Tsitsos 2001; Wuthnow 2004). In contrast to *adherents* of the different religious traditions, then, because *congregations* of the different religious traditions all tend to provide resources to communities, they should have similar negative effects on crime rates. Because of the strong institutional base that congregations establish in communities, it is imperative to control for them when modeling the effect of adherents on crime in communities. Without accounting for the institutional resources of religious traditions, it is not possible to isolate the network effect of their adherents.

Data

We constructed our data from a variety of sources. Because focusing on small neighborhoods may not capture the effects of social networks among residents across neighborhoods, we used counties as our unit of analysis. For the dependent variables, we used reports of offenses for specific crime types from the Uniform Crime Report (UCR) for 1998–2000. Although there has been considerable discussion regarding the use of official reports of crimes, we focused on crime that has minimal reporting inconsistencies—murder—and other types that have shown the most consistency with victimization surveys— aggravated assault, robbery and burglary (Cohen and Land 1984; Gove, Hughes and Geerken 1985). Because robbery and aggravated assault are violent crimes that have a particularly frightening effect on individuals, we combined them into a single measure. We calculated these crime rates per 100,000 population and log-transformed them to obtain a more normal distribution.

The religious tradition data come from the 2000 Glenmary Survey of American religious adherents and congregations (Jones et al. 2002). This decennial survey

of religious organizations estimates both the number of adherents and the number of congregations in a county for 149 denominations in the United States. We used this information to distinguish Catholic, mainline Protestant and evangelical Protestant adherents and congregations. Using Steensland et al. (2000) and Melton (2002) as resources, we classified Protestant denominations either as mainline or evangelical. . . . We classified those not fitting into one of these three religious traditions as other. To capture bonding networks in counties, we calculated the proportion of the county population composed of evangelical Protestant adherents. We used two measures to capture bridging network structures in counties: the proportion of the county population composed of mainline Protestant adherents and the proportion of the county population composed of Catholic adherents. As a measure of the institutional resources that religious traditions provide to counties, we calculated the number of congregations per 100,000 people for each religious tradition.

To minimize the possibility of spurious findings, we included numerous variables that past criminological research has found to predict crime in communities, constructed from the 2000 U.S. Bureau of the Census STF-3A files. Four measures that likely affect both the crime rate and the religious composition of communities are population density, southern residence, racial composition and socioeconomic status [SES]. We therefore included a measure of the population density per kilometer, a dummy variable for counties in states in the traditional South, and measures of the percentage of African-American, Latino, and white populations, with Asian and other racial groups as the omitted category. To capture SES effects, we included a measure of the education level in the community (the percentage of those with at least a bachelor's degree), the percentage of the population with an income at or below the poverty level, and both the median household income and the median household income squared to capture possible nonlinear effects of income.

We also included three other measures that past research has found to be associated with crime rates. Note that doing so provides a stringent test of the *network effects* we posit for adherents of the various religious traditions because we are controlling for other ways through which these adherents may affect crime. To capture communities with limited adult supervision, we included the percentage of single parent families in the county. Because the social disorganization model posits that residential instability of communities should affect the social networks within them, we included a measure of the average length of time residents have lived in their current homes. Finally, to account for the possible increase in offenders, we included a measure of the county unemployment rate. Our indicators are measured per capita, so we included the inverse of population in our models (Firebauqh and Gibbs 1985)....

Modeling Strategy

... For each of our three crime measures we first estimated models with the proportion of the county population composed of adherents of each religious tradition, along with our control variables. While this model does not control for the institutional resources of the religious traditions, it gives us a baseline model on which to build. We next estimated models in which we replaced the measures of adherents of each religious tradition with measures of the number of congregations of each religious tradition. This allowed us to assess the social disorganization theory that the institutional resources associated with each of the religious tradition's congregations should similarly reduce crime rates in communities. Finally, we estimated a model in which we simultaneously entered adherents and congregations of each religious tradition with our control variables. This full model enabled us to assess whether the different network structures that the adherents of religious traditions foster in communities affect crime rates net of the institutional resources that their congregations provide as well as numerous other variables shown in prior studies to be important predictors of ecological crime rates.

Results

We begin by viewing the effects of adherents of different religious traditions on the combined aggravated assault/robbery measure.... In the first model, when we do not control for the institutional resources of the religious traditions, there is evidence that counties with more Catholic and mainline Protestant adherents have lower logged rates of assault/robbery. A one percentage point increase in Catholic adherents in a county reduces the assault/robbery rate by .3 percent, while an analogous increase in the percentage of mainline Protestants reduces this rate by 1.8 percent, as seen in model 1 in Table 1. These results are consistent with our hypothesis that the bridging activity of Catholics and mainline Protestants reduces crime rates in communities. In contrast, we see that an increase in the proportion of evangelical Protestant adherents is associated with *higher* assault/robbery rates. For a one percentage point increase in evangelical Protestant adherents, the assault/robbery rate increases by .8 percent.

Tradition Adherents and Congregations, Controlling for Demographic Factors

To view the institutional effects of the religious traditions, we next estimate a model in which we replace the measures of adherents with measures of congregations from each tradition. We see in model 2 of Table 1 that Catholic and mainline Protestant congregations significantly reduce the assault/robbery rate in counties. Note that while evangelical Protestant adherents are associated with higher rates of assault/robbery in model 1, the effect of their congregations is not significant. This suggests that adherents and congregations are capturing distinct constructs and underscores the need to disentangle their effects by including both in a single model.

Next, we estimate our full model, including both adherents and congregations of each religious tradition. This model provides consistent support for our posited bonding and bridging network theory of crime rates in communities. We see evidence of the hypothesized bridging network effect of mainline Protestants in model 3 of Table 1; an increase in the proportion of adherents of this tradition is associated with lower logged assault/robbery rates in counties. Specifically, a one percentage point increase in mainline Protestant adherents is associated with a 1.3 percent reduction in the assault/robbery rate. Note that we obtain this result while controlling for the presence of congregations, as well as a host of other important variables shown in the criminological literature to affect crime rates in communities. The effect of Catholic adherents is also in the expected direction, although it does not reach significance at conventional levels. We stress that these findings are *not* simply "religious" effects, as in this same model a one percentage point increase in evangelical Protestant adherents is associated with a .9 percent *increase* in the assault/robbery rate. This is consistent with our argument that while bonding together and withdrawing from the larger community provides various benefits to group members, this behavior can have deleterious effects for the community as a whole. In this same model, we now see that the institutional resources of *all* three traditions have the expected negative effect on assault/robbery rates, but the effect is stronger for mainline Protestant

Table 1 Unstandardized Coefficients from the Regression of Various Crime Types on Religious Tradition Adherents and Congregations, Controlling for Demographic Factors

	(1) Assault/ Robbery	(2) Assault/ Robbery	(3) Assault/ Robbery	(4) Burglary	(5) Burglary	(6) Burglary	(7) Murder	(8) Murder	(9) Murder
Adherents (a) (b)									
Evangelical Protestants	.760 **		.923 **	.634 **		.833 **	.326 **		.740 **
	(.130)		(.180)	(.110)		(.152)	(.096)		(.143)
Mainline Protestants	−1.812 **		−1.298 **	−.721 **		−.410 *	−.427 **		−.391 *
	(.188)		(.234)	(.162)		(.205)	(.144)		(.189)
Catholics	−.291 t		−.236	−.286 *		−.426 **	.057		−.119
	(.161)		(.172)	(.132)		(.145)	(.110)		(.123)
Congregations (c)									
Evangelical Protestants		.001	−.014 **		.001	−.014 **		−.009 **	−.020 **
		(.003)	(.004)		(.002)	(.003)		(.002)	(.003)
Mainline Protestants		-.038 **	−.019 **		−.022 **	−.014 **		−.016 **	−.008 t
		(.004)	(.005)		(.003)	(.004)		(.003)	(.004)
Catholics		-.057 **	−.047 **		−.029 **	−.017 **		−.025 **	−.018 **
		(.007)	(.007)		(.006)	(.006)		(.006)	(.006)
R²	.48	.48	.50	.30	.31	.32	.37	.39	.40

Note: Numbers in parentheses are standard errors; N = 3,157. All models include measures of inverse population, population density, education, poverty, median income, median income squared, African-American, Latino, white, unemployment rate, residential instability, single parents, south, and other religious adherents and congregations

(a): reference group is percent nonreligious; (b): measured as percent of county population; (c): Measured as number of congregations per 100,000 population

** $p < .01$ (two-tail test), * $p < .05$ (two-tail test), t $p < .05$ (one-tail test).

and especially Catholic congregations. A one-unit increase in the number of congregations per 100,000 reduces the assault/robbery rate by 1.4 percent for evangelical Protestant congregations, 1.9 percent for mainline Protestant congregations, and 4.7 percent for Catholic congregations....

Next, we test whether bonding and bridging social capital affect the property crime of burglary. We see similar patterns here as those for aggravated assault/ robbery. In the model without the congregation variables, Catholic adherents and mainline Protestant adherents are associated with lower burglary rates, while evangelical Protestant adherents are associated with higher burglary rates, as seen in model 4 in Table 1. As with aggravated assault/robbery, mainline Protestant and

Catholic congregations are associated with lower rates of crime when measures of adherents are not included in model 5 of Table 1. Our full model shown in model 6 once again is consistent with our predictions. While congregations of all three religious traditions have the expected negative effects on the burglary rates of counties, we again see that only the bridging networks of Catholic and mainline Protestant adherents reduce these rates. A one percentage point increase in either Catholic or mainline Protestant adherents is associated with about a .4 percent lower burglary rate. Importantly, we see the hypothesized *positive* relationship between evangelical Protestant adherents and this crime type. A one percentage point increase in evangelical Protestant adherents is associated with a .9 percent increase in the burglary rate. We thus again identify suppressor effects for the evangelical Protestant tradition in the models that do not include both their adherents and congregations....

Finally, we see that the effects of bonding and bridging social capital work similarly for county murder rates. In model 7 with just the measures of adherents, mainline Protestants and evangelical Protestants show the hypothesized effects. The congregations of all three religious traditions have negative effects on murder rates in model 8, suggesting that they provide important institutional resources to communities. As with the previous two crime outcomes, our full model in model 9 indicates that the bridging activity of mainline Protestant adherents has an additional negative effect on county murder rates beyond the institutional effect of their congregations. In contrast, evangelical Protestant adherents are associated with *higher* rates of murder. For a one standard deviation increase in evangelical Protestant adherents (17 percent), the county's murder rate increases by 13 percent. We emphasize again that our argument is *not* that evangelical Protestants are committing murders, but rather that their bonding activity gives rise to network structures that make communities as a whole more vulnerable to this and other types of crime....

Discussion and Conclusion

Social capital has become an increasingly popular concept in the social sciences for explaining a range of positive outcomes at various units of analysis. However, a growing number of scholars have begun to criticize this single-minded focus on the positive consequences of social capital, calling for more theoretical and empirical attention to the potential "dark side" of social capital (Fiorina 1999; Paxton 1999, 2002; Portes 1998; Putnam 2000:350–363). Responding to this call, we distinguished between bonding and bridging social capital that groups cultivate in communities and explicated how these different types of social capital can have differing effects on crime rates in communities. By generally creating only tightly knit internal network ties among members, bonding groups do not forge ties with others in the wider community, which hinders the flow of communication and collective action efforts in communities and thus makes them more susceptible to crime. Bridging groups, however, by creating broadly linked network structures in communities,

facilitate the diffusion of information and mobilization of collective resources, reducing the risk of crime....

Despite the difficulty of testing empirically our theoretical model, it points to directions for future research. One especially difficult issue is the geographical unit of analysis. While our study employed counties as the unit of analysis, this unit is arguably too large and thus provided a conservative test of our hypotheses. Measuring bonding and bridging network structures of a community would ideally consist of a multilevel approach in which small neighborhoods are nested within larger areas. In other words, although studies focusing on small neighborhoods would miss the important bridging ties that can link residents and groups in areas together, studies looking at larger communities face the daunting task of attempting to measure all the ties in these communities. One approach for dealing with this difficulty is to focus on a particular community. While this approach precludes generalizing findings to other areas, several such studies would be able to test the robustness of our theoretical model. There is also the issue of specifying the exact mechanisms through which bonding and bridging social capital influence crime in communities. Future research would benefit from identifying whether collective efficacy mediates the observed relationship between bonding and bridging social capital and crime (Sampson et al. 1997).

Finally, because we are aware of no other available data on social capital that allow the distinction between bonding and bridging groups to be drawn, we believe that data on adherents of America's major religious traditions are a valuable resource for future explorations of the relationship between social capital and other community-level outcomes. This fact notwithstanding, adherents of American religious traditions are certainly not the only way to operationalize bonding and bridging social capital in communities. For example, Paxton (2002) adopted a strategy of measuring isolated and connected associational ties of individuals by focusing on the extent to which memberships in organization types overlapped. While the study used this measure in the context of cross-national data on democracy, scholars could adopt this strategy to capture network structures in local communities by specifying whether organizational linkages among residents are generally narrow or broad in scope. Although collecting such data presents a challenging task for researchers, our model suggests that other measures that are able to capture the bonding and bridging nature of groups in communities will observe similar effects on crime rates. Regardless of the measurement strategy taken, our conceptual framework provides a useful lens through which to view how the different *forms* of social capital that groups cultivate in communities can constrain or facilitate outcomes that are desirable for communities as a whole.

Discussion Questions

1. How can bonding social capital benefit individual members of a group but negatively influence the larger society?

2. How can bridging groups lower the rate of crime in a community?

CHAPTER 10

Reconsidering Peers and Delinquency

How Do Peers Matter?

Dana L. Haynie and D. Wayne Osgood

Adolescents engage in higher rates of delinquency if they have highly delinquent friends or if they spend a great deal of time in unstructured socializing with friends. However, the normative influence of peers on delinquency is more limited than indicated by most previous studies. These influences from the peer domain do not mediate the influences of age, gender, family or school.

Introduction

Interpersonal relations are a critical link between individual lives and the larger social structure. In this paper, we examine the contribution of peer relations to juvenile delinquency from the perspective of two sociological traditions. The first is the set of theoretical orientations that point to interpersonal relations as the avenue for normative influence, including symbolic interaction theory (Mead 1934), reference group theory (Newcomb 1950) and related conceptions of social influence (Simmel 1955; Sutherland and Cressey 1955). Here the attitudes, values and behaviors of individuals are influenced to become similar to those of their associates, and we will refer to that generic process as normative influence or socialization by peers. The second tradition is the social ecological approach seen in Hawley's (1950) work and elaborated in the routine activity perspective of Cohen and Felson (1979). From this perspective, interpersonal relations are relevant as part of the process by which the social structure shapes the spatial and temporal contours of social life, thereby increasing opportunities for some behaviors and decreasing opportunities for others.

Peer relations have long been central to the study of delinquency (Short 1957), and for good reason.

Adolescents spend much time with their friends, attribute great importance to them, and are more strongly influenced by them during this period than at any other time in the life course (Brown 1990). Also, delinquency has long been described as a companionate activity that typically involves co-offenders (Erickson and Jensen 1977; Hindelang 1976). The similarity of delinquency among friends remains one of the most consistent and strongest relationships in the literature (e.g., Agnew 1991; Elliott, Huizinga and Ageton 1985). Evidence of this association comes from observational research (Thrasher 1927), official data (Shaw and McKay 1942), and self-report studies (Short 1957).

Despite this history of interest, the contribution of peer relations to delinquency remains unclear. Though some theorists interpret peer similarity in delinquency as evidence of normative influence (Akers 1985; Sutherland and Cressey 1955; Warr 2002), others view it as a spurious result of peer selection (Glueck and Glueck 1950; Gottfredson and Hirschi 1990). Some of these issues have recently been resolved with Haynie's (2001, 2002) elaboration of the social network processes that contribute to higher levels of delinquency. Haynie's work is particularly noteworthy for its use of detailed friendship network information in the National Longitudinal Study of

Adolescent Health. These data provide measures of friends' participation in delinquency based on friends' actual responses rather than the usual approach of relying on respondent perceptions of friends' behavior. Haynie's findings indicate that although adolescent delinquency is positively associated with friends' delinquency, network structure moderates the strength of the association. Specifically, adolescents in very dense friendship networks or in very central positions within their networks exhibit stronger peer-delinquency associations.

The present study goes beyond that research by returning to a more fundamental question: How do peers matter in regards to delinquency? Though many scholars portray normative influence from peers as the most important source of adolescent delinquency (e.g., Akers 1985; Elliott et al. 1985), we believe this remains an open question due to methodological limitations of available research. The present study uses improved methods to evaluate the strength of normative influence, to assess the role of peer delinquency in mediating the effects of other factors on delinquency, and to determine whether normative influence is contingent on the nature of peer relations. We also address an alternative way that peers might contribute to delinquency by considering opportunity theory's emphasis on spending time with friends as conducive to delinquency (Osgood et al. 1996).

Theoretical Connections Between Peer Relations and Delinquency

PEERS AS A SOURCE OF NORMATIVE INFLUENCE

In most social psychological accounts of larger social phenomena, normative influence or socialization from close associates is the key process by which individuals come to conform with the norms of their group. Various theories offer alternative portrayals of the processes by which interpersonal relations produce this socialization. For example, symbolic interactionism emphasizes the importance of the individual taking the perspective of others (Mead 1934). Reference group theory treats the individual's identification with others as key (Newcomb 1950). Social learning theory focuses on reinforcement and modeling (Akers 1985). Yet all agree on the centrality of normative influence.

Socialization theories are prominent in explanations of the relationship between crime and delinquency as well. Sutherland's (Sutherland and Cressey 1955) differential association theory and Akers' (1985) extension to differential reinforcement theory are specifically devoted to this normative influence process. Though the generic socialization process applies to any ongoing and close interpersonal association, theories of crime and delinquency have been especially interested in peers as a source of normative influence. . . .

It is difficult to overstate the importance attributed to normative peer influence in the study of crime and delinquency. It is the key causal process in many theories, and studies often report peer delinquency to be the variable with the strongest influence on respondents' delinquency (e.g., Akers et al. 1979; Elliot et al. 1985; Warr 1993b). Furthermore, several studies have concluded that peer delinquency accounts for the association of delinquency with other major correlates including age (Warr 1993a), attachment to parents (Warr 1993b), and measures of normlessness and strain (Elliott et al. 1985).

METHODOLOGICAL ISSUES IN THE ASSESSMENT OF NORMATIVE INFLUENCE

One purpose of the present study is to determine whether methodological shortcomings have led to a serious overestimation of the importance of the normative influence of peers on delinquency. Assessing interpersonal influence is complex because similarity between friends could result from either normative influence or social selection. The ubiquitous tendency to choose friends who are similar to oneself holds for qualities ranging from age, sex and race to attitudes, personality and behavior (Blau 1977; McPherson and Smith-Lovin 1987). . . .

It is at least as plausible, however, that both socialization and selection would contribute to similarity. In fact, the theories of both Elliott et al. (1979) and Thornberry (1987) imply that delinquent peer groups and normative influence are reciprocally related, and there is empirical evidence that both processes are at work (Kandel 1996; Matsueda and Anderson 1998). This more temperate view of normative influence is consistent with prior studies finding that the effect of peer delinquency declines, but is not eliminated, upon the addition of controls for selection (Haynie 2002; Krohn et al. 1996; Matsueda and Anderson 1998).

A second methodological concern is that the standard approach to measuring peer delinquency contains a same-source bias that substantially inflates similarity between peers. In almost all criminological studies, information about friends comes from adolescents' descriptions of the behavior of their friends rather than from those friends' reports of their own behavior. Such measures inflate the correspondence between respondents and their peers because people tend to project their own attitudes and behavior onto their friends, a phenomenon social psychologists refer to as *assumed similarity* or *projection* (Byrne and Blaylock 1963; Newcomb 1961). Though such findings have led several scholars to caution against the use of respondents' reports about peers (Aseltine 1995; Bauman and Ennett 1994; Jussim and Osgood 1989; Kandel 1996; Wilcox and Udry 1986), there has been little recognition of this problem in research on crime and deviance. Such findings show that there is some truth in Gottfredson and Hirschi's (1990:157) argument that respondents' reports of their peers' delinquency "may merely be another measure of self-reported delinquency."

By inadequately controlling for selection processes and by using adolescents' reports of their friends' behaviors, previous studies have over-estimated the contribution of peer socialization to delinquency. Indeed, Kandel (1996) concluded that, in combination, these two methodological factors may lead to a five-fold over-estimation of normative influence on adolescent deviance. The study we present below builds upon Haynie's (2001, 2002) recent work by addressing the peer selection issue through a longitudinal research design and the inclusion of an extensive set of control variables including a measure of prior delinquency. Also, we follow Haynie in employing a network-based measure that uses friends' own reports of their delinquency.

PEERS AS A SOURCE OF OPPORTUNITY FOR DELINQUENCY

In the first tradition we considered, interpersonal relationships are important because they integrate individuals into normative communities. In contrast, the second tradition sees interpersonal relationships as important for structuring everyday life and thereby shaping opportunities for different types of behavior. This opportunity perspective need not be seen as contradicting the socialization perspective, and the causal processes it specifies may well coexist with that form of social influence.

. . . Osgood and colleagues (1996) proposed that situations conducive to deviance are especially prevalent during unstructured socializing with peers in the absence of authority figures. They argued that the presence of peers makes deviant acts easier and more rewarding, the absence of authority figures reduces the potential for social control responses to deviance, and the lack of structure leaves time available for deviance. Therefore, individuals who spend more time in unstructured socializing activities will also more frequently engage in delinquency and other deviant behavior. Osgood et al. (1996) demonstrated that within-individual change in unstructured socializing activities (but not other activities) was strongly related to delinquency and several measures of substance use.

From this opportunity perspective, peer relations are not connected to delinquency by the type of friends that one chooses. Instead, what matters is the amount of time spent with peers engaged in a common type of activity that is not inherently deviant. Following Gold (1970), Osgood and colleagues (1996) saw peers as important because delinquency is often a performance, and peers serve as the appreciative audience. This perspective is also consistent with Gold's (1970) portrayal of delinquency as similar to a pick-up game of basketball in being casual, spontaneous and loosely organized. For example, Gold noted that "more important than the particular company [that a youth keeps] was the presence of an opportunity for delinquency when everyone's mood was ripe for action" (p. 119).

A potential challenge to this opportunity explanation is the possibility that the association between delinquency and unstructured socializing is a byproduct of the socialization process discussed above. Socialization could produce this relationship if youths who spend the most time this way also have delinquent friends. Thus, one of the purposes of the present study is to determine whether unstructured socializing is still related to delinquency after controlling for peer delinquency. . . .

The Present Study

Our research addresses the following hypotheses derived from the socialization and opportunity perspectives reviewed above.

SOCIALIZATION THEORY

Primary hypothesis: Adolescents whose friends are more delinquent will engage in more delinquency themselves, even after controlling for selection processes.

Secondary hypothesis: The relationship of peer delinquency to adolescents' own delinquency will be stronger when adolescents are more attached to those peers and when they spend more time with them in unstructured socializing.

Secondary hypothesis: Peer delinquency will mediate much of the influence of other variables that are reliably associated with delinquency such as age, attachment to parents and school grades.

OPPORTUNITY THEORY

Primary hypothesis: Adolescents who spend more time in unstructured socializing with friends, away from authority figures, will engage in more delinquency even when controlling for peer delinquency.

Secondary hypothesis: Time spent in unstructured socializing may be more strongly related to delinquency if one's friends are more delinquent. Even for respondents whose friends are not at all delinquent, however, unstructured socializing will produce higher rates of delinquency to at least some degree.

Previous Evidence from the National Longitudinal Study of Adolescent Health

The present study relies on data from the National Longitudinal Survey of Adolescent Health (henceforth, Add Health), which includes the information necessary for constructing network-based measures of peer delinquency. . . .

The present study addresses hypotheses about the mediating role of peer delinquency and about interactions among peer delinquency, attachment to peers and unstructured socializing with peers. It also will explore the strength of normative influence and include the measure relevant to opportunity theory. We have refined measures of the key peer variables for peer delinquency and unstructured socializing, and improved the controls for selection of similar friends by extending the list of control variables and by adding a longitudinal analysis.

Methods

SAMPLE

The Add Health survey provides data for a nationally representative sample of adolescents in grades 7 through 12,

who were attending 132 schools selected with unequal probability in the United States in 1995–1996. Incorporating systematic sampling methods and implicit stratification into the study design results in a sample of schools representative of U.S. schools in terms of region of the country, urbanicity, school type, ethnic makeup of the schools and school size (Bearman, Jones and Udry 1997). Our research relies on the in-school and in-home surveys conducted in 1995 and on the second in-home survey conducted in 1996. The sample for the in-school self-administered questionnaire included every student (who was present on the day of the interview) in each school, whereas the in-home survey was limited to a random sample of students whose names appeared on school rosters or who were found in the school on the day of the in-school interview. Most of our measures come from the in-home survey, which was more extensive and also included more sensitive questions than did the in-school survey. The response rates for the in-home survey were 78.9 percent at Wave I and 88.2 percent at Wave II. Some of our analyses are limited to a portion of the Add Health data known as the "saturation sample," which consists of the 16 schools at which all students (rather than a random sample) were selected for the in-home interviews. (See Haynie 2001, 2002 for greater detail.)

To measure the social networks of the students at each school, the in-school survey asked students to nominate up to five of their closest female friends and five of their closest male friends (for a maximum of 10 friends). By linking these nominations to the friends' responses about their own involvement in deviant activities, researchers can construct network based measures of peer relationships and peer characteristics. (For example, see Haynie 2001, 2002.) . . .

The final sample consists of 8,838 respondents who provided information for all three phases of data collection (in-school survey, time 1 in-home interview, and time 2 in-home interview), for whom network information was available, and whose parent completed an initial in-home survey. For the supplementary analyses that involved the smaller saturation sample we draw upon interviews with 2,274 respondents.

MEASURES

Dependent variable. Our measure of delinquency derives from responses to a series of 14 delinquency items collected during both in-home interviews. To enhance anonymity, respondents listened to these pre-recorded questions on earphones and entered their responses directly into laptop computers (Bearman, Jones and Udry 1997). The 14 delinquency items include: paint graffiti, damage property, shoplift, steal something worth less than $50, steal something worth $50 or more, burglarize, steal a car, sell drugs, engage in a serious physical fight, seriously injure another, use or threaten to use a weapon, participate in a group fight, pull a knife or gun on someone, and shoot or stab someone (alpha = .86). The questions ask students to report how often during the past 12 months they have participated in these activities. Each delinquent act is coded from 0, if respondents did not participate during the past year, to 3, if respondents participated in the act several times.

We computed delinquency scores with the item response theory (IRT) scaling methods described by Osgood, McMorris and Potenza (2002). IRT scaling is especially advantageous for the highly skewed items comprising most measures of deviance because it translates the discrete categories of the response scale to a shared dimension that is continuous and has an equal-interval metric. Our IRT scoring employed Samejima's (1969) graded response model, which makes full use of the ordinal information in every item. We scored both waves of data jointly so that the two sets of delinquency scores would be fully comparable.

Peer delinquency. A central feature of our research is the use of network data to measure peer delinquency rather than relying on respondent's reports about their friends. Because each adolescent in the Add Health study had the opportunity to nominate friends during the in-school survey (time 1), and almost every adolescent in the respondent's school completed a questionnaire for the in-school survey, it becomes possible to measure most friends' behaviors based on the friends' actual responses to survey items.

To calculate peer delinquency, we first defined the respondent's peer network to include all those adolescents whom the respondent nominated as a friend, as well as any adolescents who nominated the respondent as a friend (i.e., the send-and-receive network). Our analyses made use of two measures of peer delinquency. The first is based on a brief series of questions about involvement in minor deviant acts, which was included in the in- school survey. Specifically, each friend was asked how often during the past year he or she had gotten drunk, smoked cigarettes, skipped school without an excuse, and been involved in serious physical fights (alpha = .69). Responses to each item ranged from 0, indicating never, to 5, indicating three to five days a

week. For the saturation sample, where all students in the school (rather than a sample) completed the in-home interview, we are able to create a second peer delinquency measure based on friends' responses to the same delinquency items used to measure the dependent variable (alpha = .79).

To obtain a fair assessment of the strength of normative influence, it is important to score peer delinquency in a manner that best captures its relevance to respondents' own delinquency. The method that proved most effective was to IRT score each friend's responses and to take the average of those IRT scores across the friends. . . .

Unstructured socializing. Our measure of *unstructured socializing* is based on three questions. For each friendship nomination, respondents indicated whether they met the friend after school to "hang out" and whether they spent time with the friend over the past weekend. For each question (asked for each nominated friend) responses are coded either 0, indicating no or 1, indicating yes. In addition to these two questions, respondents were asked in general "during the past week, how many times did you just hang out with friends?" and responses to this question ranged from 0, indicating "not at all" to 3, indicating "5 or more times." This measure is designed to focus more specifically on time spent socializing in a relatively unstructured way. Even so, the included items are not strictly limited to time away from authority figures, as stated in Osgood et al.'s (1996) opportunity theory. To the degree that our measure did not fully isolate the type of time use specified by the theory, our results are likely to be a somewhat conservative estimate of the, relevant effects. . . .

Control variables. We include a large set of control variables to account for possible selection effects. Among these are a variety of demographic variables that have often been associated with delinquency in prior research: *gender* (1 female, 0 = male), *race* (measured with two dummy variables: one coded as one for African American respondents and the other coded as one for races other than African American and non-Hispanic white; thus, non-Hispanic white is the reference group), *family structure* (1 = lives with two married parents, 0 = other family structures), *age* (measured in years) and age squared (to allow for a curvilinear relationship), and two measures of *social class* based on responses from parents elicited during the in-home interview. These are a measure of parent's educational level indexing the highest level of schooling achieved (of the more educated parent) which ranges from 0 = no formal education to 9 = professional training beyond a four-year college or university, and receipt of public assistance (1 = received public assistance during the past year, 0 = did not).

Social control variables. Measures of social control served as additional control variables. Though previous research does not support Hirschi's (1969) prediction of a social control effect of attachment to peers, a measure of this variable is necessary for testing the socialization perspective's hypothesized interaction effects. We measured *peer attachment* through responses to the question, "How much do you believe that your friends care about you?" Responses range from 0, not much at all, to 5, they care very much about me. It would be more consistent with previous measures of attachment if the question inquired about the respondents' sentiments toward their friends (e.g., Hirschi 1969). Unfortunately, no such item was available, so we must rely on the general tendencies for respondents to assume that their friends feel similar to themselves.

Unlike peers, there is consistent evidence that social controls in other domains reduce delinquency. We include two measures of parental controls. *Attachment to parents* is measured as an index combining responses to the following questions; "how close to you feel to your [mother/father]" and how much do you think your [mother/father] cares about you? (alpha = .69). The second is a measure of *parental supervision* (alpha = .60) based on adolescents' responses to six questions about their mother's and father's physical presence in the home at various times of day: when the adolescent leaves for school, returns from school, and goes to bed. Responses ranged from 1, never, to 5, always. Though this measure does not exhaust relevant aspects of supervision, it does tap the critical component of parental availability.

In addition to control by parents, we include social controls in relation to school. The first of these is the adolescent's self-reported *grade point average* (based on grades earned during the past year in math, science, English and history), which would reflect commitment to conventional lines of success. The second is the respondent's *attachment to school* (measured as an index combining responses to the following questions: "do you feel close to people at your school," "do you feel like you are part of your school," and "are you happy to be at your school") (alpha = .78). The last social control variable we include is a measure of the *importance of religion* to the respondent. This is based on one item that asks respondents to indicate: "how important is religion to you: very important, fairly important, fairly unimportant, or not important at all?" . . .

Analytical Strategy

SELECTION EFFECTS

. . . To control for selection effects we must take into account the factors that lead adolescents to choose a particular group of friends and that are also associated with their own delinquency. We take two approaches to this problem. The first is to control for the 13 factors listed above, which previous research has shown to be associated with delinquency, a far more extensive list than included in most studies of peers and delinquency.

The limitation of this first approach is that there may well be unmeasured variables that affect both peer selection and delinquency. Recent longitudinal analyses by Ackerman (2003) suggest that this problem is not too dramatic in the Add Health data; a more limited set of controls was sufficient to account for almost all of the tendency to select friends with similar levels of delinquency. Another approach to eliminating all possible selection factors would be, in effect, to control for the dependent variable. We can accomplish a version of this by treating delinquency at Wave 2 as the outcome measure while using the Wave 1 measures of peer relations as explanatory variables and the Wave 1 measure of delinquency as a control variable. . . .

We therefore view the two sets of estimates as upper and lower bounds on the effects of peer relations on delinquency. The first set, providing the upper bound, come from a cross-sectional analysis of Wave 1 delinquency, using Wave 1 measures of all explanatory and control variables. The second set, providing the lower bound, come from a longitudinal analysis of Wave 2 delinquency, again using Wave 1 measures of all explanatory and control variables, and also controlling for Wave 1 delinquency.

Statistical model. When testing for statistical interactions, it is especially important to select a statistical model that is well-suited to the distribution of the outcome measure (Osgood and Rowe 1994). The IRT measurement approach we used to scale delinquency produces a measure that approximates the normal distribution except for a substantial floor effect due to the many respondents who report committing none of the delinquent acts

(43 percent in wave 1 and 54 percent in wave 2). Following Osgood et al. (2002a), we analyze our data using the tobit regression model, which is designed for such a truncated normal distribution (Long 1997). They demonstrated that the tobit model is well-suited to delinquency data, provided that the measure has been transformed to approximate normality. Preliminary analyses indicated that the tobit model was an equally good match to our IRT measure of delinquency. Coefficients from tobit have the same interpretation as those from OLS regression, except that they refer to the untruncated dimension presumed to underlie the observed measure.

Results

OVERALL EFFECTS OF PEER RELATIONS

Peers as a source of normative influence. The results . . . address our primary hypotheses about how peer relations would be associated with delinquency. We assess socialization, or the normative influence of peers, by the effect of the delinquency of the respondents' friends. This effect is statistically significant both after controlling for many other potential causes of delinquency (the cross-sectional model) and also after controlling for a contemporaneous measure of delinquency (the longitudinal model). Therefore, we are confident that peer socialization has a meaningful causal influence on delinquency, contrary to claims that this association is entirely attributable to respondents choosing friends who are similar to themselves.

Yet our findings also show that most studies have substantially overestimated normative influence by relying on respondent's reports about their friends and by failing to control for selection processes. Such studies typically conclude that peer delinquency is an exceptionally powerful predictor of delinquency, dominating all other social influences on delinquency with a standardized effect of about .5 (e.g., Akers et al. 1979; Elliot et al. 1985; Matsueda 1982). In contrast, our estimate for the standardized effect of friends' delinquency is an upper bound of .14 and a lower bound of .05. Thus, normative influence is no more important to delinquency than are many other well established predictors. . . .

Peers as a source of opportunity. Our second theoretical perspective focuses on interpersonal relations as a potential source of opportunities for deviance, which we

measure in terms of time spent in unstructured socializing. Our central question about this perspective is whether the association of delinquency with unstructured socializing is a spurious byproduct of the influence of delinquent friends. . . . [T]his is not the case. Unstructured socializing is significantly associated with delinquency in both the longitudinal and cross-sectional analyses, with standardized coefficients of .13 (upper bound) and .04 (lower bound). The magnitude of the effect of unstructured socializing is comparable to that of normative influence and also to the effects of relations with parents and school, all of which are long established as central to theories of delinquency and adolescent deviance.

INTERACTIVE EFFECTS OF PEER RELATIONS

We find no evidence that the impact of friends' delinquency is greater either when respondents feel closer to their friends or when they spend more time in unstructured socializing with their friends. Indeed, none of the interaction effects approach statistical significance, and three of our four estimates of the interaction are in the opposite direction.

For socialization theories, the importance of this result is that the degree of normative influence is relatively independent of these other dimensions of peer relationships. Given our large sample size, we would be able to detect even a moderate interaction effect. If adolescents regard one another as friends, they tend to influence one another whether or not they feel strongly attached to one another or spend an exceptional amount of time together. The interaction results provide critical support for a routine activity perspective on peers and delinquency. Spending lots of time "hanging out" with friends is conducive to delinquency, even if those friends are not especially delinquent themselves. This finding answers a fundamental challenge to the socialization explanation by showing that the relationship of activities to delinquency is not a secondary byproduct of normative influence by peers. Thus, these findings are consistent with interpreting this relationship as reflecting the contribution of situational opportunities.

NORMATIVE INFLUENCE AS A
MEDIATOR OF EFFECTS OF OTHER VARIABLES

The final substantive issue we investigate is the degree to which normative influence is an essential causal process that accounts for the relationship to delinquency of other important variables. To address this, we turn to the variables that have served as statistical controls in the previous analyses, which include prominent correlates of delinquency such as gender, age and school performance. We compared the coefficients for those variables from two models, the first without peer delinquency (a reduced form model) and the second including peer delinquency. To the degree that normative influence mediates the contributions of those variables, their coefficients will be closer to zero in the second model.

The comparison between these models indicates that the mediating role for peer delinquency is limited in both cross-sectional and longitudinal analyses. The greatest proportionate reduction in coefficients was for public assistance, importance of religion and grade point average; peer delinquency accounts for 10 to 20 percent of the relationships of these variables to respondents' delinquency. The relationships of age and race to delinquency actually became stronger after adjusting for peer delinquency. In sum, our findings are in contrast to studies indicating that peer delinquency fully mediates the effects of age (Warr 1993a) and attachment to parents (Warr 1993b) on delinquency. Our mediation findings are not surprising, however, in the context of the rest of our results. Our improved controls for selection and independent assessment of peer delinquency produced a much lower estimate of normative influence than was found in those studies, which in turn means that peer delinquency has little potential to mediate the effects of other factors. . . .

Discussion

This study has examined the contribution of peer relations to juvenile delinquency from two perspectives about the role of interpersonal relations in linking individual lives to the social structure. The socialization perspective views peers as a source of normative influence, whereas the opportunity perspective focuses on time spent with peers as a potential source of opportunities that promote delinquency. As we noted earlier, the two perspectives are compatible with one another, and our results provide support for both.

For the opportunity or routine activity perspective, we addressed the critical question of whether the connection of delinquency to time spent with peers is better explained by opportunity processes or by normative

influence. Osgood and colleagues' (1996) routine activity explanation claims that adolescents who spend more time in unstructured socializing with peers, away from authority figures, have higher rates of delinquency because they more often encounter situations conducive to deviance. This explanation would not hold, however, if the relationship between time use and delinquency could be accounted for by the delinquency of the respondents' friends.

Our results support the validity of the opportunity explanation. The relationship between unstructured socializing and delinquency remained after controlling for friends' delinquency. Furthermore, tests for interaction effects revealed that the association between time use and delinquency was at least as strong for respondents with more conventional friends as for those with delinquent friends. This pattern supports Osgood and colleagues' (1996) supposition that support for "subterranean values" (Matza and Sykes 1961) is sufficiently widespread that even relatively non-delinquent youth can spur one another on to deviant behavior.

Considering the central place of socialization explanations in the study of deviance, it is disappointing that research on this question has been plagued by long-known methodological shortcomings. Our efforts to overcome those weaknesses produced a picture of normative influence as a modest influence on delinquency, much weaker than is claimed by researchers who portray this socialization as its dominant proximal cause. . . .

It is important to remember that, because we consider only influence from *friends,* our analysis is restricted to a limited range of attachment to peers. Findings regarding attachment might be quite different if we also assessed influence from peers who were not friends. Gold and Osgood's (1992) study of influence among incarcerated adolescents indicates that this may be the case. Those peer groups were in near- constant interaction, but members had virtually no choice about their associates. In that setting there was greater influence when respondents felt more closely attached to peers.

In sum, our findings paint a complex picture of delinquency as arising from many sources and by several processes. Two sociological perspectives have guided our work, and we have found that they both provide valuable insights about how relations with peers are linked to individual delinquency: Adolescents engage in more delinquency if they have delinquent friends or if they spend a great deal of time in unstructured socializing with friends. Yet these influences from the peer domain are no more or less important than social control processes in the realms of family and school. Finally, despite controlling for a large set of predictors associated with many of the prominent theories of crime and delinquency, the standard demographic variables of sex, age and race/ethnicity remain strongly related to delinquency, meaning that those theories do not appear to account for these fundamental relationships.

Discussion Questions

1. How would you use the findings in this article if you were to design social policies for combating delinquency?

2. How is this article an example of the importance of using appropriate methodologies when conducting research?

Source: "Reconsidering Peers and Delinquency: How Do Peers Matter?" by Dana L. Haynie and D. Wayne Osgood, excerpted and with notes & references omitted from *Social Forces*, Vol. 84, No. 2, December 2005. Copyright © 2005 by the University of North Carolina Press. Used by permission of the publisher, www.uncpress.unc.edu.

CHAPTER 11

Exposure to Community Violence and Childhood Delinquency

Justin W. Patchin, Beth M. Huebner, John D. McCluskey,
Sean P. Varano, and Timothy S. Bynum

Although crime and deviance tend to concentrate in areas of disadvantage and disorder, not all residents of disorganized neighborhoods participate in proscribed activities. This study finds that controlling for the effects of neighborhood disadvantage and other correlates of delinquency, youth who witnessed more violence in their neighborhoods were more likely to self-report assaultive behavior and weapon carrying.

The effect of neighborhood environment on child development has received significant scholarly attention in recent years (Brooks-Gunn, Duneau, Klebanou, & Sealand, 1993; Burton & Jarrett, 2000; Chaiken, 2000; Elliott et al., 1996). Research has suggested that children reared in disadvantaged neighborhoods are at an elevated risk to engage in deviant behaviors (Herrenkohl, Hawkins, Chung, Hill, & Battin-Pearson, 2001). Other research, however, has shown that the vast majority of children who grow up in disorganized environments fail to initiate serious offending (Blumstein, Cohen, Roth, & Visher, 1986; Wolfgang, Figlio, & Sellin, 1972). The goal of this research is to examine why some children, raised in neighborhoods with similar structural and economic disadvantages, engage in delinquent behaviors, whereas others abstain from crime.

Traditionally, researchers have explored the effects of community context on delinquency using social disorganization theory (Bursik, 1988; Bursik & Grasmick, 1993; Sampson & Groves, 1989; Shaw & McKay, 1942). Specifically, it has been argued that disadvantaged, disorderly, and decaying neighborhoods foster an environment in which deviance becomes widespread (Sampson & Lauritsen, 1994). In addition, these characteristics preclude

the development of social networks within the neighborhood that could potentially redress the maladies associated with crime and deviance (Bursik & Grasmick, 1993; Kornhauser, 1978; Sampson & Groves, 1989; Sampson, Raudenbush, & Earls, 1997).

The social disorganization literature has shed considerable light on the between-neighborhood processes associated with delinquency. However, less is known about the within-neighborhood mechanisms associated with delinquency. Specifically, little research has been conducted on the role of witnessing community violence on delinquency. This dearth in the literature is surprising given that researchers have found that exposure to violence is commonly reported among youth living in disorganized neighborhoods (Bell & Jenkins, 1993; Crouch, Hanson, Saunders, Kilpatrick, & Resnick, 2000; Scarpa, 2001; Schwab-Stone, Chen, Greenberger, Silver, Lichtman, & Voyce, 1999).

The purpose of this study is to extend previous research by examining the effect of exposure to community violence on delinquency among a sample of 9- to 15-year-old youth who reside in disorganized neighborhoods. Although numerous studies have examined the relationship between neighborhood context and delinquency, as noted above, few researchers have considered the effect of exposure to violence on delinquency or the effects of exposure to community violence net of delinquency correlates and neighborhood disadvantage. Inclusion of multiple controls for neighborhood disadvantage and delinquency correlates (e.g., attachment to school) helps isolate the effects of exposure to community violence. The sample selected for examination is unique in that efforts were made to include active offenders and youth who are most at risk to engage in delinquent activities. The examination of early, serious delinquency is also of particular importance because research has shown youth who engage in delinquent behaviors prior to the age of 14 are at high risk to continue participation in crime and deviance throughout the life course (Loeber & Farrington, 1998, 2001). Data for the study were obtained from youth interviews and the *U.S. Decennial Census* (U.S. Census Bureau, 2000). Ordinary least squares and logistic regression models are estimated to test the hypothesis that youth who witness more violence in their neighborhoods are more likely to report assault and weapon carrying.

Literature Review

Scholars in the Chicago School of Sociology (Shaw & McKay, 1942) and elsewhere have argued that "characteristics of the urban environment are critical to explaining the emergence of crime in specific communities" (Eck & Weisburd, 1995, p. 2; see also Sampson, 2002). Specific theoretical and empirical attention has been devoted to structural characteristics such as residential mobility, concentrated disadvantage, and population heterogeneity (Bursik, 1988; Bursik & Grasmick, 1993; Kornhauser, 1978; Shaw & McKay, 1942; Wilson, 1987). Each of these elements is thought to have direct and indirect effects—through decreased informal social control capabilities—on crime (Sampson, 2002). In addition, researchers have also argued that the deviance that occurs within disorganized neighborhoods may negatively affect the residents by making them feel compelled to use violence as a response to a threatening urban environment (Anderson, 1999; Durant et al., 1994; Stewart, Simons, & Conger, 2002).

Ecological research has consistently linked community disadvantage to between-neighborhood differences in violence and crime. More recently, researchers have begun to examine the factors within neighborhoods that are associated with delinquency, specifically exposure to community violence. The results from this research have been mixed. For example, Stewart and colleagues (2002)

found that neighborhood affluence was significantly related to preadolescent violence, whereas neighborhood violence was not. They reason that neighborhood-level factors may be less important for younger children than for older adolescents, who may be more embedded in the neighborhood culture (see also Brooks-Gunn et al., 1993; Elliott et al., 1996; Wikström & Loeber, 2000). Similarly, Wilson and Herrnstein (1985) argued that serious and persistent offenders begin offending very early in life—before contextual factors such as antisocial peers or neighborhood disorganization can negatively affect their development. Other research has indicated that youth who are consistently subjected to violence in their neighborhoods become desensitized to it and are therefore not negatively affected by it (Farrell & Bruce, 1996; Garbarino, Kostleny, & Dubrow, 1992). . . .

Exposure to community violence may also contribute to the generation of learned aggressive behaviors. The use of aggressive situational responses or adoption of weapons for self-defense could be viewed as "learned" responses, consistent with social learning theory (Bandura, 1973) and cultural perspectives. As Anderson (1999) noted, children quickly "learn to deal with their social environment" (p. 67). In a violent environment, willingness to express toughness is often revered. Youth who understand this "code" may be more inclined to engage in assaultive behaviors or to carry a weapon such that they gain respect from their peers.

Studies in other fields (notably public health) have also linked exposure to community violence with negative behavioral outcomes in children and adolescents, most notably aggressive behavior (Aneshensel & Sucoff, 1996; Colder, Mott, Levy, & Flay, 2000; Cooley-Quille, Turner, & Beidel, 1995; Durant et al., 1994). For example, Colder and colleagues (2000) found that perceived neighborhood danger was associated with positive beliefs about aggression. In addition to promoting aggressiveness, exposure to violence promotes dysfunctional defensive responses such as weapon carrying and fighting behaviors. Durant and colleagues (1994) analyzed data on a sample of African American adolescents and also found a strong positive association between exposure to violence and the use of violence by adolescents. Similarly, Sheley and Wright (1994) found youth's gun possession was strongly related to a self-reported need for protection. In short, exposure to violence may directly influence aggressive behavior through the changing of the mental calculus of those most often exposed.

Recently, scholars have attempted to better understand the complex relationship between individual- and community-level factors and adolescent development (Sampson, 1997; Wikström & Loeber, 2000). For example, Wikström and Loeber (2000) found that "there is a significant direct effect of neighborhood disadvantage on well-adjusted children influencing them to become involved in serious offending as they reach adolescence" (pp. 1133–1134). They concluded that "community context may have an important indirect influence on early onsets through its potential impact on the development of individual dispositions and, particularly, aspects of the individual social situation (family, school, peers) related to serious offending" (Wikström & Loeber, 2000, p. 1134). In short, individual and environmental attributes interact to influence the behavior of adolescents. This study serves to expand on this line of research by isolating the effect of exposure to community violence on delinquency from that of neighborhood disadvantage and individual social situation.

Method

Data

Data for the study were drawn from a larger research project designed to examine the efficacy of police-centered intervention programs in reducing serious, violent behavior among preadolescent and adolescent youth. Individual-level data were obtained through comprehensive interviews of youth, and community-level data were acquired from the U.S. Census Bureau (2000). Personal interviews conducted with 187 youth between the ages of 9 and 15 living in a moderately sized midwestern city served as the foundation of the research. Youth who resided in neighborhoods within the northwest quadrant of the city were targeted for the study because the area had been identified by city officials as disproportionately disadvantaged. In addition, the target area had been designated in 1993 as a Weed and Seed community where proactive citywide response was necessary to address many prevailing community concerns.

Specifically, youth were selected to be included in the study in one of three ways. First, youth were recruited to be interviewed from the middle school in the target area. Teachers informed youth in their classes about the project, and interested students were required to have their parent or guardian sign and return a permission slip to participate. Because of this active consent procedure, the participation rate was relatively low (about 25%). Second, youth were recruited from two recreation

centers in the neighborhood. Flyers were distributed, and the supervisors at each center agreed to solicit participants. Active consent was also secured from the parents of these youth. Finally, youth who lived in the target neighborhoods who were arrested during a 3-year period were also included in the sample. Arrested youth were generally interviewed within a few weeks of coming into contact with the criminal justice system. All youth were given $20 for a 30- to 40-minute interview. In total, 34% of the youth were interviewed at the school, 29% were recruited from the recreation centers, and 37% were included because they were arrested. . . .

Data on neighborhood disadvantage were obtained from the 2000 U.S. Decennial Census. Census data included in this analysis were aggregated to the block group area—the smallest unit commonly available to the general public. Census data were linked to the individual based on the block group area in which the youth reported living at the time of the interview. Sample members lived in a total of 40 different block group areas within the same general area of the city. In the city examined here, there are 148 block group areas, with an average of 1,500 residents and 600 housing units within each area. . . . As described above, the target area is generally more disadvantaged than the city as a whole. For example, there are a higher proportion of families below the poverty level, households receiving public assistance, and unemployed residents who live in the target area than in the city. Moreover, there is a higher proportion of abandoned buildings and more concentrated disadvantage in the target area.

Measures

Dependent Measures

The goal of this research is to examine the effect of exposure to community violence on child participation in serious personal delinquency, controlling for individual-level demographic factors and delinquency correlates. The main research question, then, is as follows: Are youth who live in disorganized neighborhoods, or who perceive their immediate environment to be violent, more likely to carry a weapon or engage in assaultive behavior? Because juvenile weapon involvement and violence continue to be national public health concerns (Thornton, Craft, Dahlberg, Lynch, & Baer, 2002), identifying the community-level factors associated with the early initiation of such behaviors aid in our overall understanding of those activities.

Self-reported weapon possession and assaultive behavior serve as dependent variables. The personal assault measure is dichotomous (1 = individual reported that he or she had assaulted an adult, assaulted a peer, or thrown rocks or bottles at others during the previous 12 months; 0 = respondent did not report assaultive behavior during the past 12 months). The weapon possession measure includes individuals who reported that they had carried a weapon for any reason during the previous 12 months (1 = youth reported possessing a weapon on one or more occasions during the last 12 months; 0 = youth did not report weapon possession). . . .

[E]ven though the average age of the sample was quite young (mean = 12.0), the participants reported substantial involvement in serious delinquency during the prior year. More than half (58%) of sample members reported that they had committed assaultive behavior during the past year, and 18% of youth indicated that they were in possession of a weapon during the past 12 months. Specifically, of those youth who were in possession of a weapon, 54% reported carrying a knife, and 41% reported carrying a gun. The type of weapon was unspecified for the remaining respondents.

Neighborhood Influences

Two measures of neighborhood influence are included in the models. The first variable, exposure to community violence, measured at the individual level, was designed to reflect personal experience with neighborhood violence and is operationalized using a seven-item additive scale (Cronbach's α = .857). Respondents were asked how often in the previous 12 months they heard gun shots, saw somebody arrested, saw drug deals, saw someone being beaten up, saw someone get stabbed or shot, saw gangs in their neighborhood, and saw somebody pull a gun on another person. Response items ranged from 1 to 4 (1 = *none*, 2 = *once or twice*, 3 = *a few times*, 4 = *many times*). . . .

Individual Characteristics and Delinquency Correlates

Consistent with previous delinquency research, a number of individual-level variables are included in the model as controls. Two dichotomous variables are included in the models as measures of gender and race. Gender was dichotomized into male respondents and female respondents (1 = male, 0 = female). Race was dichotomized into non-White and White (1 = African American, Asian, Hispanic, or other race; 0 = White). The

age variable represents the youth's age in years. A final dichotomous, individual-level measure is included in the models to control for previous arrests (1 = individual had one or more arrests during the past year; 0 = youth was not arrested during the past year). The previous arrest measure was included to control for the fact that those who were arrested have a greater likelihood of self-reporting deviant behaviors, irrespective of the community-level variables of primary interest in the current study. . . . Sixty-four percent of youth in the sample were male, 58% were non-White, and 37% had a previous arrest.

In addition, research has also suggested that factors such as parenting (Brooks-Gunn et al., 1993; Coley & Hoffman, 1996; McNulty & Bellair, 2003), peer relationships (Elliott et al., 1996; Jencks & Mayer, 1990; Veysey & Messner, 1999), and school relationships (Bowen & Bowen, 1999) may influence the relationship between community context and delinquent outcomes (see also Stewart et al., 2002). For example, youth who are strictly supervised by a parent may be less likely to witness or be negatively affected by violence that occurs in their neighborhood. Stem and Smith (1995) found that neighborhood disadvantage was related to delinquency both directly and indirectly through decreased involvement and supervision by parents. Similarly, recent research has found peer networks moderate the relationship between social disorganization (socioeconomic status, ethnic heterogeneity, residential stability, family disruption, and level of urbanization) and delinquency (Veysey & Messner, 1999). Finally, features of school environments (e.g., school climate) are important considerations and can reduce the negative effects of neighborhood environments. Youth who are strongly attached to school may spend more time with prosocial adults in that context, thereby limiting their exposure to community violence.

Informed by these previous studies, four variables are included in the models as delinquency correlates, both to control for their individual effects and to determine their potential relationship to neighborhood-level factors in terms of serious childhood violence. Family context is measured in relationship to family structure and parental supervision. The single-parent family construct reflects whether the child lived with only one primary caregiver or otherwise (1 = child currently resides with only one parent/guardian; 0 = child resides in a two-parent/guardian household). Family supervision is measured using a five-item additive scale (Cronbach's α = .724). Respondents were asked, "How much does your primary caregiver know about: who your close friends are; what you do with your friends; who your close friends' parents are; who you are with when you are not at home; and, what you are doing in school?" Response items were 1 *(knows nothing),* 2 *(knows very little),* 3 *(knows something),* and 4 *(knows everything).*

In addition, a four-item additive scale was designed to measure the respondent's attachment to school (Cronbach's α = .675). Individuals were asked to report their agreement with the following statements: "I try hard in school," "Education is so important that it is worth it to put up with things I don't like," and "In general, I like school." Response items ranged from 1 to 4 and included the following: 1 = *strongly disagree,* 2 = *disagree,* 3 = *agree,* and 4 = *strongly agree.* Students were also asked to respond to the item "Homework is a waste of time" using the following response options: *strongly agree, agree, disagree,* and *strongly disagree.*

Finally, an eight-item additive scale is included representing peer delinquency (Cronbach's α = .823). Respondents were asked in the past year how many of their friends drank beer, wine, or liquor; used a weapon or force to get money or things from people; attacked someone with a weapon or with the idea of seriously hurting him or her; hit someone with the idea of hurting him or her (e.g., fist-fighting); stole something worth more than $100; stole something worth more than $5 but less than $50; damaged or destroyed someone else's property on purpose; or took a car for a ride without the owner's permission. Response items ranged from 1 to 4 and included *none of them, a few of them, some of them,* and *all of them.*

Analyses

The goals of the research are twofold. The primary goal is to estimate the effect of exposure to community violence on weapons possession and assaultive behavior. In response to research that suggests that factors such as parenting, peer relationships, and school attachment affect the relationship between community context and delinquency outcomes (see Sampson, 1997; Wikström & Loeber, 2000), the second goal of the research is to assess the effects of exposure to community violence on personal assault and weapon possession through a series of delinquency correlates. . . .

Findings

Neighborhood Influences and Correlates of Delinquency

. . . [E]xposure to violence had a moderately strong and significant effect on each of the delinquency correlates,

net of individual controls. Youth who indicated personal exposure to neighborhood violence reported lower levels of parental supervision and school attachment and were more likely to associate with delinquent peers. As expected, community disadvantage had little effect in the models. Because youth resided in the same general neighborhoods, there was little variation in the level of disorganization. Nevertheless, it appears that youth's perceptions of neighborhood violence are more indicative of delinquency correlates than the global indicator of neighborhood disadvantage.

The effect of individual characteristics on delinquency correlates also deserves mention. Gender was the only significant predictor in the school attachment model, with males more likely to report reduced school attachment. Age, gender, and previous arrest were all significantly and positively related to peer involvement in delinquency. None of the individual demographic measures was significantly related to parental supervision. . . .

Personal Assault

Three separate logistic regression models are estimated to ascertain the unique effects of individual characteristics, neighborhood influences, and delinquency correlates on personal assault. In Model 1, males and youth with a previous arrest were more likely to report committing an act of personal assault in the previous 12 months. The strength of the relationship between arrest history, gender, and personal assault was quite strong. Both males and individuals with a previous arrest were greater than 3 times as likely to report a personal assault when compared with females and individuals without previous exposure to the criminal justice system. . . .

The inclusion of neighborhood influences in Model 2 improved the explanatory power of the model, even though the exposure to violence construct was the only measure found to be statistically significant. . . . The results of this model also support the study hypotheses. Individuals who reported higher levels of exposure to violence in their community were significantly more likely to report participation in personal assault behaviors over the previous year. However, the strength of association for community violence exposure was small; for every 1 unit increase in the exposure to violence construct, youth were 1.16 times more likely to report personal assault.

None of the delinquency correlates was found to be statistically significant in the final model (Model 3). Moreover, the inclusion of the delinquency correlates did little to change the effect of exposure to violence on personal assault. . . .

Weapon Possession

. . . In Model 1, the inclusion of individual characteristics generated only one significant predictor. Namely, individuals with previous arrest histories were significantly more likely to report possessing a weapon during the past year. In fact, youth with previous arrest histories were nearly 14 times more likely to report possessing a weapon. . . .

The importance of considering exposure to community violence when estimating youth involvement in serious, personal delinquency was further confirmed in Model 2. The exposure to community violence measure was significantly related to weapon possession; for each unit increase in the exposure to violence measure, youth were 1.22 times more likely to report the possession of a weapon during the past year. Consistent with the results from the personal assault model, neighborhood disadvantage was not significantly associated with weapons possession. . . .

Contrary to the assault model, peer influence was significantly related to weapon possession. . . . The effect of peer delinquency was particularly strong, with a 1-unit increase in the measure of peer delinquency associated with a 23% increase in the likelihood of weapons possession. This finding highlights the importance of peer influences in understanding certain forms of serious personal delinquency, specifically weapons possession.

Discussion

Before discussing the implications of the study, a few limitations merit acknowledgement. First, the sample size is small and was not randomly collected from a discrete population. As noted, the sample is disproportionately composed of very young youth with prior experience with the criminal justice system. Although this attribute is a strength in the sense that it allowed us to look at the serious violence of a very young cohort, the vast majority of youth at this age are not carrying weapons or engaging in serious assaultive behavior. There may be differences between youth in the current sample and youth who do not come into contact with the criminal justice system that were not accounted for in the analysis. Because this is a unique sample, the generalizability of the findings to a larger population is difficult. Nevertheless, the results are informative and build on previous research in this area.

Another limitation is that the individual-level data are self-reported perceptual measures. That is, the actual violence that occurs in one's neighborhood may be different from that which is perceived. Future studies should seek to supplement resident perceptions with actual measures of violence in the neighborhood (i.e., official crime or observational data; e.g., Sampson & Raudenbush, 1999). Finally, due to the cross-sectional nature of the data, causality cannot necessarily be inferred. Although it appears that youth who witness violence are impelled to carry a weapon or engage in assaultive behaviors, it could also be that youth who get into fights or carry a weapon are more likely to witness community violence (perhaps because they are a party involved in the violence). Future analyses should measure community-level variables at one time period and delinquency at a future time point to ensure proper temporal ordering.

Despite these limitations, the study was able to build on previous research by more fully exploring the neighborhood-level variables associated with childhood violence. The specific research question posed was as follows: What community-level factors differentiate offenders from nonoffenders who live in the same communities? Results from the analyses supported the hypothesis that individuals who are exposed to more community violence are more likely to engage in serious personal violence. Youth who reported higher levels of exposure to community violence were significantly more likely to report possessing a weapon and engaging in personal assault. As noted, previous research has primarily focused on the relationship between community violence and psychological outcomes; this study finds similarly negative effects on violent behavior in a sample of youth.

In contrast, larger social indicators of neighborhood disadvantage did not have a significant effect on delinquency. This is not to suggest that disadvantage, per se, is unimportant. Indeed, several of the studies reviewed above testify to its salience. It could be that the level of disadvantage in the target area is not comparable to that of communities from other studies. For example, having 13% of families living in poverty is much less than the cutoff Wilson (1987) designated as a neighborhood truly disadvantaged (40%). A more plausible explanation relates to the nature of the target neighborhoods considered in this analysis. The target area as a whole was more disadvantaged than the city; however, there may not have been enough variation in level of disadvantage within the targeted area to reveal a significant relationship. Nevertheless, research that simply tests the relationship between structural or physical attributes of the community may miss another important variable, namely, the exposure to community violence that often occurs in these contexts.

The research also highlights the importance of considering the potential effect of delinquency correlates in understanding involvement in serious, personal delinquency. Exposure to violence was significantly related to parental supervision, school attachment, and peer delinquency. The effect was particularly strong for the peer delinquency model as evidenced by a standardized beta of 0.56 for the exposure indicator. It is noteworthy that the exposure to violence measure remained significantly associated with childhood violence, even after controlling for other common correlates of delinquency. Although associating with delinquent peers does appear to influence the relationship between exposure to violence and weapon possession, exposure to violence did have a significant effect on weapon possession and personal assault, net of controls for individual demographic characteristics and delinquency correlates.

These findings offer important implications for policy. First, the study suggests a need for a more comprehensive notion of victimization, that is, a vision that extends beyond the immediate victim to others in the community who witness the incidents. As victim advocates and other concerned groups call for a more victim-centered approach to criminal justice, consideration must also be given to the potentially harmful effects to others not directly related to the incident.

The current research also speaks to the importance of developing broader community intervention models. Efforts that build a sustained community capacity to intervene with those directly and indirectly involved in violence hold the potential to prevent violence in the future. Furstenberg, Cook, Eccles, Elder, and Sameroff (1999) argued that these sorts of neighborhood resources have both direct and indirect effects on child development and increase the chances that children will successfully navigate the most deleterious, dangerous, and disorganized environments.

Finally, results of this study support the development of social networks within one's community as a way to control both unruly adolescents (Sampson & Groves, 1989) and crime more generally. Findings suggest that a proximal approach to delinquency prevention may be to protect youth from the deviance and social disorder that occurs within their neighborhoods. This protection could come in the form of more supervised after-school activities for youth or more positive mentoring by parents or other prosocial adults. This suggestion warrants further exploration because the current study found evidence that exposure to violence was inversely related to parental supervision but that parental supervision itself was not directly related to participation in delinquent behaviors. Organized activities may limit exposure to violence; and parents, teachers, or other overseers could immediately step in to comfort children if they witness violence. Moreover, parents and teachers can be proactive by discussing community violence in schools and at home. This may help youth cope with what they see in the streets. Even though results stress the virulent effects of witnessing community violence as opposed to disorder or disadvantage per se, community mobilization that enables citizens to proactively protect adolescents, particularly those most at risk for delinquency, appears to be a viable crime reduction strategy.

Discussion Questions

1. Why do you think it is important to determine if exposure to community violence is related to childhood delinquency?

2. What social policies do the authors suggest? Do you think that they would be helpful? Why or why not?

Source: "Exposure to Community Violence and Childhood Delinquency" by Justin W. Patchin, Beth M. Huebner, John D. McCluskey, Sean P. Varano, and Timothy S. Bynum, excerpted and with notes & references omitted from *Crime & Delinquency*, Vol. 52, No. 2, April 2006, pp. 307–332. Reprinted by permission of Sage Publications.

CHAPTER 12

Bullies Move Beyond the Schoolyard

A Preliminary Look at Cyberbullying

Justin W. Patchin and Sameer Hinduja

This article discusses the nature of bullying and its transmutation to the electronic world and the negative repercussions that can befall both its victims and instigators. Findings are reported from a pilot study designed to assess empirically the nature and extent of online bullying.

The home, neighborhood, and school are all recognized as important social and physical contexts within which adolescents develop. Bullying—an all too common form of youthful violence—has historically affected children and teenagers only while at school, while traveling to or from school, or in public places such as playgrounds and bus stops. Modern technology, however, has enabled would-be bullies to extend the reach of their aggression and threats beyond this physical setting through what can be termed *cyberbullying*, where tech-savvy students are able to harass others day and night using technological devices such as computer systems and cellular phones. Computers occupy a significant proportion of the homes in which children reside and are frequently used for social, entertainment, academic, and productivity needs (National Telecommunications and Information Administration [NTIA], 2002). Moreover, cellular phones are gaining widespread popularity and use among the younger age groups because they are perceived as a status symbol, allow for conversations with friends in different physical spaces, and provide a virtual tether of sorts for parents, allowing for supervision from afar.

Though they are intended to positively contribute to society, negative aspects invariably surface as byproducts of the development of new technologies such as these. The negative effects inherent in cyberbullying, though, are not slight or trivial and have the potential to inflict serious psychological, emotional, or social harm. When experienced among members of this highly impressionable and often volatile adolescent population, this harm can result in violence, injury, and even death (e.g., Meadows et al., 2005; Vossekuil, Fein, Reddy, Borum, & Modzeleski, 2002) and later criminality for both the initiator and recipient of bullying (e.g., Olweus, Limber, & Mihalic, 1999; Patchin, 2002). One particularly horrendous anecdotal account deserves mention. In May of 2001, viciously offensive messages denigrating and humiliating a high school sophomore girl who suffered from obesity and multiple sclerosis were posted anonymously to an online message board associated with a local high school in Dallas, Texas (Benfer, 2001). In time, the bullying crossed over to the physical world as the victim's car was vandalized, profanities were written on the sidewalk in front of her home, and a bottle filled with acid was thrown at her front door—which incidentally burned her mother. This example vividly depicts how bullying online can lead to physical harm offline.

Little research to date has been conducted on cyberbullying. However, research on the correlates of traditional bullying can assist in comprehending the reality and growth of this new phenomenon. To begin, the desire to be and remain popular takes on almost life-like proportions among kids and teenagers during certain stages of their life, and their self- esteem is largely defined by the way that others view them. Although it is unclear exactly when self-esteem increases or decreases during a child's life (Twenge & Campbell, 2001), it unquestionably shapes a child's development in profound ways. According to the social acceptance model, self-esteem stems from the perceptions that others have of the individual (Cooley, 1902). When individuals perceive themselves to be rejected or otherwise socially excluded, a number of ill effects can result (Leary, Schreindorfer, & Haupt, 1995). Much research has validated this theory (Leary & Downs, 1995; Leary, Haupt, Strausser, & Chokel, 1998; Leary, Tambor, Terdal, & Downs, 1995) and has pointed to the following potentially negative outcomes: depression (Quellet & Joshi, 1986; Smart & Walsh, 1993), substance abuse (Hull, 1981), and aggression (Coie & Dodge, 1988; French & Waas, 1987; Hymel. Rubin. Rowden, & LeMare, 1990; Paulson, Coombs, & Landsverk, 1990; Stewart, 1985). In addition, low self-esteem tends to be found among chronic victims of traditional bullying (Hoover & Hazler, 1991; Neary & Joseph, 1994; Rigby & Slee, 1993). It is expected that cyberbullying can similarly cripple the self-esteem of a child or adolescent, and without a support system or prosocial outlets through which to resolve and mitigate the strain, the same dysphoric and maladaptive outcomes may result. Despite these solemn possibilities, there has been very little empirical attention to date devoted toward better understanding the electronic variant of this deviance (exceptions include Berson, Berson, & Ferron, 2002; Finn, 2004; Ybarra & Mitchell, 2004).

This research seeks to fill this gap by exploring cyberbullying and examining its potential to become as problematic as traditional bullying—particularly with society's increasing reliance on technology. Its goal is to illuminate this novel form of deviance stemming from the intersection of communications and computers and to provide a foundational backdrop on which future empirical research can be conducted. First, what is known about traditional bullying will be summarized to provide a comparative point of reference. Second, data collected from various media sources will be presented to describe the technology that facilitates electronic bullying and to portray its prevalence. Third, preliminary findings from a pilot study of adolescent Internet users will be presented, highlighting the characteristics of this group and their involvement (both as victims and offenders) in the activity. Finally, suggestions for future empirical research will be offered as guidance for additional exploration of this subject matter.

Traditional Bullying

BULLYING DEFINED

A variety of scholars in the disciplines of child psychology, family and child ecology, sociology, and criminology have articulated definitions of bullying that generally cohere with each other. To begin, the first stages of bullying can be likened to the concept of harassment, which is a form of unprovoked aggression often directed repeatedly toward another individual or group of individuals (Manning, Heron, & Marshal, 1978). Bullying tends to become more insidious as it continues over time and is arguably better equated to violence rather than harassment. . . .

Providing perhaps the most panoptic definition, Nansel et at. (2001) asserted that bullying is aggressive behavior or intentional "harm doing" by one person or a group, generally carried out repeatedly and over time and that involves a power differential. Many characteristics can imbue an offender with perceived or actual power over a victim and often provide a sophistic license to dominate and overbear. These include, but are not limited to, popularity, physical strength or stature, social competence, quick wit, extroversion, confidence, intelligence, age, sex, race, ethnicity, and socioeconomic status (Olweus, 1978, 1993, 1999; Rigby & Slee, 1993; Roland, 1980; Slee & Rigby, 1993). Nonetheless, research on the relevance of these differences between bullies and their victims has been inconclusive. For example, differences in physical appearance was not predictive of one's likelihood of being a bully or a victim (Olweus, 1978), but physical shortness (Voss & Mulligan, 2000) and weakness (Leff, 1999) were found to be relevant in other research.

Although the harassment associated with bullying can occur anywhere, the term *bullying* often denotes the behavior as it occurs among youth in school hallways and bathrooms, on the playground, or otherwise proximal or internal to the school setting. Bullies can also follow their prey to other venues such as malls, restaurants, or neighborhood hangouts to continue the harassment. In the past, interaction in a physical context was required for victimization to occur. This is no longer the case thanks to the increased prevalence of the Internet, personal computers, and cellular phones. Now, would-be bullies are afforded technology that provides additional mediums over which they can manifest their malice. The following sections outline the scope, breadth, and consequences of traditional bullying as a reference point from which cyberbullying can subsequently be viewed and understood.

Extent and Effects of Traditional Bullying

It is unclear exactly how many youth are bullied or bully others on any given day. In 1982, 49 fifth grade teachers from Cleveland, Ohio, reported that almost one fourth (23%) of their 1,078 students were either victims or bullies (Stephenson & Smith, 1989). More recently, a nationally representative study of 15,686 students in grades 6 through 10 identified that approximately 11% of respondents were victims of bullying, 13% were bullies, and 6% were both victims and bullies during a year (Nansel et al., 2001). Additional research conducted by the Family Work Institute substantiated these findings through interviews with 1,000 youth in grades 5 through 12. Their study found that 12% of youth were bullied five or more times during the previous month (Galinsky & Salmond, 2002). Finally, the Bureau of Justice Statistics reports that 8% of youth between the ages of 12 and 18 had been victims of bullying in the previous 6 months (Devoe et al., 2002). That said, conservative estimates maintain that at least 5% of those in primary and secondary schools (ages 7–16) are victimized by bullies each day (Björkqvist, Ekman, & Lagerspetz, 1982; Lagerspetz, Björkqvist, Berts, & King, 1982; Olweus, 1978; Roland, 1980).

Many young people are able to shrug off instances of being bullied, perhaps because of peer or familial support or higher self-efficacy. Nonetheless, others are not able to cope in a prosocial or normative manner or reconcile the pain experienced through more serious episodes or actions. Suicidal ideation, eating disorders, and chronic illness have beset many of those who have been tormented by bullies, whereas other victims run away from home (Borg, 1998; Kaltiala-Heino, Rimpelä, Marttunen, Rimpelä, & Rantanen, 1999; Striegel-Moore, Dohm, Pike, Wilfley, & Fairburn, 2002). In addition, depression has been a frequently cited consequence of bullying (e.g., Hawker & Boulton, 2000) and seems to perpetuate into adulthood, evidencing the potentially long-term implications of mistreatment during adolescence (Olweus, 1994). Finally, in extreme cases, victims have responded with extreme violence such as physical assault, homicide, and suicide (Patchin, 2002; Vossekuil et al., 2002).

Following the fatal shootings at Columbine High School in Littleton, Colorado, in 1999, the educational system was challenged to address bullying because the two teenagers involved in the massacre were reported to have been ostracized by their classmates. Additional

school violence research of 37 incidents involving 41 attackers from 1974 to 2000 found that 71% (29) of the attackers "felt bullied, persecuted, or injured by others prior to the attack" (Vossekuil et al., 2002, p. 21). It was also determined that the victimization played at least some role in their subsequent violent outburst. Other less serious but equally as negative outcomes can result from repeated bullying. For example, students who are constantly harassed may attempt to avoid the problems at school as much as possible, leading to tardiness or truancy (BBC News, 2001; Richardson, 2003; Rigby & Slee, 1999). Truancy has been identified as a significant antecedent to delinquency, dropout, and other undesirable outcomes in the juvenile justice literature (Farrington, 1980; Garry, 1996; Gavin, 1997; Nansel et al., 2001). Based on these findings, it is clear that victims of bullies are at risk to have a discontinuous developmental trajectory for many years.

The aggressors in the bullying dyad also appear to be more likely to engage in antisocial activities later in life (Tattum, 1989). For example, approximately 60% of those characterized as bullies in grades six through nine were convicted of at least one crime by the age of 24, compared to 23% who were not characterized as either bullies or victims (Olweus et al., 1999). Further underscoring the relationship between bullying and future criminality. Olweus and colleagues (1999) found that 40% of bullies had three or more convictions by the age of 24, compared to 10% of those who were neither instigators nor victims of bullying.

Based on this brief review, it is clear that both bully victims and offenders are at an increased for developmental problems that can continue into adulthood. As such, it is imperative that researchers seek to better understand the antecedents and consequences of bullying behavior, for practitioners to develop and implement antibullying programs in schools and for societal institutions to better understand the ways in which bullying behaviors are carried out, both in traditional and nontraditional settings.

Cyberbullying

Because of the advent and continued growth of technological advances, the transmutation of bullying has occurred—from the physical to the virtual. Physical separation of the bully and the victim is no longer a limitation in the frequency, scope, and depth of harm experienced and doled out. As instances of bullying are no longer restricted to real-world settings, the problem has matured. Although a migration to the electronic realm is a seemingly logical extension for bullies, little is currently known regarding the nature and extent of the phenomenon. In short, we define *cyberbullying* as willful and repeated harm inflicted through the medium of electronic text. Based on the literature reviewed above, the constructs of malicious intent, violence, repetition, and power differential appear most salient when constructing a comprehensive definition of traditional bullying and are similarly appropriate when attempting to define this new permutation. To be sure, cyberbullies are malicious aggressors who seek implicit or explicit pleasure or profit through the mistreatment of other individuals. Violence is often associated with aggression and corresponds to actions intended to inflict injury (of any type). One instance of mistreatment, although potentially destructive, cannot accurately be equated to bullying, and so cyberbullying must also involve harmful behavior of a repetitive nature. Finally, because of the very nature of the behavior, cyberbullies have some perceived or actual power over their victims. Although power in traditional bullying might be physical (stature) or social (competency or popularity), online power may simply stem from proficiency. That is, youth who are able to navigate the electronic world and utilize technology in a way that allows them to harass others are ma position of power relative to a victim. . . .

There are two major electronic devices that young bullies can employ to harass their victims from afar. First, using a personal computer, a bully can send harassing e-mails or instant messages, post obscene, insulting, and slanderous messages to online bulletin boards, or develop Web sites to promote and disseminate defamatory content. Second, harassing text messages can be sent to the victim via cellular phones.

PERSONAL COMPUTERS

Research by the U.S. Department of Commerce noted that almost 90% of youth between the ages of 12 and 17 use computers, and by age 10, youth are more likely than are adults to use the Internet (NTIA, 2002). Demonstrating the broad reach of instant messaging and chat programs, 20 million kids between the ages of 2 and 17 logged onto the Internet in July 2002, and 11.5 million used instant messaging programs (NetRatings, 2002). Similarly, according to a study of 1,081 Canadian parents conducted in March 2000, 86% stated that their kids used the Internet, 38% had their own e-mail address,

28% used ICQ (an instant messaging program short for "I seek you"), and 28% regularly spent time in chat rooms (Network, 2001). Indeed, America Online (AOL, 2002, 2003)—the most popular Internet service provider with more than 35 million users—states that members join in on more than 16,000 chat sessions and send more than 2.1 billion instant messages per day across their network. As a point of reference, 1.9 billion phone calls are made each day in the United States. Finally, the Internet relay channels provide a venue for many other users on a daily basis. For example, on the morning of an average Saturday in May 2005, there were more than 1 million users online in more than 800 chat rooms (Gelhausen, 2005). . . .

According to the Pew Internet and American Life Project (2001), approximately 29% of youth younger than 12 regularly go online. Among teenagers, approximately 95% of girls and 89% of boys have sent or received e-mail, and 56% of girls and 55% of boys have visited a chat room. Almost three fourths of teenagers (74%; 78% of girls and 71% of boys) in the study use instant messaging to communicate with their friends, with 69% using the technology several times a week. Almost half (46%) of respondents who report using instant messaging programs spend between 30 and 60 minutes per session doing so, whereas 21% state that they spend more than 1 hour in the activity in an average online session. Testifying to the benefits of textual communication over verbal communication, 37% used it to say something they would not have said in person. Underscoring the potential for harassment and negative treatment online, 57% have blocked messages from someone with whom they did not wish to communicate, and 64% had refused to answer messages from someone with whom they were angry.

CELLULAR PHONES

In the United States, more than 150 million individuals, including half of the youth between 12 and 17 years of age, own cellular phones (Fattah, 2003). It is estimated that 74% of Americans between the ages of 13 and 24 will have a wireless device by 2006 (O'Leary, 2003). Cell phone usage is much higher among teenagers and young adults in Europe compared to the United States, 60% to 85% compared to 25% (O'Leary, 2003). Research estimates that by 2007 nearly 100 million individuals will use the text messaging service on their wireless device (Fattah, 2003). Statistics compiled in November 2001 by UPOC (2001)—a wireless communications firm in the United States—found that

43% of those who currently use text messaging are between the ages of 12 and 17. . . .

ISSUES SPECIFIC TO CYBERBULLYING

Gabriel Tarde's (1903) law of insertion suggests that new technologies will be applied to augment traditional activities and behaviors. Certain characteristics inherent in these technologies increase the likelihood that they will be exploited for deviant purposes. Cellular phones and personal computers offer several advantages to individuals inclined to harass others. First, electronic bullies can remain virtually anonymous. Temporary e-mail accounts and pseudonyms in chat rooms, instant messaging programs, and other Internet venues can make it very difficult for adolescents to determine the identity of aggressors. Individuals can hide behind some measure of anonymity when using their personal computer or cellular phone to bully another individual, which perhaps frees them from normative and social constraints on their behavior. Further, it seems that bullies might be emboldened when using electronic means to effectuate their antagonistic agenda because it takes less energy and fortitude to express hurtful comments using a keyboard or keypad than using one's voice.

Second, supervision is lacking in cyberspace. Although chat hosts regularly observe the dialog in some chat rooms in an effort to police conversations and evict offensive individuals, personal messages sent between users are viewable only by the sender and the recipient and are therefore outside regulatory reach. Furthermore, there are no individuals to monitor or censor offensive content in e-mail or text messages sent via computer or cellular phone. Another contributive element is the increasingly common presence of computers in the private environments of adolescent bedrooms. Indeed, teenagers often know more about computers and cellular phones than do their parents and are therefore able to operate the technologies without worry or concern that a probing parent will discover their participation in bullying (or even their victimization; NTIA, 2002).

In a similar vein, the inseparability of a cellular phone from its owner makes that person a perpetual target for victimization. Users often need to keep it turned on for legitimate uses, which provides the opportunity for those with malicious intentions to send threatening and insulting statements via the cellular phone's text messaging capabilities. There may truly be no rest for the weary as cyberbullying penetrates the walls of a home, traditionally a place where victims could seek refuge.

Finally, electronic devices allow individuals to contact others (both for prosocial and antisocial purposes) at all times and in almost all places. The fact that most adolescents (83%) connect to the Internet from home (Pew Internet and American Life Project, 2001) indicates that online bullying can be an invasive phenomenon that can hound a person even when not at or around school. Relatedly, the coordination of a bullying attack can occur with more ease because it is not constrained by the physical location of the bullies or victims. A veritable onslaught of mistreatment can quickly and effectively torment a victim through the use of these communications and connectivity tools.

DOES HARM OCCUR?

Of course, cyberbullying is a problem only to the extent that it produces harm toward the victim. In the traditional sense, a victim is often under the immediate threat of violence and physical harm and also subject to humiliation and embarrassment in a public setting. These elements compound the already serious psychological, emotional, and social wounds inflicted through such mistreatment. One might argue that a victim of bullying in cyberspace—whether via e-mail, instant messaging, or cellular phone text messaging—can quickly escape from the harassment by deleting the e-mail, closing the instant message, and shutting off the cellular phone and is largely protected from overt acts of violence by the offender through geographic and spatial distance. Such an argument holds much truth; however, the fact remains that if social acceptance is crucially important to a youth's identity and self-esteem, cyberbullying can capably and perhaps more permanently wreak psychological, emotional, and social havoc. . . .

With regard to public embarrassment, life in cyberspace is often intertwined with life in the real world. For example, many kids and teenagers spend days with their friends in school and nights with those same friends online through instant message programs and chat channels. That which occurs during the day at school is often discussed online at night, and that which occurs online at night is often discussed during the day at school. There is no clean separation between the two realms, and so specific instances of cyberbullying—disrespect, name calling, threats, rumors, gossip—against a person make their way around the interested social circles like wildfire.

Does the mistreatment experienced through online bullying lead to the same feelings that result from traditional bullying—such as self-denigration, loss of confidence and self-esteem, depression, anger, frustration, public humiliation, and even physical harm? This remains to be clearly depicted through empirical research but seems plausible based on the linchpin role of self-esteem among children and teenagers previously described and on anecdotal evidence specifically related to online aggression (BBC News, 2001; Benfer, 2001; Blair, 2003: Meadows et al., 2005; ÓhAnluain, 2002; Richardson, 2003).

. . . Because more information is clearly warranted, a study was designed to explore the nature and extent of cyberbullying.

Current Study

METHOD

The current study involved an analysis of youthful Internet users in an effort to assess their perceptions of, and experiences with, electronic bullying. It is difficult to individually observe the nature and extent of electronic bullying among adolescent Internet users because of the "private" nature of e-mails, cellular phone text messages, and instant messages and one-on-one chat messages within online chat channels. To be sure, if the instances of cyberbullying occur in a public forum such as a popular chat channel and in the view of all chat room members, then direct observation and consequent analyses may be possible. Most of the time, however, they occur through private (nonpublic), person-to-person communications. A survey methodology was therefore designed to collect data by requiring participants to recall and relate their cyberbullying practices and experiences via a questionnaire that was linked from the official Web site of a popular music artist revered by the target age group. An electronic format was selected as it allows for efficiency in collecting data from a large number of participants (Couper, 2000; McCoy & Marks, 2001; Smith, 1997). The survey was active between May 1, 2004, and May 31, 2004. . . .

FINDINGS

Because this was an Internet-based survey, anyone could participate. Even though the survey was associated with a teen-oriented Web site, individuals from all ages also frequent the site and therefore completed the survey. . . . [O]ut of the 571 total respondents, 384 were younger than 18 (67.3%; henceforth referred to as the *youth sample*). In both groups, the vast majority of respondents were female. This finding is likely attributable to the nature of the Web site on which the survey was linked (a female pop music star). Similarly, the vast majority of respondents were Caucasian. There are several potential interpretations of this finding. First, individuals from different racial and ethnic backgrounds may be less interested in this particular entertainer than are others and may therefore be unlikely to visit the Web site to see the survey solicitation. Alternatively, the over-representation of Caucasian respondents could be evidence of the oft-mentioned digital divide, where some populations are not privy to the access and use of technology such as computers and the Internet. As expected, most respondents were between the ages of 12 and 20, and the average age of the youth sample was 14.1. Moreover, more than 70% of respondents from the complete sample were in grades 2 through 12. High school respondents (9th through 12th grade) represented the modal category of respondents for both groups. As might be expected, the vast majority of all respondents came from English-speaking countries (the Web site and survey were written in English), and about 60% of respondents in both groups reported living in the United States. It must be mentioned that because online identity is completely malleable (Hafner, 2001; Turkle, 1995), the demographic data obtained may not be completely accurate because of a lack of trust in our research project, mischief, or purposeful obfuscation. Research performed over the Internet cannot entirely preempt this problem—at least in its current stage of technological development—and so a caveat is justified.

The remainder of the findings discussed relate only to those respondents who were younger than 18 when they completed the survey ($n = 384$). Online bullying was specifically defined on the questionnaire for respondents as behavior that can include bothering someone online, teasing in a mean way, calling someone hurtful names, intentionally leaving persons out of things, threatening someone, and saying unwanted, sexually related things to someone. . . . Almost 11% of youth reported bullying others while online, more than 29% reported being the victim of online bullying, and more than 47% have witnessed online bullying. Cyberbullying was most prevalent in chat rooms, followed by computer text messages and e-mail. Bullying using newsgroups or cellular phones was not as prominent for members of this sample. Indeed, although it is clear that all who responded to the survey have access to a computer, it is unknown what proportion of respondents have access to a cellular phone.

. . . [Y]outh were asked a general question regarding their involvement in online bullying. In addition, youth were asked to relate whether they experienced a number of behaviors that may be associated with bullying. . . . Notably, 60.0% of respondents have been ignored by others while online, 50.0% reported being disrespected by others, almost 30.0% have been called names, and 21.4% have been threatened by others. In addition, a significant proportion of youth were picked on by others (19.8%) or made fun of by others (19.3%) or had rumors spread about them by others (18.8%).

In addition to asking respondents whether they have experienced bullying online, researchers also asked youth how frequently the bullying occurred during the previous 30 days. . . . Eighty-three reported being victimized in a chat room an average of 3.36 times during the previous 30 days. One youth reported being bullied in a chat room 50 times during the previous 30 days. Bullying via computer text messaging and e-mail also occurred frequently during the previous 30 days.

[There were significant] negative effects associated with online bullying on victims. For example, 42.5% of victims were frustrated, almost 40.0% felt angry, and more than 27.0% felt sad. Almost one third (31.9%) reported that it affected them at school, whereas 26.5% reported that it affected them at home. Only 22.1% were not bothered by the bullying they experienced, and less than 44.0% stated that the bullying did not affect them.

. . . Notably, almost 20% of victims were forced to stay offline, whereas almost 32% had to remove themselves from the environment in some capacity or way. Victims also revealed a hesitation to tell authority figures about their experiences. Even though most confided in an online friend (56.6%), fewer than 9.0% of victims informed an adult.

Additional analyses were conducted to attempt to uncover correlates of online bullying. There were no statistically significant associations among age, race, or gender and who is likely to be a victim of online bullying. The lack of relationship among race or gender and victimization may be more a function of the homogeneous nature of the data than any substantive finding and must he further tested. In accordance with intuition, youth who participate in more activities online (represented by a variety score of 13 different activities) were more likely to experience online bullying. Also not surprising, youth who bully others were more likely to

be victims of online bullying. In all, 75% of youth who have bullied others online have been victims of bullying, whereas fewer than 25% of youth bullies have never been on the other end of such malicious actions ($\chi^2 =$ 42.866; $p < .001$). Future research should seek to better understand what additional factors are associated with online bullying.

Discussion

The results of this study point to a number of key issues. First, bullying is occurring online and is impacting youth in many negative ways. Almost 30% of the adolescent respondents reported that they had been victims of online bullying—operationalized as having been ignored, disrespected, called names, threatened, picked on, or made fun of or having had rumors spread by others. Admittedly, being ignored by another person may simply reflect obnoxious behavior that warranted the outcome rather than actual and willful aggression. We were not able to parcel out the stimuli of instances when people were ignored but chose to include a measure of it in the current analyses. This is because universal social acceptance is still largely desired by children and adolescents, even if as adults we understand that it is impossible to please everyone at all times. Being ignored would introduce dissonance and instability to the already tenuous relational and social equilibria sought by youths and may accordingly be considered a passive-aggressive form of bullying. Along similar lines, although some of this harassment may be characterized as trivial (e.g., being ignored by others or being disrespected), more than 20% reported being threatened by others. Anger and frustration was a commonly reported emotional response to the harassment. Finally, almost 60% of victims were affected by the online behaviors at school, at home, or with friends.

Several policy implications stem from the aforementioned findings. It is hoped that this harmful phenomena can be curtailed by proactively addressing the potentially negative uses of technology. Parents must regularly monitor the activities in which their children are engaged while online. Teachers, too, must take care to supervise students as they use computers in the classrooms. Police officers must investigate those instances of cyberbullying that are potentially injurious and hold responsible parties accountable. Unfortunately, there are no methods to discern which harassment involves simple jest and which has the potential to escalate into serious violence. Future research must analyze case studies and anecdotal stories of cyberbullying experiences to help determine when intervention by authority figures is most appropriate. Overall, parents, teachers, police officers, and other community leaders must keep up with technological advances so that they are equipped with the tools and knowledge to identify and address any problems when they arise. . . .

DIRECTIONS FOR FUTURE RESEARCH

The current study provides the framework for future empirical inquiry on electronic bullying. Indeed, the authors are currently involved in a more comprehensive study that involves both Internet-based research and traditional paper-and-pencil surveys. As with any social scientific endeavor, replication is necessary to more fully understand the phenomena under consideration. There are several questions future research in this area must address. First, data must be collected to more accurately ascertain the scope, prevalence, and nuances of cyberbullying. For example, it is important to discover whether cyberbullies are simply traditional bullies who have embraced new technologies to accomplish their intentions or if they are youth who have never participated in traditional, school-based bullying. Moreover, do personal computers enable the stereotypical victims of bullies (i.e., those who are smart, physically small, and/or socially challenged) to retaliate using means that ensure their anonymity? It would also be important to determine whether commonly accepted stimuli for traditional bullying—the need to (a) exert power and dominate, (b) compensate for victimization in another area of one's life, (c) cope with one's insecurities, and (d) attract attention and popularity—are similarly predictive in cyberspace-based instances of the deviance.

Also of interest is the extent to which electronic bullying results in harm to adolescents in their physical environments (e.g., at school or in their neighborhoods). Are threats made in cyberspace followed through on the playground? Are victims of cyberbullying the same individuals who are also victims of traditional bullying, or are they distinct groups? What about offenders? One could hypothesize that the victims of traditional bullying may turn to the Internet to exact revenge on their schoolyard aggressors. That is, the

victim becomes the offender by using his or her technological knowledge to inflict harm on the original bully. . . .

Finally, future research efforts ought to more thoroughly examine the results of this preliminary investigation using more rigorous methodology that ensures a more representative sample of responses. As indicated, the intent of this research is to generate scholarly interest in this unique form of adolescent harassment and therefore should be viewed simply as a small, but we think significant, platform on which further research efforts should be built.

CONCLUSION

The preceding review provides a description of bullying in cyberspace for the purposes of introducing it as a topic meriting academic inquiry and underscoring its often inescapable pernicious nature. Indeed, 74% of the youth in this study reported that bullying occurs online, and almost 30% of the youth reported being victimized by others while online. Some may dismiss electronic bullying as normative behavior that does not physically harm anyone. To be sure, some have this perception regarding traditional bullying, dismissing it as a rite of passage or an inevitable and even instructive element of growing up. Because of the familiarity and memorability of bullying as almost unavoidable in both the schoolyard and neighborhood milieu during one's formative years, perhaps the reader may share those sentiments.

Because no consensus exists when considering whether cyberbullying merits increased attention because of society's continued progression into a wired world, perhaps it should just be considered another contemporary cultural challenge that kids often face when transitioning into adulthood. Conceivably there is no need to panic when introduced to the concept that online bullying does and will continue to take place as children seek to carve out an identity for themselves and cope with various pressures associated with their development. Alternatively, perhaps there is a need for alarm as both those who bully and those who are bullied might yield readily to other criminogenic influences and proceed down a path of deviance online, offline, or both. Regardless, cyberbullying is very real, and it is hoped that this work has highlighted its relevance for the purposes of inspiring additional interest in its etiology and consequences.

Discussion Questions

1. According to Patchin and Hinduja, how does the harm of cyberbullying compare to that of traditional bullying?

2. Do you think cyberbullying takes place among college students to the same extent it occurs among high school students? Why or why not?

Source: "Bullies Move Beyond the Schoolyard: A Preliminary Look at Cyberbullying" by Justin W. Patchin and Sameer Hinduja, excerpted and with notes & references omitted from *Youth Violence and Juvenile Justice*, Vol. 4, No. 2, April 2006, pp. 148–169. Reprinted by permission of Sage Publications.

PART IV

SOCIAL STRATIFICATION AND POWER

In Part IV, we turn our attention to *social stratification,* how societies distribute the things valued in their society and rank groups of people according to their access to what is valued. Today, money is highly valued in almost every society, and the gap between those who have money and those who do not is increasing. In the United States, the top one percent of households now own more wealth than *all* of the bottom 90% combined!

As the gap widens, the social distance between rich and poor increases, and it becomes harder for those who have little to attain more. Today, those who hope to gain jobs that pay well must have a high level of education and, in many cases, connections to those in power. Those who have neither are in deep trouble. In the first article, "Mass Imprisonment and the Life Course: Race and Class Inequality in U.S. Incarceration," Becky Pettit and Bruce Western show that one group of people who fall into this category, Black men who are high school dropouts, have a nearly 60% chance of going to prison.

In "Talk of Class: The Discursive Repertoires of White Working- and Upper-Middle-Class College Students," Jenny M. Stuber reveals that working-class students are much more aware of social class differences than are upper-middle-class students. Her findings show that, while wealthier students tend to think of themselves as less well off than those who have *more* money, they tend not to think about how much better off they are than their poor and working-class classmates. They seem not to be aware of the growing gap between the poor and the wealthy.

The authors of the last two articles reveal how social class is created and maintained through interpersonal interactions. In "A Place in Town: Doing Class in a Coffee Shop," Carrie Yodanis shows how women in a coffee shop create class distinctions among the different subgroups in the shop through their conversations about their work (or volunteer work), families, and leisure activities and tastes. In "Professorial Capital: Blue-Collar Reflections on Class, Culture, and the Academy," Mary Kosut uses her own experience as a graduate student to describe how interactions in the upper level of academia reproduce inequality and benefit middle- and upper-class students at the expense of working-class students.

As you read the articles in this section, keep in mind the following points:

- The gap between the very rich and everyone else in U.S. society is wider now than any time since the Great Depression in 1929.
- A college education is now a crucial step toward entry into the middle class.
- Our prisons are disproportionately full of poor high school dropouts.
- The culture of academia is geared toward middle- and upper-class students.
- We create social class distinctions in our everyday interactions with one another.
- Working-class and upper-middle-class college students perceive social class in very different ways.
- The most content populations live in societies in which workers are organized.

CHAPTER 13

Mass Imprisonment and the Life Course

Race and Class Inequality in U.S. Incarceration

Becky Pettit and Bruce Western

The risks of being incarcerated are highly stratified by race and education. Among Black men born between 1965 and 1969, 30 percent of those without college education and nearly 60 percent of high school dropouts went to prison by 1999. Incarceration has emerged as a new stage in the life course of young, low-skill Black men.

Has the growth of the American penal system over the past thirty years transformed the path to adulthood followed by disadvantaged minority men? Certainly the prison boom affected many young black men. The U.S. penal population increased six fold between 1972 and 2000, leaving 1.3 million men in state and federal prisons by the end of the century. By 2002, around 12 percent of black men in their twenties were in prison or jail (Harrison and Karberg 2003). High incarceration rates led researchers to claim that prison time had become a normal part of the early adulthood for black men in poor urban neighborhoods (Freeman 1996; Irwin and Austin 1997). In this period of mass imprisonment, it was argued, official criminality attached not just to individual offenders, but to whole social groups defined by their race, age, and class (Garland 2001a:2).

Claims for the new ubiquity of imprisonment acquire added importance given recent research on the effects of incarceration. The persistent disadvantage of low-education African Americans is, however, usually linked not to the penal system but to large-scale social forces like urban deindustrialization, residential segregation, or wealth inequality (Wilson 1987; Massey and Denton 1993; Oliver and Shapiro 1997). However, evidence shows incarceration is closely associated with low

wages, unemployment, family instability, recidivism, and restrictions on political and social rights (Western, Kling and Weirnan 2000; Hagan and Dinovitzer 1999; Sampson and Laub 1993; Uggen and Manza 2002; Hirsch et al. 2002). If indeed imprisonment became commonplace among young disadvantaged and minority men through the 1980s and 1990s, a variety of other social inequalities may have deepened as a result.

Although deepening inequality in incarceration and the pervasive imprisonment of disadvantaged men is widely asserted, there are few systematic empirical tests. To study how the prison boom may have reshaped the life paths of young men, we estimate the prevalence of imprisonment and its distribution among black and white men, aged 15 to 34, between 1979 and 1999. We also compare the prevalence of imprisonment to other life events—college graduation and military service—that are more commonly thought to mark the path to adulthood.

Many have studied variation in imprisonment but our analysis departs from earlier research in two ways. First, the risk of incarceration is usually measured by an incarceration rate—the overnight count of the penal population as a fraction of the total population (e.g., Sutton 2000; Jacobs and Helms 1996). Much like college graduation or military service however, having a prison record confers a persistent status that can significantly influence life trajectories. Our analysis estimates how the cumulative risk of incarceration grows as men age from their teenage years to their early thirties. To contrast the peak of the prison boom in the late 1990s with the penal system of the late 1970s, cumulative risks of imprisonment are calculated for successive birth cohorts, born 1945–49 to 1965–69. Second, although economic inequality in imprisonment may have increased, most empirical research just examines racial disparity (e.g., Blumstein 1993; Mauer 1999; Bridges, Crutchfield, and Pitchford 1994). To directly examine how the prison boom affected low-skill black men, our analysis estimates imprisonment risks at different levels of education. Evidence that imprisonment became disproportionately widespread among low-education black men strengthens the case that the penal system has become an important new feature of American race and class inequality. . . .

Race and Class Inequality

High incarceration rates among black and low-education men have been traced to similar sources. The slim economic opportunities and turbulent living conditions of young disadvantaged and black men may lead them to crime. In addition, elevated rates of offending in poor and minority neighborhoods compound the stigma of social marginality and provoke the scrutiny of criminal justice authorities.

Research on carceral inequalities usually examines racial disparity in state imprisonment. The leading studies of Blumstein (1982, 1993) find that arrest rates—particularly for serious offenses like homicide—explain a large share of the black-white difference in incarceration. Because police arrests reflect crime in the population and policing effort, arrest rates are an imperfect measure of criminal involvement. More direct measurement of the race of criminal offenders is claimed for surveys of crime victims who report the race of their assailants. Victimization data similarly suggest that the disproportionate involvement of blacks in crime explains most of the racial disparity in incarceration (Langan 1985). These results are buttressed by research associating violent and other crime in black neighborhoods with joblessness, family disruption, and neighborhood poverty (e.g., Crutchfield and Pitchford 1997; Messner et al. 2001; LaFree and Drass 1996; Morenoff et al. 2001; see the review of Sampson and Lauritsen 1997). In short, most of the racial disparity in imprisonment is attributed to high black crime rates for imprisonable offenses (Tonry 1995, 79).

Although crime rates may explain as much as 80 percent of the disparity in imprisonment (Tonry 1995), a significant residual suggests that blacks are punitively policed, prosecuted, and sentenced. Sociologists of punishment link this differential treatment to official perceptions of blacks as threatening or troublesome (Tittle 1994). The racial threat theory is empirically supported by research on sentencing and incarceration rates. Strongest evidence for racially differential treatment is found for some offenses and in some jurisdictions rather than at the aggregate level. African Americans are at especially high risk of incarceration, given their arrest rates, for drug crimes and burglary (Blumstein 1993). States with large white populations also tend to incarcerate blacks at a high rate, controlling for race-specific arrest rates and demographic variables (Bridges et al. 1994). A large residual racial disparity in imprisonment thus appears due to the differential treatment of African Americans by police and the courts.

Similar to the analysis of race, class disparities may also be rooted in patterns of crime and criminal processing. Our analysis captures class divisions with a measure of educational attainment. Education, of course, correlates with measures of occupation and employment status that more commonly feature in research on class and crime (for reviews see Braithwaite 1979; Hagan, Gillis, and Brownfield 1996). Just as the social strain of economic disadvantage may push the poor into crime (Merton 1968; Cloward and Ohlin 1960), those with little schooling also experience frustration at blocked opportunities. Time series analysis shows that levels of schooling significantly affect race-specific arrest rates (LaFree and Drass 1996). While a good proxy for economic status, school failure also contributes directly to delinquency. Whether crime is produced by the oppositional subculture of school dropouts, as Cohen (1955) suggests, or by weakened networks of informal social control (Hagan 1993), poor academic performance and weak attachment to school is commonplace in the biographies of delinquents and adult criminals (Sampson and Laub 1993, ch. 5; Hagan and McCarthy 1997: Wolfgang, Figlio and Sellin 1972). High incarceration rates may therefore result from high crime rates among young men with little schooling.

As for racial minorities, researchers also argue that the poor are perceived as threatening to social order by criminal justice officials (e.g., Rusche and Kirchheimner 1968; Spitzer 1975; Jacobs and Helms 1996). The poor thus attract the disproportionate attention of authorities, either in the way criminal law is written or applied by police and the courts. Consistent with this view, time series of incarceration rates are correlated with unemployment rates and other measures of economic disadvantage, even after crime rates are controlled (Chiricos and Delone 1992). Few studies focus on education, as we do, but class bias in criminal sentencing is suggested by findings that more educated federal defendants receive relatively short sentences in general, and are less likely to be incarcerated for drug crimes (Steffensmeier and Dernuth 2000). Thus, imprisonment may be more common among low-education men because they are the focus of the social control efforts of criminal justice authorities. . . .

Imprisonment and the Life Course

In addition to increasing race and class inequalities in incarceration, mass imprisonment may mark a basic change in the character of young adulthood among low-education black men. From the life course perspective, prison represents a significant re-ordering of the pathway through adulthood that can have lifelong effects. Consequently, the prison boom—like other large-scale social events—effects a historically significant transformation of the character of adult life.

PRISON AS A LIFE COURSE STAGE

Life course analysis views the passage to adulthood as a sequence of well-ordered stages that affect life trajectories long after the early transitions are completed. In modern times, arriving at adult status involves moving from school to work, then to marriage, to establishing a home and becoming a parent. Completing this sequence without delay promotes stable employment, marriage, and other positive life outcomes. The process of becoming an adult thus influences success in fulfilling adult roles and responsibilities.

As an account of social integration, life course analysis has attracted the interest of students of crime and deviance (see Uggen and Wakefield 2003 for a review). Criminologists point to the normalizing effects of life course transitions. Steady jobs and good marriages offer criminal offenders sources of informal social control and pro-social networks that contribute to criminal desistance (Sampson and Laub 1993; Hagan 1993; Uggen 2000). Persistent offending is more likely for those who fail to secure the markers of adult life. The life course approach challenges the idea that patterns of offending are determined chiefly by stable propensities to crime, that vary little over time, but greatly across individuals (Uggen and Wakefield 2003).

Imprisonment significantly alters the life course. In most cases, men entering prison will already be "off-time." Time in juvenile incarceration and jail and weak connections to work and family divert many prison inmates from the usual path followed by young adults. Spells of imprisonment—thirty to forty months on average—further delay entry into the conventional adult roles of worker, spouse and parent. More commonly military service, not imprisonment, is identified as the key institutional experience that redirects life trajectories (Hogan 1981; Elder 1986; Xie 1992). Elder (1987:543) describes military service as a "legitimate timeout" that offered disadvantaged servicemen in World War Two an escape from family hardship. Similarly, imprisonment can provide a chance to re-evaluate life's direction (Sampson and Laub 1993, 223; Edin, Nelson, and Paranal 2001). Typically, though, the effects of imprisonment are clearly negative. Ex-prisoners earn lower wages and experience more unemployment than similar men who have not been incarcerated (Western, Kling and Weiman 2001 review the literature). They are also less likely to get married or cohabit with the mothers of their children (Hagan and Dinovitzer 1999; Western and McLanahan 2000). By eroding employment and marriage opportunities, incarceration may also provide a pathway back into crime (Sampson and Laub 1993; Warr 1998). The volatility of adolescence may thus last well into midlife among men serving prison time. Finally, imprisonment is an illegitimate timeout that confers an enduring stigma. Employers of low-skill workers are extremely reluctant to hire men with criminal records (Holzer 1996; Pager 2003). The stigma of a prison record also creates legal barriers to skilled and licensed occupations, rights to welfare benefits, and voting rights (Office of the Pardon Attorney 1996; Hirsch et al. 2002; Uggen and Manza 2002). In short, going to prison is a turning point in which young crime-involved men acquire a new status involving diminished life chances and an attenuated form of citizenship. The life course significance of imprisonment motivates our analysis of the evolving probability of prison incarceration over the life cycle. . . .

Calculating the Cumulative Risk of Imprisonment

A life course analysis of the risks of imprisonment was reported by Bonczar and Beck (1997) for the Bureau of Justice Statistics (BJS). Using life table methods and data from the 1991 Survey of Inmates of State and Federal Correctional Facilities, Bonczar and Beck (1997) estimate that 9.0 percent of U.S. males will go to prison at some time in their lives Significant racial disparity underlies this over all risk. The estimated lifetime risk of imprisonment for black men is 28.5 percent compared to 4.4 percent for white men. The risk of entering prison for the first time is highest at ages 20 to 30, and declines significantly from age 35.

The BJS figures provide an important step in understanding the risks of incarceration over the life course, but the analysis can be extended in at least two ways. First, the BJS age-specific risks of incarceration are not defined for any specific birth cohort; instead the incarceration risks apply to a hypothetical cohort that shares the age-specific incarceration risks of all the different cohorts represented in the 1991 prison inmate surveys. This approach yields accurate results if the risk of incarceration is stable over time. However, the incarceration rate and the percentage of men entering prison for the first time grew substantially between 1974 and 1999. The percentage imprisoned more than doubled during this period. We address this problem by combining time-series data on imprisonment (1964–1999) with multiple inmates surveys (1974–1997). These data allow estimation of cumulative risks of imprisonment to age 30–34 for five-year birth cohorts born between 1945–49 and 1965–69. This approach provides a direct assessment of how the prison boom may have changed the life course of young men.

Second, like virtually all work in the field, cumulative risks have not been estimated for different socioeconomic groups. Motivated by claims that the prison boom disproportionately affected the economically disadvantaged, as well as African Americans, we study how the risks of imprisonment differ across levels of education.

While our data sources and specific techniques differ, we follow Bonczar and Beck (1997) in using life table methods. These methods are used to summarize the mortality experiences of a cohort or in a particular period. The cumulative risk of death, for example, can be calculated by exposing a population to a set of age-specific mortality rates. Life table methods can be applied to other risks including the risk of incarceration. Our estimates arc based on multiple-decrement methods in which there are several independent modes of exit from the life table. The analysis allows two competing risks: the risk of going to prison and the risk of death.

Life Table Calculations

Calculations for the cumulative risk of imprisonment require age-specific first-incarceration and mortality rates. . . .

Cumulative risks of imprisonment are estimated for three levels of education: (1) less than high school graduation, (2) high school graduation or equivalency, and (3) at least some college. Table 1 reports the distribution of black and white men by education for cohorts born 1945–49 and 1965–69. By age 30 to 34, the three-category code roughly divides the black and white male population into the lower 15 percent, the next 35 percent, and the top 50 percent of the education distribution. Census data (1970–1990) are used to estimate population counts at each level of education. To adjust for differential

Table 1　Percentage of Non-Hispanic Men at Three Levels of Educational Attainment, Born 1945–1949 and 1965–1969, in 1979 and 1999

	White Men (%)	Black Men (%)
Born 1945–1949 in 1979		
Less than high school	12.3	27.3
High school or equivalent	32.9	38.2
Some college	54.8	34.5
Born 1965–1969 in 1999		
Less than high school	7.5	14.2
High school or equivalent	33.4	43.0
Some college	59.1	42.8

Note: Cell entries adjust for the incarcerated population, adding prison and jail inmates to the counts at each level of education. Data from the Current Population Survey.

mortality by education we use figures from the National Longitudinal Mortality Study which reports mortality by education for black and white men. These figures are used to calculate multipliers for each age-race group to approximate education-specific mortality rates. Finally the surviving fraction of inmates is adjusted to account for additional education attained after admission to prison. The National Longitudinal Survey of Youth (NLSY) was used to estimate the proportion of inmates who go on graduate from high school or attend college in each subsequent age interval.

We assume that mortality rates for men going to prison arc the same as those for non-prisoners and educational inequality in mortality is unchanging. Neither assumption substantially affects our results because mortality rates are low compared to imprisonment rates for men under age 35. Thus, a wide variety of morality assumptions yield substantively identical conclusions about the risks of imprisonment. For example, the poor health of prisoners and their exposure to violence likely increases mortality risk compared to men who have not been to prison. We conducted a sensitivity analysis in which the mortality rate of men who have entered prison was set to twice that for those who had never been to prison; under this assumption the results are essentially identical to those reported below.

Although we combine a wide variety of data to estimate the cumulative risks, our key data source is the *Survey of Inmates of State and Federal Correctional Facilities,* 1974–1997. Descriptive statistics from the surveys show that the state prison population became more educated between 1974 and 1997, increasing the number of high school graduates from 38 to 60 percent. The percentage of whites in prison also declined, due largely to the increasing share of Hispanic men in state prison. . . .

Results

THE PREVALENCE OF IMPRISONMENT

The full table for non-Hispanic black and white men, born 1945–49 and 1965–69, illustrates the life table calculations (Table 2). The risk of first-time imprisonment is patterned by age, cohort, and race. In contrast to crime where offending peaks in the late teens, the risk of first-time imprisonment increases with age and peaks for men in their late twenties. Not just an event confined to late adolescence and young adulthood, men in their early thirties remain at high risk of acquiring a prison

record. The life table also clearly indicates cohort differences. Between ages 25 and 29, black men without felony records had almost a 10 percent chance of imprisonment by the end of the 1990s (Table 2, column 3). This imprisonment risk is 2.5 times higher than that for black men at the same age born twenty years earlier. The probability of imprisonment for white men was only one-fifth as large. High age-specific risks among recent birth cohorts of black men sum to large cumulative risks. Black men born 1945–1949 had a 10.6 percent chance of spending time in state or federal prison by their early thirties. This cumulative risk had climbed to over 20 percent for black men born 1965–69. The cumulative risk of imprisonment grew slightly faster for white men. Among white men born 1965–1969, nearly 3 percent had been to prison by 1999, compared to 1.4 percent born in the older cohort (Table 2, column 7).

Table 3 reports cumulative risks for different birth cohorts and education groups and compares these to the usual prison incarceration rates, Incarceration rates are highly stratified by education and race. High school dropouts are 1 to 4 times more likely to be in prison than those with 12 years of schooling. Blacks, on average, are about 8 times more likely to be in state or federal prison than whites. By the end of the 1990s, 21 percent of young black poorly-educated men were in state or federal prison compared to an imprisonment rate of 2.9 percent for young white male dropouts. . . .

Like incarceration rates, the cumulative risks of imprisonment fall with increasing education. The cumulative risk of imprisonment is 3 to 4 times higher for high school dropouts than for high school graduates. About 1 out of 9 white male high school dropouts, born in the late 1960s, would serve prison time before age 35 compared to 1 out of 25 high school graduates. The cumulative risk of incarceration is about 5 times higher for black men. Incredibly, a black male dropout, born 1965–69, had nearly a 60 percent chance of serving time in prison by the end of the 1990s. At the close of the decade, prison time had indeed become modal for young black men who failed to graduate from high school. The cumulative risks of imprisonment also increased to a high level among men who had completed only 12 years of schooling. Nearly 1 out of 5 black men with just 12 years of schooling went to prison by their early thirties. . . .

Prison time has only recently become a common life event for black men. Virtually all the increase in the risk of imprisonment falls on those with just a high school education. For non-college black men reaching their thirties at the end of the 1970s, only 1 in 8 would go to

Table 2   Life Tables for Cumulative Risks of Prison Incarceration and Mortality for Non-Hispanic Men Born 1945–49 and 1965–69

Age (years) (1)	nMIx (2)	nqIx (3)	N1x (4)	Ndix (5)	N (6)	Cumulative Risk (7)
White Men						
Born 1945–1949						
15–19	.0006	.0032	100000	318.5	318.5	.32
20–24	.0008	.0040	99444	393.4	712.0	.71
25–29	.0008	.0040	98768	396.3	1108.3	1.11
30–34	.0006	.0030	97429	289.0	1397.3	1.40
Born 1965–1969						
15–19	.0008	.039	100000	394.6	394.6	.39
20–24	.0007	.0033	99392	332.5	727.1	.73
25–29	.0024	.0118	98847	1163.2	1890.4	1.89
30–34	.0021	.0105	96817	1018.2	2908.6	2.91
Black Men						
Born 1945–1949						
15–19	.0040	.0197	100000	1972.9	1972.9	1.97
20–24	.0064	.0313	97747	3056.8	5029.7	5.03
25–29	.0078	.0379	94291	3569.1	8598.8	8.60
30–34	.0045	.0222	88504	1962.6	10561.4	10.56
Born 1965–1969						
15–19	.0042	.0206	100000	2064.4	2064.4	2.06
20–24	.0084	.0409	97742	3997.3	6061.7	6.06
25–29	.0205	.0964	93448	9006.6	15068.3	15.07
30–34	.0137	.0657	82720	5436.6	20504.9	20.50

Note: Cumulative risks are for incarcerations (in the presence of mortality).

$_nM_x^l$ = age-specific incarceration rate

$_nq_x^l$ = probability of incarceration in the interval

$_nl_x^l$ = number at risk (adjusted for mortality)

$_nd_x^l$ = number of incarcerations in the interval

N = cumulative number of incarcerations

prison, and just 1 in 16 among high school graduates. Although these risks are high compared to the general population, imprisonment was experienced by a relatively small fraction of non-college black men born just after World War Two.

The final panel of Table 3 adds mortality risks to the risks of imprisonment. Again, non-college black men born in the late 1960s experience high risks. Estimates show that one-third die or go to prison by their early thirties. The table also indicates that the risk of imprisonment is much higher than the risk of death, so the results are not significantly altered by the addition of mortality. . . .

Imprisonment Compared to Other Life Stages

Finally, we compare imprisonment to other life experiences that mark the transition to adulthood. We report levels of educational attainment, marital and military service histories for all and non-college men, using data from the 2000 census. To make the incarceration risks comparable to census statistics, our estimates are adjusted to describe the percentage of men, born 1965–69, who have ever been imprisoned and who survived to 1999.

The risks of each life event varies with race, but racial differences in imprisonment greatly overshadows any other inequality. Among all men, whites in their early thirties are more than twice as likely to hold a bachelor's degree than blacks. Blacks are about 50 percent more likely to have served in the military. However, black men are about 7 times more likely to have a prison record. Indeed, recent birth cohorts of black men are more likely to have prison records (22.4 percent) than military records (17.4 percent) or bachelor's degrees (12.5 percent). The share of the population with prison records is particularly striking among non-college men. Whereas few non-college white men have prison records, nearly a third of black men with less than a college education have been to prison. Non-college black men in their early thirties in 1999 were more than twice as likely to be ex-felons than veterans. This evidence suggests that by 1999 imprisonment had become a common life event for black men that sharply distinguished their transition to adulthood from that of white men.

Table 3   Imprisonment Rate at Ages 20 to 34, and Cumulative Risk of Imprisonment, Death, or Imprisonment by Ages 30 to 34 by Educational Attainment, Non-Hispanic Men

	All (1)	Less than High School (2)	High School/GED (3)	All Noncollege (4)	Some College (5)
Imprisonment Rate (%)					
White Men					
1979	.4	1.0	.4	.6	.1
1999	1.0	2.9	1.7	1.9	.2
Black Men					
1979	3.2	5.7	2.7	4.0	1.5
1999	8.5	21.0	9.4	12.7	1.7
Cumulative Risk of Imprisonment by Ages 30–34					
White Men					
BJS	3.0	—	—	—	—
NLSY	4.3	11.3	3.7	5.1	1.5
1979	1.4	4.0	1.0	2.1	.5
1999	2.9	11.2	3.6	5.3	.7
Black Men					
BJS	24.6	—	—	—	—
NLSY	18.7	30.9	18.8	19.3	7.2
1979	10.5	17.1	6.5	12.0	5.9
1999	20.5	58.9	18.4	30.2	4.9
Cumulative Risk of Death or Imprisonment by Ages 30–34					
White Men					
1979	3.8	7.8	3.5	4.9	1.5
1999	5.0	14.0	5.5	7.7	1.7
Black Men					
1979	15.6	23.8	11.6	17.8	8.7
1999	23.8	61.8	21.9	33.9	7.4

Note: The Bureau of Justice Statistics (BJS) figures are reported by Bonczar and Beck (1997) using a synthetic cohort from the Survey of Inmates of State and Federal Correctional Facilities (1991). The National Longitudinal Survey of Youth (NLSY) figures give the percentage of respondents who have ever been interviewed in a correctional facility by age 35 (whites N = 2171, blacks N = 881). The NLSY cohort was born 1957–1964. The 1979 cohort is born 1945–1949; the 1999 cohort is born 1965–1969.

Discussion

This analysis provides evidence for three empirical claims. First, imprisonment has become a common life event for recent birth cohorts black non-college men. In 1999, about 30 percent of such men had gone to prison by their mid-thirties. Among black male high school dropouts, the risk of imprisonment had increased to 60 percent, establishing incarceration as a normal stopping point on the route to midlife. Underscoring the historic novelty of the prison boom, these risks of imprisonment are about three times higher than 20 years earlier. Second, race and class disparities in imprisonment are large and historically variable. In contrast to claims that racial disparity has grown, we find a pattern of stability in which incarceration rates and cumulative risks of incarceration are, on average, 6 to 8 times higher for young black men compared to young whites. Class inequality increased, however, as a large gap in the prevalence of imprisonment opened between college-educated and non-college men in the 1980s and the 1990s. Indeed, the lifetime risks of imprisonment roughly doubled from 1979 to 1999, but nearly all of this increased risk was experienced by those with just a high school education. Third, imprisonment now rivals or overshadows the frequency of military service and college graduation for recent cohorts of African American men. For black men in their mid-thirties at the end of the 1990s, prison records were nearly twice as common as bachelor's degrees. In this same birth cohort of non-college black men, imprisonment was more than twice as common as military service.

In sum, excepting the hypothesis of increased racial disparity, our main empirical expectations about the effects of prison boom on the life paths of young disadvantaged men are strongly supported. Because racial disparity in imprisonment is very high and risks of imprisonment are growing particularly quickly among non-college men, the life path of non-college black men through the criminal justice system is diverging from the usual trajectory followed by most young American adults.

The high imprisonment risk of black non-college men is an intrinsically important social fact about the distinctive life course of the socioeconomically disadvantaged. Although the mass imprisonment of low-education black men may result from the disparate impact of criminal justice policy, a rigorous test demands a similar study of patterns of criminal offending. Increased imprisonment risks among low-education men may be due to increased involvement in crime, if patterns of offending follow economic trends, declining wages among non-college men over the last 20 years may underlie the growing risk of imprisonment. Researchers have examined the consequences of race differences in offending for official crime and imprisonment, but relatively little is known about educational differences in offending within race groups. To determine whether the shifting risks are due to policy or changing patterns of crime, we thus need to develop estimates of crime rates for different race-education groups.

Mass imprisonment among recent birth cohorts of non-college black men challenges us to include the criminal justice system among the key institutional influences on American social inequality. The growth of military service during World War Two and the expansion of higher education exemplify projects of administered mobility in which the fate of disadvantaged groups was increasingly detached from their social background. Inequalities in imprisonment indicate the reverse effect, in which the life path of poor minorities was cleaved from the well-educated majority and disadvantage was deepened, rather than diminished. More strikingly than patterns of military enlistment, marriage, or college graduation, prison time differentiates the young adulthood of black men from the life course of most others. Convict status inheres now, not in individual offenders, but in entire demographic categories. In this context, the experience of imprisonment in the United States emerges as a key social division marking a new pattern in the lives of recent cohorts of black men.

Discussion Questions

1. Give three possible reasons why incarceration has become a new stage in the life course of a majority of young, low-skilled Black men.

2. What social polices should be implemented to address the phenomenon described in this article? Do you think the policies you suggest will be put into place? Why or why not?

Source: "Mass Imprisonment and the Life Course: Race and Class Inequality in U.S. Incarceration" by Bruce Western and Becky Pettit, excerpted and with notes & references omitted from *American Sociological Review*, 2004, Vol. 69, April: 151–169. Reprinted by permission of American Sociological Association.

CHAPTER 14

Talk of Class

The Discursive Repertoires of White Working- and Upper-Middle-Class College Students

Jenny M. Stuber

Interviews of 60 White working- and upper-middle-class college students reveal that, while there are some similarities in how the two groups of students discuss social class, the working-class students are much more aware of class issues. Students from both social class groups compare themselves to members of the social class above them.

Understanding how lay people make sense of social inequality is critical for understanding how social inequalities get reproduced. . . .

My research explores the cultural underpinnings of social inequality by investigating how college students talk about social class. Using in-depth interview data from sixty college students, I ask: What kinds of *discursive repertoires* (Frankenberg 1993) do college students use for talking about social class? How does their "talk of class" compare across class lines? Examining the social class constructions of a group of individuals within a particular context—such as a college campus—is important because status processes and dynamics of inclusion and exclusion take place within specific social contexts and in interaction with concrete others (Sander 2005). College students are an important group to study because they are positioned to become society's next generation of gatekeepers; hence, their constructions of social class speak to future processes of social reproduction. . . .

How Americans Think and Talk about Social Class

Motivated by their discipline's interest in social class and social inequality, many sociologists have endeavored to

understand precisely how Americans think and talk about social class. . . .

One of the persistent themes in the research on how Americans think and talk about social class deals with their *class awareness*. Class awareness refers, in part, to the tendency to see society as partitioned into two or more social classes (Rothman 2002). Researchers find that even if Americans lack a common vocabulary for talking about social class and speak about it in highly variable ways, they still exhibit a sense of class awareness. Although they may not agree on how many classes there are or what lines demarcate these social groupings, lay persons do adhere to the general belief that society is divided into at least two classes (Coleman and Rainwater 1978). . . . While including both economic and cultural factors, Americans tend to place particular importance on economic factors, especially income, in shaping a person's social standing.

Further evidence of Americans' class awareness is their ability to locate themselves within a particular class location and claim a fairly high level of salience for their class identity. Although results depend on how the question is worded (Centers 1949), high percentages of Americans readily identify themselves as members of a class, with the working and middle classes each being claimed by about 40% of the respondents (Jackman and Jackman 1983; Smith 1996). Beyond simply identifying with a social class,

Jackman and Jackman (1983) also report that affective class ties are stronger than might be expected: more than three-quarters of respondents in one national sample expressed an either very or somewhat strong attachment to their social class (Jackman 1979). . . .

A second theme . . . in the research on how Americans think and talk about social class focuses on their sense of *class consciousness* (Mann 1973): their sense of whether and how social class matters. Consistent with the dominant American ideology, Americans are much less likely than are their European counterparts to support government efforts at redistribution and are much more likely to emphasize the role of individual effort in shaping class outcomes (Ladd 1994). In addition, a majority of Americans believe that social inequality can have a positive impact on society (Ladd and Bowman 1999). . . .

The third and final strand of research on how Americans think and talk about social class deals with *symbolic boundaries* and cultural constructions of social class. Symbolic boundaries are the conceptual distinctions made by actors to categorize objects, people, and practices (Lamont and Molnar 2002); because they also "constitute a system of rules that guide interaction by affecting who comes together to engage in what social acts," symbolic boundaries "not only create groups; they also potentially produce inequality" (Lamont 1992, 12). Through their boundary work, individuals constitute the self, claim membership in a group, and draw a line between the pure (themselves) and the polluting (others). As such, *symbolic boundaries* are a necessary, but not sufficient, condition for the construction of *social boundaries* (Lamont and Molnar 2002).[1] . . .

Although understandings of social class are an important object of study, their meanings cannot be taken as a given; rather, they must be understood as situated constructions that emerge organically, dynamically, and contextually. This research responds by asking, How do college students make sense of social class within the college environment? I build on this research by using qualitative data to unpack the cultural meanings that lie beneath the insights generated by survey research on the topics of Americans' class awareness and class consciousness. In addition, I use the insights of cultural sociology to investigate where the rising generation draws its class lines. Throughout, I argue that although the class talk of young Americans is complex and sometimes contradictory, it is important because it sheds light on the relationship between cultural constructions of social class and processes of social reproduction.

Research Design and Methods

During the 2003–2004 academic year, I conducted in-depth interviews with sixty students attending two institutions of higher education within the same Midwestern state; half of the respondents were enrolled in a large public university ("Big State") and half were enrolled in a small, private liberal arts college ("Benton College"). In-depth interviews are ideal for understanding the meanings that people attach to their social experiences; here, they are used to illuminate how college students construct understandings of social class. College students are an important group to study because they are positioned to become the next generation of gatekeepers and hence play a critical role in institutional and interactional processes of inclusion and exclusion. This population is also of interest because schools function as sites of class socialization, and much of the differentiation and stratification that takes place in these settings is mediated through peer interactions (Bettie 2003; Eckert 1989; Holland and Eisenhart 1992).

To understand how social class backgrounds influence how people construct understandings of social class, I drew respondents from the relative poles of the socioeconomic spectrum. . . . The sample is fairly evenly divided between first-generation, working-class students ($n = 28$) and non-first-generation, upper-middle-class students ($n = 32$). I define students as "working class" if their parents or guardians have not completed a four-year degree and if they hold jobs in lower-skilled, lower-paying manual or service occupations. "Upper-middle-class" students, by contrast, are those whose parents have completed at least a four-year degree and hold jobs in higher-skilled, higher-paying professional or managerial occupations.[2] I designate this group upper-middle class rather than simply middle class because these parents have jobs as upper-level managers and professionals, rather than lower-level managers and semiprofessionals (Gilbert and Kahl 1982). . . .

Respondents were recruited using both random and purposive sampling methods. Potential respondents were contacted via e-mail and invited to participate in the study. For those who replied, I used a set of screening questions to determine how well they fit the sampling frame. Individuals were excluded if they did not fit the operationalization for the working- or upper-middle-class categories.[3] Respondents were asked to participate in two interviews, each lasting approximately 90 minutes; six of the sixty respondents chose not to participate in the followup interview. The average total interview length is 165 minutes; interview length does not vary by gender or social class background. Within this sample, males and females are represented in roughly equal numbers ($n = 28$ and 32, respectively); all of the respondents were traditional-age sophomores or juniors (19–21 years old) at the time of the interview. Interviews were taped and transcribed verbatim. Although the quotes presented are verbatim, some have been edited for easier reading. All names are pseudonyms. Finally, because I interviewed only white students, these analyses speak only to the class constructions of a group of white, traditional-aged college students. . . .

Findings

Within the interview context, college students constructed understandings of social class that were remarkably complex and contradictory. Each respondent, whether over the course of an interview or within one conversational turn, talked about social class using a variety of discursive repertoires and moved back and forth between these modes with ease. Indeed, working- and upper-middle-class individuals alike talked about social class in ways that alternately acknowledged and rejected the significance of social class. Despite this similarity, differences emerged between working- and upper-middle-class students in their *class awareness,* their *class consciousness,* and the kinds of *symbolic boundaries* they draw. Although any claims about their link to social inequalities must necessarily remain speculative, their accounts provide some hints at how talk of class might be linked to processes of social reproduction.

SEEING SOCIAL CLASS: ASSESSING STUDENTS' CLASS AWARENESS?

Researchers argue that for individuals to possess a sense of class consciousness, they first need to possess a sense of class awareness. Class awareness, in its simplest form, refers to the belief that society can be divided into two or more class groupings (Rothman 2002); in its more complex manifestation, it also means identifying with a particular class and being able to recognize and talk about class distinctions (Jackman and Jackman 1983). Students from different social class backgrounds had varying levels of class awareness and differed in the extent to which they felt that social class is something that can easily be detected. The majority of upper-middle-class students described themselves as being unaware of social class differences and argued that class is not something that can be easily or reliably determined from external cues. Working-class students, by contrast, were more likely to describe themselves as aware of social class differences. In addition, unlike their more privileged counterparts, they did not hesitate to label the class differences they saw.

Although upper-middle-class students were quick to acknowledge their privilege and could label their own class positions with relative ease, they also tended to describe themselves as having little social class awareness. Fully half of these students remarked spontaneously that their class awareness was limited because they grew up surrounded by people from similarly privileged class positions. In the words of Benton College's Andrea Barnett, "I really was not that aware. I still don't think I'm that aware. Just because I grew up in a wealthy community and a lot of the people were in the same situation that I was." Whereas a handful of students said that they developed some sense of class awareness while riding the school bus through different neighborhoods, others said that what class awareness they did have was largely hypothetical: that is, it was something they learned about from televisions, movies, or books.

Whereas approximately one-third of these students said they had developed greater awareness of class differences while at college, the majority still characterized themselves as rather unaware and indeed spoke in rather vague terms about their exposure to class differences on campus. For a significant minority, their new college environments seemed no more diverse than the environments in which they grew up, hence providing little opportunity to learn about class differences. For Big State's Nick Wrede, the high costs of higher education led him to conclude that his peers can basically fall into two and only two categories: "extremely wealthy and wealthy enough so you can go to college. I mean, we're in college, so people have to have some sort of money."

A deeper look into the discursive repertoires of these upper-middle-class students reveals a high degree *of equivocation* in their class talk. More than half of these respondents displayed a palpable sense of uncertainty over precisely what class is, how to read a variety of potentially class-coded cues, and generally how one might go about identifying a person's social class. Even when these upper-middle-class students did offer some schema that might be used to identify a person's social class, they often seemed unwilling to commit fully to this point of view:

> Like some girls might wear the nice, new fall line, and others don't, but I don't know if that's class, 'cause like some people. . . . Well, I guess that would be class, 'cause I guess if you're in the upper class, you might focus on that stuff, maybe. I don't know. I guess it's kind of a stereotype, but. . . . (Ryan Connors, Benton College).

. . . A common refrain among upper-middle-class students was that "you just can't tell" what social class a person might belong to. A majority of these students discounted their ability to "pick out" or label a person's social class and were particularly adamant that a person's social class cannot be read from their appearance. In the words of Big State's Stacey Sandefer:

> I don't think that if you walked outside you would really know who has money and who doesn't. I feel like people who don't have the same amount of money as everyone else will find some way to have the things that other people have, so it's not as apparent. I don't think you can tell based on appearance.

Indeed, status pressures—as suggested by Stacey—combined with the recent upscale marketing of budget-minded retailers like Target and Old Navy, may make it increasingly difficult to identify a person's social class by what they wear or how they present themselves. For fellow student Kendall Baker, how one presents oneself is largely a matter of personal choice and individual priorities, rather than a reflection of social class:

> Clothes don't really matter all that much, 'cause somebody can spend all their money on clothes and not have anything else. Or some people take better care of themselves than others, but who's to say that they didn't just get up late that morning and run to class? So no, I wouldn't say that you can tell. . . . That doesn't necessarily mean they're not the same status, but maybe they just don't care.

Indeed, nearly a third of these upper-middle-class students offered the example of the rich hippie student, the one who is "loaded" but you would "never know," to explain why outward appearance cannot reliably be used as an indicator of social class.

. . . These students equivocated, then, as they moved back and forth in their assessments of what a person's house or clothing might reveal about their class position. For many upper-middle-class students, their hesitancy to act as experts in the realm of social class is often paired with assertions of their ignorance of class-related issues. This sentiment emerges most clearly in the words of Big State's David Gold, who said, "That's one of the negatives about growing up where I grew up and then coming here, is that I haven't really seen much about social class." Thus, like white people who argue that they do not know much about race because they are white and have grown up surrounded largely by white people, these students suggest that they are not qualified to make claims about social class because they have grown up in largely class-homogeneous environments.

In contrast to their more privileged peers, the majority of working-class students described themselves as aware of social class differences; they were also quicker to draw various inferences about social class. For these students, an early awareness of their own and others' class situation was something they developed as they moved through a variety of mixed-class environments,[4] including their schools and their neighborhoods. For some, like Benton's Jenny Wilson, this class awareness emerged through contact with her own extended family: "My dad's side is actually wealthy and my mom's side is definitely not wealthy. So I was very aware very early on because I had the two complete opposites to compare." More often, though, an awareness of social class is something these students developed within their own immediate families. According to Benton College's Bobby Sanders, "I've been aware of it all my life because we've always struggled to pay the bills. I've always known that we were not upper class, or even middle class." For fellow student Tiffany Morrison, childhood experiences similarly shaped her awareness of social class: "Like when churches are bringing you your Thanksgiving dinner, or when the church gives you Christmas dinner and your Christmas gifts and, like, back to school supplies, you're aware of it." The words of Bobby and Tiffany are noteworthy and stand in stark contrast to those of their more privileged peers, in that they claim that an awareness of social class is something they hardly could have avoided.

Rather than equivocate when talking about social class dynamics on campus, less-privileged students tended to construct quick and forthright judgments about social class. Their discursive strategy was to "tell it like it is."[5] Free of the hesitations and self-consciousness that characterized many upper-middle-class students, these speakers were more decisive in talk of social class. When asked, for example, what her first impression was of her peers at Benton College, junior Suzanne Sorensen responded flatly: "A bunch of rich preppy kids." Matching her certainty were the voices of other students who similarly claimed that "you could just tell right off" that some kids grew up in a higher social class. Although many respondents elaborated their claims by referring to a number of appearance-based signifiers (Burberry scarves, Tiffany jewelry, Northface jackets), they also claimed that a person's social class can easily be detected by the way students act. Benton College sophomore Jenny Wilson said: "It's very obvious to me when people are from a higher social class, just by their demeanor and the way they present themselves. The way they act is very much like an 'I'm-better-than-you' kind of attitude." For Jenny and the thirteen other working-class students who invoked this phrase, the sense that their more-privileged peers were looking down on them came from interactional cues such as eye-rolling, not engaging in conversation, not laughing at their jokes, or offering only the shortest of replies. Appearing only a few times in the accounts of more privileged students—sometimes even to characterize their own behavior—these interactional cues were frequently used by less-privileged students as a way to name social class. . . .

WHAT'S CLASS GOT TO DO WITH IT?
ASSESSING STUDENTS' CLASS CONSCIOUSNESS

In addition to a sense of whether or not classes exist and can be easily detected, *class consciousness* also encompasses beliefs as to whether differences between social classes matter (Mann 1973). Students across the class spectrum offered rich and frequently contradictory accounts of the significance of social class. When asked directly, both working- and upper-middle-class students refuted the significance of social class; a more comprehensive look at their narratives, however, reveals that respondents also talked about social class as something that does matter. Ultimately, the narratives of working- and upper-middle-class students diverged as working-class students more decisively arrived at the conclusion that social class does, in the final analysis, matter.

Assessments of students' class consciousness were made by looking at how students responded to both direct and indirect questions about social class. For example, when asked directly whether they thought social class matters on campus, nearly half of both privileged and less-privileged students suggested that social class does not matter. These students did not, in other words, see social class as significantly structuring one's college experiences. Students from both working- and upper-middle-class backgrounds variously commented that they did not think about social class in their daily lives, that they did not choose friends on the basis of social class, and that their own lives would not be substantially different if they came from a different social class background. Whereas some students suggested that social class may matter more outside the classroom than inside, a significant minority rejected the power of social class to shape students' lives in social, academic, or extracurricular realms.

In responding to these direct questions, students used a variety of discursive strategies to explain why social class does not matter. A number of privileged students said that social class does not matter because financial aid and scholarships exist for both regular college tuition and for programs like study abroad. These students tended to see college as a level playing field. Another common notion was that everyone, regardless of social class, was in "the same boat." Angel Curtis, a working-class sophomore at Big State, put it this way: "I think

we all kind of walk into the class with a common goal. We're all doing the same things. We're getting up, we're throwing on clothes, and we're going to class."

Finally, other students downplayed the power of social class by emphasizing the power of *individuals* to construct their own college experiences. Students argued that plenty of opportunities are out there and that anyone can take advantage of them if they are motivated. When asked if class matters in terms of the kinds of experiences students have at Benton College. Brook Marshall, a soft-spoken upper-middle-class student, offered this particularly succinct articulation:

> I don't really think so. If you're involved enough and work hard enough to immerse yourself in the campus and try hard to have every experience you can, then it really doesn't matter. It shouldn't shape who you are and what you want to do.

Like others, Brook argues that individual efforts can override the influence of social class on what students get out of their college experiences. Brooke's response, then, reflects a more general pattern among college students: denying the significance of social class by invoking a rather egalitarian, meritocratic imagery.

In contrast to these responses to direct questioning, a more comprehensive analysis of their accounts shows that virtually all of these students also talk about various ways in which social class does matter at college. Upper-middle-class students gave several indications of how social class can exert its influence on the college experience. They stated, for example, that whereas social class did not matter in regard to participation in Greek life as a whole, it might matter in a few specific houses; it might—particularly at Big State—affect where you live on campus and the people with whom you make friendships,[6] and as suggested above, it can make opportunities such as study abroad more feasible. Many of these students also acknowledged their own privilege and praised their parents for enabling them to attend the college of their choice. . . . [H]owever, even when upper-middle-class students did acknowledge the significance of social class, they frequently retreated from the brink and returned to their original position that it does not, ultimately, matter. . . .

Indeed, the tendency to construct class as a moving target, one that alternates between significance and insignificance, is typical among these upper-middle-class students. The question then becomes, Why do these students alternately acknowledge and refute the significance of social class? One piece of this puzzle may be that the dominant American ideology is so deeply embedded in these students' minds that rejecting the influence of social class is, for many of them, virtually automatic. A key part of this ideology is the emphasis on individual achievement, or the belief that each member of society is in control of his or her fate. This sentiment, whose pervasiveness has been noted by both classic (de Tocqueville 1966) and contemporary observers (Lipset 1996), is particularly evident in the constructions of those upper-middle-class students, as they argue that what matters is not so much social class as individual effort. Closely connected to this belief in individual achievement is the image of society—particularly its educational institutions—as a meritocracy (Turner 1960). Thus, students spontaneously reject the possibility that social class matters in the classroom or that professors would give it any weight in evaluating students' performance. Indeed, Benton's Jordana Lindholm ties together both of these notions as she says:

> I don't think any professor would treat you any differently because of social class. And I don't think they would grade you any differently because of social class, so as far as GPA goes, I would think that if you put in the same effort as someone else you would get the same sort of results.

For Jordana and others who view schools as formally class-neutral institutions, their rejection of the significance of social class seems to rest, in part, on their immediate invocation of a cultural frame that places the dominant American ideology at the center. . . .

Although just more [than] a third of working-class students denied the significance of social class when asked directly, most of them provided more uniform and more extensive constructions of how social class matters. With some exceptions, compared with their upper-middle-class peers, these students responded more quickly and more extensively to questions of social class. Throughout their interviews, these working-class students claimed that class matters in that it gives one a "different outlook," puts pressure on one to work harder, results in weaker academic preparation, and reduces one's ability to take advantage of the many opportunities offered in college. Several young men also commented on how social class limited their dating life, worrying that they did not have the financial means necessary to engage in the traditional courtship process. Ty Mills, a member of a Greek house at Big State, put it this way:

> When it comes to dating, it's hard for me to be like, "Hey, let's go see a movie," or "Hey, let's go out to dinner," 'cause I can't always do that. Not only that, but when you get closer in relationships you always feel

uncomfortable, you know, telling them about your past. You wonder if they're going to think less of you. Or if you were to meet their parents, are they going to accept you? They'll ask you, like, "So what do your parents do?"—and you don't even live with your parents.

Expanding on this point, some students continued to tell it like it is by offering virtually encyclopedic accounts of how they felt social class mattered. When asked if she thought there was a class system on campus, Big State junior Anna Barlow replied: "I think there's a class system everywhere; everywhere you go there's always, I think, going to be social class." . . .

In a society in which discussions of money and social class are considered gauche, it is not surprising that individuals would struggle to arrive at neat and tidy conclusions about the meaning of social class. Indeed, individuals from both working- and upper-middle-class backgrounds spoke in ways that alternately acknowledged and rejected the significance of social class. The stories of working-class students, however, more consistently argued that social class does matter. In addition, like the lower-income high school students described by Brantlinger (1993), these students' accounts were rife with emotion and tales of the "hidden injuries of class" (Sennett and Cobb 1973). Even if those lower down in the stratification system may not call for radical social and economic change, they are still less likely than are their more privileged counterparts to embrace the dominant ideology (Kluegel and Smith 1986; Ladd 1994); this may help explain why these working-class students were slightly less likely to invoke the dominant ideology and more likely to tell a consistent story of their class consciousness. Thus, although Americans in general have difficulty talking about social class, their class position clearly shapes the kinds of class stories they tell.

Where Do You Draw The Line? Assessing Students' Symbolic Boundaries

Because symbolic boundaries play an important role in shaping very real social, or material, boundaries within society, it is important to examine the types of symbolic boundaries drawn by this group of students. The types of boundaries they draw are also revealing because they tell us more about their class consciousness; that is, to the extent that these students are conscious of class differences, what are these differences and how do they matter? My analysis reveals that students from both working- and upper-middle-class origins tend to draw boundaries between themselves and those above them, rather than between themselves and those below them. Rarely, if ever, did they construct a sense of self, or mark out a symbolic boundary, by comparing themselves with those occupying lower or more disadvantaged class positions. Whereas the tendency to "draw up" makes sense for working-class students, in that they are surrounded by a far greater concentration of more privileged students, it is somewhat surprising that upper-middle-class students would look upwards to construct boundaries between themselves and those they perceive as being even more privileged than themselves.

Like earlier research on the construction of symbolic boundaries among working-class individuals (Gorman 2000a; Lamont 2000), these data show working-class people drawing boundaries between themselves and others based on claims of moral superiority. These less moral "others," however, are most frequently those situated higher up in the stratification system. In part, these working-class students drew a boundary between themselves and their more privileged peers by condemning or critiquing the values and behaviors of the middle- and upper-middle classes. In general, these students charged their peers with being spoiled and used to getting what they want, valuing the wrong things (e.g., looking good, being popular, etc.), being lazy and not picking up after themselves, not taking care of their possessions, and of taking their privileges and life experiences—including their education—for granted. On numerous occasions, these students proclaimed that they would not want to be like these more privileged students and that they were glad that they did not grow up in similar circumstances. When asked about what she'd learned about social class since coming to Benton College, for example, Jodie Brewer gave this reply:

Interviewer: Are there groups of students or individuals on this campus who simply didn't exist in your high school? In other words, did you encounter new kinds of people on this campus?

Jodie: That's hard. Just I never thought that I would really have any close contact with anyone who was like super rich or anything like that, and that also kind of tells me that I don't want to be like that. You know, my aspiration is not to become filthy rich when I get older. I just want to be happy and not be like them.

Interviewer: Why don't you want to be like them?

Jodie: I don't want to feel like I'm making other people inferior. Because, I don't know, that's just not me. I don't want to feel like I'm too good for anyone to come and talk to me or too good for—I don't know, I just don't want to be seen as that kind of a person.

Whereas Jodie's critique of middle-class values comes in response to some of the "hidden injuries" (Sennett and Cobb 1973) she's experienced at college and centers on the importance of treating others with a sense of dignity, fellow student Eric Carpenter argues that the middle-class experience is a morally impoverished one, one that fails to transmit key social values:

Some people can just spend their money on stuff that they don't need; like they've just grown up with a silver spoon and stuff like that. And I just don't want to be that. I would hate to be that, actually, because they have no sense of values, you know, of what it's like to have to work to come to school here. I would like to see a lot of the guys here work on a farm, like I did, and see how long they last.

For Eric, to claim that some of his peers have "no sense of values," then, is to say that they lack a strong work ethic—something he identifies with and takes pride in.

The above cases show working-class students drawing a line between themselves and their more privileged peers by critiquing the values and behaviors of the middle- and upper-middle classes; they extend this theme by simultaneously *embracing* the values and behaviors of the working-class. These students, then, claim a sense of superiority by both pushing themselves away from those higher up and pulling themselves toward those lower down. As suggested by Eric above, this embrace of working-class values centers on notions of a stronger work ethic, greater self-sufficiency, and being more "laid-back" and humble. . . .

Cultural values such as these are not cultivated in a vacuum; rather, individuals develop their norms and values neatly tailored to the opportunities and constraints of their actual life circumstances (Swidler 2001). Thus, in a context where these working-class students find themselves surrounded by many students who they perceive as having experienced success with relatively little struggle or hard work, they face the challenge of constructing a dignified sense of self; they do this by claiming an alternate set of standards—one that privileges moral worth above the socioeconomic (Lamont 2000). . . .

In contrast to much of the literature on symbolic boundaries, rather than construct a sense of self vis-à-vis those below them in the stratification order (Lamont

1992), upper-middle-class students drew the strongest boundaries against those students they perceived as more privileged than themselves. Although these upper-middle-class students were able to *characterize* members of the lower classes—variously describing them as less confident, less adept with grammar, and more humble and laid-back—never did they *compare* themselves with these students. Instead, they drew boundaries that distanced themselves from students they perceived as more privileged than themselves, and in doing so claimed the moral high ground and minimized their own privilege.

When asked to compare themselves with other students, the equivocal strategies for talking about social class among upper-middle-class students soon fell away. Many of the students who previously claimed that they were unable to identify social class now constructed a rather sophisticated set of distinctions to articulate where they stand with respect to other students. More often than not, their gaze turned upward, to students they perceived as being at the top of the status hierarchy. In these accounts, the very kinds of status markers that were previously rejected as having any particular meaning return as the bearers of incredible social significance. Students drew distinctions, for example, among everything from the brands of alcohol one drinks, to the brand of wallet or purse one has, to the newness of one's golf clubs, to how many items of a particular brand-name good they possess. Upper-middle-class students also frequently situated their own class positions by comparing their own car with the cars owned by other students on campus. Erika Douglas, a Big State sophomore, claimed that she's not "a rich girl" because while other students are driving their BMWs around campus, she just drives her "little Jeep Wrangler." . . . Stories of spring break followed a similar pattern. Numerous upper-middle-class students lamented, for example, the fact that they "only" went to Florida for spring break and had to rent a cheap hotel room rather than stay in a friend's time share. In constructing such boundaries, these students made no reference at all to their fellow peers who do not own cars or who did not go on any kind of spring break trip but rather returned to their hometowns to earn money for school.

In making these comparisons and mapping the symbolic boundary between themselves and their peers, upper-middle-class students also constructed moral arguments that allowed them to claim a position of superiority. In general, these students offered considerable criticism of other privileged students, frequently referring to them as snobby, high-maintenance, materialistic, and elitist. At the same time, they scrupulously insisted that they were cut from a different cloth. Indeed, many of these students argued that they have a different—and

ostensibly better—relationship to their possessions than their more "materialistic" peers. This theme emerges in Emily Chase's (Big State) account of the tensions she had on a recent trip with some of her sorority sisters, where they spent much of their time shopping:

> There's just a certain attitude I get from them. For me, it's just that I like things that are nice. I may have these $50 Tiffany earrings that I got as a gift, but I *appreciate* what I get. I kind of see that they maybe they don't have the same kind of appreciation.

A similar sentiment is found in the words of Big State's Peter Ashbaugh, who said, "I mean, I have that kind of stuff [Northface jackets and backpacks] as well, but I guess I just don't value it as high as maybe those other people do." For these students, there appears to be a right way and a wrong way of relating to one's possessions; the right way, from the perspective of these students, is not to flaunt or fetishize their goods, but to have a more casual, but respectful, attitude toward them. By marking this boundary, these students are able to claim a sense of moral dignity for themselves.

Other boundary-making strategies had the effect of minimizing one's own privilege. In comparing himself with his fraternity brothers, for example, Benton's Kyle Kempner suggests that it is not so much that he is a "rich kid" who has a lot of disposable income but that he makes thrifty financial decisions:

> I do have nice clothes and my room is really nice; I definitely went all out in trying to make my room the best I possibly could. But at the same time. I'm smart about it. I got all of the stuff for my room on sale; I shop around and stuff.

Kyle effectively minimizes his privilege by tying his ability to have nice things to a behavioral or personality trait rather than a socioeconomic position. Mollie Weinstein—who was using her trust fund to pay for her education at Big State—similarly minimizes her privilege by using a number of status markers to draw a boundary between herself and the *truly* wealthy:

Interviewer: So how would you say the students at Big State compare to the students you went to high school with?

Mollie: Much more image conscious. I didn't even know what a Coach [brand] bag was until I came to this campus. I just didn't think that so many people were so rich and so beautiful and so skinny.

Interviewer: But you don't identify with that?

Mollie: I'm not that rich, that's the thing. My mom won't, she won't get me Gucci sunglasses.

Interviewer: But I can see that you have some Tiffany jewelry on.

Mollie: Yeah, but I don't have a real Prada purse or a Coach purse, and that's what makes me different. I don't really feel that spoiled. I mean, I can get my mom to do whatever I want her to do, but it's at a lower level, I feel, than some people. I just feel like I'm maybe a little less arrogant.

. . . The relentless focus on those above carries reproductive potential to the extent that it results in a partial view of social class dynamics and inequalities. The tendency to draw up when constructing symbolic boundaries suggests that students are generally more aware of those they perceive as standing above them in the status hierarchy than they are of those standing below. Compared with their rather anemic descriptions of less-privileged students on campus, these students exhibit a wealth of interest in and knowledge about the lives of other privileged students. This way of looking at social class becomes potentially problematic to the extent that the construction of such boundaries results in greater invisibility for those below. These students remain unaware of the existence of less-privileged students, their day-to-day experiences, and the challenges they may face within a college environment. Furthermore, as they position themselves in relation to more privileged students, they effectively minimize their own, albeit relative, privilege. . . .

Discussion and Conclusions

. . . This research shows that although there are noteworthy similarities in how working- and upper-middle-class college students talk about social class, their constructions ultimately diverge and suggest two rather different understandings of social class. In terms of similarities, students up and down the class hierarchy talked about social class in ways that were complex and contradictory, both accepting and rejecting the significance of social class. They did so, sometimes, within the same breath. In terms of differences, respondents varied in the extent to which they felt that they could detect social class: whereas privileged students tended to equivocate on this question, less-privileged students claimed the power to see social class. In addition, despite their occasional egalitarian claims of the insignificance of

social class, the narratives of working-class students, in their totality, show a greater sensitivity to social class and a greater likelihood of concluding that social class does matter. Finally, these students also share the tendency to draw symbolic boundaries between themselves and those above. The social and cultural implications of their boundary work, however, differ. For upper-middle-class students, the tendency to draw boundaries against those above them may play into processes of social reproduction; for working-class students, although they are engaged in processes of social transformation, their boundary-drawing strategies hint at the possibility of leveled aspirations and the limiting of their own mobility.

The construction of symbolic boundaries among upper-middle-class students deserves further elaboration. By defining themselves in relation to other privileged students, they largely disregard less-privileged students. This, coupled with a professed inability to identify social class, highlights the presence of certain "blind spots" in the accounts of upper-middle-class students. These blind spots are noteworthy for a number of reasons, some negative and some positive. On one hand, the virtual invisibility of working-class students may be negative in that it limits class consciousness and reinforces the notion that class does not matter. To the extent that individuals are unaware of social inequality or the dynamics of social class, they will be less likely to be receptive to social changes—whether on campus or in society as a whole—aimed at ameliorating such inequalities. On the other hand, if we take these narratives at face value, they can be construed positively in that that they suggest that social class matters less for these social actors than is often assumed. It is possible that these students are not particularly attuned to social class differences, not particularly concerned with class dynamics, and hence not particularly adept at orchestrating processes of social exclusion.

Adopting a more "naturalist" gaze (Harris 2003), one might also ask why social class is not more salient in the stories of these upper-middle-class students. One possibility is that, as young adults, they are still in the process of developing their class-decoding and gatekeeping skills. Although researchers find that even children have some implicit understanding of the class system (Simmons and Rosenberg 1971), our national vocabulary for talking about social class is still rather limited, and thus it is reasonable to assume that the ability to engage with the concept in complex ways develops over time. A second possibility is that these students *are* aware of social class and *do* act on the basis of social class but are not conscious of the ways in which they do so. Perhaps social class has become embodied in them and their peers, in the manner of Bourdieu's (1977, 1984) "habitus" or Williams's (1961, 1977) "structures of feeling," so that it is a lived, but not necessarily named, reality. Thus, they may, in fact, be engaging in a variety of class-exclusionary practices but do not define them as such. A third and final possibility is that the class consciousness of these upper-middle-class students remains muted because their working-class counterparts are not doing much to raise their class consciousness. Indeed, despite discussions of both their "hidden injuries" and the ways in which class matters, many working-class respondents said that they were not likely to engage their friends or classmates in discussions of social class. Thus, their own silence may play a role in reinforcing the class *un*consciousness of their privileged peers. . . .

An important contribution of this research is that it examines constructions of social class within a particular setting. Much of the previous research, whether conducted through surveys or in-depth interviews, tended to elicit more general evaluations of social class. Such evaluations, however, are limited in that they shed little light on how individuals act within specific situations and in concert with concrete social actors. This research transcends that limitation by looking at how college students make sense of social class within the college environment. Similarly, looking at constructions of social class within a particular setting is crucial because it is within concrete settings, with concrete others, that processes of inclusion and exclusion play out. Many of the situations they discuss are not merely hypothetical but rather illustrate specific examples of decisions they have made or boundaries they have drawn, which may have repercussions down the line. A limitation of this approach, however, is that this research cannot speak more broadly about these students' understandings of social class. Their responses would surely differ had they been interviewed in a different setting or if their attention had been drawn to different comparisons. In fact, to make inferences about class differences or inequalities, students sometimes drew their attention to the lower-income citizens of the surrounding communities rather than their classmates. This further reinforces the finding that many privileged students are not particularly aware of inequalities and class dynamics within the college

environment, but it also illustrates the importance of context by showing that their class awareness, class consciousness, and symbolic boundaries may be constructed differently within a different context.

NOTES

1. Social boundaries refer to objectified forms of social difference. Cultural sociologists have not reached consensus on the conditions under which symbolic boundaries translate into social boundaries. Lamont and Molnar (2002) suggest that symbolic boundaries are more likely to translate into social boundaries when they are widely held. Suzanne Shanahan (personal communication, May 2005), by contrast, argues that boundaries are never simply either symbolic *or* social.

2. It is possible to argue that the analyst's imposition of class labels on these students violates a fundamental assumption of constructionist approaches to social inequality (Harris 2004). It is also important to point out that other scholars would propose rather different models of class measurement. I have decided to use these labels for three reasons: (1) because they are supported by other class theorists, (2) because these two categories allow for a more streamlined class language, and (3) because this study is not specifically about how the respondents understand the content of particular class categories. If the present study were about the meaning of different class *categories,* my use of these labels would be quite problematic. This study, however, focuses on students' class awareness and their evaluations of the significance of social class.

3. Respondents were excluded, for example, if only one parent had graduated from college.

4. Whereas thirteen of twenty-five upper-middle-class students said that the lack of diversity within their own neighborhoods prevented them from developing an awareness of social class, only four of twenty-five working-class students made this claim.

Discussion Questions

1. According to Stuber, what were some of the similarities and differences in how White working- and upper-middle-class college students talked about class issues?

2. Why do you think working-class students were more likely to notice class differences and believe that class matters than upper-middle-class students? How can groups of people noticing or not noticing class differences influence society?

Source: "Talk of Class: The Discursive Repertoires of White Working- and Upper-Middle-Class College Students" by Jenny M. Stuber, excerpted and with references & some notes omitted from *Journal of Contemporary Ethnography*, Vol. 35, No. 3, June 2006, pp. 285–318. Reprinted by permission of Sage Publications.

CHAPTER 15

A Place in Town

Doing Class in a Coffee Shop

Carrie Yodanis

During observed interaction in a coffee shop, women use work, family and leisure-related behaviors, values, and tastes associated with socioeconomic positions in the process of class categorization. No set hierarchy results, doing class involves an ongoing struggle to situate one's own class category higher than the others.

The Coffee Shop is a small breakfast and lunch spot in a rural fishing community. . . .

The Coffee Shop sits in the middle of the town of 500 permanent, year-round residents. To me and the tourists who passed through the shop, the Coffee Shop first appears to be a friendly spot for local women to gather. Tricia, who managed the store, described the gathering spot as "Joe's Bar for women." After becoming a regular myself, however, I began to notice patterns in the interaction between women. The women did not all socialize together. Instead, they segregated themselves into distinct groups. These groups discussed different topics and behaved in unique ways. The interaction between the groups of women was characterized by patterned association and avoidance.

In this paper, I describe the interactions of women in the public space of the Coffee Shop over the course of a summer. In doing so, I provide an example of how social class is "done" during interaction. In the way they act and treat others, the women assign themselves and each other to classes. Class categorization is something the women do during their time in the Coffee Shop. Embedded in this process is a constant negotiation for a place in the stratification system with no clear ranking emerging. . . .

The Coffee Shop

The Coffee Shop sits in the middle of an interesting town. Situated on a remote coast, most of the full-time, year-round residents work in the fishing or small tourist industry. A number of residents also work for summer residents on the exclusive colony of mansions to the south of the town. Since the 1800s the summer residents have had a striking influence over the local residents, providing not only employment but also financial support to the town, including funding for the town library and medical center and individual families (paying for houses and cars). There are also a number of other "people from away," who have moved to the area. Some of these people are affiliated with the military base, sitting to the north of the town. Others are back-to-the-landers who moved to the town over the past decades to enjoy the slower pace of rural life and work on their art or farms. The symbolic meaning of these diverse populations for the year-round residents of the town comes into play as they do class in the Coffee Shop.

Each weekday morning from 8:00 until 10:30, nine women and I came to the Coffee Shop. Although these women have known each other for years and some for their whole lives, they segregated themselves into groups. Nancy, Sharon, and Holly sat at the counter. They were the first to arrive when the Coffee Shop opened at 8:00 and sat at their "regular stools" at the counter, rarely turning around to even acknowledge the other women in the Coffee Shop. Around 9:15, Gigi, Jean, and Helen arrived and sat together at a table toward the front of the Coffee Shop. Guests visited their table only when invited, and invitations were infrequent. Amy, Dorothy, and Tricia formed a third group. They sat at the far back table. They got together less regularly than the other women, but were in the Coffee Shop at least a few days each week.

These seating arrangements, which were rarely if ever violated, were the most obvious way in which women created boundaries and distinctions among themselves. . . .

While there are similarities across the groups and important exceptions within each group, the groups tended to be somewhat differentiated by levels of education, occupation, and income and wealth. The women at the counter tend to have lower socioeconomic positions. Nancy and her husband have high school degrees. She worked for years as a cook, at local factories and fish dealers, as a housekeeper, and as a clerk at local stores. Recently, she got a job as a teacher's aide. While school was out for the summer, she was not working for pay. Her husband works on fishing boats and as a maintenance worker. Sharon did not graduate from high school, but her husband did. During the summer of 1996, she worked at the fish plant in the neighboring town and has worked at a number of factories and as a housekeeper throughout the years. Her husband works for a local construction company. Holly graduated from technical school and has some college education. She worked at the Coffee Shop, as a nurse's aide, and as a housekeeper. Her partner has a high school degree and works as a fisherman.

In comparison, the women at the front table are generally wealthier. Gigi is from the elite summer colony. Her husband is a lawyer, and she is president of the women's board of a hospital in her home city. During the summer, she had no work to do. Helen is also of a higher socioeconomic status. She has a college degree and her husband has a PhD. She has worked intermittently for pay throughout her life. During the summer, she was in the Women's Club, works in the library, and volunteers for retirement homes. Jean is an interesting exception, because compared to the other women she is not wealthy. She has technical school training and is a home-duty nurse's aide. She is also active in many community organizations. She was not married, but her former husband was in the military.

Among the final group of women at the back table, Tricia managed the Coffee Shop during the summer season

and worked for pay sporadically during winter, making wreaths or assisting at a day care. She has a college degree, but her husband did not go to school beyond high school. He works as a gardener for the summer colony. Dorothy has technical school training and works part-time as a secretary. Her husband also has technical training and owns a small retail store. Amy went to college for a while but did not complete her degree. She works sporadically for pay throughout the year as a substitute teacher, in retail stores, and making crafts to sell. Her husband has some technical school training and is a fisherman.

So there are socioeconomic differences between the women. Nonetheless, differences in income, occupational prestige, and education in and of themselves were not sufficient for creating class categorization. Within the seating arrangements that physically created the groups, the women continually use or reject behaviors, tastes, and values during interaction to categorize themselves and the other women into three classes. As a result, Nancy, Sharon, and Holly became working-class women, with a strong work ethic. Gigi, Helen, and Jean became upper-class women, enjoying high culture and fine dining and dedicated to their volunteer work. Tricia, Dorothy, and Amy became new middle-class women, dedicated to intellectual and liberal, politically active pursuits. In the rest of the paper, I describe these interactions, based in different orientations to work, leisure, and family, which I observed during my time in the Coffee Shop.

Work

In the Coffee Shop, different orientations toward work were continually acted out. While in the Coffee Shop, the working-class women worked and talked about work. Even when hanging out in a restaurant, a supposed leisure activity, they managed to work. Among Nancy, Sharon, and Holly, the overwhelming topic of conversation was work. While at the Coffee Shop, they often commented on how they are being lazy or a "slug" by sitting around. Yet their actions and conversations always contradicted this. They came into the Coffee Shop the earliest and left the soonest. While sitting having coffee, they discussed the paid or household work they did before or would do after leaving the shop. Nancy, who was not employed for the summer, emphasized work by talking about the housework she did. . . . Describing the amount of work they did became almost competitive between the working-class women. . . .

The most obvious behavior was the work that Nancy and Holly did while at the Coffee Shop. Holly was employed at the Coffee Shop and rarely sat to talk.

Instead, she held conversations from behind the counter while she washed dishes, prepared food, and cleaned up. When Holly was in the Coffee Shop and not working, she was always stopping on her way to her other nursing or housekeeping work. Although not employed at the Coffee Shop, Nancy frequently worked while there. She got up from her stool and did the dishes, made egg salad or coffee, or changed the displays. She started doing this without pay, but later in the summer was asked to fill in on the weekends for pay. Yet, she continued to help out during the week even if she was not on the payroll.

At times, Sharon did not come to the Coffee Shop for a few days. When she did return, she would report that she had been working double shifts at the fish plant, and she talked about the hours she put in this week and how she only got one day off a week. She also showed her hands and the cuts, dirty nails, and stained fingers as a sign of her work at the factory.

The working-class women used these values to distinguish themselves from others. In addition to acting out their work ethic, the working-class women talked about how lazy others are. Holly, who cleans houses for the summer colony, was telling me about how the job varies depending on the family She told the story about one family who never puts the new roll of toilet paper on the holder. They always just put it on top, and she has to put it on the holder. She said she really doesn't understand—they have nothing else to do while they are just sitting there, so can't they just do that one simple job? . . .

At the same time, however, the other women in the Coffee Shop treated the working-class women as inferior based on these values. They were treated by the other women as being lazy, although they were the only women working while at the Coffee Shop. Although they were there far fewer hours than the other women, the other women and customers would comment on how often they were in the Coffee Shop. It was not uncommon to hear someone say to Nancy, "You should have your name engraved in that stool." They were often asked if they were "working hard" and were praised when they started a new job. For example, Sharon had been working double shifts for most of the summer at the fish-processing plant. The work is hard, hot, and dirty. She had only one day off a week. Yet, the following excerpts from my field notes show how the other women view her:

Jean [an upper-class woman] came into the Coffee Shop. Sharon was sitting at the counter and said that she had worked 13 days in a row. Jean asked in a very condescending way, "So you got a job? Where are you working?" and then after Sharon answers, she said, "Now you finally have work and now you are working

too hard. . . . You jumped right into it. You went from nothing to overtime."

So while the working-class women acted out a strong work ethic, the other women acted to undermine and downgrade their orientations and values. This created bounded categories between the women and began the struggle for hierarchies between the groups.

In sharp contrast, the upper-class women acted according to a volunteer rather than a paid work ethic. In the Coffee Shop, Gigi, Jean, and Helen were all highly involved in community organizations and presented this work as their primary concern whether or not they also worked for pay. When they said, "I have to work," they were referring to their community activities. They frequently talked about the unpaid community work that they were doing and often left stating that they had some community work to conduct. Gigi had to return to the city because September was going to be a busy month for the women's board at the hospital. Helen had to go to dance practice for a retirement home. Jean had to sell tickets to raise money for a new roof for a historic hall in town.

Jean does not have the socioeconomic class standing of Gigi or even Helen and thus was most active in creating her class category through interaction in the Coffee Shop. She is a good example of how class categorization does not necessarily correspond to one's socioeconomic position. Nearly everyday, Jean talked about the unpaid work she was conducting in the town, noting how important this work is to the social foundation of the town. Jean talked about the many hours she puts into running the plays and described the plays as providing worthwhile leisure activities and cultural experiences for the young people in town. She discussed the scholarships and charity work which were conducted by the Women's Club. She mentioned the "anonymous" charity work that she did on her own. She distributed and posted fliers advertising the plays or fundraisers which she organized. She sold tickets for community events from the card table that she set up on the sidewalk right outside of the Coffee Shop. She would laugh and call the Coffee Shop her "office" for her community work.

Describing their time in the Coffee Shop, Jean, Gigi, and Helen explained "that is what we do here, we form a community." They sat near the door and watched and greeted everyone who came into the Coffee Shop. They saw these actions as important for building community and presented themselves as community-minded residents. As compared to the working-class women, they stayed the longest at the Coffee Shop.

While acting as volunteers, the upper-class women never acted as paid workers. Helen and Gigi did not work for pay. Jean, on the other hand, financially needed to work for pay. She worked as a private home nurse's aide, cleaned the summer cottage that her sister owns and rents, and filled in for her friend at his art shop. She worked anywhere from 3 to 6 days a week, but never discussed her paid work in the Coffee Shop. When listing her day's activities, her paid work was never mentioned. On days when she was unable to come to the Coffee Shop because she had to work, she did not provide an explanation unless she was asked directly and then only gave a brief answer. When she did talk about her work as a nurse's aide, she discussed it in terms of volunteer work. She was "taking care of an older woman in town" or "giving a massage to a woman who had an injury."

The upper-class women also used their work values in an effort to gain status in the class hierarchy of the Coffee Shop. The upper-class women distinguished themselves from others by talking about the apathy in town, referring to the lack of interest in joining community organizations or volunteering for tasks or positions within the organizations. Jean frequently talked about the frustration she felt when others were not willing to help and often criticized the projects that she sees as so essential to the community. Gigi and Helen agreed and saw it within their own community work. . . .

The middle-class women acted according to yet another orientation toward work—a commitment to progressive, political work—in the process of doing class and being categorized as members of the new middle class of intellectual, liberal professionals. In complete contrast to the working-class women, they lacked a paid work ethic and openly share it. Like the upper-class women, they kept later hours at the Coffee Shop, often hanging out until the middle of the afternoon. While Holly and Nancy, working-class women, worked in the Coffee Shop, Tricia, who also worked at the Coffee Shop, left her work and joined Amy and Dorothy at their table in the back. In my first conversation with Amy at the Coffee Shop, she presented her lack of a paid work ethic to me when she told me, "The two most important things about the Protestant work ethic is that religion should be first and the work should be second in importance, and neither are very important to me."

Tricia, Amy, and Dorothy are political. They are all involved in local politics, serving on the school board and other committees, and this work was a near daily topic of conversation at the Coffee Shop. Who was at the town meeting? When will the teachers' contract be settled? If the military leaves, how will that impact the town? Will the town buy the water company? They also talked about national and state politics—public policies,

the presidential campaigns, and the candidates for state government. Tricia closed the Coffee Shop or had someone fill in for her so that she could do work for the school board in the state capital.

Their political orientation was very specific, however. They defined themselves as "liberal" and presented themselves as such. They distinguished themselves from the people in the town who have sexist, homophobic, and racist ideas and acted as social change agents trying to enlighten people to change their backward ideas. . . .

Actions of the middle-class women confirmed their values. Amy parked her van, with a bumper sticker supporting gay and lesbian rights, outside of the Coffee Shop. During a referendum regarding a gay rights bill, Tricia wore a button to work which revealed her support for gay and lesbian rights. She listened to National Public Radio while working.

The Coffee Shop is a public place where women "do class." The women could have just done different jobs and work outside of their time at the Coffee Shop, but that would not necessarily translate into categorization into particular social classes. Without acting according to class-associated work values and orientations, they would not be identified as members of a particular social class based on their work. By doing hard work, Nancy, Sharon, and Holly acted to be categorized as working class; while emphasizing volunteer work, Gigi, Helen, and Jean sought categorization as upper class; and through their political work, Amy, Tricia, and Dorothy did class as intellectual, liberals of the new middle class. I argue here that these repeated, patterned actions were not random but rather involved the women acting according to behaviors and values associated with a particular social class. These behaviors categorized women into social classes in their daily interactions in the Coffee Shop.

Leisure

As with work values and orientations, the women in the Coffee Shop also used leisure in the process of doing class. In this section, I show how their tastes for leisure activities were used in interaction for class categorization. In other words, preferences in leisure do not just emerge from socioeconomic positions but are in fact used to place meaning on and categorize people according to these differences.

The working-class women downplayed leisure as they emphasized their work ethic. Nonwork activities were rarely a topic of conversation. When I would ask

Nancy or Sharon, "How was your weekend?" or "Did you get to enjoy this beautiful day?" they answered according to how productive the day or weekend was, such as "I got a lot done" or "Didn't get enough done." . . .

Among the upper-class women, Gigi, a member of the elite summer colony, was the clearest symbol used by Jean and Helen in their leisure. By sitting and being seen with Gigi, leisure time was very important for acting out affiliation with the summer colony, and Gigi's friendship continued to be used in interaction even when she was not there. For example, after Gigi had returned to her permanent residence in the fall, she wrote a note to Jean. In the setting of the Coffee Shop, Jean shared the letter with the women in the Coffee Shop, demonstrating her personal ties and knowledge of Gigi:

> Jean announced that she got a card from Gigi. She said that "She said to say Hi to everyone, Helen, Carrie, Tricia and someone else. . . . Oh, Sharon" (and laughed). "She will be back at the end of October. She said that she is back into her routine which she enjoys although she 'whines' about it a lot. She is such a real person."

In contrast to the working-class women, the upper-class women frequently discussed their leisure activities, in particular those related to high culture. Indeed, discussion of high culture dominated their daily conversations. They discussed experiences in Europe and tropical vacation spots. Almost 20 years ago, Jean lived in Germany, Hawaii, and the Philippines as a result of her former husband's military career. Yet, she used these experiences in her interactions to display orientations toward high travel. . . .

One day, she brought me a stack of *Condé Nast Traveler* magazines. The vacation spots covered in the magazines range from "55 Islands of Desire" to Rome, Thailand, and Latin America. Although she had not been outside of the country since her divorce and her travel was a result of military assignments rather than exotic vacations, both her subscription to this magazine and bringing them to the Coffee Shop were important actions in her display and creation of class category. In contrast, although Amy, another woman in the Coffee Shop, also lived in Europe as a result of her husband's work in the military, she never discussed her experiences as engaging in high culture.

Tastes for high culture pervade their actions. One day, Jean explained that during the afternoon she and a friend who was visiting were planning to have tea at 4:00

on the rocky shore of the summer colony. Her friend's sister in law, a concert flutist who teaches at a private school, was going to play the flute. Helen, nearly every day, talked about listening to classical music and attending musical performances. She shared her knowledge about high culture by listing performers and evaluating the technical quality of performances. Jean kept everyone updated on the progress of the local plays she was organizing. She brought in a tape of classical music to share with Helen. The upper-class women openly made plans to attend the opera and the local plays together, excluding the other women in the Coffee Shop.

At the same time, the upper-class women showed disdain for the local working-class culture of the town. In doing so, they continued to categorize themselves as upper class and strove to gain a superior position relative to the working class. They talked openly about avoiding the Diner, a casual seafood restaurant in town where many of the fishermen and other local families hang out. Their criticism centered on the atmosphere, which they did not see as on their level. Jean said she doesn't like the Diner: "I am going to sound snobby, but [pause] it is the level of conversation that goes on." . . .

In comparison, upper-class women often discussed dinner at the Dining Room, a more formal, expensive seafood restaurant, where residents of the summer colony often ate. They talked about the excellent meals they had and the good service they received. They invited me to meet them at the Dining Room for dinner. As Jean explained one day, she and a friend wanted to go to dinner, but she was getting sick of the Dining Room because they went so frequently.

Related to this, Jean had very high standards for service at the Coffee Shop, which other women approached as very casual. Every day when she came in, she demanded that her service be prompt and that her tea and popcorn were prepared just right. She got visibly upset and annoyed if she did not receive the service she expected. . . .

Like the upper class and unlike the working class, the middle-class women engaged in conspicuous leisure during their interactions in the Coffee Shop. For example, Tricia did not work on the weekends in the Coffee Shop. Rather, she had younger women fill the Saturday and Sunday shifts. In addition, she often took an additional day off to make the weekend longer and provide more time for leisure activities. Amy came into the Coffee Shop to socialize on days when she had turned down substitute teaching jobs because she was feeling ill.

What was unique about their leisure was the focus on new age, liberal, intellectual interests and hobbies. For example, Tricia, who manages the Coffee Shop, did the purchasing for the small gift shop in the back of the store. She included aromatherapy and environmentally friendly and Native American print greeting cards in the stock. By selecting these items for the store, Tricia displayed her class-associated values and interests. Similarly, Amy one day asked me, while ignoring the upper-class women I was sitting with, if I would like to visit an herb shop with her in a neighboring town. I agreed, and we visited two herb shops and an organic farm along the way. Throughout the trip, Amy shared her knowledge of herbs for both artistic and medicinal purposes.

The middle-class women also often discussed films and books. For example, one day they were talking about an author whose books they have all read. The author writes about Hasidic Jews. None of them are Jewish, and they all loved the books. Tricia said that she was "thrown off" by the author's last book because it was about African Americans. She quickly explained that there was "nothing wrong" with a book about African American culture, but that she was "just really in a mood for a book about Hasidic Jews." Another day, I referred to the movie *Bound*. Tricia, who hadn't seen it, asked what it was about. I described it as a "lesbian Mafia movie," to which Sharon, a working-class woman, joked, "Maybe we shouldn't talk to Carrie anymore," and Tricia replied, "That sounds really interesting." Nancy and Sharon laughed with each other when Amy and Tricia talked about how much they enjoy visiting bookstores.

These values ran through all of the leisure activities they discussed in the Coffee Shop. Amy talked about the interesting guests who were on *Oprah* the day before, especially the lesbian congressperson. Tricia talked about an article she read in *Ms.* magazine. Amy talked about how she wants to visit the Holocaust Museum while visiting her children in Washington, D.C. . . .

While it first appeared when entering the Coffee Shop that all of the women were there to enjoy some leisure time, upon closer observation it became apparent that the three groups of women acted out different values and tastes toward leisure. Leisure was then used by the women to associate themselves with others seeking the same class category and to distance themselves from the other women.

Family

In the process of doing class in the Coffee Shop, women brought their family members into the action. The women in the Coffee Shop selectively used expectations and accomplishments of children as they "did" class.

The working-class women deemphasized socio-economic mobility among their children. Instead, they encouraged them to stay and work in the town, for which a university education is not necessary and instead usually results in children moving away. Nancy's discussion of the future plans of her 17-year-old daughter, who was soon graduating from high school, provides a good example. Nancy said her daughter's friend left to go to school in Florida and that her daughter was dead set on going to a college outside of the state—something she discouraged. Instead, Nancy showed her preference that her daughter stays in town. A few months later, her daughter decided to enlist in the military. Nancy was afraid of her daughter traveling and being so far away from the town. One day at the Coffee Shop, Nancy said that she thought that her daughter was changing her mind and no longer wanted to leave. When pushed by other women to explain further, she admitted that her daughter never actually said that she did not want to go, but that she just sensed it. In the presentation of her daughter's future plans, Nancy stressed the importance of maintaining her relationship with a local young man. She told other women at the Coffee Shop that she asked her daughter about her plans for her new relationship after she leaves town: "Are you going to break up and just be friends, or are you going to try to make it work?" Nancy described their relationship to the other women as "very serious," although her daughter is only 17 and they have only been dating 2 months. Thus, within the public setting of the Coffee Shop, Nancy demonstrated how she discouraged her daughter from social mobility. Instead she presented her desire for her daughter to stay in the area and maintain a local relationship rather than travel in the military. Nancy's daughter later took steps to retract her commitment to the military and remain in town in order to maintain her relationship with the young man. Nancy supported her decision.

What Nancy did not say in the public setting is just as important as what she did. There were aspects of her daughters' lives, especially those based in educational attainment, which Nancy did not talk about. For example, her older daughter was taking, very interested in, and doing well in Advanced Placement English classes in her high school. Yet, Nancy never mentioned this among the other women. Furthermore, her younger daughter was the only student in the local grammar school class who got straight A's consistently every semester. Yet I learned this only from reading the local newspaper. Nancy did not talk about this. She could have easily presented this information in the Coffee Shop. But in the process of "doing" class, Nancy buried her daughters' socioeconomic mobility.

In comparison, the upper-class women bragged about educational and financial success in their families. Helen, whose children have acquired the greatest educational and financial success, most frequently talked about the accomplishments of her children. She talked about her son's success in college, where he applied and was accepted to graduate school for engineering, and where he works. As the following field note shows,

> Helen said that her daughter got straight "A's" because she was an over-achiever. Gigi said that her daughter, too, was an overachiever. Helen talked about her son and how he was very smart, was told to do liberal arts, but wanted to do sciences and that he was very good at science. He went to Stanford. Gigi added, "Like your husband?"

As stated before, however, what women hid is just as important as what they showed in the process of doing class. Jean rarely mentioned her two daughters who had not attained educational and occupational mobility. Her daughters had not graduated from college, do not hold prestigious jobs, and are married to men who perform physical work. Because they do not fulfill the expectations for children which correspond with her desired class category, she never mentioned her daughters in the Coffee Shop.

The middle-class women used a third set of expectations of their children during the process of class categorization in interaction. Amy, Dorothy, and Tricia neither encouraged nor discouraged socioeconomic mobility. Rather, they emphasized knowledge and worldly experiences. During our interview, Amy described her daughter as follows:

> My daughter went to school in Pennsylvania and she actually remarked several times about how she felt that she was more aware of things going on in the world, like independence and getting along and that kind of stuff, than a roommate she had one year who was from New York City. . . . She is the curious kind of a person that would be more aware. . . . Of course, everybody has their own interpretation of what success is, but Barbara is one of those kids that will definitely be a success in her eyes and in other people's eyes. It's just because she really loves life, enjoys life,

is curious and wants to know. She doesn't sit down and read novels very often, but she always is reading something that non-fiction kind of things. . . . Even though she came from a small town, she's pretty with what's going on in the world and everything. And very liberal social ideas.

Here she emphasized that her daughter is not "small town" but is knowledgeable of the ways of the world, even in comparison to young women from New York City. Her knowledge came from her intellectual curiosity and being well-read. In the end, she connected her daughter's knowledge to liberal social ideas. . . .

The thing Tricia would not tolerate would be her children doing what Nancy, a working-class woman, wanted for her daughter:

> I would be real upset if [my daughter] got married when she was 18 or 19. I mean very upset. And the same with [my son]. . . . I don't what him graduating from high school, then just marrying the first girl that he dated and stay living here for the rest of his life.

Thus, the women used expectations for their children in the process of doing class. Upper-class women presented socioeconomic mobility, while the working-class women did not. The middle-class women pushed for knowledge of and experience with diverse cultures and people outside of the small town. . . .

Conclusion

The Coffee Shop provides a setting for observing how class is "done" in microlevel interactions of everyday life. Each morning, women were continually creating and re-creating local social class distinctions and working to categorize themselves into social classes. They did this by acting against or according to behaviors and tastes which are associated with a particular socioeconomic position. They also selectively associated with or distinguished themselves from other women and acted to gain status relative to other women based on their behaviors, values, and tastes.

As many researchers have documented over the decades, there is no question that socioeconomic differences matter. But these structural differences in and of themselves are not sufficient for creating class categorizations, identities, and ranking. Rather, it is through interactions that given socioeconomic positions take on meaning in the daily lives and encounters with other people. Without these actions, involving the taking and acting out of class symbols, there would not be class categories in the Coffee Shop.

There are similarities in what occurs in the Coffee Shop and previous literature on class. For example, the value of a physical work ethic has been found in studies of working classes (Halle 1984; Ferree 1987; Rosen 1987; Rubin 1976, 1995), the significance of volunteer work has been found among upper-class women (Ostrander 1984; Daniels 1987), and the new middle classes, comprised of highly educated professionals such as academics and artists, tend to value liberal political and social orientations in their work (Brint 1985; Lamont 1987; Brooks and Manza 1997). Bourdieu (1984) outlines the preferences for music, food, reading material, sports, travel, and entertainment that demarcate socioeconomic positions, some of which correspond to what I found in the Coffee Shop.

Yet these studies assume two things that I did not find in the Coffee Shop. First, these studies define class membership based on occupation, income, and wealth. In the Coffee Shop, these objective criteria were neither necessary nor sufficient for class categorization. For example, while the new middle class is usually believed to be comprised of highly educated professionals, within the Coffee Shop and town, Amy sought a similar class category although she had not graduated from college, works as a substitute teacher, and makes crafts to sell locally rather than working as a professor or professional artist. Similarly, Jean was able to be categorized with Gigi, a wealthy summer resident, and distanced from the working-class women at the counter. Thus, class categories are not merely about wealth, education, and occupational prestige. Rather, they are outcomes of performances and interaction. This is similar to what Anderson (1976) and Warner and Lunt (1941) find—stratification systems are

systems of patterned and selective, symbolic action and interaction.

What I observed in the Coffee Shop, however, is also different from what Anderson (1976) and Warner and Lunt (1941) found. In the Coffee Shop, there was a class system but no set stratification system. Unlike Anderson's study, no one group deferred to another. Instead, there was an ongoing struggle between the groups to gain status relative to each other with no one accepting a lower rank. What emerges from the Coffee Shop is that the process of doing class does not necessarily result in a set system of inequality but rather involves efforts to situate one's own class higher, not lower, than the others in any resulting system of inequality. . . .

In this paper, I discuss what I found in the Coffee Shop. It is admittedly a unique setting. Yet it is situated in a town where similar patterns emerge (Yodanis 2002). Throughout the town, women and men use socioeconomic-associated behaviors, tastes, and values, often represented by the wealthy summer colony, the back-to-the-landers "from away," or the hardworking local way of life to do class. In other micro situations, with different local symbols of social class and with greater intersections in the process of doing class, gender, and race, people may well do class in different ways. Other research approaches, including more constructionist, discursive approaches, may also reveal additional perspectives on how people do class. The opportunities for future research remain wide open.

Discussion Questions

1. What are some of the ways that the different groups of women in the coffee shop "do" class?

2. Why do you think it is so important to these women that they are seen as legitimate members of their respective coffee shop groups?

Source: "A Place in Town: Doing Class in a Coffee Shop" by Carrie Yodanis, excerpted and with notes & references omitted from *Journal of Contemporary Ethnography*, Vol. 35, No. 3, June 2006, pp. 341–366. Reprinted by permission of Sage Publications.

CHAPTER 16

Professorial Capital

Blue-Collar Reflections on Class, Culture, and the Academy

Mary Kosut

Merging theory with autoethnographic reflections, the author critically explores the relationship between social class and the reproduction of inequality within the upper ranks of the academy, while reflexively and purposefully challenging traditional modes of academic discourse. Drawing from her experiences as a blue-collar sociology doctoral student, the concept of an academic class ceiling is elaborated.

Introduction: Where I Am Coming From

Social science education did not prepare me to write from the heart, to touch other people, or to improve social conditions. My education taught me to write in a way that would bring respect from a small, elite group of colleagues (Ellis, 1997, p. 135).

Although our memories are often fleeting and fuzzy, interpretations of lived events we rewrite and edit throughout our lives, some memories echo in our minds with clarity. Instead of drifting farther away from us over time, they remain distinctly audible. . . .

"Mare, what's goin' on? It's dear old Dad just checkin' in to see how you're doin'."

"Hey, Dad. I'm good. Just working on a take-home final essay exam," I said trying to mask my regret for having picked up the phone. I was on a roll and had hoped to finish my final and shut down my computer so that I could get to bed by midnight.

"I gotta hand it to ya. I couldn't do what you're doin,'" he said with sincerity.

"Yeah, sometimes it gets pretty tiring, especially when work gets hectic. With graduate school and my job, I have no time to have a life."

"Oh, but you know it will be worth it. Teachers are state workers, and they have good benefits and retirement. I was talking to your uncle about you, and he said that you should definitely teach kindergarten kids or first graders 'cause when they are little, they listen to you. When they get to be junior high or high school age, then they start actin' up and givin' you crap," he offered.

"Dad, umm, as I have told you many times before, I am getting my doctorate. I plan to teach in a college. I am going to conduct research and write books and articles. I will be a Ph.D., a professor," I said with consternation and patronization.

After a long uncomfortable pause, he replied, "Oh. I see, a college professor," in a mockingly haughty voice.

Even though I had been in graduate school pursuing a doctorate in sociology for more than 5 years, most of my blue-collar, non-college-educated family members did not have a clue as to what I was doing. Some of them understood that I was going into the field of education, but they could not comprehend why it was taking so long. They were worried. I was worried too but for different reasons. Even though I understood why the titles *Ph.D.* and *professor* were virtually meaningless to them, I had to confront the reality that I knew their culture, yet they did not know the culture I was entering. It became clear to me that the closer I got to the title of Ph.D., the more distance was being wedged between myself and my blue-collar familial roots. I began to feel detached from my family because I found it harder to pass in their world. I made it a point not to use academic jargon or fancy words, so I would not sound like a snob. At the same time, I did not feel comfortable in the academy. I consciously strived to mask evidence of my blue collarness in hopes of gaining acceptance and credibility as a student scholar and eventually a professor. I felt like an outsider who had snuck in. For roughly 7 years, I lived in what hooks (2000) describes as a state of class limbo. Now that I am on the inside, I have a privileged platform through which to communicate my experiences.

. . . I contend that a class ceiling inhibits working-class students from entering the so-called knowledge factory (Tokarczyk & Fay, 1993). Much like the glass ceiling limits women from rising to upper-level positions in the labor force, a class ceiling exists within the upper levels of the academy impeding less privileged students from achieving the same levels of success as their more privileged colleagues. The class ceiling is supported by everyday practices as illustrated in my elaboration of a theory of professorial capital. I suggest that achieving recognition and success in a humanities or social science doctoral program is directly related to the levels of professorial capital a student possesses.

Professorial capital is based on Bourdieu's (1984, 1986) concept of cultural capital. In *Distinction: A Social Critique of the Judgement of Taste,* Bourdieu (1984) theorizes that our social class position reflects four kinds of capital that are inherently interconnected: economic, social, cultural, and symbolic. According to Bourdieu, members of the dominated classes have not only little economic capital but also less cultural capital. All members of society are born with varying amounts of cultural capital that are reproduced through what he refers to as the habitus, or "internalized, embodied, social structures" (Bourdieu, 1984, p. 468). For example, those born into the upper class will have access to elite institutions and hereditary privileges (private schools, seats at the symphony) that function to reproduce their elite cultural capital and social location. Likewise, members of the working class will reproduce their social location through the habitus by engaging in low-status activities such as playing pool and watching TV. The concept of habitus and cultural capital are valuable because they link individuals with macrostructures, providing a greater understanding of how structure is reproduced by individuals in action.

I propose that professorial capital functions as a specific type of cultural capital that reproduces class stratification within the upper tiers of the academy. Professorial capital consists of four different cultural tools that a doctoral student may possess: discursive, aesthetic cultural, cognitive, and temporal. These four forms are dialectically related and enable a privileged class of academics to monopolize academic discourse and culture. Graduate students with high levels of professorial capital benefit because they possess valuable cultural knowledge that may translate to success in doctoral programs, eventually opening the doorway to the academy. . . .

Forms of Professorial Capital: A Series of Clicks

. . . In the following section I present a series of clicks: biographical moments embedded in my memory that contributed to the formation of my own class consciousness. I conceptualize these autoethnographic clicks as mundane everyday interactions that reproduce a hidden curriculum: They send implicit messages about who has a place in the academy and who does not. Although each click is a highly subjective micronarrative, when fused together, they narrate a larger story about exclusion and inequality in American education. These clicks are the foundation of a theory of professorial capital.

CLICK 1: DISCURSIVE CAPITAL

The setting is a classroom in an urban university. The room is decorated in the classic institutional style: beige walls, florescent lighting, oversized simulated wood grain seminar table in center of the room, and an absence of windows. Fifteen graduate students are waiting for the professor to arrive. Some talk quietly in groups, some reread their notes, and others gaze listlessly at random objects. It is the second time the class will meet, and the inaugural semester of my Ph.D. student career. I feel nervous, confused, inept, and frazzled. I pan the room looking for symbolic signs of hope. No visible tattoos, black concert t-shirts, facial piercings, or other obvious cues of unconventionality. I wonder to myself, "My god, what have I done?" The White male student in his late 20s sitting next to me breaks my solipsistic silence.

"So did you finish the readings?" he said.
    "Ah hah," I nodded back.
    "What did you conclude?"

"Umm, yeah, I concluded that some sociologists are crappy writers. I mean, some of that stuff was pretty hard to figure out," I offered sincerely. "Ahhh, I like what Adorno had to say about the culture industry, but the way he writes is pretty confusing and alienating. . . . Why do they have to write like that? Although, writing style aside, he writes some cool shit to think about." I stop talking because I realize he is furrowing his brow. I get the feeling I gave the wrong answer.

"Perhaps you should invest some time in a more thoughtful reading of the text or consult some secondary sources if you are unable to process the material," he said in a condescending tone. His body turns away from mine. I am shut down.

"Yeah, perhaps I should do that," I replied in a cocky tone. I take a lungful of air and utter the word *asshole* under my breath. We are both relieved when the professor enters the room and takes his spot at the center of the table.

I sat quietly in anger, mulling over the exchange. I did not speak the entire class because I knew I would sound stupid. To sound stupid is to be stupid. I feared that my peers and more importantly, my professor, would discover I was an intellectual charlatan. I remembered what my friend Tom said: "Just be quiet and people will think you are smart." I thought to myself, "Where did that guy learn to talk like that? Who the hell talks like that?" Click.

. . . A doctoral student's success hinges on his or her ability to communicate ideas verbally. Oral examinations and dissertation defenses allow professors to determine whether a student possesses the discursive skills that are the signature of a legitimate academic. However, professors assess a student's intelligence and creativity via forms of talk from the start of the institutionalization process. Students from less privileged backgrounds are at a major disadvantage on entering doctoral programs because they often do not possess the vocabulary, speech patterns, and pronunciation skills of their colleagues. Working-class, uneducated families communicate in a language distinctively different from academic discourse (Belanoff, 1993; Bernstein, 1971). In addition, working-class students are less likely to hone their communication skills at school. The state colleges that I attended did not prepare me for institutional discourse. Because of large classes and predominantly unidirectional dialogue from professor to student, I learned to listen, write, and memorize. I did not know what a seminar course was prior to graduate school.

When I first encountered doctoral seminar speak, I became acutely aware of how insufficient my vocabulary was. I quickly determined words that I commonly used, such as *cool, good,* and *sucks,* needed to be replaced by *fascinating, tenable,* and *problematic* if I wanted to stay competitive. This took a lot of practice as I grew up in a house that engaged in fights, not polemics. . . .

Lack of discursive capital puts working-class students at a disadvantage because they are less likely to be recognized as bright or intelligent. They are also less likely to speak, fearing their own language would be appallingly inappropriate. Students with high amounts of discursive capital receive rewards that translate into real opportunities. For example, they are mentored by high-ranking professors, are more likely to receive the most prestigious academic awards and scholarships, and most important, are identified as having promise. Without the right communication codes, blue-collar students remain silent and invisible.

CLICK 2: AESTHETIC-CULTURAL CAPITAL

The setting is the hallway outside of my professor's office. I sit on the floor with my legs crossed, impatiently wondering if I will be able to meet with her today. More than 20 minutes have passed, and I glance at my watch again. It is almost 4 p.m. I will have to try again next week. I unlock my body and look up from my notes. I recognize a classmate coming down the hall. She has a big grin on her face.

"Hey, waiting to see Dr. X?" she asked.

"Yeah, it ain't happening today. One of the boys is monopolizing her office hours," I halfheartedly complained. "Where are you coming from?"

"Oh, I just had an excellent meeting with Dr. B," she beamed. "I wrote this paper that references Mandelstam, and as it turns out, Dr. B is a big fan of his. He seemed really impressed. He was drooling over my paper. I think I am going to ask him to be on my thesis committee."

"Who is Mandelstam?" I asked.

"Osip Mandelstam. He is a Polish-born writer who grew up in Saint Petersburg. He often gets lumped into the category of the great Russian writers, like in the tradition of Tolstoy or Nabokov," she chattily replied.

"Oh, is he still alive?"

"No, he died in the early 1940s," she said authoritatively. There is a brief moment of awkward silence, "Well, I guess I better run. I am meeting my boy-friend at the opera tonight, and I want to go home and change first," she said as she walked backwards away from me.

"Have fun," I said rather lamely. I stood there for a moment and watched her gaily bounce away. I never met people in their 20s who went to the opera. I never read Mandelstam. (I never even heard of Mandelstam.) I never read Tolstoy or Nabokov. "Maybe she would run into Dr. X or Dr. B at the opera," I thought to myself. Click.

This particular click, a casual friendly conversation, illustrates how a doctoral student's career may be positively influenced by the level of aesthetic-cultural knowledge they possess. Aesthetic-cultural capital refers to knowledge of the humanities and arts, from Aristotle and Kant to Proust, Wilde, and Manet. Students that can drop names, make links between disciplines, and use examples from obscure literary references stand out. Aesthetic-cultural knowledge may accumulate through attendance of elite institutions (including primary and secondary schools) that promote a classic, liberal, well-rounded education. Aesthetic-cultural knowledge may also be transferred via the family. For example, children who are socialized by highly educated parents are more likely to be exposed to a variety of academic concepts and disciplines before entering college. They are also more likely to have been exposed to different types of books. Aside from newspapers and magazines, my parents did not read regularly. The small bookcase my family owned contained an assortment of knick-knacks, a set of encyclopedias, a few self-help books, and a best seller or two. Russian literature, philosophy, and feminist theory were noticeably absent from my childhood. . . .

Click 3: Cognitive Capital

The scene takes place in a large square-shaped classroom. A balding White male professor in a rumpled, gray, wool jacket is pacing back and forth in front of the chalkboard. He looks like a living cliché. The professor lectures, reads passages from a text, and scrawls random words on the board with great urgency. I sit amid 25 students; some are avidly listening and furiously writing down every word the professor utters. I am one of those students. However, others appear to be less than engaged. A few students are visibly annoyed; they shift in their chairs, sigh from time to time, clear their throats aggressively, and one or two men appear as if they will physically explode if they are not given a chance to be heard. The professor's homily is interrupted by a student's unsolicited interjection.

"I disagree with your argument. Bauman's thesis is highly problematic to me. I think that it is erroneous to

suggest that institutional moorings have been weakened," said White Male Student A addressing the professor directly.

"You are sounding like a modernist," said White Male Student B (who cuts off White Male Student A in midsentence). Students A and B debate back and forth for a few minutes as the class silently watches the intellectual sparring. The professor referees and takes power back. The professor is delighted by the outburst. He seems energized by the exchange. I sit in a state of disbelief. "Where do they get the guts to talk like that?" I think to myself. "Who do they think they are challenging the professor?" Moreover, "what gives them the right to rip apart Bauman?" Click.

Cognitive capital refers to a particular way of knowing, perceiving, and interacting within the academy. Cognitive capital can also be described as an attitude that is synonymous with self-assurance. As Smith (1997) pointed out, "some students learn their own voices have authority, they count and should be heard" (p. 1149). Because of their privileged, educated upbringings, some students not only are more at ease within university environments, but they also have learned the correct way to think. Thinking the correct way means challenging, deconstructing, and questioning the material with which you are presented. As a potential academic, you must successfully digest the canon and be prepared to quote passages verbatim. However, in doing so, you must demonstrate the understanding that all theories and treatises are imperfect, if not fundamentally flawed in some fashion. It is commonly understood in academia that "the A students do not memorize, they question" (Peckham, 1995, p. 270). As a first-generation college student who spent the initial 22 years of her life trapped in a small, economically wounded industrial region, who was I to challenge academic authority? What gave me the right to question a professor, let alone a French poststructuralist?

Drawing from Bernstein (1971), Gos (1995) argues that working-class students are less likely to challenge academic authority because they are socialized in authoritarian position-oriented rather than person-oriented households. Person-oriented families are composed of idiosyncratic individuals, each having their own rights, who are taught to creatively negotiate roles (Bernstein, 1971; Gos, 1995). As a result, privileged children are taught to think imaginatively and challenge various perspectives. These skills are fundamental to achieving success within extremely competitive doctoral programs. Unlike privileged families, working-class families are hierarchically ordered according to positions, such as role (with father at the top) or birth order (Bernstein, 1971; Gos, 1995). The authority and legitimacy of a statement derives from social relationship rather than reasoning. For example, if a working-class child asks a parent why he or she must perform a task, the response will likely be "because I am your mother and I said so." If the child fails to comply, power is transferred vertically to someone with more authority as in "now you will have to deal with your father." . . .

CLICK 4: TEMPORAL CAPITAL

The setting is an intimate seminar room with a small table that seats approximately 10 people. It is 3:20 p.m., and class begins in 10 minutes. Students are trickling in sporadically. They strategically position themselves around the seminar table and begin to organize their individual spaces—coffee, note-books, photocopies, pens, highlighters, and cough drops are a few of the props that decorate the scene.

"Hey, what's goin' on?" I said as I entered the room crashing in the first available chair next to a male colleague.

"Hi, where you coming from—you look a little freaked," he calmly returned.

"Oh, I just rushed here from work. It was so cold that I had to take the subway and the damn A train was late. I needed to stop and get a cup of coffee because I was so tired. I tried to get through the readings last night, but I was dying on the vine. I was afraid I was going to be late, but I needed that coffee. It's so busy at work and my boss is insane . . . ," I trailed off in midsentence, realizing I was rambling. I also realized I had forgotten to go to the bathroom. "So what's up with you?" I sincerely offered.

"I've been so into this subcultural theory. I spent the morning rereading this stuff, and I just can't wait to discuss it with Professor K. I like McRobbie a lot, but 'Resistance Through Rituals' is rather theoretically empty. It's like this big build up, and then you are left saying, so what?" he said enthusiastically.

"Um, yeah," I lamely offered. I still needed to pee. "You don't work in the daytime?"

"No, I work full-time on school."

"Oh, that's cool," I said. "Excuse me." I run quickly to the bathroom. "Man, I can't believe that people can live in New York City and don't have to work," I thought as a walked down the hall. "Full-time on school? It is not my imagination. He really does go to every meeting and event on campus," I obsessed. Click. "He looks well-rested because he is

well-rested." Click. "What a privilege it would be to devote all of my energy into school." Click. "Man, I could sound smarter if I didn't have to work." Click. Click. Click.

Out of all of the forms of professorial capital, temporal capital is the most straightforward and obvious. Temporal capital is the amount of time a student has available to devote to study, research, and writing. Students from the privileged classes are less likely to work as many hours in the labor force, if at all, compared to blue-collar students. Quite simply, some students work their way through college and some do not. Having free or discretionary time to study when you are in the mood or write at a time when you are most productive can translate into a high level of preparedness and productivity. Also, those that have significant amounts of temporal capital can ensure more face-to-face interaction with professors as they have the time and flexibility to wait outside professors' offices during office hours. Temporal capital allows students to attend scholarly presentations or seminars recommended by professors. Attendance at these events shows you are a serious and committed student who is active in all phases of the scholarly community. As one colleague put it, "It's time to go show my face." Working-class students who have to juggle doctoral work and labor-force work have a substantial deficit of temporal capital. Like discursive, aesthetic-cultural, and cognitive capital, temporal capital supports the class ceiling. . . .

Conclusion

Feminist scholars such as Smith (1987, 1997) and hooks (1984, 1993, 2000) and sociologists such as Bourdieu (1984, 1986), Bourdieu and Passeron (1977), and Willis (1977) have shed light on the relationship between the Other, the academy, and the reproduction of the status quo. The notion that universities reproduce inequality, while at the same time promoting the ideology of meritocracy, must continue to be explicitly problematized from a theoretical and pedagogical perspective. It is crucial to connect existing social structures and the resulting cultural distinctions that they produce with individual experience and everyday practices. Social structures possess an everyday component or microcomponent because it is people who reproduce them. The practices that sustain the class ceiling actively reinforce institutional inequality when they are enacted or performed in graduate classrooms, professors' offices, and other mundane institutional contexts. Educational institutions that promote egalitarianism are guaranteeing that the upper ranks of the academy will continue to be dominated by the culture of the elite. In turn, this supports inequality and oppression outside of institutions, creating a cultural and economic gap between the working and privileged classes.

As less privileged students learn the ropes and struggle in isolation to gain access into the academy, those with professorial capital quickly advance because they are presumably brighter and more hardworking. The voices of graduate students with low levels of discursive and cognitive capital will continue to be obscured, or as is often the case, remain mute if professors do not take radical, purposeful steps to address the power dynamics of the classroom. . . .

Critically deconstructing multiple voices is a central component in what Giroux (1997) calls border pedagogy. He argues that when educators engage this practice in the classroom, it can help to facilitate students' ability to communicate, write, and listen. No longer marginalized and mute as border crossers, blue-collar graduate students have the potential to become agentic, engaged individuals who are more intellectually and emotionally equipped to confront, cross, and remap borders between established academic knowledge and experiential knowledge. Through the act of border crossing, professorial capital, particularly discursive and cognitive, is directly challenged. . . .

The everyday dynamics of class exclusion within the academy must be further explored. Just as feminist scholars exposed institutional sexism and racism, the class ceiling must be made visible. I propose that a theory of professorial capital may contribute to developing a greater understanding of how class works in social science and humanities doctoral programs because it explicitly links experience to structure. It is my contention that professorial capital supports the class ceiling through everyday practices. Those of us who identify as members of the working classes who are lucky enough to join the professoriate must work to change the system from the inside. Because of our unique class standpoint (outsiders who have made it in), I believe that we have a responsibility to make class visible.

We did not get an invitation, but it is time to crash the party.

Discussion Questions

1. According to Kosut, how does "professorial capital support the class ceiling through everyday practices"?

2. What is your social class background? How has it influenced your college experience?

Source: "Professorial Capital: Blue-Collar Reflections on Class, Culture, and the Academy" by Mary Kosut, excerpted and with notes & references omitted from *Cultural Studies/Critical Methodologies*, Vol. 6, No. 2, 2006, pp. 245–262. Reprinted by permission of Sage Publications.

PART V

RACE AND ETHNICITY

We turn to issues of race and ethnicity in Part V. Some of the articles here grapple with how race is constructed and interpreted and the repercussions of differing interpretations. Other articles in this section examine, respectively, the changing racial and ethnic makeup of the United States and racial inequality in our school systems.

Social structural factors, like class, are at the heart of Herbert Gans's "Race as Class." Gans makes the case that skin colors and other physical features used to define classes are based on the social class hierarchy of the United States. He points out that the relationship between race and class and the class competition inherent in a capitalist nation like the United States make it very difficult for those on the lowest rung of the racial hierarchy to rise above their position.

We all know that over the past four decades the United States has become more ethnically and racially diverse. However, in "A Distorted Nation: Perceptions of Racial/Ethnic Group Sizes and Attitudes Toward Immigrants and Other Minorities," Richard Alba and his co-authors find that different racial and ethnic groups have starkly different perceptions of the extent of that diversity. Their study reveals that approximately half of all Americans, particularly minority-group members, think that Whites are now a numerical minority (they are not!). The perceptions of White Americans relates to their attitudes toward racial minorities, with those who think there are more minorities in the United States than there really are having the most negative attitudes toward them.

In "College Access, K–12 Concentrated Disadvantage, and the Next 25 Years of Education Research," John Yun and José Moreno look at how racial/ethnic inequality in higher education is related to students' experiences in the K–12 education system. Using data from California, they show that educational disadvantage is clustered in schools with high percentages of racial/ethnic minority students. This inequality in schooling in the pre-college years puts young racial/ethnic minorities at a disadvantage when they apply to enter a college in the race-neutral California higher education system. Yun and Moreno's findings make it obvious that those who want to promote equitable access to higher education should focus first on addressing inequality in the lower grades.

In the last article in this section, "Circles of Influence and Chains of Command: The Social Processes Whereby Ethnic Communities Influence Host Societies," Anthony M. Orum looks at how immigrant groups influence the United States. Much of the earlier sociological literature examined how immigrants adapt to their new nation. However, Orum points out means by which immigrant groups have helped shape the United States.

As you read the articles in this section, keep in mind the following points:

- Race is related to social class.
- Many Americans have a distorted idea of the racial and ethnic makeup of the United States.
- Organized immigrant groups have influenced the United States in many ways.
- Race is a social construction but can have very real consequences on the health and well-being of racial group members.
- Social structural factors influence how racial groups are defined and how they are treated.
- Racial/ethnic inequality in higher education is tied to racial/ethnic inequality in the K–12 system.

CHAPTER 17

Race as Class

Herbert J. Gans

Why does the idea of race continue to exert so much influence in the United States? Because the skin colors and other physical features used to define race were selected precisely because they mirror the country's socioeconomic pecking order.

Humans of all colors and shapes can make babies with each other. Consequently most biologists, who define races as subspecies that cannot interbreed, argue that scientifically there can be no human races. Nonetheless, lay people still see and distinguish between races. Thus, it is worthy asking again why the lay notion of race continues to exist and to exert so much influence in human affairs.

Lay persons are not biologists, nor are they sociologists, who argue these days that race is a social construction arbitrary enough to be eliminated if "society" chose to do so. The laity operates with a very different definition of race. They see that humans vary, notably in skin color, the shape of the head, nose, and lips, and quality of hair, and they choose to define the variations as individual races.

More important, they lay public uses this definition of race to decide whether strangers (the so-called "other") are to be treated as superior, inferior, or equal. Race is even more useful for deciding quickly whether strangers might be threatening and thus should be excluded. Whites often consider dark-skinned strangers threatening until they prove otherwise, and none more than African Americans. . . .

Never mind for the moment that the skin of "whites," as well as many East Asians and Latinos is actually pink; that Native Americans are not red; that most African Americans come in various shades of brown; and that really black skin is rare. Never mind either that

color differences within each of these populations are as great as the differences between them, and that, as DNA testing makes quite clear, most people are racially mixed origins even if they do not know it. But remember that this color palette was invented by whites. Nonwhite people would probably divide the range of skin colors quite differently.

Advocates of racial equality use these contradictions to fight against racism. However, the generate public also has other priorities. As long as people can roughly agree about who looks "white," "yellow," or "black" and find that their notion of race works for their purposes, they ignore its inaccuracies, inconsistencies, and other deficiencies. . . .

Race, Class, and Status

In fact, the skin colors and facial features commonly used to define race are selected precisely because, when arranged hierarchically, they resemble the country's class-and-status hierarchy. Thus, whites are on top of the socioeconomic pecking order as they are on top of the racial one, while variously shaded nonwhites are below them in socioeconomic position (class) and prestige (status).

The darkest people are for the most part at the bottom of the class-status hierarchy. This is no accident, and Americans have therefore always used race as a marker or indicator of both class and status. Sometimes they also use it to enforce class position, to keep some people "in their place." Indeed, these uses are a major reason for its persistence.

Of course, race functions as more than a class marker, and the correlation between race and the socioeconomic pecking order is far from statistically perfect: All races can be found at every level of that order. Still, the race-class correlation is strong enough to utilize race for the general ranking of others. It also becomes more useful for ranking dark-skinned people as white poverty declines so much that whiteness becomes equivalent to being middle or upper class. . . .

True, race is not the only indicator used as a clue to socioeconomic status. Others exist and are useful because they can also be applied to ranking co-racials. They include language (itself a rough indicator of education), dress, and various kinds of taste, from given names to cultural preferences, among others.

American English has no widely known working-class dialect like the English Cockney, although "Brooklynese" is a rough equivalent, as is "black vernacular." Most blue-collar people dress differently at work from white-collar, professional, and managerial workers. Although contemporary American leisure-time dress no longer signifies the wearer's class, middle-income Americans do not usually wear Armani suits or French haute couture, and the people who do can spot the knockoffs bought by the less affluent.

Actually, the cultural differences in language, dress, and so forth that were socially most noticeable are declining. Consequently, race could become yet more useful as a status marker, since it is so easily noticed and so hard to hide or change. And in a society that likes to see itself as classless, race comes in very handy as a substitute. . . .

The Historical Background: African-American Exceptionalism

The only population whose racial features are not automatically perceived differently with upward mobility are African Americans. Those who are affluent and well educated remain as visibly black to whites as before. Although a significant number of African Americans have become middle class since the civil rights legislation of the 1960s, they still suffer from far harsher and more pervasive discrimination and segregation than nonwhite immigrants of equivalent class position. This not only keeps whites and blacks apart but prevents blacks from moving toward quality with whites. In their case, race is used both as a marker of class and, by keeping blacks "in

their place," an enforcer of class position and a brake on upward mobility.

In the white South of the past, African Americans were lynched for being "uppity." Today, the enforcement of class position is less deadly but, for example, the glass ceiling for professional and managerial African Americans is set lower than for Asian Americans, and on-the-job harassment remains routine.

Why African-American upward economic mobility is either blocked or, if allowed, not followed by public blanching of skin color remains a mystery. Many explanations have been proposed for the white exceptionalism with which African Americans are treated. The most common is "racism," an almost innate prejudice against people of different skin color that takes both personal and institutional forms. But this does not tell us why such prejudice toward African Americans remains stronger than that toward other nonwhites. . . .

A better explanation might focus on "Negroid" features. African as well as Caribbean immigrants with such features—for example, West Indians and Haitians—seem to be treated somewhat better than African Americans. But this remains true only for new immigrants; their children are generally treated like African Americans.

Two additional explanations are class-related. For generations, a majority or plurality of all African Americans were poor, and about a quarter still remain so. In addition, African Americans continue to commit a proportionally greater share of the street crime, especially street drug sales—often because legitimate job opportunities are scarce. African Americans are apparently also more often arrested without cause. As one result, poor African Americans are more often considered undeserving than are other poor people, although in some parts of American, poor Hispanics, especially those who are black, are similarly stigmatized.

The second class-based explanation proposes that white exceptionalist treatment of African Americans is a continuing effect of slavery: They are still perceived as ex-slaves. Many hateful stereotypes with which today's African Americans are demonized have changed little from those used to dehumanize the slaves. (Black Hispanics seem to be equally demonized, but then they were also slaves, if not on the North American continent.) Although slavery ended officially in 1864, ever since the end of Reconstruction subtle efforts to discourage African-American upward mobility have not abated, although these efforts are today much less pervasive or effective than earlier.

Some African Americans are now millionaires, but the gap in wealth between average African Americans and whites is much greater than the gap between incomes. The African-American middle class continues to grow, but many of its members barely have a toehold in it, and some are only a few paychecks away from a return to poverty. And the African-American poor still face the most formidable obstacles to upward mobility. Close to a majority of working-age African-American men are jobless or out of the labor force. Many women, including single mothers, now work in the low-wage economy, but they must do without most of the support systems that help middle-class working mothers. Both federal and state governments have been punitive, even in recent Democratic administrations, and the Republicans have cut back nearly every antipoverty program they cannot abolish.

Daily life in a white-dominated society reminds many African Americans that they are perceived as inferiors, and these reminders are louder and more relentless for the poor, especially young men. Regularly suspected of being criminals, they must constantly prove that they are worthy of equal access to the American Dream. For generations, African Americans have watched immigrants pass them in the class hierarchy, and those who are poor must continue to compete with current immigrants for the lowest-paying jobs. If unskilled African Americans reject such jobs or fail to act as deferentially as immigrants, they justify the white belief that they are less deserving than immigrants. Blacks' resentment of such treatment gives whites additional evidence of their unworthiness, thereby justifying another cycle of efforts to keep them from moving up in class and status.

Such practices raise the suspicion that the white political economy and white Americans may, with the help of nonwhites who are not black, use African Americans to anchor the American class structure with a permanently lower-class population. In effect, America, or those making decisions in its name, could be seeking, no necessarily consciously, to establish an undercaste that cannot move out and up. Such undercastes exist in other societies: the gypsies of Eastern Europe, India's untouchables, "indigenous people" and "aborigines" in yet other places. But these are far poorer countries than the United States.

Some Implications

The conventional wisdom and its accompanying morality treat racial prejudice, discrimination, and segregation as irrational social and individual evils that public policy can reduce but only changes in white behavior and values can eliminate. In fact, over the years, white prejudice as measured by attitude surveys has dramatically declined, far more dramatically than behavioral and institutional discrimination.

But what if discrimination and segregation are more than just a social evil? If they are used to keep African Americans down, then they also serve to eliminate or restrain competitors for valued or scarce resources, material and symbolic. Keeping African Americans from decent jobs and incomes as well as quality schools and housing makes more of these available to all the rest of the population. In that case, discrimination and segregation may decline significantly only if the rules of the competition change or if scarce resources, such as decent jobs, become plentiful enough to relax the competition, so that the African-American population can become as predominantly middle class as the white population. Then the stigmas, the stereotypes inherited from slavery, and the social and other arrangements that maintain segregation and discrimination could begin to lose their credibility. Perhaps "black" skin would eventually become as invisible as "yellow" skin is becoming.

Discussion Questions

1. According to Gans, how might "'black' skin . . . become as invisible as 'yellow' skin is becoming?" Do you think this will ever happen? Why or why not?

2. Before reading this article, were you aware that Irish and Italian Americans were once perceived as non-White? Why do you think so few Americans are now aware of this historical fact?

Source: "Race as Class" by Herbert J. Gans, excerpted and with notes & references omitted from *Contexts*, Vol. 4, No. 4, pp. 17–21, Fall, 2005.

CHAPTER 18

A Distorted Nation

Perceptions of Racial/Ethnic Group Sizes and
Attitudes Toward Immigrants and Other Minorities

Richard Alba, Rubén G. Rumbaut, and Karen Marotz

As of 2000, roughly half of Americans, particularly minority-group members, believed that Whites had become a numerical minority. Minority-group respondents' perceptions of the relative sizes of minorities affect their attitudes toward immigrants, Blacks and Hispanics, with those having the most distorted perceptions holding the most negative attitudes.

As Herbert Blumer (1958) famously observed, racial prejudice is connected to a sense of group position. The changing racial and ethnic composition of the United States, spurred largely by contemporary immigration, would seem to challenge the sense of group superiority of native Anglos, i.e., non-Hispanic whites, by altering rapidly and, in some cases, radically the compositions of schools, neighborhoods, workplaces, shopping malls and voting booths. Since immigration resumed on a large scale in the late 1960s, some regions of the United States have undergone remarkable demographic transformations. In California, for example, whites went from two-thirds to less than half of the population between 1980 and 2000. Equally great shifts are forecast for the future; population projections suggest that the numerical dominance of Anglos could end in the nation as a whole by the middle of the century (National res4earch Council 1997). It will certainly end in many cites and metropolitan regions long before that—as indeed it already has in some major urban centers such as Los Angeles, San Francisco, Houston, San Antonio, Miami and New York.

Sociological literature, exemplified by Blalock's (1967) well-known theoretical analysis, has long connected changing racial/ethnic demography with the perception of threat to the majority and the institutionalization of exclusionary barriers to preserve its social privileges (Bobo 1983; Williams 1947). Among those barriers are hostility and other forms of prejudice directed towards demographically expanding minorities. Lincoln Quillian (1995), for example, has found that prejudice against immigrants in European countries varies in accordance with the size of the immigrant population; Fossett and Kiecolt (1989) have found the equivalent linkage in the United States between the black percentage of the population in an area and the anti-black attitudes of its white residents.

Yet between the macro-sociological plane of demographic shift and the micro-level phenomenon of individual prejudice as registered in surveys lies *perception*. How do individuals whose horizons are largely bounded by their everyday social contexts, which may be highly segregated, perceive the changing demography of their society, its potential impact on them, and its effect on the position of the groups to which they belong? Some recent survey research complicates the demography 'threat' prejudice linkage. It finds that many Americans misperceive the sizes of the major racial and ethnic minority groups, inflating their numbers well beyond any demographic reality; whether this is in any way a change from the past cannot be ascertained (Kaiser Family Foundation 2001; Nadeau, Niemi and Levine 1993; Sigelman and Niemi 2001). On one hand, exaggeration of minority-group sizes could be argued to reflect a heightened sense of threat among the members of the majority group (Gallagher 2003). On the other, insofar as these misperceptions are shared by members of majority and minority groups, it suggests that other mechanisms, including cognitive ones, may be at work. . . .

The present paper reexamines the issue of group-size perceptions with data from the 2000 General Social Survey, which asked respondents to estimate the percentage sizes of the major racial/ethnic populations in the United States, including whites. This inclusion of the estimated seize of the majority group allows us to examine group size in a relative sense, which probably corresponds better than the absolute one with the notion of threat in Blumer's and Blalock's frameworks. The General Social Survey also provides a range of attitudinal data about race, which was expanded in the 2000 survey to include additional questions about attitudes toward immigration and immigrant groups. Consequently, we can address how group-size perceptions correspond with the attitudes that respondents hold. . . .

The GSS Data

The General Social Survey is a nationally representative survey of the non-institutionalized, English-speaking population of the Untied States, conducted biannually. For the 2000 version of the survey, the GSS Board of Overseers developed a module entitled "Multi-Ethnic United States," or MEUS, which was intended as a test of new questions on respondent attitudes towards immigration and the racial and ethnic minorities developing from it. The MEUS module was presented to one of the two 2000 samples, or 1,398 respondents. It included a battery of open-ended questions asking respondents to estimate the sizes of racial/ethnic groups, including whites. The instructions to the interviewers emphasized that respondents were to be encouraged to give their best guesses, without worrying about mathematical consistency

Just your best guess—what percentage of the United States population is each group? [INSTRUCTIONS: PERCENTAGES DO NOT HAVE TO ADD UP TO 100% AND THE LISTED GROUPS MAY OVERLAP. ENCOURAGE ESTIMATES FOR ALL GROUPS, BUT DISCOURAGE RESPONDENTS REVISING THEIR ESTIMATES.]

	%
a. Whites	_____
b. Blacks/African-Americans	_____
c. Jews	_____
d. Hispanics or Latin Americans	_____
e. Asian Americans	_____
f. American Indians	_____

A similar set of questions was posed about "the people who live in your community." In addition the survey inquired into a number of immigration- and race-related attitudes. Our analysis draws on these to investigate the consequences of group-size perceptions. One important domain of potential consequences is immigration-related. Here, for example, we will analyze an index constituted by three questions in MEUS that solicited opinions about the consequences of immigration for U.S. society:

What do you think will happen as a result of more immigrants coming to this country? Is each of these results very likely, somewhat likely, not too likely, or not likely at all?

A. Higher crime rates?

B. Making the country more open to new ideas and cultures?

C. People born in the U.S. losing their jobs?

. . . In examining the consequences of group-size perceptions for racial attitudes, we draw on the large repertoire of race-related items in the GSS. Some of these items are parts of rotating sets that are asked of partial samples and thus not of all MEUS respondents. (For a discussion of the rotation and the "ballot" design of the survey, see Davis, Smith and Marsden 2001: 1527–7). Illustrative of the kinds of attitudes we analyze is:

Here are some opinions other people have in connection with Black-white relations. Which statement on the card comes closest to how you yourself, feel?

A. African Americans shouldn't push themselves where they are not wanted. (Responses are: Agree strongly, agree slightly, disagree slightly, disagree strongly.)

The Problem of Innumeracy

Inspection of the estimates given by respondents reveals a significant problem of innumeracy, of numbers that are highly implausible as perceptions of group sizes. Some respondents, it appears, cannot easily translate their perceptions into numerical terms or they have very imprecise perceptions. Thus, there are respondents who provide the same estimate for every group or estimate one group to be 100 percent (or 0 percent).

A consistent problem throughout the estimates is a lack of precision; respondents are, after all, not usually demographers. They tend to give estimates that are divisible by 5 when they are not divisible by 10. In fact, some 60 percent of the estimates are multiples of 10. Further, respondents seem to be wary of underestimating groups' sizes: and thus half of the estimates of minority-group size are 20 percent or more. Thus, there are patterns in the way respondents express themselves in numbers that would appear to inflate minority group sizes, especially for the smaller groups such as Asians and American Indians. . . . The Asian percentage of the population ere counted at not quite 4 percent in the 2000 Census, but two-thirds of the GSS respondents estimated it to be at least 10 percent.

The ramifications of these tendencies are made clear when one adds up the estimates for the groups of the so-called ethno-racial pentagon (Hollinger 1995), the five mutually exclusive categories that should include virtually everyone in the U.S. population (whites, blacks, Hispanics, Asians and American Indians); the percentages add up to nearly 150 percent on average for GSS respondents.

This brief overview of numeracy (and innumeracy) issues leads to three conclusions: (1) the estimates of some respondents are highly implausible as reports of their perceptions of sociological reality; (2) the absolute sizes of the estimates of minority-group size are untrustworthy and need to be related to some other magnitude, most plausibly, the respondent's estimate of the size of the majority population; (3) and the estimate of the smallest minorities, Asians, American Indians and Jews, tend to be more error-prone than the others. For the last two reasons, our analysis will focus on the relative sizes of the black and Hispanic populations compared to non-Hispanic whites—that is, of the two largest minorities, who together comprised about 25 percent of the total U.S. population in the 2000 Census, compared to the majority population, which comprised 70 percent.

The "Endangered" White Majority

Although respondents tended to overstate minority-group size, they did not do the same for whites.

Indeed, . . . they tended instead to underestimate the white percentage of the population. The 2000 Census showed whites to be almost 70 percent of U.S. residents. (We assume that, for most respondents, "whites" do not include Hispanics; if respondents are using the term in the literal sense of demographers would give it, thus including white Hispanics, then the degree of misperception of the majority group's size obviously worsens.) If, as a rough measure of an accurate estimate, we accept any in the 60- to 80-percent range, then slightly more than half of the sample has a good grasp of the white proportion. While a small group of respondents overestimates whites' size, a substantial group—nearly 40 percent of respondents—thinks that whites make up a significantly smaller part of the population than they do in reality.

Thus, the tendency to overstate minority-group size combined with that to understate whites' population proportion does indeed suggest that many respondents exaggerate the sizes of minority groups. In fact, these two tendencies combined suggest further that, for some respondents, whites' majority status is in question. . . .

Nearly 20 percent of the respondents depict whites as a minority in an absolute sense, estimating their population percentage to be less than 50. An even greater number of respondents assigns whites a population share of at least 50 percent, but nevertheless presents them as a minority relative to blacks, Hispanics or a combination of the two. Thus, 6 percent believe that one of these two minority groups—usually blacks—is at least as large as whites; an additional 23 percent believe that the two minority groups together outnumber whites. Obviously, this last fraction would increase further if we added Asians and American Indians into the mix. Thus, a conclusion that roughly half of Americans no longer perceive whites to be the majority seems fair.

To some extent, this incorrect perception is a result of minority respondents overestimating the size of their own groups, Table 1 shows how respondents belonging to the three largest racial/ethnic populations perceive, on average, the composition of the population. (There are too few Asian and American Indian respondents in the GSS sample to include their estimates here.) For whites' percentage of the population, Blacks and Hispanics give slightly, but not significantly, lower average estimates than whites do. Blacks appear to give slightly higher estimates of their own percentage of the population, while Hispanics more substantially overestimate their fraction. (For similar results, see Kaiser Family Foundation 2001: 4.) Members of all three groups overestimate the Asian and American Indian percentages, but Hispanics appear to do so to a slightly greater extent.

Table 1   Mean Group-size Estimates by Race/Ethnicity of Respondents

	% White	% Black	% Hispanic	% Asian	% American Indian	N
Estimated by:						
Whites	58.8	29.1	22.3	15.7	12.2	945
Blacks	56.4	37.8	27.1	20.3	16.0	158
Hispanics	56.6	34.8	39.3	26.8	20.3	94
F statistic	2.27	15.57**	31.81***	19.31**	10.28***	
df	(3/1230)	(3/1230)	(3/1230)	(3/1204)	(3/1196)	

Source: General Social Survey, 2000.

***p < .001.

The Impact of Residential Contexts on Perceptions of National Demography

An individual's everyday social context is a likely source of his or her perceptions of the sizes of different groups, and earlier research has supported the hypothesis that the racial/ethnic demography of the residential area exerts a substantial influence on these perceptions (Nadeau, Niemi and Levine 1993). However, on theoretical grounds, the relationship has been argued in two ways: on one hand, some researchers have suggested that the perceptions of relative group sizes in the society as a whole are the results of faulty generalizations from everyday experience, ad this is what Nadeau, Niemi and Levine (1993) in fact found; on the other, it can be argued that exaggerated estimates of group sizes result from lack of intergroup contacts and thus an absence of the realism introduced by experience (Gallagher 2003). Either way, one could attribute distorted perceptions of the nation's racial and ethnic composition to the high levels of residential segregation in the United States (Logan 2001).

In the GSS, we find that the most usable measures of local context stem from a series of questions, paralleling those on national group sizes that call for perceptions of the sizes of different groups in "your community." In Comparison to perceptions of groups at the national level, perceptions of groups in the neighborhood appear to be much better grounded, and the estimates have far greater numerical plausibility. As Table 2 reveals, the average perceived size of whites is 67 percent. This is obviously not much below the percentage one would expect on the basis of whites' percentage of the population. Likewise, at

20 and 14 percent, the estimates of blacks' and Hispanics' sizes are more realistic than is the case for the national estimates. As a consequence, the sum of the estimates for the five populations in the ethno-racial pentagon averages 112 percent, close to the ideal of 100 percent.

Table 2   Mean Group-size Estimates for Community and Nation

Race/ethnicity:	% in Community	% in Nation
Whites	66.5 (1,223)	58.4 (1,234)
Blacks	19.7 (1,205)	30.8 (1,234)
Hispanics	14.4 (1,184)	24.2 (1,234)
Asians	7.2 (1,173)	17.2 (1,208)
American Indians	4.6 (1,155)	13.4 (1,200)

Source: General Social Survey, 2000.

Note: Ns in parentheses.

The demographic composition of their neighborhoods, as respondents see it, is quite powerfully related to the perceptions they have of groups in the national population. . . . More specifically, these influences stem from perceptions of minority-group sizes rather than perceptions of the white population. The latter may be redundant here because, given the apparently greater realism of the neighborhood perceptions, whites' proportion among residents is, at least in an approximate sense, implied by the minority-group proportions. In any event, adding the estimated neighborhood percentages of blacks and Hispanics to the equation predicting the logged ratio of minority to majority sizes in the nation substantially raises the explained variance.

The Consequences of Perceived Group Sizes for Attitudes

So far, the analysis has treated the distorted perceptions of group sizes as "error." . . . The question now to be addressed is whether these misperceptions make any sociological difference: are they echoed, for example, in the attitudes that respondents hold about racial and ethnic diversity, as one would expect from the theoretical reasoning of Blalock and Blumer, cited earlier? We adhere to this reasoning by limiting the analysis to members of the racial/ethnic majority group, i.e., non-Hispanic whites, who are presumably threatened by increasing minority-group size in ways that members of the minority groups are not.

There are two "objects" for which we examine attitudes: immigrants and immigration, and African Americans. . . .

[A]nalyses demonstrate that perceptions of group sixes bear fairly systematic relationships to what majority-group respondents think about immigration and racial minorities, although the effects are of moderate strength at best. . . . [R]espondents' perceptions of immigration become more unfavorable as their perceptions of group sizes tilt away from whites' majority status.

Accordingly, attitudes toward continued immigration are shaped by perceptions of contemporary demography. The larger that non-Hispanic whites perceived minority groups to have grown in numbers relative to themselves, the more they desire to see immigration restrictions imposed. Moreover, the perception of threat implicit in distorted perceptions of group sizes corresponds to a hierarchy in the majority group's preferences for immigrants. The effect of logged ratio on the desire for immigration restriction is greatest for Latin American immigrants and least for those from Europe, with immigrants from Asia in between.

The impact on attitudes towards racial minorities is more scattered than is true with respect to immigration. . . . One leitmotif in the items where effects appear concerns the potential for minority intrusion in the social worlds of persons ethnically like the respondents. Thus, the logged ratio is associated with responses to the statement, "African-Americans shouldn't push themselves where they're not wanted." The more distorted their perceptions of group sizes, the more likely white respondents are to agree with the statement and to do so strongly. The same holds for agreement that they are hurt by affirmative action. ("What do you think the chances are these days that a white person won't get a job or promotion while an equally- or less-qualified black person gets one instead?") The only set of stereotypes that appears to be affected by misperceptions of group sizes concerns minority violence. Respondents who perceive minorities as dominant in the national population tend also to believe that blacks and Hispanics are more violent than average. . . .

Conclusion

This research demonstrates that many Americans have highly distorted perceptions of the racial and ethnic composition of the United States; and that these distortions are of consequence for the attitudes they hold towards immigration and immigrant groups and towards other minorities. The extent of the distortion is revealed by our rough approximation that in the year 2000, about half of Americans believed that whites were already a minority in the total population. This belief was held even more by members of minority groups than by whites themselves.

As other research has also found, the misperceptions about group sizes are related to the everyday social environments in which respondents live: the more they encounter members of racial and ethnic minorities in their communities, the larger they perceive these groups to be on the national plane. This finding does not imply, however, that the attitudinal effects of group-size perceptions are attributable to community contexts. Our analyses show that, even with the compositions of these contexts controlled, misperceptions have significant influences on attitudes for members of the majority group.

We have improved upon past research by uncovering a confounding between numeracy, or numerical ability, and perceptions of racial and ethnic group sizes. This occurs when the measure of perception of group size is formulated in terms of absolute, rather than relative, numbers. Future research should probably include an independent measure of numerical ability to disentangle the two phenomena. In addition, our testing of the linkage between group-size perceptions and attitudes has been more systematic than in the past, and in particular we have shown for the first time a substantial connection to attitudes towards immigrants and immigration. Given the huge impact of immigration on the demography of the nation, this connection may carry large implications for attitudinal divisions in the future.

It appears to us that this research leads to an additional, quite practical conclusion. For as long as social scientists have investigated forms of prejudice, they have recommended educational programs to counteract it (Allport 1954). By now, the persistence of prejudice in the face of decades of educational effort has led to a jaundiced view of the benefits. However, in this case, misperceptions truly appear to have consequences that could be addressed by better information.

Social scientists themselves may have to take some of the blame for these misperceptions. In their own zeal to prepare Americans for the racial and ethnic changes that are likely in the next decades, they have emphasized or allowed others to emphasize, scenarios stemming from population projections for 2050. These scenarios, moreover, tend to reify the broadest racial and ethnic categories (e.g., "white" and "Asian"), thus overlooking their historically contingent nature and the likelihood that they will change as the underlying demography of the united States does. A consequence of the emphasis on projections a half century into the future is that even some generally well-informed Americans appear confused about the nation's demography, as is apparent in this passage written in 1998 by the historian Garry Wills:

> The explosion of ethnic diversity guarantees that affirmative action of some sort will be needed so that everyone feels a stake in a country that is literally changing complexion everyday: *whites will be a minority by early in the next century.* (Wills 1998: 67, our emphasis)

Unlike Wills, many Americans appear to feel less welcoming towards affirmative action as a result of misperceiving whites' continuing majority status. Their attitudes are better summarized by Ron Unz, the Silicon Valley entrepreneur who spearheaded Proposition 227 in California, "English for the Children," which drastically limited bilingual education. In "California and the End of White America" (1999). Unz saw two possible ethnic futures, both shaped by "the political reality of a shrinking white minority:" the assimilationism of a "new American melting pot" (represented by his Proposition 227), or "the coming of white nationalism" (represented incipiently by Proposition 187, the 1994 anti-immigrant "Save Our State"

initiative, which passed with 59 percent of the statewide vote, but was ruled unconstitutional by the courts). Both visions are focused on a world in which "Americans of European ancestry fall increasingly into minority status during the first half of the new century." Blumer (1958) might have seen both as reactions to a felt challenge to a historically evolved sense of group position.

Perhaps, with less emphasis on a hypothetical demography 45 years in the future and based on fixed racial/ethnic classifications, and more on contemporary demography and the changes to be anticipated in the near term, the widespread misperceptions and their attitudinal consequences could begin to be addressed. While bigotry cannot be eliminated by education alone, the perceptual distortion of the nation, which exacerbates prejudice, may be reduced with such corrective lenses. Such a correction would be a contribution, however modest, to the creation of conditions under which the sense of group position recedes and racial prejudice declines.

Discussion Questions

1. What do the authors mean when they say "social scientists, themselves, may have to take some of the blame for these misperceptions about racial/ethnic group size"? What is problematic about making projections about racial demographics?

2. What is the connection between White Americans' attitudes toward continued immigration and distorted perception of racial/ethnic group sizes? How does this finding relate to the current national debate about immigration?

CHAPTER 19

College Access, K–12 Concentrated Disadvantage, and the Next 25 Years of Education Research

John T. Yun and José F. Moreno

Clustered inequality in California's K–12 schools puts young racial/ethnic minorities at a disadvantage when they apply to enter a college in the race-neutral California higher education system. Those who want to promote equitable access to higher education should focus first on addressing inequality in the lower grades.

The U.S. Supreme Court decisions in *Gratz v. Bollinger* (2003) and *Grutter v. Bollinger* (2003) allowed colleges and universities to continue using race and ethnicity as a part of their admissions processes in order to ensure a racially and ethnically diverse learning environment for students. While using racially inclusive affirmative action can be an important policy tool for preserving equitable access to selective colleges and universities, access to such institutions does not begin and end simply at the point of admissions. Ultimately, access to higher education depends on many factors, including the interaction between K–12 systems (wherein students acquire the tools and credentials to support their college applications) and university admissions policies-an interaction in which inequalities can be either acknowledged and mitigated or propagated and solidified. In fact, the majority opinion in Grutter acknowledges the importance of the K–12 system in higher education admissions. In that opinion, Justice Sandra Day O'Connor wrote: ". . . . [I]t remains the current reality that many minority students encounter markedly inadequate and unequal educational opportunities. . . . As lower school education in minority communities improves, an increase in the number of such students [among college applicants] may be anticipated" (2003, p. 346).

Supporting O'Connor's analysis of educational systems, the literature on the factors that contribute to K–12 inequities is extensive. Over the past several decades, scholars have documented the effects that various types of disadvantage—such as racial/ethnic segregation (Hanushek, Kain, & Rivkin, 2002; Orfield & Yun, 1999; Rumberger & Palardy, 2005), economic background (Coleman, Campbell, Hobson, McPartland, Mood, Weinfeld, et al. 1966; Kahlenberg, 2001; Kreuger, Rothstein, & Turner, 2004), difficulty with English (Gandara, 2000), shortage of qualified teachers (Darling-Hammond, 2000), and limited access to college-prep curricula—have on equitable schooling outcomes, as well as their impact on college access (Oakes, Rogers, Silver, Horng, & Goode, 2004). While the educational equity literature about the independent impact of these factors is expansive, few studies have simultaneously examined the impact on educational outcomes of multiple layers of disadvantage combined with race/ethnicity and class.

Recent studies have begun addressing these issues of concentrated schooling disadvantage within racially/ethnically isolated schools. Using California Department of Education data, Oakes et al. (2004) and Teranishi, Allen, and Solorzano (2004) document the separate and unequal schooling conditions that undermine educational equity. Specifically, Oakes et al. (2004) found that, on average,

Latino and African American students attend schools where 81% and 78% of students, respectively, are nonWhite; and that 63% of White students attend majority-White schools. Further, Oakes et al. found that "the worst school conditions and fewest educational opportunities converge in the State's racially isolated schools. . . . Forty-two percent of predominantly non-white schools have several opportunity problems, compared with only 7 percent of majority-white schools" (p. i). Reporting similar findings, Teranishi et al. (2004) examined the relationship of these school-structured inequalities to college admissions criteria and college participation in California's public higher education system. They found that students across all racial/ethnic groups who attended majority Latino and/or African American schools had lower college eligibility and participation rates, fewer advanced placement (AP) courses, and fewer experienced teachers, than did students from White-majority schools. Despite these studies, which begin to explore this phenomenon, most researchers have either ignored concentrations of disadvantage or attempted to isolate individual factors to explore how each independently affects the measures of student achievement used in college eligibility and admissions decisions.

The purpose of this article is twofold: first, to present a methodology—cluster analysis—that may be used to conduct exploratory analyses describing concentrated disadvantages in the K–12 system in a more complex and nuanced way than previous analyses do; and, second, to examine how such findings can be used to generate, as well as answer, questions about the link between the K–12 system and college access. For this article we operationalize concentrated disadvantage multidimensionally, reflecting a combination of various types of schooling disadvantage (e.g., high proportion of English learners [EL], high percentage of students eligible for free or reduced-price lunch, lack of AP and college preparation classes, poor teacher preparation, and racial/ethnic isolation) generally cited as being related to negative schooling outcomes. We examine whether these negative outcomes are concentrated in ways and at levels that affect students differentially vis-à-vis university eligibility. It is important to note that, although we examine the impact of concentrated disadvantage by race/ethnicity, we do not mean to imply that disadvantage is a function of the presence of minority students or that particular racial/ethnic groups are culturally deficient. Instead, we focus on whether these disadvantages cluster together disproportionately in schools where racial isolation is prevalent. Our findings suggest that concentrated disadvantage in the K–12 system, combined with rigid university eligibility criteria,

create differential opportunities to attend public universities in California. We further posit that opportunity differentials affect students unequally by race/ethnicity and that these inequitable opportunities to attend public universities can further exacerbate already critical issues of racial/ethnic inequality.

The questions that we chose to guide this exploration of our cluster analysis and to operationalize our purpose are as follows: How are selected schooling disadvantages in California's public schools clustered? Using these clusters, what can we learn about how these schooling disadvantages interact with eligibility requirements for the University of California (UC) and California State University (CSU)? What can this approach tell us about the racial/ethnic distribution of these disadvantages? And finally, what are the implications of these results for educational policy and for Justice O'Connor's goal, as stated in the *Grutter* decision, of eliminating the use of race in admissions decisions within 25 years?

The California Context

California is an ideal site for this exploratory analysis for three reasons. First, as the country becomes more racially/ethnically diverse, it is important to examine the interactions between diversity and the public schools. California is a highly diverse state in which nearly 6.3 million students were enrolled in the K–12 system during the 2003–2004 school year, with enrollments approximately 46% Latino, 33% White, 11% Asian, 8% African American, and 1% American Indian (California Department of Education, n.d.). Given the level of racial/ethnic diversity in the state, California is an important exemplar that should be examined as other states experience similar racial/ethnic demographic changes.

Second, California has a clearly articulated and well-defined higher education eligibility and admissions policy. The Master Plan for Higher Education, adopted in 1960, established admissions eligibility criteria that called for the UC system to admit the top 12.5% of California high school graduates, the CSU system to admit the top 33%, and the Community Colleges to serve as open enrollment institutions. The criteria for establishing these tiered admissions policies included a highly structured course-taking pattern, grade point average in those courses, and scores on standardized tests (SAT or ACT). Using these criteria, the CSU and UC systems have established an eligibility index whereby students with high enough grade point averages in A–G courses[1] and high enough overall SAT or ACT scores are guaranteed a seat by the Master Plan. However, this plan, while egalitarian on its face, has resulted in important gaps in college access by race and ethnicity (Moreno, 1999; Spring, 1994). For example, in the most current analysis of UC/CSU eligibility rates in the state, the California Postsecondary Education Commission found that while 14% and 29% of California public high school students were UCor CSU-eligible, respectively, only 6% to 7% of African American, American Indian, and Latino students were eligible for UC admission and only 16% to 20% were eligible for CSU admission. What is most startling is that, combined, these three groups make up 42% of high school graduates in California (California Postsecondary Education Commission, 2004).

Finally, California, as prohibited in state law by Proposition 209, may not explicitly use race/ethnicity in its higher education admissions formula. The ability of California's schoolchildren to reach the Master Plan's goal of "universal access" is largely predicated on all students having an equal opportunity to compete for a place among the top 12.5% for UC admissions or the top 33% for CSU admissions. Without an equal starting line, such standards, in the absence of racially/ethnically inclusive admissions policies, may make the goal of universal access largely unattainable for those racial/ethnic groups faced with multiple disadvantages within their school settings. Given the important implications of college access policies, California's size, demographic composition, and policy environment present an important opportunity to examine how all of these conditions come together to structure disadvantage or opportunity for all public school students in California interested in attending its public colleges and universities.

To describe the structure of opportunity in K–12 education we analyzed publicly available school-level data, which include data on all public schools in California, from the California Department of Education. California collects and makes available school data drawn from its California Basic Education Data System through numerous sources using many different templates. We have chosen to merge data using both the School Accountability Report Card (SARC) and the state's Web-based Data Quest tool. Because we are looking specifically at college eligibility in relation to the quality of K–12 educational settings, we chose to examine only public high schools. We determined our sample by choosing all schools that had 12th-grade students enrolled. We further restricted our sample by dropping schools with enrollments below the 5th percentile in enrollment (schools

with fewer than 62 students), to better represent institutions that were comprehensive high schools and not smaller special program schools. After restrictions, we were left with 899 schools in our sample, which represents 95% of all comprehensive public high schools in California.

An Exploration of Concentrated Disadvantage

To describe the patterns of concentrated disadvantage present in California's public high schools by racial/ethnic group, and to highlight the value added of using an exploratory cluster analysis, we first provide a descriptive reading of the data, followed by our cluster approach. In this descriptive approach we calculate average school characteristics weighted by the number of students attending those schools by race/ethnicity. This allows us to examine the composition of the "average" school attended by the "average student" of a particular race/ethnicity. To provide a more complex picture of the schooling geography, we then introduce cluster analysis, a more novel strategy to identifying school-based inequities. Cluster analysis[3] allows us to classify schools into similar groups given observable characteristics (Afifi & Clark, 1996; Aldenderfer & Blashfield, 1984)—in this case, characteristics that have been linked to student success and failure, such as percentage of students eligible for free and reduced lunch, percentage who are English language learners, percentage of certified teachers, and degree of school racial/ethnic isolation. . . . This technique allows us to examine the types of school characteristics that tend to cluster together, how large such clusters are, and what types of schools fall within these clusters. How these characteristics cluster in schools captures the type of disadvantage that students in those environments face. For instance, students who attend schools where they are racially isolated, with relatively low numbers of certified teachers, few AP classes, and large numbers of English language learners, are likely to attend schools that are overtaxed in their attempt to meet the requirements for university eligibility. This situation creates potentially greater challenges for schools than would high levels of any single disadvantage. In addition, some characteristics may factor more heavily in the equation than others. For instance, do schools that have high numbers of English learners but no other factors associated with differential educational outcomes have lower levels of college eligibility indicators when compared with schools with high numbers of free/reduced-lunch-eligible students? In short, we ask the question, Are all "risk" factors considered equal? These substantive questions help us to define our clusters conceptually by defining levels of educational disadvantage.

Once we define our clusters empirically and conceptually, we confirm their existence by applying the technique of discriminant analysis, which allows us to use the school racial/ethnic enrollments and measures of disadvantage to build a model that predicts school assignment into particular clusters. Using this method, we can measure the extent of misclassification of schools into their clusters and provide support for their further use in the analysis. Once they are specified and validated, we then use these clusters to examine "achievement indicators" of schools (e.g., percentage of students completing college-prep course-taking pattern, percentage who are proficient-to-advanced on state exams, percentage taking the SAT) across the clusters and compare those indicators with the racial/ ethnic school enrollments to examine whether particular types of disadvantage are differentially experienced by students of different racial/ethnic backgrounds. Finally, we suggest subsequent analyses that may illuminate how particular types of students interact with particular clusters of concentrated disadvantage. It should be noted that cluster analysis can result in many different results depending on the specification of the input variables. Because of this variation, we present the clusters in an exploratory manner to highlight the limitation of previous research that applies race, class, school curriculum, teacher qualifications, and language proficiency as if they were independent factors each unaffected by the presence of the others. Our exploratory presentation is intended to suggest alternative avenues of important research.

Implications for Educational Access and Equity

To address the implications for access and equity of our analytic approach, we first need to ask the question, How are schooling disadvantages in California's public schools clustered? . . . Previous studies showing the schooling experiences of the "average" student of each racial group [found that on] average, White students' schooling environments have the most positive outcomes and the lowest levels of disadvantage but have high levels of racial isolation (55.4%), second only to Latino students (57.8%). In addition, the average Black or Latino student shows the highest level of disadvantage and the lowest average level of positive outcomes. For example, the average experience

for all students in our sample would be a school with 36.0% of its students eligible for free/reduced lunch (FLE),[2] 15.8% English learners, 87.3% of its teachers certified, and 36.7% of graduates completing A–G courses, as well as 41.2% of students taking the SAT. When compared with other groups, the average White student would attend a school with much lower percentages of FLE students (22.9%) and English learners (9.0%). In addition, the average White student attends a school with a higher percentage of certified teachers (91.0%) and a higher percentage of graduates completing A–G courses (40.0%). Black and Latino students face a substantially different reality, in schools with an average of 42.3% and 48.5% FLE students, respectively, and 16.6% and 22.5% English learners. When compared with their White counterparts, Black and Latino students also attend schools with a lower percentage of certified teachers and A–G completers. While these differences may not seem large (approximately 7 percentage points), when they are seen as an average number across the entire state, they are substantial. Asian students show an interesting pattern distinct from all other groups. They seemingly have the best outcomes (42.1% A–G completion and 48.5% SAT participation) of all students. They also have higher percentages of poor students (31.5%) and EL students (15.0%) in their schools than White students, but lower percentages of these disadvantages when compared with Black and Latino students.

These numbers reflect the literature cited earlier and describe substantive differences in educational opportunity distributed by race/ethnicity. However, because such descriptive analysis can hide patterns of advantage and disadvantage that are created because of uneven distributions of students across schools, other types of analysis that can detect these distributional variations are necessary. One methodology that can provide such vision is cluster analysis.

The clusters that we identified within the data are specified in Table 1. To form our groupings, we used the percentage for each racial/ethnic group (including multiracial, which we omitted from the table for space), percentage of EL, percentage of FLE, percentage of certified teachers, and number of AP courses offered. Each of these school characteristics was selected because it was readily available in the state data and because each represents an important aspect of school disadvantage. For instance, percentage of FLE has been widely used as an important factor in the assessment of school quality because the association between schools with large proportions of poor students and poor academic performance is well established. We also use the number of AP courses to reflect opportunities for students to take high-level courses in the school. We use courses instead of classes in our analysis because we believe that the opportunity to learn is related to the presence of a course (i.e., AP English), while many classes of the same course (i.e., five sections of AP English) may simply be reflective of school size. We isolated nine clusters in the data and validated their existence by using discriminant analysis. With this process, we found that approximately 85% of the schools were assigned properly in their clusters. This analysis provides some empirical evidence that the clusters do exist in the data. However, our goal for this article is more modest than establishing the correct clusters to specify all of California's public schools. We intend only to demonstrate the usefulness of this approach and to show the various type of information that can be obtained using the technique. In fact, because our aim is exploratory and in some fashion generative of questions for research, we argue that robustness of cluster specification is not the most important value in this research approach. Indeed, the most important factor may be the uncovering of various lenses with which to view the opportunities and barriers faced by schools and the students attending those schools. Thus the exact nature of the clusters is not as important as the descriptive information that we can derive from the analysis.

In Table 1, the "Cluster Description" column represents a substantive understanding of the cluster's mean characteristics. The cluster types were described by racial/ethnic composition, percentage of EL students, percentage of students who were poor (defined by free-lunch eligibility, or FLE), percentage of certified teachers, and number of AP courses . . . The "low," "mid," and "high" labels were created using quartiles with the bottom quartile representing low levels of racial isolation, the middle two quartiles representing the mid group, and the top quartile representing high levels of racial isolation. These cluster labels are in many ways subjective, but they are reasonable given the average values of the school cluster characteristics.

Note also in Table 1 that more than 601,000 students (nearly 37% of high school students) attended isolated White schools (Cluster 3) without substantial levels of schooling disadvantage. The percentage of EL students is substantially higher in Clusters 5 through 9, schools with larger numbers of Latino students, and highest in Cluster 7, the hyper-isolated Latino schools. Notably, there are two clusters of Latino–White schools, Clusters 4 and 8, both with only mid-levels of EL students (~12%) despite the fact that these clusters have 40.8% and 33.5% Latino enrollment, respectively. However both

types of schools differ with respect to poverty levels and access to AP courses, with Cluster 4 averaging 31.1% free-lunch-eligible students and an average of 8.4 AP courses, while Cluster 8 averaged 64.6% free-lunch-eligible students and an average of 3.9 AP courses. Clearly these school clusters, which are so similar in racial/ethnic enrollment and EL proportions, differ in important ways with respect to educational access—ways that would not have been exposed in the previous aggregate analysis. This nuance is true for Asian students as well.

Asian students appear in their largest proportions in Clusters 1 and 5, Asian–White schools and Asian–Latino schools; however the students attending Asian–White schools are exposed to substantially lower levels of schooling disadvantage than those attending Asian–Latino schools—another important finding that would have been hidden by more traditional methods of analysis.

Given the clusters that we have isolated, what can we learn about how these selective schooling disadvantages interact with eligibility requirements for the UC and CSU? What can this approach tell us about the racial/ethnic distribution of these disadvantages? To address these questions, we sorted our clusters by our chosen outcome measure of educational opportunity as measured by percentage of graduates who completed the A–G requirements for UC/CSU eligibility. This outcome is critical to the university participation of students in California because UC/CSU eligibility is dependent on the completion of these requirements; students who do not complete them have not met minimum requirements for eligibility and thus are simply ineligible for UC/CSU admission. We also report percentage of graduates who took the SAT, the mean combined SAT scores of graduates in these clusters, and the mean percentage of students scoring in the "proficient" and "advanced" categories on the California high school exit examination. SAT scores can be seen as demonstrating the link to access because they are required for eligibility and admission to the UC/CSU system; and the state test results can be used as a measure of how well a school is preparing students to graduate because the state exam is intended to be a requirement for graduation. If fewer students pass the test and thus fewer graduate from certain schools, the level of access to higher education for students who attend those schools is certainly compromised. In this context, Table 2 provides a picture that shows much larger differences in higher education opportunity and access by race/ethnicity than [the picture from previous studies] and enables us to examine the mean levels of these opportunity indicators by the

Table 1 Descriptive Statistics Characterizing the Fitted School Clusters, 2003–2004

Cluster	Cluster Description	Enrollment	Number of Schools	% Asian	% Black	% Latino	% White	% EL	% FLE	% Certified Teachers	Number of AP Courses[a]
Cluster 1	Asian–White schools, low-EL, low-poverty, high-teacher-certification, high AP	78,549	39	52.7	3.5	11.0	31.1	8.1	11.5	91.3	11.6
Cluster 2	Isolated Black schools, mid-EL, mid-poverty, low-teacher-certification, mid-AP	15,227	9	5.3	63.8	27.7	2.5	12.3	40.1	77.3	7.3
Cluster 3	Isolated White schools, low-EL, low-poverty, high-teacher-certification, mid-AP	601,620	376	7.3	3.2	17.1	68.5	5.2	17.2	92.1	8.0
Cluster 4	Latino–White schools, mid-EL, mid-poverty, mid-teacher-certification, mid-AP	330,698	159	12.9	11.7	40.8	32.8	13.5	31.1	87.1	8.4
Cluster 5	Asian–Latino Schools, high-EL, high-poverty, mid-teacher-certification, mid-AP	108,553	52	40.5	15.1	31.7	11.3	23.2	50.3	88.9	8.2
Cluster 6	Isolated Latino schools, high-EL, high-poverty, mid-teacher-certification, mid-AP	306,402	145	8.3	6.2	69.8	14.9	25.7	57.1	83.7	8.0
Cluster 7	Hyper-isolated Latino schools, high-EL, high-poverty, low-teacher-certification, mid-AP	130,934	51	2.6	3.1	90.6	3.3	41.6	77.9	78.8	7.7

(Continued)

Table 1 (Continued)

Cluster	Cluster Description	Enrollment	Number of Schools	% Asian	% Black	% Latino	% White	% EL	% FLE	% Certified Teachers	Number of AP Courses[a]
Cluster 8	Latino–White schools, mid-EL, high-poverty, mid-teacher-certification, low-AP	37,078	43	3.9	3.9	33.5	48.2	11.5	64.6	88.1	3.9
Cluster 9	Latino–Black Schools, high-EL, high-poverty, low-teacher-certification, low-AP	36,377	25	4.9	28.6	60.9	4.3	29.4	58.7	50.4	4.5

Note: We chose to drop American Indians from this table because on average they made up less than 1% of each cluster. Data are from the California Department of Education SARC Data, 2003–2004, for public use.

a. We use courses instead of classes because the presence of a course indicates opportunity, whereas multiple classes may simply be reflective of school size.

N = 899.

Table 2   Factors of Disadvantage and Achievement by Cluster Type and Percentage of Each Racial/Ethnic Group Attending Each School Type, 2003–2004

Cluster	Measures of School Quality and Opportunity					Percentage of Students Attending Cluster Type by Race/Ethnicity				
	% Graduates A–G Completers	% Seniors Taking SAT	Mean SAT Total	% Advanced/ Proficient in ELA	% Advanced/ Proficient in Math	% Asian	% American Indian	% Black	% Latino	% White
Cluster 1	59.7	69.1	1131.4	63.3	48.1	19.3	2.3	2.1	1.3	4.0
Cluster 2	51.5	58.4	803.1	16.8	2.3	0.3	0.3	7.5	0.7	0.1
Cluster 3	39.7	44.3	1059.4	49.3	24.8	24.2	54.8	16.9	17.0	65.7
Cluster 4	35.7	38.7	980.6	36.1	14.7	19.6	16.7	30.7	20.3	17.9
Cluster 5	35.5	42.9	934.0	30.6	17.0	20.4	5.6	12.3	5.2	2.0
Cluster 6	30.0	31.9	902.5	23.6	9.6	12.7	11.0	15.9	32.1	7.1
Cluster 7	25.7	33.7	824.9	15.0	6.4	1.6	1.4	3.7	18.1	0.4
Cluster 8	22.2	31.4	961.4	30.1	12.4	1.0	7.3	1.7	2.1	2.7
Cluster 9	15.6	33.2	791.6	9.9	3.1	1.0	0.5	9.2	3.2	0.1
Overall average	35.9	40.9	988.0	38.1	18.7	100.1[a]	99.9[a]	100.0	100.0	100.0

Note: ELA = English Language Arts. Data are from the California Department of Education SARC Data, 2003–2004, for public use.

a. Numbers may not add up to 100% because of rounding.

N = 899.

149

proportion of students of various racial/ethnic groups who have access to these public high schools.

First, it is important to note that the two types of schools that have the highest levels of A–G completion (above 50%) are extremely different from one another. Cluster 1 averages low levels of all categories of disadvantage (Table 1) and the highest levels of achievement across all of our measures (Table 2). Nearly 20% of all Asian students attend these schools, whereas, overall, only about 5% of all students attend them. Cluster 2 represents isolated Black schools with similarly high levels of A–G course completers and seniors taking the SAT; however, the mean SAT scores of these two clusters differ by more than 300 points, and fewer than 17% of students in Cluster 2 are advanced or proficient in English Language Arts; fewer than 3% of students are either advanced or proficient in math on the state exit examination. This school cluster enrolls 7.5% of all Black students even though it enrolls only 1% of students overall. The differences between these two school types is vast and suggests that there may be many ways for schools to facilitate the completion of the requirements imposed on students by colleges and universities. Some may be more successful than others in particular contexts. For instance, these data suggest that the isolated Black schools in Cluster 2, while graduating a high proportion of A–G students, may not be preparing students as well as some schools that are graduating far fewer students that complete A–G courses. These findings suggest two possible explanations: (a) Other institutions are not doing all that they can to provide the classes or guidance necessary for students to complete A–G courses; and/or (b) isolated Black schools have higher proportions of students completing A–G courses at the seeming expense of moving them toward proficiency on the state examinations. Given either explanation, students concentrated in Cluster 2 schools appear to be experiencing a system that limits their opportunities. In the former scenario, students (disproportionately from isolated Latino and Black schools) are not taking or are not given the opportunity to take the college preparatory courses, while in the latter scenario they are exposed to college preparation courses that are not preparing them at levels equal to their counterparts in other schooling contexts. The exact mechanism for these discrepancies cannot be determined from these analyses; nevertheless, the ability to identify these schools is important because it allows researchers to isolate and examine places of interest or concern and enable policymakers to help modify or create policies that ultimately will improve the quality of education and equalize these opportunities across racial/ethnic groups.

Clusters 3 and 4 enroll more than 50% of the high school students in California and more than 80% of the White students. These schools have levels of our opportunity indicators above or very near the state average. However, when compared with Cluster 4, Cluster 3, the isolated White school cluster, enrolls more students (37% of all students and 65.7% of White students), has much higher percentages of students scoring in the proficient and advanced categories in both math and English Language Arts (24.8% and 49.3%, respectively), and has average SAT scores approximately 80 points above those of Cluster 4. The disproportionate representation of White students in the top four clusters (nearly 90% of White students attend these schools, as compared with nearly 60% of Black students and 40% of Latino students) suggests a disturbing racial/ethnic disconnect between the K–12 school system and the indicators necessary for inclusion in the pool of college-eligible students.

Clusters 6 and 7, representing both isolated and hyper-isolated Latino schools, enroll more than 50% of all Latino students and expose them to much lower levels of postsecondary opportunity when compared with their White and Asian peers. This 50% represents some 330,000 Latino high school students attending racially isolated to hyper-isolated educational institutions. In fact, nearly 130,000 of these students attend hyper-segregated Latino schools. Not only do these schools have lower levels of A–G completion rates when compared with their less isolated peers, but they also have substantially lower levels of preparedness as measured by exit test scores.

It is important to note that 9.2% of Black students and 3.2% of Latino students attend Cluster 9 schools, which have the lowest average percentage completing A–G courses (15.6%). Students in Cluster 9 attend schools that, on average, have nearly 60% of their students categorized as reduced/free lunch eligible and only 50% of their teachers certified (Table 1). On average, only 9.9% and 3.1% of the students tested proficient-to-advanced in the state math and English Language Arts exams, respectively. More than 36,000 students attend these schools with extremely high levels of concentrated disadvantage, and more than 90% of those students are Latino and African American (Table 1). Latino enrollment in these schools represents only 3.2% of the overall Latino population, but, because the number of Latino students enrolled overall is so high, this relatively small percentage represents more than 21,000 students who are being educated in schools with extremely high levels of concentrated disadvantage.

Finally, the findings discussed above provide evidence to support the hypothesis that racial/ethnic patterns of concentrated disadvantage exist in California's high schools; but, just as important, the findings show that many students in historically disadvantaged groups also find footholds in relatively advantaged schools. Thus this type of analysis could be expanded to examine whether historically disadvantaged students in relatively advantaged schools are performing as well as their historically advantaged peers within the same schooling context. More specifically, if A–G completion data by race/ethnicity within schools were available for this set of data, we would be able to see if Asians in Black–Latino schools perform similarly or differently from their peers in the school, or alternatively if Black or Latino students in isolated White schools perform as well as their White peers. While prior research (e.g., Teranishi et al., 2004) has demonstrated that there exist differential patterns of access within schools by race/ethnicity—often referred to as "resegregation"—cluster analyses with this type of data allows us to identify such schools and differential outcomes on a larger scale than does the limited sample of schools identified in prior research. This type of analysis is necessary but is difficult to accomplish without this type of clustering organizational approach.

Conclusion

Given our examination of the literature and the geography of schooling in California, what are the implications of these results for educational policy and for O'Connor's goal of eliminating the use of race in admissions policies within 25 years? Our analysis suggests that schooling disadvantage in the state is concentrated largely in schools where African American and Latino students are located. Thus these students incur grave disadvantages when compared with their Asian and White peers. These findings underscore the importance of understanding the relationships between schooling contexts, college eligibility indicators, and racial/ethnic composition of schools. Such discussions need new tools to address these complex problems. In this article we have suggested one such approach. We believe that it may provide answers to many questions that researchers have not yet begun to ask and may identify schools and interactions that have been missed thus far in systematic analyses. In particular, this cluster analysis approach is one that policymakers can use as they deliberate changes in statewide policies that may disproportionately affect different groups of students. For example, as a greater number of

high school graduates become UC/CSU-eligible, without construction of new campuses these university systems inevitably will feel the need to raise eligibility standards. By conducting cluster analyses that enable us to examine the extent to which varied groups have equitable access to those criteria, policymakers can better shape policies to mitigate or contextualize the varied geography of schooling advantage and disadvantage in the state.

In her *Grutter* (2003) opinion, Justice O'Connor mentioned the possibility of ending any Court-sanctioned use of race in admissions policies within 25 years. Underlying this aspiration is the expectation that educational opportunity will be afforded equitably to all students regardless of racial/ethnic background. This can realistically be accomplished only if the inequities that we have documented here are mitigated or eliminated. Our data suggest that the most direct policy approach, simply mandating that students take A–G requirements and take the SAT, or reformulating eligibility criteria for university admission, may not necessarily lead to greater or equitable preparation of students. Instead of policies narrowly designed to meet eligibility requirements mandated by the university system, an effort needs to be made to address the context of public schools that allow high levels of poverty, low levels of teacher preparedness, and racial/ethnic segregation to exist in any setting, particularly when those settings are concentrated largely in minority and poor communities. Any one of the disadvantages illustrated here is difficult to address and mitigate in isolation, but when multiple needs and requirements are concentrated in a school, they can be too much for the school to untangle without targeted and substantive assistance, rather than simple mandates and changes in course titles. We should take Justice O'Connor's goal of 25 years as a challenge, but recognize that this challenge will require a fundamental restructuring and reallocation of resources and advantage throughout our public schools. Without these changes, we must continue to develop and apply college access policies that take into account the multiple disadvantages under which students are asked to perform. Furthermore, additional research and methodologies are needed if we are to more fully understand how multiple types of disadvantage act to compound the unequal opportunities present in the K–12 system and, more basically, how to conceive of multiracial, multidimensional phenomena (Yun & Kurlaender, 2004). Tools and methodologies such as the ones outlined in this article may help direct that work, identify the school contexts that most disadvantage students within current eligibility criteria, and move us closer to the legitimate ending of race/ethnicity as a factor in admissions, and more broadly to the elimination of disadvantages that further reify and sustain racial/ethnic disparities in schooling outcomes.

NOTES

1. A–G courses are those that are required for eligibility to apply for admission to either the UC or the CSU system.

2. Students qualifying for the federal free-or-reduced-price lunch program are considered poor. This criterion is generally thought to produce a low estimate of poverty in high schools because older students are less likely to apply for such aid, but it is the most readily available and widely used indicator of school poverty in the research literature.

Discussion Questions

1. According to Moreno and Yun, why is California a good state in which to conduct research on ethnic/racial inequality in the K–12 public school system?

2. After reading this article, do you think Supreme Court Justice O'Connor's goal of eliminating racial preferences in higher education within 25 years is a realistic one? Why or why not?

Source: Yun, J. and Moreno, J. (2006). College access, K–12 concentrated disadvantage, and the next 25 years of education research. Excerpted and with references and some notes omitted from *Educational Researcher*, Vol. 35, No. 1, pp. 12–19. Reprinted by permission of Sage Publications.

CHAPTER 20

Circles of Influence and Chains of Command

The Social Processes Whereby Ethnic Communities Influence Host Societies

Anthony M. Orum

Research into immigration, especially by sociologists, has focused most of its attention on the issue of how immigrants adapt to host societies. But the most interesting questions arise as to how immigrants influence the host country. This paper proposes a sociological theory to account for such influence and provides empirical examples.

Introduction

During the past four decades, millions of new immigrants have entered the United States. As of 2002, more than 32 million new residents, or approximately 11 percent of the total U.S. population, have been added in this manner (U.S. Census, February 2003). This stream of new immigrants has come to America from places very different than in the past. As the result of a major overhaul of immigration policy—evident in the 1965 Hart-Celler Immigration Act—the long-time preference for settlement given to immigrants from Western Europe was dropped; in its place new criteria shifted the basic flow of immigrants to Asia, Africa and Latin America.

The large majority of these newcomers today, about 50 percent, arrive from countries in Latin America (U.S. Census, February 2003), mostly Mexico. In 2000, 9.2 million immigrants, or roughly 30 percent of the total foreign-born U.S. residents were from Mexico (U.S. Census, December 2003). The newcomers also are concentrated regionally and in major metropolitan areas. The foreign-born tend to favor the West and Northeast, and are least likely to live in the Midwest (U.S. Census, December 2003). For example, fully 26 percent of the

population of California is foreign-born. In 2000, four major metropolitan counties were home to 22 percent of the total U.S. immigrant population (U.S. Census, December 2003). The counties were Los Angeles, California; Miami-Dade, Florida; Cook County, Illinois; and Queens County, New York.

As the numbers have multiplied in recent years, it has become abundantly clear that this new generation of immigrants has begun to exercise a dramatic impact on the character of this nation. There are many diverse indications of the nature of the impact. Among them is the growth of a number of new ethnic businesses outside of the local enclaves, especially new ethnic restaurants. In addition, one can find a more prevalent use of non-English languages in the conduct both of private and public business. Many ATM outlets in major metropolitan areas such as Chicago, for instance, now allow users to conduct their business in English or Spanish. In other parts of the country, such as Boston, ATM users are given a choice of seven languages. On the West Coast, Wells Fargo recently added Spanish with audio capacity to 2,700 of its ATM machines (ATM Marketplace.com 2004, 2003, 2001). For several years, the state of Illinois has provided driver's examination booklets in three languages—English, Polish and Spanish. There are an increasing number of bilingual education programs in public schools—even as the debate rages about the appropriateness of such education programs. There also are a greater number of newspapers, radio stations and television outlets in different languages—among them, Chinese, Russian, Polish and, of course, Spanish. In brief, there are a host of signs heralding the growth of ethnic and linguistic diversity throughout American society.

The growth of this ethnic diversity, especially in major metropolitan areas, appears to go beyond the development of diverse ethnic neighborhoods. There is, it would seem, a more pervasive influence, one that affects the language of everyday life, the discourse of business, the variety of menus available in restaurants, and the like. America has become enriched by a cornucopia of different languages, symbols and cultural paraphernalia. Cultural diversity, in other words, once simply an ideal promoted by liberal political groups, has gradually become a fact of life for millions of Americans.

Why has this happened? But, even more to the point, how can we as social scientists provide a compelling theoretical explanation for this growing cultural and ethnic diversity—now as well as in the future? . . .

Conceptions of Immigrants and Host Societies

At the outset it is important to acknowledge that the usual theories employed by immigration researchers do not admit to the possibility that immigrants can change or alter institutions of the host society. All such models are premised on the fundamental assumption that immigrants, if they are to remain in the United States (or any host society for that matter), will be compelled to adapt to its institutions. Failing to do so, the assumption appears to be that the foreigners will simply exit or remain marginal and thus problematic. In other words, the current models of the social sciences do not permit immigrants, as groups, to exercise any form of agency over the institutions of the new societies they confront. They are, at best, contentious players, engaged occasionally in conflict with the host institutions, but never permitted, in any serious theoretical fashion, either to challenge or to change them. . . .

There are, however, a number of significant developments that give a new twist to our world today, ones that are likely to affect the capacity of immigrants and ethnics to reshape American institutions. The ability of people to

move from one nation to another has increased immeasurably (Castles and Miller 1998). Moreover, the capacity of such people to retain both their cultural heritage as well as their general sense of purpose, most observers agree, is much greater today than it was in the past. Part and parcel of these changes are new developments, such as the emergence of transnational communities of migrants, people that move easily back and forth among nations while maintaining a separate transnational community (Glick Schiller 1999). The net effect has been to enable large numbers of immigrants to retain a great degree of autonomy and power in the conduct of their daily lives. It is only natural, therefore, for us to expect that today's immigrants might be able to change and refashion American institutions or those of any host society in ways perhaps inconceivable in the past. Indeed, once we acknowledge this possibility, it not only gives a new perspective on the relationship between immigrants and host institutions today, but also provides a fresh look at the past as well.

A Model of the Ethnic Community and Its Avenues of Influence

How, then, shall we think about the impact of immigrants today on the United States, in particular, on American social and spatial institutions? I offer below a relatively compact theory that can help us account for changes in a host society, such as the United States, and for tracing those changes back to the immigrant populations. I shall do so, in part, by postulating a model of power and influence. It is that kind of model, I would argue, that can help answer the question of how immigrants alter and change institutions in the United States. . . .

THE ETHNIC COMMUNITY

Let me begin first with the concept of an *ethnic community*. I shall use this concept in two different but equally important ways. First, it can refer to a very specific and concrete community that is located in space—in a particular metropolis or even village. It can also refer to a broader community, one that can be found in different quarters and places across a metropolitan area or even a nation, and is not confined to a specific geographical area. In addition, we may think of the ethnic community as a collective actor in much the same way that other theorists think of status groups as actors (Weber in Gerth and Mills 1958). The ethnic community, in other words, possesses a life all its own. Accordingly it is capable of collective and concerted action designed to attain specific ends and goals.

CONSTITUTIVE ELEMENTS

My concept of ethnic community is composed of a number of key elements. There exist a variety of definitions of community, of course. I have identified those elements that seem to constitute the most comprehensive definition of the ethnic community. They are: (1) a group of people who define themselves as members of a common ethnic community or who share a common ethnic identity (Gordon 1964); (2) organizations that are unique to the ethnic community in terms of the products and services they offer, such as stores that sell ethnic goods, but also clubs and political agencies that promote the cause of the ethnic group; (3) an ongoing conscious and deliberate effort to ensure the survival of the community through activities that create a legacy and celebrate a common heritage, all actively pursued by institutions such as the family, school and church (or mosque or temple); and (4) spatial and/or social boundaries that distinguish between the ethnic community and the larger society, such as physical demarcations such as streets, but also social markers including membership and/or activity in the organizations and institutions of the ethnic community. . . .

BOUNDARIES

The boundaries that lie between ethnic communities and the larger society, I believe, are of crucial importance to understanding the nature of the ethnic community (Barth 1969; for an excellent recent analysis, see Sanders 2002). They are significant in two respects. First, they define what lies inside and outside the ethnic community. If this distinction does not exist or if it cannot be drawn, then one could not speak of the effect or influence of the ethnic community on the larger society. It is thus of conceptual significance in examining and understanding the nature of the ethnic community and its impact.

Second, boundaries are also important in terms of understanding the variations among ethnic communities, differences that will manifest themselves in the likely effect of ethnic communities on the larger society. In particular, the permeability of these boundaries varies widely among ethnic communities. Some ethnic communities are highly bounded, thus impermeable in the sense that they are cut-off and isolated from influences outside

themselves. This may be the result either of a voluntary decision on the part of the ethnic community or, alternatively, because of actions taken by powerful institutions of the larger society, specifically the state or its equivalent. Other ethnic communities, by contrast, seem highly permeable and thus much more subject both to influencing and being influenced by the larger society. . . .

POWER AND INFLUENCE

Following Max Weber, I shall use the concept of *influence* to describe actions that result in changes of policy and/or practice taken by organizations, groups and/or individuals outside the ethnic community that advance the activities and interests of the ethnic community (Weber, in Gerth and Mills (1958), p. 194). Influence, furthermore, may assume one of two forms: (1) *direct influence,* which is the actual and successful action by an ethnic community that results in the projected changes of policy and/or practice by non-ethnic parties; and (2) *indirect influence,* which is a change in policy and/or practice taken by non-ethnic parties that, even in the absence of any direct action by the ethnic community, both acknowledges and advances the ethnic community's interests (Dahl, 1963). An example of the exercise of direct influence by an ethnic community would be the election of a representative of an ethnic community to a political office in local government, in which the majority of the ethnic community votes for that representative. An example of the exercise of indirect influence would be the increased use of an ethnic community's language, for example Polish, by local businesses outside the Polish community even in the absence of any direct action taken by the Polish community to produce that result.

CIRCLES OF INFLUENCE AND CHAINS OF COMMAND

I propose, then, that there are two principal social structures through which an ethnic community is able to exercise its influence over the institutions of the larger, or host, society. One is what I shall term the *circle of influence.* By this concept I mean all those organizations, businesses, clubs and individuals that lie outside the boundaries of the ethnic community and through which the ethnic community is able to make its influence felt. Circles of influence can be conceived in two forms, parallel to the nature of an ethnic community, itself. First, they can be the circles of groups and individuals that surround a spatially-defined ethnic community. The wider the circle of influence by an ethnic group, the greater the number of organizations, businesses, clubs and individuals spatially adjacent to the ethnic community that have taken steps to acknowledge and advance the interests of the ethnic community. The circle of influence can also be conceived in non-spatial and territorial terms as the array of groups, organizations and individuals lying outside the broad ethnic community that have taken steps to acknowledge and to advance the interests of the ethnic community.

An example of the first circle of influence would be the use of bilingual education, say Spanish and English, in public schools that lie within the immediate vicinity of a Spanish-speaking ethnic community. In contrast, an illustration of the second broad form of a circle of influence would be the proportion of members of a local city council who represent and advance the interests of the local Chinese community in a city. Another example would be the growth of Latino music in the United States, especially the recent introduction of the Latino Grammy Awards, an effort spearheaded by Latino artists including Gloria Estefan.

The second social structure through which the ethnic community manages to exercise its influence is what I shall call the *chain of command*. By this concept I mean the chain of command—or line of authority—within an institutional or organizational sector of a given area (a metropolis or even a society). It can refer to any institutional sector, thus to the church, public schools and even to the legal system. Just as the circle of influence is designed to point our attention to the broad lateral array of parties through which an ethnic community may exercise its influence, the chain of command is designed to point our attention to the hierarchical dimension through which authority is exercised. This can be an exceptionally important element to the exercise of influence, generally, and to its exercise by ethnic communities, specifically.

For example, when the Rev. Jesse Jackson seeks to get a nationwide corporation to take actions that will acknowledge and/or advance the interests of African-Americans, he seeks to persuade not all the principal officers of local outlets but rather the chief officers, those who stand at the top of the chain of command. If Jackson is successful, then he has taken a particularly effective route to exercise influence for change in policy and/or practice. Initiated at the top of the organization, these actions will generally be binding on all those officials and businesses lower in the hierarchy. Similarly, if a specific ethnic community wishes to get certain policies adopted by public schools, it is a far more effective strategy to seek to persuade the top school officials rather than simply local school officials.

Basic Theoretical Propositions and Evidence

Let me now advance my central theoretical propositions about the links among ethnic communities, circles of influence and chains of command. I furnish below illustrations and examples to support each of the main propositions. This evidence is, I must emphasize, illustrative and intended to showcase the manner in which ethnic communities have in fact influenced the institutions of host societies in the past. I also have made a conscious effort to select a variety of examples from different places as well as different historical eras. My intent in so doing is to suggest the broad relevance of the concepts as well as the different forms that both circles of influence and chains of command may assume. . . .

I turn, then, to the major proposition:

> Ethnic communities are able to influence or to otherwise shape the actions of non-ethnic parties in the larger society through two social mechanisms: circles of influence and chains of command.

There are three illustrations that I shall use to support this proposition. The first is the classic historical case of Tammany Hall in New York City. It furnishes a clear example of how an ethnic community can use the chain of command in an organization to wield influence over the larger metropolis. Tammany Hall is one of the great political machines in the history of American politics. With origins as a patriotic and fraternal organization in the late 18th century, it was captured by Irish immigrants in the 1830s and, over the next half century or so, became a vehicle whereby the Irish were able to exercise considerable power in New York City. The machine established its roots by providing a variety of benefits to new immigrants, among them jobs and shelter. Those at the top of the chain of command, especially during the heyday of William "Boss" Tweed, exercised their power and influence almost recklessly; indeed, Tweed eventually was toppled by charges of corruption. At the lower levels of the organization, the workings of influence provided a model that other machines and politicians would come to emulate over the years. The extraordinary story of all of this is told in the famous recollections of George Washington Plunkitt, that estimable machine politician who claimed, "I seen my opportunities and I took 'em." Plunkitt was an exemplary influence-peddler, using the resources of the machine to wield influence over local residents and thereby spread the influence of the machine, and the Irish immigrants who composed it, across the city (Riordan 1995; Allen 1993).

A variety of illustrations for the ways in which ethnic communities can widen their circles of influence to embrace spatially proximate organizations and groups comes from Cohen's study (1991) of the development of the working class and unions in Chicago during the 1920s and 1930s. Cohen explored the making of three different ethnic communities in Chicago in the 1920s—Poles, Jews and Italians. Each group developed its own particular organizations and clubs, and each established a variety of ways in which to celebrate their ethnic heritage. For each group, moreover, its religious organization came to play an essential role. Indeed, among the Poles, the parish became the center of the ethnic community around which there grew additional clubs and organizations (Erdmanns 1998). Moreover, the Poles and the Jews established local schools for their children, thus providing a means of passing on their heritage.

Beyond the core social and religious arrangements, however, there were other organizations and groups that came to fall under the influence of each community. In effect, each of the three different communities extended its influence outward, taking in public spaces and organizations and using them for their own purposes. For example, each of the ethnic communities found its own pubs and taverns in which to gather, and these places came to be known as the Polish pub or the Italian tavern. More importantly, however, the community's influence came to include new forms of entertainment that, by their very nature, had nothing to do with the essential character of the ethnic community, itself. For example, motion pictures were just emerging as a popular form of entertainment, and local entrepreneurs began to build motion picture theatres in different parts of Chicago. Soon, in each community, the movie theatre ran only motion pictures that were in the language of and appealed to the local residents be they Jews, Poles or Italians. In fact, as Cohen beautifully illustrates, the motion pictures became the place where a contest developed between the special interests of the ethnic community and the growing use of a mass culture. Eventually the mass culture won out, but not before the motion picture theatres had become sites where each of the different ethnic groups could gather and, through celebrations on the screen, create and recreate their own sense of ethnic heritage in Chicago.

My third illustration comes from research on how some ethnic communities dominate specific occupational sectors of the labor market. This is an instance where the influence of ethnic communities extends into the economy and thereby can eventually become very widespread.

Some of the most interesting work on this topic comes from Waldinger (1996); see also Light and Gold 2000. In his study of ethnicity and labor markets in New York City, Waldinger makes a variety of discoveries that show how specific ethnic communities, both long ago and at present, come to extend their circle of influence by gaining dominance in particular occupations. In the past, for example, the Jewish community in New York City was especially concentrated in the garment industry, whereas now it has gained niches in legal services, accounting and education. More recently, African-Americans have gained an especially strong foothold in the public sector, while Dominicans and West Indians have gained strong footholds in the hotel industry. Occupational niches such as these provide a means for exercising considerable influence because the ethnic communities become, in effect, gatekeepers, determining who can and cannot enter particular local job markets (Light and Gold, 2000). . . .

These three examples, then, reveal how different ethnic communities can come to exercise their power via circles of influence and chains of command—and how it can happen both in spatial and non-spatial forms. . . .

Robust ethnic communities will be likely to possess a wide circle of influence.

This proposition means simply that robust communities possess the institutional and organizational resources necessary to extend their influence outward over the institutions of the host society. . . .

A notable study of the development of the Korean community in Philadelphia nicely illustrates the manner in which a robust ethnic community can establish a circle of influence (Goode and Schneider, 1993). Koreans began to migrate to Philadelphia in the early 1970s. Eventually they developed fairly sizeable and flourishing communities in a number of sites. Each community was notable for its businesses and stores. Moreover, each was controlled and developed by a relatively small number of figures that exercised a decisive influence over the internal organization of the community. These leaders eventually came to represent the face of the Korean community to the larger metropolis, especially to the key leaders and political figures in Philadelphia. As Goode and Schneider note, "(o)nce the networks of city influentials came to know these individuals, they became universal referrals for anyone who wanted to approach 'the community.' As we (the authors) sat on the boards of programs for the arts, museums, and human-rights networks, it became apparent that this was the way things worked" (p. 85). . . .

This particular case perfectly illustrates how the leaders of an ethnic community can develop a circle of influence and how both the ethnic community and the leadership of the larger metropolis may embrace one another as representatives of their respective groups. Moreover, it is clear that this circle of influence, through the formal channels, is a major, if not the major, path by which Koreans are able to exercise their influence in Philadelphia.

Robust ethnic communities will be likely to exercise their influence high up the chain of command of a particular organizational or institutional sector.

... One of the best illustrations of this proposition today can be found in the Cuban community of Miami (Portes and Stepick 1993). This community, of course, has often been singled out as unusual, even unique. But in terms of the framework I advocate here, Miami's Cuban community simply provides a prototype of how a robust ethnic community can exercise influence over both local and national circumstances. Stepick and his colleagues (2003) give us a rich description of the many ways in which the Cubans have become dominant in Miami, not only in local institutions but also in their relations with other groups. Assessing the overall local influence of the community, they note:

In 1983, Latinos captured a majority in Hialeah, the county's second largest city. The Miami City Commission turned majority Cuban American in 1985 and has had a Cuban American mayor almost continually since then. In 1996, Alex Penelas became the county's first Cuban American mayor In addition, the County Commission achieved a Cuban American majority The City Commission of Miami Beach, the county's third largest city became majority Cuban American in the fall of 1999. Two Miami Cubans are in the U.S. House of Representatives, and the Miami-Dade County state legislative delegation along with the Miami-Dade County School Board are dominated by foreign-born Latinos, especially Cubans. (21)

While this community has been unusually effective in exercising its influence in local quarters, Stepick and his colleagues observe that after Janet Reno, Attorney General of the Democratic Clinton Administration, forced the return of the young boy, Elian Gonzalez, to his father in Cuba, the Cubans of Miami turned out in record numbers to vote for Republican George W. Bush in 2000—thereby punctuating their influence and demonstrating it even in the national arena. . . .

Impermeable ethnic communities, by definition, will be less likely both to influence and to be influenced by non-ethnic parties, regardless of the robustness of their institutional resources.

This is a very important proposition, and it is meant to draw a distinction between the internal nature of an ethnic community and its capacity to influence or be influenced by non-ethnic parties. Thus, there can be very robust ethnic communities, but unless those communities possess boundaries that are permeable they will be unable to exercise any influence over the institutions of the larger society. One example of this is the case of the Bronzeville area of Chicago. In the 1930s and 1940s, Drake and Cayton (1945) could describe this area as one rich with a local social and civic live. Storefront churches were everywhere. There were a variety of voluntary associations among residents and a very lively political life. Its robust character notwithstanding, however, it was a community unable to influence Chicago for one simple but powerful reason: it was a segregated community, actively enclosed and cut off from the rest of the metropolis by the political organization and officials in metropolitan Chicago. . . .

THE GENERAL CONCEPT OF ETHNIC COMMUNITY

... As I have suggested above, an ethnic community is a rich and complex phenomenon whose elements range from a sense of common identity to the existence of boundaries between itself and the larger society. My conception emphasizes especially the institutional components of such communities precisely because institutions, I believe, represent the very foundations of ethnic communities. While such communities also entail complex social networks among people, what really sustains them over time is the presence of vigorous and credible institutions, such as the church or the family, that work to retain and to advance the unique cultural heritage and legacies of the ethnic group. In the absence of such institutions, I would argue, the ethnic community simply will disappear. Indeed, I would further speculate that when such basic institutions as the church (or synagogue or mosque) or school diminish in strength, then ultimately the fate of the ethnic community is sealed and it will become extinguished.

THE SPATIAL CONCENTRATION OF THE ETHNIC COMMUNITY

One of the most observable traits of an ethnic community lies in its concentration in a specific spatial area. One can easily argue that where an ethnic community is most spatially concentrated—in terms of its institutions and members—it would be most likely to exercise an influence over the host institutions in its immediate vicinity (assuming its boundaries are permeable). Yet how this influence makes itself manifest will depend, in large part, on the specific nature of the host institutions. Political institutions, in particular can often gerrymander the quarters occupied by an ethnic community, and, therefore, limit the political influence of that community. Such a strategy, however, only works when the local political system is constructed on the basis of district—not at-large—voting.

SPHERES OF INFLUENCE AND THE RELATIVE STRENGTH OF ETHNIC COMMUNITIES AND HOST SOCIETIES

One of the most important matters to consider is the institutional sector within which an ethnic community can exercise its influence. In particular, are there certain kinds of institutions wherein an ethnic community can make its influence felt more easily, even more substantially, than other kinds of institutions? We might phrase this theoretical concern in a slightly different, but equally compelling, manner: are there spheres, or institutions, wherein the host society holds a decided advantage over the resources of the ethnic community, and can thereby limit its influence? . . .

In keeping with my effort at conceptual parsimony, I want to suggest that, in general, where an ethnic community enjoys an ease of social access to a group or institution then it will be more likely to extend its circle of influence and/or ascend the chain of command in that sphere than in a sphere where it does not enjoy such access. Let us consider several illustrations of such access. Spatial proximity provides such access, and it can be used to explain why an ethnic community first expands its circle of influence among those businesses, people and groups immediately spatially adjacent to it. These are the parties that lie within the easiest social reach of the community, and therefore they are the ones likely to be most susceptible to changing in ways that will advance the community's interest. Ease of access can also explain why it is that public institutions, such as schools and the police force, show evidence of the influence by an ethnic community in programs such as bilingual education rather

than in private organizations such as large corporate businesses. Public institutions are most directly subject to federal and local mandates that require them to provide opportunities for education and employment to all groups regardless of origin. Entry into such public institutions, in other words, is much easier than it is into private ones. Finally, ease of access would also help to explain why specific ethnic communities are able to gain control over certain occupational sectors. The presence of co-ethnics in a particular labor market, say hotels, provides an initial social foothold or point of entry. And once that foothold is established, access is made much easier for others of the same ethnic origin and easier than for job seekers of different ethnic origins (Waldinger 1996). . . .

Conclusion

This paper has offered a way to conceptualize the manner in which the new immigrants, and the ethnic communities they have established in the United States leave their imprint on American institutions. I have offered some historical illustrations to support the general theoretical propositions, but these propositions can only be affirmed through much more extensive research into the nature of ethnic communities and their ties to various circles of influence and chains of command.

Of course, one must always remind oneself that the patterns observed in the past as well as the present may be evanescent and impermanent. Among other things, it is clear that if immigration to America had continued well beyond 1928 when the 1924 laws went into effect, the history of ethnicity in the United States would also have been far different than it is today. There seem to be indications of a growing diversity in America, but only the future will tell us whether they shall remain. As Gerstle (1997) and Higham (1955) remind us, the history of America and its experience with ethnicity and immigration is one that wavers between periods of "constraint" and those of "liberty." We seem to live today in a period of somewhat less freedom than in the past, but unexpected events such as war and terrorism can always intervene to force the state to exercise even greater constraint on those entering a country and what happens to them upon entry. Whether the changes we observe today will remain tomorrow or whether the ethnic communities will be as vibrant depends ultimately on historical events over which we have very little control.

Nevertheless, I offer a means both of explaining and of beginning to answer the question of how immigrants today have had an impact on American institutions. One of the matters that remains to be explored in greater depth is the nature of the changes, themselves. I sense that there are many such changes, ranging from the greater use of languages, such as Spanish, in quarters well beyond the Latino enclaves, to the greater diversity of restaurants and general cultural paraphernalia brought in by the new immigrants. But future research obviously will have to carefully spell out the specific empirical accounts of these changes. What I have attempted to clarify is the critical nature of the difference between the ethnic community and non-ethnic parties. Boundaries are essential to thinking about these matters. Indeed, it is at the boundaries, as history has shown, that contests over the rights of the ethnics and the power of the state often are fought. Such issues, I hope, also will be explored by future research.

I hope, moreover, to have provided a firmer sociological foundation to understanding the process whereby such changes might happen; for both circles of influence and chains of command lie at the very foundations of that which is sociological. In addition, I encourage further exploration, especially how it is that today's diversity can happen even when there is an apparent absence in many places of organized and concerted political action. As I suggest, changes may occur as a result of indirect influence and thus even in the absence of direct political action by ethnic communities. But perhaps the deeper and more satisfying change, from the point of view of ethnic communities, is that which results from the work of organizations such as MALDEF [the Mexican American Legal Defense and Educational Fund] that, using the courts, seeks to influence the chain of command in the legal system, and ultimately those laws that influence our everyday lives.

Discussion Questions

1. Why is unity among ethnic group members necessary in order for the group to influence a host society?

2. Considering that Latin American immigrants come from many different countries, do you think that Latinos, as a group, will be able to have a strong influence on U.S. society? Why or why not?

PART VI

SEX AND GENDER

While the gap in social, economic, and political power between men and women has decreased over the past few decades, Part VI shows that a gender divide still exists. The first two articles in this section look at gender equity in the household and on the playing field. The third article examines how race and citizenship influence women's interpretation and understanding of sexual harassment. The last two articles observe how traditional masculine attributes are highly valued, albeit in different ways, by different high school male subcultures and how gender neutral socialization has stalled due to the linking of gender nonconformity with homosexuality.

In "Divorce Culture and Marital Gender Equality," Carrie Yodanis reveals that marital equality is greatest in cultures where divorce is accepted. However, her findings also show that women still do most of the house and child work throughout the globe. Meanwhile, in "I Just Want to Play," Lee McGinnis and her co-authors reveal that institutional and interactional barriers to women's golf participation are still alive and well. The authors of both of these articles point out that laws that uphold equal rights for women have worked to diminish, but not close, the gap in power between men and women.

In " 'I'm Not Thinking of It as Sexual Harassment' ": Understanding Harassment across Race and Citizenship," Sandy Welsh and her co-authors show that the current legal definition and enforcement of sexual harassment legislation tends to benefit White, middle-class women. Their findings reveal that Black women and women without full citizenship are likely to interpret sexual harassment differently and are more likely to fear retribution for reporting it. The authors point out the importance of recognizing race and citizenship status when constructing such legislation.

In "Multiple Masculinities? Teenage Boys Talk about Jocks and Gender," C. J. Pascoe describes how boys from different high schools and student subcultures shape, in various ways, their own sense of masculinity. He notes that they do so in relation to the masculinized attributes associated with jocks, such as competence, heterosexual sexual exploits, and dominance. The theme of heterosexuality and gender norms also appears in Karin A. Martin's "William Wants a Doll. Can He Have One? Feminists, Child Care Advisors, and Gender-Neutral Child Rearing," Martin suggests that, while feminists have had some success in influencing childrearing practices, the goal of some second-wave feminists to promote gender neutral child-rearing is still not fully accepted. Martin points out that the perceived link between gender non-conformity and homosexuality is one of the reasons gender neutral child-rearing has not become fully accepted in our society.

As you read the articles in this section, keep in mind the following points:

- Legal understandings of sexual harassment tend to be based on the experiences of White, middle-class women.
- Despite the improvements in gender equity in sports due to Title IX, institutional and inter-actional barriers to women's participation in sports still exist.
- The dominant masculine "jock" culture in high school influences how non-jocks, as well as jocks, establish their masculine identities.
- Gender roles vary over time and from society to society.
- Many guides to parenting intentionally or unintentionally reinforce the notion that gender non-conformity is linked to homosexuality.

CHAPTER 21

Divorce Culture and Marital Gender Equality

A Cross-National Study

Carrie Yodanis

Based on multilevel analysis of data from 22 countries, results indicate that a divorce culture on the national level is associated with greater marital equality; that is, where divorce is accepted, the distribution of work between women and men in marriage is more equal. These findings support the enhanced equality hypothesis that the possibility of divorce provides women with leverage to gain more equal status within marriage.

Marital Gender Inequality in a Divorce Culture

Most studies on divorce examine the consequences of personally experiencing divorce for individual women, men, and children. However, divorce can also be viewed as part of a macro, cultural-level phenomenon affecting people throughout a society regardless of whether they individually experience divorce. In her book *Marriage in a Culture of Divorce,* Karla Hackstaff (1999) contrasts marriage culture and divorce culture. A marriage culture includes the belief, assumption, and practice that marriage is a given and forever. A divorce culture, in comparison, is a set of beliefs and practices that define marriage as optional and conditional, with divorce being an option if the marriage does not work.

Research on the consequences of rising divorce rates and especially changing attitudes toward divorce on a national level is limited. There is some evidence that high national divorce rates are related to lower fertility rates, later age at marriage, and lower rates of spousal violence (Gibson 1976; Lester 1996; Sleebos 2003; Stevenson and Wolfers 2003; Wolfinger 2003). In addition, some research suggests that women's increasing labor force participation is an outcome of high divorce rates. In societies characterized by high divorce rates, women may be less willing to be financially dependent on men in marriage and therefore more likely to participate in the labor force throughout the life course (Diekmann 1994; Hou and Omwanda 1997). Most notably, a debate continues regarding how a growing divorce culture affects gender equality in intact marriages. This article contributes to this debate.

Bargaining theory focuses on how couples negotiate agreements in the relationship, including how to divide the work. According to bargaining theory, partners have options both within and outside of marriage, and each partner's ability to negotiate in the bargaining process is based on the options that are available to him or her. Particularly relevant is the concept of a "divorce threat point." When bargaining occurs within the context of the possibility of divorce, partners consider their alternatives if their relationship should end, and the attractiveness of their anticipated alternatives affect their negotiations (Lundberg and Pollak 1996; Manser and Brown 1980; Muthoo 2000).

The divorce threat point operates on an individual level and is dependent on environmental factors, such as the level of public assistance to divorced single mothers and divorce laws regarding the division of property (Lundberg and Pollak 1996). Stevenson and Wolfers

(2003) find support for the importance of the contextual dimension of the threat point when they find that the introduction of no-fault divorce laws across U.S. states is related to significant decreases in rates of spousal violence in the states. In other words, when it became easier to leave a relationship, gender dynamics within the relationship improved. As they conclude, "unilateral divorce changed the bargaining power in marriage and therefore impacted many marriages—not simply the extra few divorces enabled by unilateral divorce" (p. 19).

This article adds a cross-national component to this argument. Nations, more so than the 50 states in the United States, have varying laws and dominant ideologies that make it easier or harder for individuals to divorce whether or not they want to. In the context of strict laws and attitudes against divorce, individual divorce threat points will be high or nonexistent.

Building on bargaining theory, the literature outlines two possible ways that a divorce culture on a national level can affect the level of gender equality in marriages. An enhanced equality hypothesis suggests that divorce culture may increase equality between partners. Unlike in a marriage culture where women stay in the relationship no matter how unsatisfied or unequal they are, men risk losing women in a divorce culture if the relationship does not move toward equality. Thus, divorce becomes a tool that women use to secure change and greater equality in marital relationships. . . .

In a counter diminished equality hypothesis, a divorce culture may increase inequality between marriage partners. The divorce alternative increases men's power relative to women's. In a marriage culture, men stay in the marriage no matter what. In a divorce culture, in comparison, women risk losing men if they push for change in the relationship. Divorce can be a threat that men use against women in an effort to thwart their attempts at marital equality and thereby can reduce women's power in marriage. Given that women often experience declines in economic well-being with divorce, this threat can be powerful in controlling women's attempts to strive for equality. In her classic study of dual-career couples, Hochschild (1989) finds support for the diminished equality hypothesis that women are not able to push for change in the unequal distribution of work in relationships because of the threat of divorce. . . .

In this article, I address the question, How is a divorce culture, measured as both national practices and attitudes toward divorce, related to gender equality in marriage on an individual level? In addressing this question, this article provides a cross-national examination of the enhanced and diminished marital equality hypotheses of divorce culture. Most of the research about these hypotheses is based on data from the United States, a country with a very high divorce culture. Looking across nations makes it possible to see if the theories hold up in different cultural contexts and if variation between countries in divorce culture is related to variation in marital relationships (Kohn 1987). This is what I set out to do in this article. . . .

Method

The data used in this article come primarily from the International Social Survey Programme (ISSP). The ISSP, analogous to a cross-nationally comparative General Social Survey, is an annual social survey conducted in countries throughout the world. Since 1986, a different topic is selected each year as a module of focus in addition to the repeated items. For this analysis, data from the 1994 Family and Changing Gender Roles module are used.

The data are gathered through a 15-minute questionnaire, conducted as a supplement to regular national surveys or as a separate survey. The samples for each country are national household probability samples. The questionnaire is originally written in English and translated into the national language(s) for conducting the survey. The data are then compiled into English-language data sets.

Twenty-two countries are included in the analysis. In the 1994 ISSP data set, Spain and the Netherlands were dropped due to insufficient data. For this analysis, I use two levels of data: country and individual level. At the individual level, the total sample is 9,529 married women. To be included in the sample, participants had to be currently married. People who were currently cohabiting were dropped from the sample. Only women were included in the analysis. This decision was made based on the nature of the research questions as well as the fact that key variables about wives, such as education, age, gender ideology, and opinions about women's employment, were available only for the respondent.

At the country level, data are based on the entire sample, including married and not married women and men. This decision is based on the need to measure the overall dominant ideology and practices of the country.

OUTCOME VARIABLE: MARITAL GENDER INEQUALITY

The level of marital gender inequality is measured using the division of household labor. The distribution of housework between husband and wife is measured using reports of who does the following four household tasks:

shopping for groceries, deciding what to have for dinner, doing the laundry, and caring for the sick. Responses include "always or usually the woman," "equally," "usually or always the man," and "a third person." Those who responded that a third person did the task were dropped. A mean score was computed by summing the responses and dividing by the number of completed answers for each case. The scale has a Cronbach's alpha of .68. A high score indicates a traditional division of labor with women doing more housework than do men. . . .

INDIVIDUAL-LEVEL INDEPENDENT VARIABLES

Gender role ideology is conceptualized as beliefs about gender roles in marriage. The variable is a composite measure of the following three questions from the ISSP: "Do you agree or disagree . . . (1) A job is all right, but what most women really want is a home and children, (2) Being a housewife is just as fulfilling as working for pay, (3) A man's job is to earn money; a woman's job is to look after the home and family." For each statement, respondents indicated whether they *strongly agree, agree, neither agree nor disagree, disagree*, or *strongly disagree*. These three indicators were confirmed for selection based on factor analysis and theory. The composite measure was created by summing the scores on the items and dividing by the number of the responses given. A high score indicates a nontraditional gender ideology. The scale has a Cronbach's alpha of .68. The range in average scores across countries is not large. The most traditional ideology is found in Russia, with a mean score of 2.16, and the most nontraditional ideology is in East Germany, with a mean score of 3.80.

Relative earnings is included to account for the relative resource theory of marital gender equality, which explains that valued resources, including income, can be exchanged within the relationship to opt out of doing housework (Brines 1993). This variable measures who earns more, the husband or wife. The five responses include "the man earns much more," "the man earns a bit more," "we earn about the same amount," "the woman earns a bit more," and "the woman earns much more." A high score indicates the woman earns more. . . . Slightly more than 68 percent of the women are employed either full- or part-time or retired. In nearly 77 percent of the couples, the man earns much or a bit more, while in 10 percent of the couples, women do. . . .

Age is included in the equation to control for cohort effects in marital relations. The respondent's age is measured in years. For the sample, the mean age is 45 years.

Education is constructed as a dummy variable, indicating whether the respondent has a university degree (1 = university degree). Nearly 11 percent of the sample has a university degree.

Cohabitation is also associated with greater marital equality (Batalova and Cohen 2002). Thus, a dummy variable is included in the equation, indicating whether the couple lived together before marrying (1 = cohabited). Nearly 29 percent of the sample cohabited before marriage. . . .

Divorce attitudes are based on the following three questions from the ISSP: "Do you agree or disagree . . . (1) Divorce is usually the best solution when a couple can't seem to work out their marriage problems, (2) When there are children in the family, parents should stay together even if they don't get along, (3) Even when there are no children, a married couple should stay together even if they don't get along." Responses are given on a 5-point Likert-type scale ranging from *strongly agree* to *strongly disagree*. Items were coded so that a high score indicates an acceptance of divorce or high divorce culture. Items were combined by summing the scores and dividing by the number of responses given. The scale has a Cronbach's alpha of .57. . . .

COUNTRY-LEVEL INDEPENDENT VARIABLES

Divorce culture is a composite measure of attitudes toward divorce and divorce rates. The measure is a factor score combining these two items using principal components analysis. National aggregates of divorce attitudes, based on the mean score on the divorce attitudes measure for each country, are used. Divorce rates are based on data from the 1997 and 1998 *United Nations Demographic Yearbooks*. . . .

Gender role ideology. A second country-level variable, dominant gender ideology, is included to account for the fact that part of the country-level effect of a divorce culture on marital equality may be spurious since nontraditional values are related both to greater marital equality (Komter 1989) and to a higher divorce culture. Gender ideology on the country level is measured using the mean score for each country on the individual-level gender role ideology index. The correlation between the national measures of divorce culture and gender role ideology is rather weak ($r = .386, p = .076$).

ANALYSIS

. . . The analysis presented in this article incorporates two levels of data—individual- and country-level variables on the outcome variable, marital equality.

On the individual level, relative income, individual gender ideology, age, education, and divorce attitudes are centered at the grand mean. To explore the country-level impact, I test if the intercept of the individual-level equation varies by levels of divorce culture and gender ideology. Both country-level variables are centered at the grand mean. Age, education, relative income, cohabitation, presence of children, and individual divorce attitudes have fixed effects across countries.

Results

COUNTRY-LEVEL DESCRIPTION OF DIVORCE CULTURE AND MARITAL EQUALITY

. . . Countries are ranked according to the level of divorce culture. Surprisingly, given the vast variation between countries in their history, religion, family laws, and the status of women, there is not a large amount of variation in attitudes toward divorce. Austria has the strongest acceptance of divorce (with a mean score of 4 on a 5-point scale), and Japan has the lowest acceptance (with a mean score of 2.87). Divorce rates range from a high of 4.29 in the United States to lows of .46 in Italy and 0 in Ireland and the Philippines, where divorce is not legal. The United States has the strongest divorce culture. Catholic, familialistic, and collectivist countries, including Italy, Ireland, Poland, and the Philippines, have the lowest culture of divorce.

Turning to average measure of marital equality across countries, again it is interesting to see that despite large variation between the countries, the housework on average remains unequally distributed, with women being responsible for most of the work. In no country was the housework on average distributed equally or primarily done by men (as would be indicated by a score of 1 to 3).

MULTILEVEL ANALYSIS

Individual-level effects. Looking first at the relationship between individual-level variables and the division of housework, findings from previous research are supported. . . . Model 1 shows the effects of individual-level variables commonly used to explain the division of household labor. Supporting resource theory, the more women earn relative to men, the more equal the division of housework. In addition, women with university degrees report a more egalitarian division of labor than women with less education. In models 1 and 2, the nonresponses for the income variable do not differ significantly on the division of household labor. In the later models, there is a small yet significant difference.

Previous findings regarding the effect of gender ideology on the distribution of housework are also supported. When women have a nontraditional gender role ideology, the division of labor is less unequal. In addition, as a cohort effect would expect, older women do significantly more housework compared to younger women. Women who cohabited before marriage are significantly more likely to report greater equality in the distribution of housework, and the number of people in the household is related to women's doing more housework relative to men. . . .

Country-level effects. Model 3 adds the country-level measure of divorce culture, the focus of this article. In this multilevel model, the intercept of housework, or the mean distribution of housework across countries of average divorce culture for women of average age, gender ideology, and relative income; with no university education; and who did not cohabit before marriage, is 3.98, indicating a general tendency toward women's doing most of the work. The divorce culture of a country is related to the distribution of housework within marriage. The stronger the divorce culture, the more equal the division of housework. Specifically, controlling for women's resource contribution, gender role ideology, and other characteristics found to be related to marital equality, with each increase of 1 on the divorce culture index, the average score on the housework index decreases by .09, moving toward a more equal division of labor. The size of the effect is not very large but is not inconsequential given the rigidity of the gendered division of labor across cultures. This is addressed in more detail in the Discussion. Model 4 adds the country-level variable, dominant gender ideology, to the model. The gender ideology of a country is not directly related to the distribution of housework.

Comparing the variance components between models 1 and 2, individual-level divorce variables do not explain additional variation in the division of household labor. Looking at model 3, it is apparent that national divorce culture explains a substantial portion of the variation in the intercept across countries. Divorce culture reduces the amount of unexplained variance in the intercept by a third.

Discussion

The main objective of this article is to examine the cross-national relationship between a divorce culture on a national level and gender equality in intact marriages. In particular, I look across countries to see if there is more support for the argument that a divorce culture is associated with enhanced or diminished equality for women in marriage.

Overall, the results provide support for the enhanced equality theory over the diminished equality hypothesis. A strong divorce culture on the national level is associated with a more, not less, equal distribution of work in marriages. Thus, it appears that the concern that divorce would limit women's ability to push for equality in marriage does not appear to be the overall pattern. In countries where divorce is more accepted and widely practiced, women's position within marriages is better.

In addition, the national divorce culture of a country, rather than individual divorce attitudes or experiences, appears to be particularly important. This adds confirmation to the argument that divorce threat points and, correspondingly, women and men's options and perceived alternatives within relationships are influenced by social and cultural context. If divorce is not an accepted or available option within a society, the divorce threat point is remote, limiting the extent to which alternatives to the relationship can be used to bargain for equality within the relationship.

. . . While much research shows the potential negative consequences of divorce, this study provides support for the often overlooked positive correlates of a divorce culture. Researchers have long argued that divorce can provide physical and psychological safety for women and children by providing opportunities to leave abusive or unhealthy relationships (Katz et al. 1995). This study adds to the evidence that there may be benefits to the availability of divorce that extend beyond extreme, life-threatening situations and ironically may contribute to the strengthening of marriages. At a time when efforts such as the implementation of covenant marriages are trying to reverse the divorce culture and make it more difficult to leave marriages, understanding the positive outcomes of a divorce culture is more important than ever (Rosier and Feld 2000). . . .

Gender role ideology is included in the analysis to try to rule out some possible spurious national-level factors that might explain the relationship between divorce culture and marital gender equality. There are likely to be other variables that affect this relationship. For example, religious history and culture unquestionably explain variation in the divorce culture across countries. Some of these variables, such as religion, may be less likely to have direct relationships to marital equality than indirect relationships through such variables as gender ideology. Other variables such as women's political and occupational status relative to men's may also explain part of the relationship. . . .

In research focusing on a few countries, it is possible to consider the detailed specifics of each case and variable, such as marital gender equality, and to consider the complex factors that led to variation in divorce cultures across countries. This unquestionably is an interesting future direction for cross-national research on divorce culture. Such questions, however, involve a different type of cross-national research than the one presented in this article. This study seeks to examine patterns across a larger sample of countries—an approach that Kohn (1987) calls "country as the unit of analysis." While this approach necessitates a loss in the depth of detail for each specific variable and case, it provides the advantage of a breadth of information across more cases. Using this approach, Kohn argues that it is not imperative to explain how the countries got to their current status. Such questions are better left to other cross-national research designs. Rather, the focus is on studying the correlates of the current social circumstances of nations, regardless of the various historical or cultural processes that lead to them.

Discussion Questions

1. According to Yodanis, how does a divorce culture influence *intact* marriages?

2. To what does Yodanis relate the "consistency in women's responsibility for household labor across countries that vary greatly in culture, social structures, and social institutions"? How was household labor distributed in your family of origin? Why?

Source: "Divorce Culture and Marital Gender Equality: A Cross-National Study" by Carrie Yodanis, excerpted and with references omitted from *Gender & Society*, Vol. 19, No. 5, October 2005, pp. 644–659. Reprinted by permission of Sage Publications.

CHAPTER 22

I Just Want to Play

Women, Sexism, and Persistence in Golf

Lee McGinnis, Julia McQuillan, and Constance L. Chapple

This study explores the institutional and interactional barriers to women's golf participation and uncovers strategies women use to negotiate playing and persisting in golf. The women report heightened visibility and experiences with typecasting on the golf course, much like women in predominantly male occupations.

Since the implementation of Title IX, more American women are playing sports and exceeding previous expectations of women's athletic possibilities (Messner, 2002). Such advances raise our expectations of the possibility of gender-integrated sports. Why then has golf, ostensibly a sport that accommodates a wide range of abilities, remained a "man's game" (Maas & Hasbrook, 2001), despite the notable efforts made by women professional golfers? We sought to answer this question by interviewing recreational women golfers who have persisted in the sport. We learned about the barriers and constraints that they overcame to persist and the strategies they employed.

The physical barriers to women's integration into traditionally male sports are disappearing; however, profound social and psychological barriers and constraints remain. Inspired by the interviews, and insights from the extensive research tradition on women and the labor market, we suggest that similar to many occupations, people often frame golf as masculine. This framing marks women golfers as different or unexpected (Snyder, 1977). For most people, the term *golfer* immediately brings to mind a man, requiring the phrase "lady golfer" for women. In addition, the disproportionate number of men compared to women on the course heightens women's visibility and encourages tokenism. Institutional barriers such as an unequal distribution of work and leisure time for women and institutionalized sexism inhibit women's participation in golf much the same way discrimination inhibited women's entrance into male-dominated occupations. We suggest that the framing of golf as masculine and women's experiences with conscious and nonconscious sexism, social closure, and tokenism in golf settings have important ramifications for women's participation and persistence in golf. . . .

Our research addresses two questions: What barriers and constraints to participation do women experience on the course and what strategies do women use to negotiate playing and persisting in golf? We also investigated how the institution of golf is structured to privilege men and whether institutional practices on the course can become "woman friendly." By examining women who stay involved in golf, we gain insight into the strategies women use to overcome institutionalized sexism in an area dominated by men. By making visible the structures and dynamics that privilege men in golf and women's agency to overcome these barriers and constraints, we contribute to ongoing research traditions in the sociology of sport and the sociology of gender. . . .

Research on Tokenism, Statistical Discrimination, and Social Closure

We combine the feminist literature on the sociology of sport with literature from occupational sex segregation (statistical discrimination and tokenism) to help explain the sexism women experience on the golf course. Feminist theorists have conceptualized institutionalized barriers as practices that require little effort to maintain; they take on a life of their own as they are built into the formal structure of work organizations (Acker, 1990). According to Reskin and Hartmann (1986), institutionalized barriers that maintain sexism need not have their origins in prejudice but can be byproducts of administrative rules and procedures that were established for other reasons (Reskin & Hartmann, 1986). Institutionalized sexism is often the hallmark of imbalanced sex ratios in occupations, or in our case, sports.

As only 24.2% of all golfers (Liberman, 2004) are women, the sex ratios of professional and recreational golf are similar to male-dominated occupations. In fact, Kanter (1977) considered occupations that contain 16% to 34% of women to be "tilted" and women in these tilted occupations are often treated as tokens. This issue becomes even more apparent in golf when examining the percentage of women compared with men in the Professional Golfer's Association (PGA) of America, which is the golf industry's largest supplier of club professionals. Less than 4% of the members and apprentices in this program are women (Kinney, 2003).

Although the concept of tokenism is rarely applied outside of research on occupations, tokenism can have profound psychological impacts on minority group members (Kanter, 1977; Yoder, 2001). Because of their status as statistical and structural minorities in male-dominated institutions, women tokens often feel performance pressure, heightened visibility, and that they must either "fly under the radar" or risk typecasting (Jackson, Thoits, & Taylor, 1995; Kanter, 1977; Yoder, 2001). Kanter (1977) suggested that women tokens often respond to increased pressure by accepting their social isolation, by turning against their own group, or by embracing their token status by adhering to stereotypical typecasting. The danger of tokenism, according to Kanter, is that women are "often treated as representatives of their category, as symbols rather than individuals" (p. 208).

The idea of tokens and sex discrimination in institutions is tied to practices of statistical discrimination (England, 1992; Jencks, 1992). Statistical discrimination involves an individual stereotype that is misapplied to the group. For instance, women often are considered slower golfers than men because on average they have shorter drives. Although it is probably true that many women have shorter drives than many men, this does not necessarily translate into a slower pace of play because shorter drives can be more accurate. Statistical discrimination occurs when an individual is treated as if he or she possesses the qualities and characteristics typical for his or her sex, regardless of his or her individual abilities. The assumption that a woman will have short drives or slow play is an instance of using stereotypical attributes of a group to predict an individual's performance; this is as true in golf as it is on the job.

As described above, golf is potentially open to all abilities and types of players but, in reality, promotes masculine hegemony with the "citizen golfer" framed as young, male, and able-bodied (Maas & Hasbrook, 2001). Coakley and White (1998) applied a "gender logic" idea in their analysis of American sports. They argued that through participation in sports, people learn and reinforce the so-called commonsense idea that women are "naturally" inferior to men in any activity requiring physical skills and cognitive strategies, even when this logic is fallacious. According to Coakley and White, even those who may not share gender logics that govern institutions must nevertheless respond to them as they organize their lives because they tend to be self-perpetuating. Similar to Ridgeway's (1997) conceptualization of nonconscious discrimination, gender logics are self-perpetuating entities that do not require one's conscious intent to create inequality; however, unless a conscious effort is made to change them, gender logics continue. Attitudes and behaviors that systematically and unnecessarily privilege men in golf and frame "good golfers" as male golfers create an unwelcoming atmosphere of social closure. . . .

Golf is one of a few sports and leisure activities currently involved in a gender equity debate. Martha Burk's protest at the 2003 Masters Golf Tournament, because of the host club's gender discrimination practices, as well as participation by women in the PGA Tour events, has elevated golf to new levels of gender-based critical analysis (Shipnuck, 2004). Because of this historical moment, identifying conscious and nonconscious gender-based discrimination in golf and offering ways to eliminate or circumvent sexist practices contributes to research on sexism in general and may help those seeking change in golf, in particular. Similar to McGinnis, Chun, and McQuillan

(2003), we argue that marketers and managers are in better positions to push for structural gender change than individual players alone. We acknowledge that the recent attempts made by women touring professionals and amateurs to participate in professional men's events can help change perceptions. However, in terms of changing female participation for the long run, marketers and managers are in better positions to enhance the experience on the local level. In addition, we offer evidence that the golf industry will also benefit by fostering greater gender equity and integration in golf. Therefore, after we describe the sample, methodological approach, and insights from the experiences of women who persevered in golf despite encountering several barriers and constraints, we describe actions that those with power in the golf industry can take to promote increased women's participation in golf.

Sample and Method

DATA COLLECTION

The first author engaged in 10 semistructured personal interviews with women golfers during a 1-year period starting in the spring of 2000 and ending in the spring of 2001. These interviews took place before Annika Sorenstam, Michelle Wie, Martha Burk, and other newsmakers in golf penetrated the national media; therefore, the data presented here do not reflect these salient events. All of the women lived in the Midwest at the time of the study, which is where the primary researcher resided at the time of the study as well. Snowball (referrals from each interview respondent) and purposive (sampling women with particular experiences; e.g., recreational but persistent golfers) sampling strategies were used to find participants with a range of experience and ability in golf. Because the interview was long and the goal was depth of experience (not generalizability), we sought participants willing to talk openly and at length about their experiences. Our purpose was to find participants who could accurately and meaningfully describe the lived experience on the golf course. A referral from a friend was a good way to establish trust for this process; however, because personal referrals were used in the selection process, participants tended to be in similar professions, as informants would often select those in their workplace as potential participants. Consequently, several informants were selected from the medical profession. Medical professionals were also likely candidates because of the fact that salaries and

leisure time inherent in these professions are commensurate with the time and money needed for golf. . . .

The participants were first asked general questions about how they started playing golf, how often they play, with whom they generally play, and what they like about playing golf. After establishing their general experience with golf, the interviews focused on specific questions about gender, sexism, and golf. Finally, each woman was asked if she had suggestions that would help make golf more welcoming for women. An important goal of the research was to learn how some women continued to play golf when so many other women quit. . . .

All of the names of the women in this article are pseudonyms, and each participant was assured confidentiality in the research process. When quotes include references to specific locations or people, we replaced them with a generic term or an X. Because no new information emerged from the last interviews and convergence developed among the major themes, we stopped with 10 interviews. Similar to other qualitative researchers (Gainer, 1995; McCracken, 1988), we found that 10 interviews generated enough data to construct analytic categories and to develop themes.

To address our research questions, we needed women with a wide range of golf experience and ability. . . . The women in our sample have played golf for an average of 14.5 years, ranging from 4 to 21 years. All of the women are White and either held professional jobs or were obtaining advanced degrees. Two women play more than 80 rounds per year, two play about 5 rounds per year, and the remainder plays between 10 and 20 rounds per year. They range in age from 25 to 70 years old. Four of the women are married, and eight are employed. Four of the 10 women say that they are serious golfers; the remaining six primarily play for fun.

Observation and Analysis

. . .

TOKENISM AND DISCRIMINATION ON THE COURSE: SLOW PLAY AND DRIVING DISTANCE

Kanter (1977) explained several social-psychological ramifications of tokenism: increased performance pressure, heightened visibility, and stereotyping of behavior. We found that the women in the current study reported feeling all these because of, in part, statistical discrimination. In particular, these feelings of tokenism and discrimination surfaced when the women discussed how they felt they were unfairly labeled as slow or "not good" golfers because of their shorter driving ability. Several participants told stories of others expecting slow play or automatically assuming that women are not good golfers. Because women make up the minority of golfers, many of the women in the current sample, as tokens, felt singled out and highly visible on the golf course. They also felt unfairly stereotyped as not good golfers.

Driving distance and the speed of play are used to frame women as not good golfers. According to the women in our sample, this is how the process of statistical discrimination in golf plays itself out. Other golfers see most women hitting shorter drives than most men and assume that all women are slower players (i.e., not good golfers). However, many players, according to the women in the current sample, do not take into account the placement of men's longer and women's shorter drives. As one participant cogently pointed out, men's errant long drives can end up slowing down play much more than women's shorter but accurate drives.

> I may not hit the ball as far as they [men], but I am more accurate than they. . . . That ball that they hit a country mile over in the next fairway . . . I just sit there and wait for them to go find their ball. I'll get them because they have to use a shot to come back, and I'll get them because I'll go straight down the middle of the fairway, maybe only a 150 yards, but it's straight down the middle of the fairway, and then I'll pitch up and my putting is real good. So I can beat most of the guys. (Doris)

Driving distance is often an easily identifiable and important marker of who deserves to be on the course. Being a new golfer and a female golfer may give women a feeling of heightened visibility and undue performance pressure. This increased performance pressure, a classic by-product of tokenism, is evidenced in several accounts. According to Fran, many of the new golfers she plays with express unjustified dissatisfaction with their play and their image as golfers based on how far they can drive the ball.

> You know, actually I do think about it when I am playing with some of my good friends. They tend to comment, "Oh I didn't hit the ball as far as you." But they forget to think that maybe they hit the ball straighter than I did or in a better position on the fairway than I did that makes it easier for their second

shot onto the green. But I still think that in many women's minds it is sort of a downfall.

Women also expressed that they wanted to feel "up to par" with the men on the course, which often translated into driving the ball a similar distance. . . .

Driving distance was a concern for many of the participants and subtly informed their identities as deserving or good golfers; however, concerns over driving distance were eclipsed by the women's preoccupation with being framed as slow players. Although slow play is common at many golf courses and with many different kinds of players, the women in the current study indicated how they felt "picked on" when it came to this problem. Feeling picked on and unduly singled out is a classic reaction to the heightened visibility and stereotyping tokens often experience. One participant claimed that a starter warned her group (three women and a young boy), before they started on the first hole, to make sure they kept up with the group in front of them. The marshal did this even though he did not talk to any of the groups of men starting the course (according to our informant) and had no idea how fast or slow these women were likely to play. Other participants described similar experiences of being singled out. One participant indicated that women play faster because they are sensitive to how others will react to them:

> Men think that women are slow. They really do think that, and when I play with all these guys, I say to them, I'd rather play with women. Women move faster than you guys, and the reason is, is that we don't hit as far, and our balls are usually pretty straight. We know our limitations; we know how far we're going to hit the ball. (Doris)

Doris's view of slow play closely resembled Fran's, who commented how men are just as slow if not slower. "I think men in my experience can be just as slow as a group of women. In my years of playing golf, I have been behind many slow groups, and, honestly, I think more of them have been men." Eileen indicated, echoing the performance pressures highlighted earlier, that she feels rushed because of the slow play label: "I'm almost overly conscientious of slow play, and sometimes actually rush when I shouldn't because I don't want to be slow." We argue that her heightened sensibilities to this treatment has made her and many other informants in the current study acutely aware of the time discrepancies between men and women, arguably making her and other women golfers' accounts more credible.

Women's feelings of frustration and stereotyping did not stem solely from the misperceptions of their driving distance or their speed of play. In the following excerpt, Nellie, a former Division I collegiate golfer who worked in a pro shop while in college, explained the poor treatment she received from the other side of the counter. She noted how some men entering the pro shop failed to respect her golf knowledge until they were notified of her collegiate golf background. In the following statement, she explained how the interactions often changed when the men found out she was a university golfer.

> The men who would come in were very ignorant. . . . They sort of treated me like, "Oh, you're a woman. You don't even know what golf is." I would say something about buying a ball, and I would say what kind of ball . . . but they didn't know what I was asking. So it was like, "What do you mean?" You know, they kind of pretended that I didn't know, and then those guys that I worked with [said], "Oh, you shouldn't talk to her like that . . . she plays for the university." And then . . . all of the sudden they would be so small, and would kiss my ass . . . you know, that sort of the thing.

Finally, several women, in reaction to the tokenism they experienced on the golf course, displayed what Kanter (1977) called "role entrapment" in which tokens embrace stereotypical roles. For some of the women in our sample, role entrapment translated into emphasizing the femininity of golf and exaggerating differences between men and women on the golf course. Some of our participants' continued interest in golf was premised on framing golf as a feminine pursuit, in line with their overall feminine identity. For the women for whom maintaining a feminine identity was critical, it was important to them to play golf in such a way as to not appear too masculine—or not too aggressive, physical, or dominating. . . .

The women interviewed clearly exhibited many of the same coping strategies expressed by female tokens in male-dominated occupations. The token women golfers reported feelings of frustration because of stereotyping, heightened performance pressures due to increased visibility, and role entrapment because of gendered expectations of behavior. Similar to the difficulties in persisting in male-dominated occupations, tokens on the golf course may have trouble persisting at golf. This is especially true if their experiences with tokenism are coupled with social closure.

SOCIAL CLOSURE: COURSE SETUP, MERCHANDISING, ROLE MODELS, AND GOLF FUNCTIONS

Women often spoke of female friendly golf courses and golf outings. We believe what the women are describing when talking about female friendly experiences is inclusive golf; when women describe situations that were not female friendly, they were experiencing social closure. Social closure occurred in several domains: course setup, merchandising, role models, and golf functions. Each of these categories overlaps to form a potentially unwelcoming atmosphere to women on the golf course, signaling to women that they are not serious, deserving golfers.

Course setup was one of the first and most frequently mentioned unwelcoming issues. Some of the women indicated that restroom facilities for women were insufficient. One woman described the possible source of limited facilities: men used the outdoors. In response to a question asking if there is "anything men might do to send signals that women are outsiders," Sheryl, who plays more than 50 rounds a year, responded: "I don't think so, except not using the bathroom. Men don't do that very often; they just go behind a tree." This action conveys a message to women that men are not concerned with their presence, thereby defining golf courses as men's spaces. We doubt that this is a common practice; however, the mere fact that it happens sends a message to women. These acts signal social closure because the golf course is essentially an extension of the male-only locker room: a so-called backstage area in which the self-restraint expected in public domains does not apply.

The limited availability of women's golf clothing and equipment was a more common complaint in the interviews. Some of the women who described the lack of merchandising pointed out that because fewer women golf than men there is less merchandise available for them. The absence of female-oriented merchandise often signaled a course that was not as Lana termed it, "female friendly." In addition to inventory disproportions, the appearance that women's merchandise is stashed in out-of-the-way places or located in less trafficked areas was discouraging for some of these women as well, even if they recognized the reality of the market. For example, Lana said:

> Maybe it's because the percentage of female golfers is lower, so naturally you have to cater more to the men. But at course X, I just had a bad vibe when I looked in there, not even a visor for the ladies. . . . Since I have been golfing, I get a lot of golf catalogs, and most have of them have just one page or two pages of female clothing.

Fran made a similar comment:

There are always small sections for women's golf shoes and women's shirts at golf clubs. So you sort of feel like, well, here off in the corner are all the women's things and everything else seems male—all oriented towards the men.

Equipment complaints were similar, with some of the remarks targeted toward the lack of clubs for women. The availability of merchandise is tied to the general male-oriented structure of golf.

Clothes, there is always just a little selection for women and those things and just the way they might be treated on the golf course. Well, they don't hit the ball as strong of course, so they don't get the same kind of respect. It's like they [women] don't know what they're doing. (Nellie)

This final comment from Nellie is particularly telling. Not only is she upset about the lack of merchandise for women, she links this exclusion to the larger dynamics that frame women as not deserving to be on the course. For Nellie, a serious golfer and a former German national golf team member, clothes and merchandise are not just representations of self but rather markers of social acceptance. Even such an accomplished golfer felt unwelcome. The lack of available clothing and merchandise resulted in many women's feeling excluded from the course. . . .

The women in the current study recognized the gender challenges of many golf courses at which they experienced tokenism and social closure but continued to play in spite of these conditions. We turn now to the strategies women employ to persist in golf in the face of many challenges.

NEGOTIATING SEXISM ON AND OFF THE COURSE: PERSISTENCE STRATEGIES

One of our earlier questions concerned how women continue to play golf despite the challenges that we described in the previous sections. We observed several persistence strategies women use to stay involved. Some of these strategies include playing with same-sex golf partners, playing on woman-friendly courses, limiting participation to off times, and fitting golf in with paid work and child care responsibilities.

Limiting play to woman friendly places, players, and times. The women interviewed indicated only a few instances

where they could participate in a "pick-up" game (where one goes to the golf course individually expecting to be placed in an unplanned group) or play by themselves. Women often prefer to play with someone they know, preferably other women (McGinnis, 2002). For many women in the current sample, the social support they received while playing is critical to their continued involvement in golf. Playing with other women provides a feeling of security on the course, typical of groups who are in disadvantaged social locations. Difficulty in finding another woman to play with severely limited when and how often many of our participants could play. Some indicated instances in which they would forgo or postpone the idea of playing until they could find their desired partner. One participant said that she prefers to play with other women because it is more comfortable.

I will play with men in a scramble if they need me. . . . I'll do that when the pressure is on, but it is more relaxing with the women, and they are professional women—I have to be honest with you. "They," are other attorneys, or finance people. They are professional women. I try to encourage women to pick up the game because it is, if you are a professional, an important game to have. It is an important game at least to be able to play in certain circumstances and to not look like a fool. The worst thing is to play and hack it; that's horrible. In that case, you should probably drive the beer cart or something and not mess around with that. (Mindy)

Mindy indicated a number of important points in this quote. In addition to describing a desire to play with other women, she echoed our participants' general need to feel worthy while on the course. She also highlighted the social and professional importance of golf and the simultaneous danger of incompetence. We contend that the desire to feel up to par affects male golfers as well; few men, however, confront the other subtle messages about driving distance and speed of play that challenge women's golf worthiness. The women we interviewed persisted in golf despite these challenges. The current study participants created a more welcoming atmosphere by finding other women to play with.

. . . Another persistence strategy that some of the women mentioned was to play when friendlier conditions prevailed. The women indicated a number of different elements that helped make golf what they call female friendly or woman friendly. These elements follow the course layout (fewer par fives or long holes), the availability of women's merchandise in the pro shop, and the general female-friendly attitude toward women by the course workers (talking to the women directly, maintaining eye contact, not hurrying them up, making women feel welcome). According to Sheryl, woman-friendly courses were more welcoming to women and treated women with respect. For Lana, female friendly translated into how she was treated in the pro shop and on the course. For many of the women, defining *woman* or *female friendly* courses and conditions was difficult. They could more easily define situations that definitely were not female friendly, such as when they felt excluded, rushed, and had their golfing ability prejudged. All of the women interviewed challenged the logic of the sexism that they encountered. Some thought carefully about the treatment they received and found it illogical or unfair because it was based simply on their gender and not their ability. Most of the women had trouble articulating their discomfort with sexism in golf; however, all of the women challenged the idea that women are less entitled to play than men. All of the women at some point implied that maybe they were unlike other women because the ideas about women golfers that they encountered did not fit their notions of themselves. This seems to be the only way that they could make sense of the negative attributions they encounter about women golfers. . . .

Conclusion and Discussion

Although women continue to take up the game of golf in great numbers, they leave almost as quickly as they enter. The purpose of the current study was to examine the barriers and constraints women face in golf by examining data from interviews with those who stay and play the game. We were interested in the persistence strategies women employed to resist the individual, interactional, and institutional discrimination they encountered. Several interesting and revealing themes emerged from our data: tokenism, discrimination, and social closure; we discuss each in turn.

As suggested by Kanter (1977), tokens can accept their isolation, turn against their own group, or adhere to stereotypical typecasting. Each of these actions was evident to some extent in the current analysis. The most prevalent action was adhering to stereotypical typecasting, as many women seemed to indicate a sense of not wanting to rock the (gender) boat. Rather than creating an unapologetic "in your face" attitude toward sexism (Broad, 2001), the women in the current study were more likely to express unwillingness to golf alone. Golfing with other women provided a way to golf and have no worries about their femininity. For women golfers, playing alone or with men made gender more salient. As indicated by

Kanter (1977), the danger in tokenism is that women are often treated as representations of their category. The women in the current study were subject to this danger as noted by the treatment they received from course personnel and male golfers in regard to their hitting distance, perceived slow play, and teeing preferences.

There are several institutional and interactional barriers to women's participation in golf. Social closure and statistical discrimination occur in golf, either consciously or unconsciously, and shape women's perceptions of the game. These gendered interactional dynamics shape women's sense of golf worthiness (i.e., good golfers) and their perception of golf as female friendly. Repeatedly encountering golf courses that are not women friendly diminishes women's desire to play golf. Experiences of social closure and statistical discrimination are serious barriers to women's persistence in golf. Similar to how gender-linked attributes are used to discriminate in employment, the presumption that gender determines driving distance and speed of play subtly contribute to the presumption that only men deserve to be on the golf course. This theme was consistent in the interviews. We recognize that a minimum driving distance is necessary to enjoy golf. Distance, however, is only one component of good golfing; accuracy is as, if not more, important. Long but inaccurate drives can incur extra time and penalties through lost balls and extra shots, contributing to more time and higher scores than shorter but more accurate drives. Some of the women in our sample clearly understood this dynamic; however, many did not. For those who did not, their short driving ability meant that they were not good golfers and, therefore, less worthy of being on the course than long-driving but often inaccurate men. . . .

In addition to these barriers to women's involvement, we learned of several strategies that help women stay involved. Finding women friendly courses, playing with other women, challenging the stereotypes of women golfers (that women can be competent, competitive players), and focusing on the benefits of golf (e.g., physical activity, beautiful surroundings, and fun competition) helped our participants stay involved. Yet, when individuals alone find ways to accommodate gendered inequity, the system remains unchanged (West & Zimmerman, 1987). Are there systematic changes at the interactional and institutional levels that golf marketers and golf managers can do to make more golf courses and golf as a whole more inviting for women?

We think there are. We see these changes not only as a way to promote gender equality but also as profitable and good for the growth of the game, an initiative often purported by the industry's governing bodies. More women want to play golf than are currently doing so. For the past 3 years the total number of rounds played has declined (Graves, 2003); however, the demand for golf persists. In the United States, 45 million people call themselves golfers (Graves, 2003); according to the National Golf Foundation (1999), approximately 41 million Americans (older than age 12) want to play golf or play more golf. This 41 million consists of four segments: (a) 14 million current players who want to play more, (b) 12 million former golfers who want to play again, (c) 7 million nongolfers who are interested in trying the game, and (d) 8 million juniors between ages 5 and 17 years who would like to learn or to play more. Of the nongolfers, 60% are women, compared to 20% who currently make up the entire golf population (National Golf Foundation, 1999). Golf associations and managers are already trying to reduce gender inequity in golf. For example, many golf courses have eliminated gendered teeing grounds altogether and are instead using markers such as front, middle, and back for teeing grounds. Some courses are using handicaps as teeing designations.

There is still room for improvement. For example, although some may chalk up the absence of merchandising for women as trivial, this was an important theme in the interviews. Merchandise for women signaled a woman-friendly course that appreciates women golfers. Unlike one participant, we are not convinced that women need special equipment or lessons to accommodate their bodies. Golf managers and marketers need to find a way to make women feel welcome without making it seem as though they need special equipment. In addition, many women described exclusionary nonverbal communication with golf personnel. For example, personnel would not address them or look at them directly but instead turned their attention to the men in their group. Training managers and course workers to treat all women as active and serious golfers will easily remedy this barrier. . . .

Research on eliminating discrimination in male-dominated workplaces can also contribute to our thinking about ways to end gender-based discrimination in golf.

Suggestions for changing workplaces include holding managers accountable, creating interdependence among employees, and neutralizing the cognitive processing that promotes categorization and differential value (Bielby, 2000; Reskin, 2000). It is likely that these strategies will work in golf as well. To these we add suggestions for making golf more inviting to women by having more women working at golf courses, providing more merchandise geared toward women, training employees to not assume that women will engage in slower play, emphasizing that teeing grounds are tied to ability not gender, emphasizing nine-hole play for economy of time, and providing affordable drop-in care close to the golf course for dependents.

Golf is an engaging context in which to observe gender dynamics. Barriers to women's participation in golf constantly emerge despite golf's apparent gender neutrality. Even though the number of women participating in golf has increased, its proportions have remained relatively constant. Although societal-level changes are necessary to make dramatic changes in women's sports participation, the microlevel adjustments we describe begin the process of greater gender integration in golf. Golf has the potential to operate as a so-called gateway sport leading to more gender equity in all sports, Many women "just want to play"; recognizing and reducing gendered barriers to their participation is a step in making that happen.

Discussion Questions

1. What suggestions do the authors make to eliminate sexism on the golf course?

2. This article focuses on the obstacles facing women golf players. However, the authors note that race and class inequities are also issues on the golf course. How does social class influence who gets to play golf? What social class advantages come with being a good golfer?

Source: "I Just Want to Play: Women, Sexism, and Persistence in Golf" by Lee McGinnis, Julia McQuillan and Constance L. Chapple, excerpted and with notes & references omitted from *Journal of Sport & Social Issues,* Vol. 29, No. 3, August 2005, pp. 313–337. Reprinted by permission of Sage Publications.

CHAPTER 23

"I'm Not Thinking of It as Sexual Harassment"

Understanding Harassment across Race and Citizenship

Sandy Welsh, Jacquie Carr, Barbara MacQuarrie, and Audrey Huntley

Diverse focus groups provide data for distinguishing women's understandings of sexual harassment based on race and citizenship. For Black women and women without full citizenship, issues of race cannot be separated from ideas about sexual harassment. Only White women identify completely with existing legal understandings of sexual harassment and believe they have the right to report it.

One frequently discussed problem in the research on sexual harassment is that women will report experiencing unwanted sexual attention but will not label those experiences as sexual harassment. This phenomenon has led some to focus on the gap between objective and subjective perceptions of harassment or the likelihood respondents will label their experiences as sexual harassment (Vaux 1993; Williams 1997). Most sexual harassment research complicates this issue because it is conducted on white women (who are predominately heterosexual with full citizenship rights and a variety of class backgrounds). Although some have recently studied the experiences of women of color (Cortina 2001; Kalof et al. 2001; Texeira 2002), there is need for more attention to how women define sexual harassment through the intersection of race, gender, and citizenship. This intersectionality may explain why some women do not define their experiences as sexual harassment.

This study is concerned with the way women talk about and define sexual and workplace harassment. While some may argue it is the legal definition of harassment that matters, we believe it is important not to be constrained by this definition. In the specific case of sexual harassment, women who experience racialized harassment alongside sexual harassment (or do not define their

sexual harassment as "sexual" but as about race) do not fit within our legal conception of sexual harassment.

This analysis examines how race and citizenship complicate women's definitions of sexual harassment while utilizing past research on intersectionality to move our arguments forward. While others have incorporated racialized processes into their harassment research (Texeira 2002), we move beyond these to demonstrate how citizenship also shapes the meaning of sexual harassment. Using focus group from a participatory action research project, we argue that race and citizenship are present in women's definitions of harassment. . . .

Interlocking Systems of Domination

. . . Sexual harassment, like rape and other forms of sexual violence, is embedded in an interlocking system of race, gender, and citizenship. As Razak notes, when rape is discussed in court or other arenas, "the rape script is thus inevitably raced whether it involves intraracial or interracial rape" for "race never absents itself from the rape script" (1998, 68–69). For example, the rape of Black women by Black or white men is taken less seriously by the criminal justice system than the rape of white women. The same can be said for sexual harassment—race and citizenship are never absent. What is often overlooked in analyses of sexual harassment is how they represent a set of interlocking social arrangements. To answer the question of how diverse women define sexual harassment, it is necessary to focus on the interlocking nature of race and citizenship. To do this, we first discuss research on race and sexual harassment and then turn to the issue of citizenship.

RACIALIZED PROCESSES AND SEXUAL HARASSMENT

. . . Recent studies use the terms *gendered racism* or *racialized sexual harassment* to describe how the harassment experiences of women of color are not simply about sexual discrimination that involves race (e.g., Banneriji 1995; Buchanan and Ormerod 2002; Texeira 2002). Mansfield et al's (1991) study of women in blue-collar occupations found that African American tradeswomen experienced gender and racial harassment. Yoder and Aniakudo (1996) provide some evidence that gender and racial harassment are intertwined for African American women firefighters. Although they focus most of their analysis on gender, their respondents consistently refused to distinguish between race and gender as the source of their differential treatment. In the words of one respondent, "it's hard to say whether it was just specifically because I was Black. With it being a double edge: being Black and being female" (Yoder and Aniakudo 1996, 266). Mecca and Rubin's (1999) analysis of African American women university students found that half of their sample perceived racial differences between their experiences and the experiences of Caucasian women. Comments about racially based features and racially based stereotypes that label African American women as promiscuous were found to be sexually harassing. These studies highlight the need to attend more closely to how race inter-plays with gender when trying to understand how women interpret sexual behaviors in the workplace. . . .

CITIZENSHIP STATUS AND SEXUAL HARASSMENT

Past research on sexual harassment makes citizenship invisible by focusing on citizens living in their country of origin. We argue that citizenship status is a visible and complicating component of women's definitions of sexual harassment. Hondagneu-Sotelo's examination of undocumented Latina domestic workers is an example of how "citizenship or legal status is a significant analytic category that might fruitfully be incorporated in our analyses of women's employment" (1997, 104; see also Arat-Koc 2001; Nakano Glenn 2000a). She finds the

harassment, intimidation, and isolation experienced by these immigrant women workers is made worse by their undocumented status. Some women report living like prisoners in their employers' homes, having no friends, and being threatened that their employer will turn them in to the Immigration and Naturalization Service. . . .

To answer the question of how diverse groups of women in Canada define sexual harassment, we draw on focus group data from a Larger study of women's harassment experiences. The analysis begins with a discussion of white women with full citizenship rights. This is followed by an analysis of how the women of color and women without full citizenship rights define sexual harassment. Finally, we conclude with a discussion of what our findings mean for definitions of harassment.

Data Collection and Method

We derive data for this analysis from focus groups collected as part of a participatory action research project in the province of Ontario, Canada. Focus groups were held in the summer and fall of 2000 and throughout 2002. For both time periods, participants were selected based on purposive sampling to allow us to refine our understanding of the intersection of race, citizenship, disability, sexuality, living in isolated rural areas, and class with women's experiences of sexual harassment. Six focus groups were completed in 2000 with Black women, Filipinas, white women in unionized male-dominated manufacturing settings (two groups), mixed-race women employed by the federal government, and a mixed-race sexual harassment support group. . . .

Two members of the research team facilitated each focus group session. Focus groups opened with a general discussion of what women thought about sexual harassment and whether they knew anything about it. This opener was followed by topics that included what women's experiences were with sexual harassment and other forms of workplace discrimination; whether women had reported these experiences; if so, what they had experienced; and what were the consequences of experiencing harassment. . . .

How Do Women Define Sexual and Workplace Harassment?

By letting women define harassment, we can discover where other forms of oppression, such as racism, homophobia, lack of citizenship, disability, and classism, intersect with sexual harassment. This helps us move beyond a monolithic understanding of sexual and workplace harassment to one that is more inclusive of the experiences of all women. Our analysis also calls into question the legal definition of sexual harassment that may serve the law well, but not necessarily diverse groups of women.

LEGALISTIC VIEW OF SEXUAL HARASSMENT: WHITE WOMEN WITH FULL CITIZENSHIP RIGHTS

Four of the focus groups (two groups of union women, the sexual harassment support group, and the federal employees group) consisted of women whose definitions of sexual harassment fit most closely with legal understandings of sexual harassment. In two focus groups, when asked specifically about sexual harassment, these predominately white women citizens stated that sexual harassment consists of "inferiorizing sexual contact, degrading and inferior"; "the abuse of power"; "a course of conduct that is unwelcome," with *unwelcome* being the key word; and "a look, something verbal, attitude, leering, etc. making you uncomfortable." In the other two focus groups, women did not explicitly define sexual harassment but rather they told their stories of harassment. These women discuss being molested, implicitly threatened with sexual assault, and other forms of unwanted sexual conduct while at work.

Most of the white women gave a fairly consistent view of sexual harassment: Sexual harassment is behavior that is unwelcome and of a sexual nature. In contrast, Giuffre and Williams (1994) find some workers draw "boundary lines" around what they consider sexually harassing behaviors and what are pleasurable and/or tolerable (see also Williams, Giuffre, and Dellinger 2004). We believe the consistency of the understanding of the white women in our study is related to two factors. First, the white women in our study have the advantage of both white privilege and citizenship status. Due to the invisibility of their whiteness and their citizenship status to themselves and to those harassing them, the white women are not harassed based on their race or citizenship status. This privilege also makes it easier for these women to see their experiences as fitting within the law. The white women may perceive more opportunities to file complaints given their privilege in the legal system over other racialized and noncitizen groups.

Second, unlike Giuffre and Williams (1994), we include women who have reported their harassment in our analysis. One interpretation of our findings is that the process of filing a complaint may impose a legalistic

understanding of sexual harassment onto women's experiences. Marshall (1998) discusses how the complaint process leads to the development of a "legal consciousness" about sexual harassment. Many of the white women, who are the ones most likely to have reported their harassment in our study, appear to have developed an understanding that sexual harassment is a legal problem with a corresponding legal discourse for describing it. And in turn, this process of filing a complaint leads to a legal consciousness that imposes a legalistic view about how sexual harassment is defined (Welsh et al. 2005). We also believe our findings point to the way in which both race and citizenship, which are normally considered absent in the analysis of white women, play out in these women's experiences. The status of being white Canadian citizens combined with either their belief that they could report or their actual reporting of their harassment, made it possible for the white women to define their experiences as sexual harassment.

WOMEN OF COLOR AND THE DEFINITION OF SEXUAL HARASSMENT

Most of the women of color in our focus groups consistently mention that it was not simply sexual harassment that they experienced or that they were not sure if they could define their experiences as harassment (Yoder and Aniakudo 1996). For example, one woman of color in the sexual harassment support group, when asked whether she experienced sexual harassment differently than the white women in her group, stated the following: "Racial comments were included. Comments about men of color, or my skin color." A Filipino live-in caregiver stated that she defined harassment in the following way: "It's like a mix. It's a mix action. You don't know if it is if that person is doing it to you because of the color of your skin and the type of the job that you have, you're doing the dirty job in the house so you don't know if it is harassment or sexual harassment." As we will discuss next, defining harassment as a "mix action" differs across the women of color and women lacking full citizenship rights in our study.

Black women with full citizenship rights. The focus group of Black women demonstrates the racialized nature of workplace harassment. Similar to other research (Buchanan and Ormerod 2002), the Black women in the focus group discuss how sexual harassment is intertwined with racial issues. At the outset, this group defined the term *sexual harassment* as less meaningful for describing their experiences compared to white women.

As part of their discussion, these women also made connections to how they do not label sexual behaviors at work as sexual harassment. As one Black woman stated, "we do not define it [sexual harassment] and I think we are offended but we have grown to accept that as a norm, within our society. 'Cause the guys think it's normal and so do we. You see the young girls. The young girls, sometimes I get offended for them when these guys with their old ugly self trying to say and do things, and they just 'hee hee hee.'" The Black women in this focus group discuss how sexual harassment has been normalized between Black women and men.

At the same time, for many of these Black women, it is difficult to separate sexual harassment in the workplace from sexual and racial harassment in society at large. This has the effect of further complicating the issue of labeling behaviors as sexual harassment. The following interchange between the facilitator and focus group members illustrates this:

Facilitator: You know it's interesting. I'm hearing something very interesting happening around the table. We came here to talk about sexual harassment, and as I'm listening to the things that people are saying, I'm really hearing a lot of very subtle, not so subtle racial harassment that goes on.

Participant A: That's exactly what it is. Yes.

Participant B: . . . The racial piece is convoluted. Quite often it is insidious.

Participant C: I think we, we as Black women would experience that, because as you see at the very beginning, I think we can handle sexual harassment. So it's not a big deal for us. Really.

Participant A: That's why we don't name it.

Participant C: Yes, that's right, we don't think of it as sexual harassment.

Participant D: That's right, we don't think of it as sexual harassment because we can handle it.

Participant E: You know, I have a little bit of a problem with that though. But it would probably get a little bit more complex. I do think that, going back to the not naming piece, I do think that Black women are harassed a lot, but that they maybe don't,

as you said before, maybe don't see it as sexual harassment. Um . . . perhaps a key, perhaps a very key piece of evidence for that whether it be the workplace, or in the social environment because we keep talking about the workplace . . . but a key piece for the social environment is perhaps even more so than the workplace. . . . They [Black women] have to go it alone.

Participant E proceeds to discuss how domestic relationships between Black women and Black men affect Black women's understanding of sexual harassment. In particular, this Black woman focuses on issues of power and abandonment between Black mothers and fathers. For this group of women, their understanding of sexual harassment in the workplace cannot be separated from the historical position of Black women, domestic relationships between Black men and women, and larger societal issues of racism. . . .

In this focus group, sexual harassment was often discussed as "easier to handle" and less pressing than racial harassment and discrimination. Sexual harassment was seen as something white women were less adept at handling on their own compared to Black women. One clue to this may be the race of the harasser: This emerged as an important factor in Black women's distinction between sexual harassment that they can handle versus sexual harassment that they do not name. Texeira's (2002) study of African American women law enforcement officers also points to the importance of the race of the harasser (see also Giuffre and Williams 1994). The African American women in Texeira's study are reluctant to report if the harasser is also African American due to the perceived need to keep a "united racial front" (Texeira 2002, 540). The Black Canadian women in our study have a slightly different take on not reporting harassment of Black men. While not explicitly discussing a reluctance to report Black male harassers, this group of women tends to view harassment from Black men as something that is normalized and hence not defined as harassment.

A second explanation for the Black women's definition of harassment can be linked to the structure of sexual harassment law in Canada. In a legal system with static categories of racial and sexual discrimination and harassment, women who experience both are forced to prioritize which experience they put forward (Crenshaw 1989). This dynamic, intertwined with systemic racism experienced by these Black women, could explain their belief that sexual harassment is easier to handle in some cases. . . .

Lack of full citizenship status, race, and harassment. For the women in our study who immigrated to Canada, the issue of citizenship status was a clear component of both their harassment experience and how they defined this experience. . . . The Filipino domestic workers face unique circumstances surrounding the intersection of their race and citizenship status. Many domestic workers come to Canada as part of the Live-in Caregiver Program. These immigrants receive an employment authorization visa that is usually valid for one year and is renewable for two years. To renew their employment authorization, immigrants must have a letter from their employer stating that the position is renewed for another year. Although immigrants can move to another employer while working under an employment authorization, the immigrant must then apply for and receive a new employment authorization before changing employers. While working under an employment authorization, immigrants are tied to a specific employer. This makes it difficult to avoid harassment by changing jobs. Unlike women with full citizenship rights, women in the Live-in Caregiver Program do not feel free to leave their job and to seek a new employer. . . .

How do Filipinas working as live-in caregivers define their harassment experiences? In one of the Filipina focus groups, the women try to decide whether one member of their focus group experienced sexual harassment by a white elderly employer or whether it was just "old age." One participant explains that her white employer is 92 years old, is a doctor, and still is "smart" and mentally capable. She continues,

> Many times he walks around the house with nothing on the bottom, only the top. I said I don't want you to walk around with nothing on. He said, what's the matter? So I said to myself, maybe just because he was a doctor so he doesn't care you know the part of the body is just like part of your face, part of your hands. Because I work in a hospital too, so I said to myself maybe that's what he thinks. It's up to me if I think something if I define it differently. So I was confused and then last night he was in the other room and I said, "Do you have something on?" Because he was just wearing his top and he said, "Nothing, but you cannot see nothing." I said, "No, I don't like it," so I gave him something to wear, but he didn't give me any malice. He's just natural.

Her concern is first dismissed by another participant, who comments, "He's old, it totally changes the behavior," and says that his behavior cannot possibly be harassment. Another participant comments that this could be a case of dementia. Yet the woman experiencing the behavior continues to defend herself by stating, "I know [it could be something else] but in this particular thing he knows that it is bad . . . because he's [not] doing that in front of the children. . . . Every time he has a visitor, he dresses good, he fixes himself, every time." The women debate whether this is harassment if the older man does not touch the woman and if it takes place in his home. The woman experiencing this behavior expresses her frustration when she states, "No one would believe me if I said my 90-year-old [employer] has nothing wrong with his mind."

At this point, the definition of what happened to the one caregiver is unresolved. Is it sexual harassment or something "natural" that the older employer should be allowed to do? For women working in homes, the ambiguity around what is natural and what is harassment is a line that must be negotiated. . . .

While the white women with citizenship were able to fit much of their experience into an understanding of what sexual harassment is in Canada, the focus group of Filipinas struggled with defining harassment in Canada. There are a myriad of forces that collide in their struggle to label this experience, including being Filipina, working for white employers, having less than full citizenship rights, and working in their employers' homes. Their understanding of the definition of harassment in Canada conflicted with their understandings of harassment in their home country, where little if anything was socially or legally defined as sexual harassment. This conflict created ambiguities in their ability to define this particular experience as harassment. . . .

Conclusion

In her analysis of intersectional theorizing, Stasiulis asks, "*Which* social relations in the seemingly dizzying array of differences should be accorded particular salience or significance in any given theoretical framework is impossible to predict a priori" (1999, 378). Our choice to focus on race and citizenship should not be seen as meaning that other identities and oppressions are irrelevant. Rather, in the analysis of our data, issues of race and citizenship emerged as dominant themes that shaped diverse women's definitions of harassment. It is not simply that white women, women of color, and women with and without legal citizenship rights have different understandings of what constitutes sexual harassment. It is more that the term *sexual harassment* and its meaning are interlocked with race and citizenship status.

The experiences of the white women with full citizenship rights in our study appear to be the most easily encapsulated by both legal and social science definitions of sexual harassment. Although white women's perceptions of sexual harassment match most closely with legal understandings of sexual harassment, it may be that it is our legal understandings that mirror white women's understandings of sexual harassment. The law is a powerful structuring mechanism for what is defined as sexual harassment.

Women of color present diverse definitions of harassment. The Black women in our study define harassment in two ways. When perpetrated by Black men, these women tend not to label their experiences as harassment. They link it back to historical issues of sexism in the Black community. When discussing sexual harassment from non-Black men, these women say harassment is something they can handle on their own and is not as pressing a problem as racism and racial harassment. Filipina domestic workers see sexual harassment in their workplaces as more ambiguous. Working for predominately white employers in their homes, it is not always clear where the boundary lines between appropriate and inappropriate behavior lie. The Filipina workers also make direct connections to their lack of full citizenship rights in terms of how this affects their ability to do anything about their experiences.

This analysis highlights how current conceptual and legal understandings of sexual harassment are not always meaningful and may not capture the experiences of many women, especially women of color. The women of color in our study do not see their harassment as being about race or gender; rather, it is about how race and gender, along with citizenship, intersect that defines their experiences. In terms of legal definitions, Crenshaw (1989) points out how Black women's employment discrimination claims have difficulty being recognized because legal arguments must be framed as either sexual or racial discrimination, not both.

Crenshaw (1989) argues that shifting our understanding of discrimination to be inclusive of women of color calls into question our current legal definitions of sexual harassment. In a precedent-setting document, the Ontario Human Rights Commission (2002) discusses the need to incorporate an understanding of intersectionality into discrimination and harassment complaint mechanisms. This includes building into reporting mechanisms the need to probe women (and men) for the ways that their experiences are unique due to overlapping oppressions and for accounting for the intersection of these oppressions when determining remedies for the harassment. For women of color and women lacking full citizenship rights who have had their experiences rendered invisible by the dominant discourses of race or gender, these are important first steps in having the legal discourse and mechanisms around sexual harassment account for their experiences.

Discussion Questions

1. According to the authors, why might existing sexual harassment laws most closely relate to White women's perception of sexual harassment?

2. What might make you *not* report being sexually harassed in the workplace?

Source: "'I'm Not Thinking of It as Sexual Harassment': Understanding Harassment across Race and Citizenship" by Sandy Welsh, Jacquie Carr, Barbara MacQuarrie and Audrey Huntley, excerpted and with notes & references omitted from *Gender & Society*, Vol. 20, No. 1, February 2006, pp. 87–107. Reprinted by permission of Sage Publications.

CHAPTER 24

Multiple Masculinities?

Teenage Boys Talk about Jocks and Gender

C. J. Pascoe

Through interviews, the author examines the ways in which boys from different school subcultures engage with the most dominantly masculine of the school's peer groups—the Jocks. Boys from less "masculine" groups maintain a sense of self as masculine by reworking meanings of group membership and gendered identity to include masculinized attributes associated with jocks, such as competence, heterosexual success, and dominance. A simplistic deployment of the "multiple masculinities" may miss some of the ways gender works in a given setting.

This article examines the gendered and generational sensibility of teenage boys coming of age in the new millennium who are, directly and indirectly, confronting third-wave feminism and growing up in society that is debating both privately and publicly new and varied ways of being teenage boys and men. Because gender is central to identity, what does it mean to be a boy in adolescence, the very time one is forming the basis of an adult identity (Erikson, 1959/1980; Kinney, 1993)? In the wake of all of the changes in gender institutionally and individually, what are the lived experiences of boys in contemporary America?

Interviews with 20 teenage boys between the ages of 15 and 18 at two California High Schools, Pinetree and Independence, indicate that a sense of masculinity is central to being a teenage boy. These interviews suggest that athleticism and sports are principal markers of masculinity in high school (Edley & Wetherell, 1997). However, not all high school boys may easily engage in or draw on the "patriarchal dividend" (Connell, 1995) granted by participation in sports. Those boys who are not "Jocks" have a more difficult time accessing the sense of masculinity bestowed on boys who are Jocks. In this study, I look at

boys who are Jocks and those who are not Jocks to investigate the ways in which this image of the Jock permeates boys' sense of themselves as masculine. Using these interviews, I show how boys' social positionings in the school's gender order affect the way in which they construct themselves as masculine in the face of this pervasive image of adolescent masculinity. I find that regardless of his actual social status, each boy is able to construct himself as sufficiently masculine by discursively reworking his individual or group identity such that it mirrors some part of the masculinity of the Jock. . . .

High School Hierarchies

High school is a staging ground for identity formation and the primary hub of social life in adolescence. One is primarily recognized by whom one hangs out with. The students' lives are, to a large extent, shaped by the structure of the school. Schools help to promote hierarchical student relations through structuring of both education and sports (Eckert, 1989). The style of masculinity in a given school often reflects the surrounding community

(Connell, 1996; Heward, 1990; Skelton, 1996). Masculinity also plays a large role in the creation of adolescent school subcultures, which, in part, function to reproduce class structure (MacLeod, 1987; Parker, 1996; Willis, 1981). Most important for this article, peer groups are hierarchically ranked and infused with gendered meanings (Adler, Kless, & Adler, 1992; Kinney, 1993; Martino, 1999; Thorne, 1993).

At Independence, social groups are highly delineated. The Preps, Jocks, and Cheerleaders rule campus. At the opposite end of the social spectrum are the PACrats. PAC is the acronym for Performing Arts Center. Rats are the students who participate in drama. Joining them on the lower end of the social hierarchy are the Freaks. Freaks, dressed in black and adorned with multiple piercings, usually spend their time smoking in an area of campus called Hell. The Bench Mob, a group of juniors who hang out in the central quad, and the Skaters, boys and some girls who are involved in skateboarding, are located somewhere in the center of this social scale.

At Pinetree, the groups are less distinctly defined but no less hierarchical. The Jocks and the students who participate in A.S.B. (the Associated Student Body—student government) sit at the top of the school's social world. A group of senior boys formed a group called the Millennium Mob and pride themselves on crashing all the student parties. By virtue of these intimidation tactics, they also sit high on the social hierarchy. At the opposite end of the spectrum, again, are the drama students and the Goths (Pinetree's version of the Freaks). At both schools exist a group of students in the middle of the hierarchy who remain unnamed. To be sure, most of the students muddle through somewhere in the middle. It is the visibility of these groups and the status each represents that provide other students a variety of identities with which to define what they are and what they are not.

At both schools, Jocks are considered the highest ranking position in the social order. It is widely acknowledged by the boys at both schools that the Jocks are usually the most popular boys in school. . . .

This is not to say that all boys who play sports are Jocks. Most of the boys I interviewed played sports, but the majority of them certainly were not considered by themselves or others to be Jocks. Being a Jock is not just playing a sport but about *what* sport one plays and one's orientation to other groups of boys and girls. To be a Jock, one must play the right type of sport, usually football, basket-ball, and depending on how the school structures and funds its sports, wrestling, baseball, or soccer. To be a Jock is to emphasize dominance over others,

whether it be on the field or in the social world, as can be seen by their position on the social hierarchy. Jocks also participate in an emphasized heterosexuality in which girls' function as status symbols or sexual objects, not as girlfriends, is emphasized.

Jocks are associated with a dominant masculinity. Often when talking about a Jock or imitating someone they identify as a Jock, boys lower their voices to simulate a more "manly" sound. Often, Jocks are portrayed, by both themselves and others, as having a dominant attitude toward other (usually non-Jock) groups of boys. Says Neil, a Jock, about playing basketball,

> You got like the guys who actually play sports and then the guys that want to play but can never make the team. So they always sit out there at lunch and play like basketball and stuff. And they can never make the basketball team. The guys who are on the teams will never actually practice unless they are forced to practice. And the guys that can't make it are always practicing, but never make it.

His voice is mocking when referring to the guys who are practicing during lunchtime. In a similar vein, Shane, a wrestler and a Jock at Independence, notes that guys "want all the guys to respect them kind of thing. They want to be able to do everything better than someone else. I know I work harder to do that. Some people just dream about it and some people just go on with it." To be a Jock is to be dominant and, in some ways, to naturalize this dominance. . . .

In part because of the school's structural emphasis on sports and in part because of broader cultural definitions of masculinity that include sports, boys, when describing themselves and their identities, refer to what they consider to be the embodiment of the male athlete—the Jock. In each interview, the boy would, when describing his identity and his position in the school's social organization, reference the Jock and position his own identity accordingly. However, when referencing the Jock, the boys are often not referring to any specific person but an image, a symbol, by which they feel they should be defining themselves. They manipulate this symbol in various ways according to their own abilities and understandings of gender. In the following vignettes, I highlight recurring themes in the boys' interactions with the symbol of the Jock. Through this image, masculinity functions as a lexicon from which boys can draw, depending on their position in the school status structure. For some boys, being an athlete functions as "Jock insurance," allowing them to include other, more "femi-nine" parts of their identities without being labeled a "fag." Frequently, when boys are perceived as not acting sufficiently masculine, they are called "homo" or "fag" (Burn, 2000; Plummer, 2001; Smith, 1998). But if one is masculine enough in one area of his identity, he may have enough "Jock insurance" to act slightly feminine, at least occasionally. When athleticism is not an option for boys, they draw on other masculine traits associated with the Jock, such as emphasized heterosexuality or dominance, to "make up for" what they lack in claims on masculinity through sports. Sport also can function in contradictory ways in which it does provide a way to assert a masculine self while simultaneously facilitating a sense of connection with other boys and men. Some boys may not attempt to claim masculinity through drawing on certain tropes of masculinity; instead, they may divest the Jocks of masculinity by feminizing them. Gender, in this sense, is understood as a relationship between social position and discursive work through which boys attempt to position themselves in ways that will be socially recognized as masculine.

Jock Insurance

Even though he has a solid claim on masculinity through his involvement in football, Adam understands himself in decidedly "non"-masculine terms. Adam is a hand-some 17-year-old senior, a dead-ringer for Tom Cruise. He is friends with the Jocks, plays football, and was a prince on the homecoming court. Initially, he tells me that sports are central to who he is. He continues through the rest of the interview to detail his close relationship with his mother, his alienation from his father, and how his friends tease him about his "feminine" traits. Adam has a complex understanding of himself in which sports consciously play a large role, but our discussion indicates that his identity is also closely tied to what he, and other teenage boys, considers "feminine" qualities such as sensitivity and emotion. . . .

Adam sees himself as "different than some guys, or than a lot of the guys I know," in that he is emotional. He describes his best friend as one of those unemotional guys from whom he is different. "Like he's totally the opposite of me. Like I'm all sensitive and feeling. And he'll like make jokes about it and make me laugh about it. Like you can tell that he totally has feelings." He believes that girls want to date "someone who understands. Someone who can share, is able to express their feelings.

'Cause I know a lot of guys who are almost afraid to express their feelings to a girl 'cause it doesn't seem manly or whatever." Again he connects being under-standing and emotionally oriented to masculinity and heterosexuality.

. . . It is exactly because he is a Jock that he is able to make up for this sort of behavior. He is also able to invoke heterosexual success with girls. Being a Jock acts as a sort of insurance for these non-Jock behaviors. Adam is able to recast supposedly feminine orientations in a het-erosexual context, invoking heterosexual "success" with girls to justify this "feminine" orientation. Adam's gender project is an interaction between a Jock identity and a more feminine sense of self. Adam is able to discursively position himself as feminine because of his positional claim on masculinity through his status as a "Jock," his "Jock insurance."

Emphasized Heterosexuality

Kevin, a large, White, 15-year-old sophomore with dark hair and a full beard, must be more careful about his pre-sentation of self as masculine because he cannot draw on athletic ability the same way Adam can. Kevin comes to the interview dressed in a stylish leather jacket and could easily, on first inspection, pass for 20 years old. Kevin's interview focuses on his choice between football and drama as his school activities and, more important, as his identity. He had recently made the decision to leave football to participate in drama. He experiences partici-pation in both drama and football as contradictory and as central to his understanding of self. He groans when I first ask him what his group of friends is like.

> Aaahhh, I have like two main groups. My first one is like all these Jocks, you know. 'Cause I'm like this football-actor. Like I'm the only football-actor that I know. And they are actually separated like that. My first group is all these Jocks. They're all like basket-ball, football guys. Then my other group is a whole bunch of like outcasts and like totally funny hilari-ous people. I actually like them better.

So he is not just participating in two different activi-ties but two different social groups at opposite ends of the campus hierarchy, both of which have implications for his gendered sense of self. At both schools, those students who participate in drama are relegated to the bottom of the social ladder. It is also important to note that boys who participate in drama are not just positioned at the bottom of the social hierarchy but at the bottom of the gender hierarchy, because often boys who participate in drama are often labeled "fags." . . .

Although drama is ranked below football in the school hierarchy, Kevin draws on some parts of a dominant masculinity to maintain a sense of self as masculine. He talks about how difficult the decision to leave football was, saying that he is too ashamed to "show my face" in the locker room any more. In drama, "the opportunity doesn't arise to pick some guy up off the ground and throw him on the ground and say [deep voice] 'Who's your daddy?!' It just doesn't arise. So it was hard."

However hard leaving football is, Kevin talks about drama excitedly. Kevin experiences drama as infused with sexuality, specifically heterosexuality. Although he attends parties given by both social groups, he describes the Jocks' parties negatively:

They're huge and so they are so big that everything is going by the time you are like a half an hour into it and you can't move. You can't, if you see a girl, you can't like go talk to her because you can't get there.

The drama parties, on the other hand, facilitate a sexually charged atmosphere. "There's like, I dunno, 50 people at most. They're all funny. They're all flirtatious, all crazy people. It's crazy. So everyone is just all, it's just like one huge sex-driven party." Like Adam, Kevin immediately relates what might be considered a nonmasculine orientation, group, or activity to heterosexuality. He in fact casts the Jock parties as parties that thwart heterosexual success and drama parties as activities that promote it.

This active heterosexuality is central to Kevin's definition of self. . . .

However, to use heterosexuality as part of his claim on masculinity, Kevin needs to be careful about how he publicly presents this sexuality. Similar to Adam, Kevin sees himself as romantic. But for high school boys, the public presentation of the heterosexual self must concentrate on the sexual, not the romantic (Martin, 1996), or else they might be teased by other boys. Kevin talks about why he would make a good boyfriend, although he is frustrated because he does not currently have a girlfriend. "'Cause I'm the type of guy that will. . . . I like to dance. I like to bring flowers. I'm just a romantic." Kevin details a romantic vision of himself as a boyfriend saying, "This is so stupid. Okay, I have to imagine myself singing, like serenading her." He says that all the girls

think this is really sweet and "all the guys are like 'Dude, you're gay!'" Kevin feels he has to guard against publicly enacting the wrong type of sexuality. Because he lacks solid claims on masculinity (unlike Adam) Kevin cannot publicly enact a more emotion-centered heterosexuality. But Kevin is able to draw on the sexuality of masculinity to make up for participating in a nonmasculine activity such as drama. He discursively reworks drama by infusing it with heterosexuality and indicating that being a Jock actually thwarts heterosexual success. . . .

Rejecting the Jock

Instead of navigating the tricky waters of sports and masculinity, some boys form their sense of masculinity by rejecting the Jock as model of masculinity. Jeff rejects the symbol of the Jock by devaluing the school's hierarchy and the centrality of competition to masculinity. Jeff exhibits a sort of "counterculture" identity and dresses, as do his friends who mill around outside the cafe where we talk, in all black, with tattooed arms, and a 1950s style, James Dean–type hairdo. Jeff is an 18-year-old senior at Pinetree who describes himself as "Rockabilly" (a cross between punk and a 1950s style).

When Jeff first describes himself, like the other boys, he references sports. He's "eclectic, a little bit of everything on the creative end. I don't play sports. I listen to music obsessively." When describing his childhood, he sets himself apart from those kids who played sports: "I was the terror of the fifth grade. Every other kid was playing soccer. And I was wearing all black and had long hair and wore combat boots and was obsessed with the Red Hot Chili Peppers."

This identity gives Jeff a way to reject the Jock identity by claiming an alternative one. . . .

Not only does Jeff reject the athlete as part of his identity but he also feminizes the Jocks. He paints it as his choice to reject the Jocks, not that he was locked out of this type of masculine achievement. He points out the contradictions in the football players' lives. "Their girlfriends always make them paint their toenails." Jeff says they are scared of others finding out about this practice. He makes fun of one football player because "he's really super homophobic." Jeff teases him about his painted toenails: "Yeah but if anyone said anything to you about it you'd be like [deep voice] 'My girlfriend made me do it!'" To which the football player responded "Yeah, you're right, I totally would." Through pointing out contradictions between the Jocks' masculine public image and their more feminine private behavior, Jeff rejects popular definitions of masculinity.

Managing Masculinity

Examining the role of the Jock in these boys' narratives reveals some of the ways in which contemporary boys experience, construct, and negotiate masculinity in adolescence. Being seen by others and by oneself as masculine is central to being a boy in high school. As these narratives indicate, understanding and portraying oneself as sufficiently masculine is not always simple, given one's social position in the school. The most recognizably masculine group at both of these schools is the Jock. To interpret their own identity as masculine, each of these boys somehow engages with that image and works it into his own narrative.

For Adam, this discursive work is easy. He has the "Jock insurance" to account for a more "feminine," emotional sense of self. But even this "insurance," it seems, won't protect him from having to continually reference heterosexual success in tandem with his discussion of sensitivity. Kevin, like Adam, experiences himself as more romantic than other boys. But because Kevin lost any possibility of "Jock insurance" when he left the football team, he infuses his romantic orientation with an emphasized heterosexuality, thus drawing on a recognizably masculine orientation toward girls. . . .

Jeff, instead of relying on emphasized heterosexuality or otherwise accounting for an apparently nonmasculine position in the social order, attempts to feminize those, specifically the football players, who are seen by themselves and by others as masculine.

What these interviews indicate is not that each boy is enacting a different type of masculinity but, instead, that they are attempting to infuse their own identity with recognizably masculine characteristics. Slotting boys into masculinity types, as is commonly done in the multiple

masculinities model, would not reveal the varying functions of the "Jock" in these boys' lives. Although several of the boys may be identified by themselves and others as "Jocks," they cannot all be analytically lumped into a single category because to do so would gloss over the varied ways in which structure, discourse, and emotion work in identity. Likewise, to cast the boys who are not Jocks as simply that—nonmasculine, non-Jocks—would be to ignore the ways these boys then work with definitions of masculinity to include those definitions in their narratives of self. These typologies would overlook the complex ways in which masculinity is discursively manipulated so that even boys who are understood as less masculine within a school's social hierarchy maintain or create a sense of self as recognizably masculine.

These boys' stories indicate the different ways in which gender in high school is navigated as they invest and divest masculinity of meaning depending on where they are in the school's social structure. These boys' narratives of their experiences of masculinity and sports indicate how structural power manifests itself in the formation of identity. It is not that all boys who are not "Jocks" reject the rules of masculinity. Instead, they rework their own narrative so that they may draw on parts of this identity. Through discursive reworking of their own sense of self as masculine, they then can draw on tropes of masculinity to create themselves as recognizably masculine to themselves and others.

Discussion Questions

1. How do the boys interviewed for this article establish a masculine identity for themselves?

2. Does the description of jocks as examples of dominant masculinity remind you of the social hierarchy at your high school? Why or why not?

Source: "Multiple Masculinities? Teenage Boys Talk about Jocks and Gender" by C. J. Pascoe, excerpted and with notes & references omitted from *American Behavioral Scientist*, Vol. 46, No. 10, June 2003, pp. 1423–1438. Reprinted by permission of Sage Publications.

CHAPTER 25

William Wants a Doll. Can He Have One?

*Feminists, Child Care Advisors, and
Gender-Neutral Child Rearing*

Karin A. Martin

Using an analysis of child care books and parenting websites, this article asks if second-wave feminism's vision of gender-neutral child rearing has been incorporated into contemporary advice on child rearing. The data suggest that while feminist understandings of gender have made significant inroads into popular advice, especially with regard to the social construction of gender, something akin to "a stalled revolution" has taken place. Children's gender nonconformity is still viewed as problematic because it is linked implicitly and explicitly to homosexuality.

> *William wants a doll, so when he has a baby some day,*
>
> *he'll know how to dress it, put diapers on double,*
>
> *and gently caress it, to bring up a bubble,*
>
> *and care for his baby as every good father should learn to do.*
>
> *William has a doll! William has a doll!*
>
> *'Cause some day he may want to be a father, too.*

"William's Doll," lyrics by Sheldon Harnick (1974)

Other societies assign roles to men and women that are quite unlike ours. But no country I know of has tried to bring them up to think of themselves as similar. Such an attempt would be the most unprecedented social experiment in the history of our species.

Spock (1974, 252)

A major thrust of second-wave feminism was the revisioning of the socialization of children. This article asks, What is the legacy of this political project? Are the goals of second-wave feminism now incorporated into contemporary child care advice? More than ever, parents, especially middle- and upper-class parents, seek advice from experts on the rearing of children (Geboy 1981; Hays 1996). According to Hochschild (1994), advice books can provide a window into how social issues are culturally understood. Contemporary child care advice books—manuals for socialization—help parents by providing culturally appropriate understandings of gender and interpretations of children's doings of gender. Analysis of these is one way to assess how gender socialization is popularly understood today. . . .

While feminist sociologists have theorized that gender has multiple locations, in identity, interaction, social structure, and discourse, one might argue that it is through socialization (and the management, negotiation, and resistance of it) that children learn how to operate in gendered structures (Lorber 1994), learn the repetitive stylized performances that constitute gender (Butler 1990), or learn how to do gender in interaction and how to avoid sanctions for doing it wrong (West and Zimmerman 1987). Furthermore, most feminist sociologists, regardless of theoretical bent, are likely to find it problematic that children's access to clothes, toys, books, playmates, and expressions of emotion are severely limited by their gender. Understanding gender socialization remains important not only to explaining gender but also to the construction of gender inequality. This article is an attempt at uncovering new ways that research on gender socialization might continue to contribute to feminist research today.

Specifically, in this article, I ask if the proper socialization of children today includes gender-neutral socialization. Through an examination of parenting books and Web sites, I find that most advice now acknowledges and even emphasizes the social component of gender, and most suggests that girls can play with boys' toys and vice versa. However, like previous researchers, I find a "stalled revolution" (Hochschild 1989). As the data below suggest, the problem of homosexuality thwarts child care advisors' embrace of gender-neutral child rearing. Just as Stacey and Biblarz (2001) reveal the heteronormative presumption that shapes the discourse and research on lesbigay families, I find that this presumption also limits the discourse and advocacy of gender-neutral child rearing among popular child care advisors. This examination of gender socialization, through a contemporary lens, points to the important connections between gender and sexuality.

Feminists and Child Care Advice

The concept of gender-neutral child rearing is a product of second-wave feminism, especially liberal feminism. Through consciousness-raising groups, early second-wave feminists developed a critique of how girls were raised and outlined the inequalities of girls' socialization (Statham 1986). Feminists wanted to open up possibilities for girls and to remove limitations on their lives. They encouraged expanded roles for girls at home, at school, at work, and in the media.

They argued for girls to have access to sports, trucks, math, science, blue jeans, and short hair, all previously off limits. Furthermore, they encouraged renouncing or at least limiting, for example, dresses, makeup, fairy tales, and housework, all understood as constraints on girls' lives.

Liberal feminists, especially, took up this issue wholeheartedly and translated it into advocating for gender-neutral parenting for both girls and boys. . . .

Gender-neutral parenting, as liberal feminists constructed it, drew from social and developmental psychology and social learning theory. "The early feminist movement enthusiastically took up the implications of social learning theory, and many if its recommendations for change were based on an implicit acceptance of behaviorist principles underlying social learning theory" (Statham 1986, 97). This perspective emphasized the socially constructed aspect of gender and critiqued biological and psychoanalytic explanations.

Given this social learning orientation, these feminists emphasized changing children's environments, especially what children played with, how they dressed, what they read, what they watched on television, and the roles that parents modeled. They also emphasized changing how parents responded to gender-nonconforming behaviors in children. *It's All Right to Cry,* sung by a former National Football League football player on the *Free to Be You and Me* (Thomas 1974) album, epitomizes this tendency.

However, the feminist call for gender-neutral child rearing, especially as it was popularized by liberal feminists as they tried to market it to the larger public, fell short of earlier, more radical feminist visions. First, the liberal feminist call for gender-neutral child rearing did not fully grapple with how sexuality is entangled with gender, nor did it fully eradicate heterosexism and homophobia from its writings about gender socialization. Liberal feminists attempted to address issues of sexuality and to critique homophobia and heterosexism but did not do so successfully. . . .

Second, as gender-neutral parenting advocates, feminists understood such parenting to be a route to social change. "For rationalist feminism had always had a program of *social* change, and not just individual empowerment" (Ehrenreich and English 1978, 289). However, as feminists set out to popularize the idea of gender-neutral child rearing, they sold it to parents as a strategy for raising successful, happy children. Liberal feminists emphasized again and again that gender-neutral parenting was good for children as individuals and a way to "raise free children," and in doing so, they muted the call for social change that it originally embodied. . . .

Feminists have continued to be critical of expert advice to mothers, especially as this advice has grown (Grant 1998; Hulbert 2003). They are critical of a variety of issues, especially how experts speak down to mothers, address advice about child rearing to mothers and not fathers, tell mothers their children will be harmed if they work, see mothers as the cause of their children's problems, and write of children as "he" and parents as "she" (Chira 1994; Grant 1998; Hays 1996; Statham 1986; Walzer 1998). Also, feminist sociologists have examined and critiqued explicitly gendered advice in women's self-help books (Hochschild 1994; Simonds 1992). However, there is no examination of how contemporary advice understands or encourages the traditional gendered socialization of girls and boys. This article seeks to fill that gap and to understand what has been the legacy of feminists' revisioning of gender socialization. To this end, I examine contemporary advice to parents in the hopes that it will also offer insight into larger cultural understandings of the gender socialization of children.

Research Design and Method

To look at contemporary parenting advice about gender, I examine 34 parenting books and 42 articles on 15 Web sites that offer advice to parents. Since there is no comprehensive list of the best sellers in parenting (Hays 1996), I generated a list of books from a variety of complementary sources. I compiled recommended book lists from a variety of organizations that provide services or advocacy for parents and children, for example, National Parenting Information Network, Pediatric Nursing Association, Civitas, I Am Your Child Foundation, Lamaze, La Leche League, American Academy of Pediatrics, Zero to Three, and National Association for the Education of Young Children.

From these lists, I chose all the books that were general child care books—books that are a comprehensive manual about parenting and not only about one aspect of parenting. These books describe child development. They are the reference books that are intended for everyday parental consultation rather than those that parents consult about a particular problem. Each book at a minimum had to include advice on children age two or older, as a quick perusal of books that were only about baby care suggested that they would unearth few concerns around gender and are more focused on physical care (diaper changing, feeding) and milestones (when baby smiles, sits up, walks). I also excluded books focused only on teens as virtually all are discipline and problem books. I also excluded books that were not comprehensive and were only about sleeping, feeding, shy children, or spirited children. This sample does not consider how advice about gender might be entangled with advice about specific issues: sleep, discipline, shyness, spiritedness. However, most of the books in the sample include discussion of these topics as well, so this sort of advice is not entirely overlooked here. I included any other books that fit these criteria and had an Amazon.com sales ranking equal to or better than the lowest ranked book on the originally compiled recommended list as an attempt to gather the best sellers that might not be recommended. Finally, I included three comprehensive books that are about parenting the Black child to examine any racial differences that might exist in advice about gender socialization; however, on this dimension, I found none.

Parenting Web sites are a prolific source of examples of expert advice. I compiled the list of parenting Web sites in the same way that I collected the book sample. I examined the Web sites during two one-week periods in September 2002 and May 2003. I included only those that were directed primarily at parents and not at professionals. I omitted any sites that were only about babies and sites that were sponsored by a product, with the exception of Disney.com and the Pampers site, both comprehensive parenting sites. Finally, I note that parenting magazines are another major source of parenting advice but did not examine these independently as many have Web sites that are included here, and many Web articles come directly from the magazines. . . .

About two-thirds of the books and all of the Web sites included explicit and substantial discussions of gender. Another five books made passing remarks about gender but did not provide any substantially developed advice about it.

From these sources, I analyze all text that explicitly offers information or advice about gender. By "explicitly," I mean all sections in the books on gender development (which often explain when a child has a sense of gender), gender behavior (can my son wear a dress?), sexuality (including genitals, where babies come from, homosexuality), and the importance of mothers and/or fathers as caretakers. I do not examine the implicit ways the books are gendered, that is, if there are more pictures of girls versus boys in the book (see Statham 1986 for such an account). I am interested not in the books' gendered biases but in their explicit advice about how to understand or manage gender in children. Finally, I pay only secondary attention to issues of how fathers and mothers should share the responsibility of care. There is a significant scholarly literature on this already (Grant 1998; Hays 1996; Hochschild 1989; Risman 1998; Walzer 1998). I examine how parents share child care responsibilities only when it arises as important to how children understand gender.

I read these materials inductively and asked the following questions: (1) Which theories of gender do experts offer to parents? (2) Do they advocate gender-neutral parenting? and (3) How do they recommend coping with a child's gender nonconformity?

Results

THEORIZING GENDER IN CONTEMPORARY ADVICE

While liberal feminists used social learning theory for understanding gender development in children, they often critiqued traditional psychoanalytic and biological theories of gender. Here I ask, Through which lens do child care advisors today understand gender development? Where I could identify a predominant theoretical underpinning for how the advisor(s) understood gender development, I categorized the sources into biological, social learning, and psychoanalytic explanations of gender development. Some sources recounted or made use of all three perspectives, and I could not discern that they favored any one in particular, and many gave no account of gender development.

Four sources emphasized biological difference. These told stories of the importance of hormones and/or fetal development and said that natural differences ultimately determine gendered behavior. While these sources sometimes said that nurturing plays a role, they describe biological differences as more important. For example,

> But while certain societal expectations relate to sex roles, there are also certain biologically based leanings, which have led some experts to suggest that the tendency to nurture girls and boys differently actually stems (at least in part) from the fact that girls and boys by nature *behave* differently. Differences in the brain and in hormones seem to manifest themselves in differences in temperament and behavior that are visible from birth. In general,

newborn boys are more physically active and more vigorous, while newborn girls are quieter, and more responsive to faces and voices. Typically, boys are more aggressive, girls more social; boys respond more to objects, girls to people. (Eisenberg, Murkoff, and Hathaway 1996, 223)

. . . Five sources emphasized a social learning perspective, which underscores how children learn the roles of men and women from parents, schools, and the media. While these sources sometimes said that biological differences played a role, they describe the learned component of gender as more influential. For example, while Drspock.com notes many "obvious" biological difference between the genders—"for example, males tend to be larger, their sexual maturation in puberty starts later and ends later, and on average their mature bodies are more muscular"—it emphasizes how gender differences generally are "more likely to be colored, largely, by the different ways boys and girls are raised in our society." The Web site has a section that outlines "different behaviors praised" (emphasizing accomplishment for boys and appearance for girls); "different ideas about play" (emphasizing differences in children's media and toys); "different chores: boys are assigned chores in the garage, in the basement, or on the lawn; girls work inside the house"; and "different expectations" (emphasizing that boys are expected to cover up feelings and girls are expected to have few capabilities in reasoning, logic, and sports). These advisers with a social learning perspective understood gender as a learned role, focused on behavior, and were less likely than other sources to emphasize how gender might be entangled with a deep sense of self.

Finally, I categorized as psychoanalytic eight sources that emphasized the importance of identification, the deep, psychological aspect of gender identity; emphasized the importance of fantasy; and/or presented some discussion about what Freud called "penis envy." For example,

> "Gender" is a complex psychological construction. It includes many different thoughts and fantasies about what it means to be male or female. Some of these thoughts and fantasies are conscious; others unconscious. (Mayes and Cohen 2002, 186)

Both boys and girls are now aware of their own gender and the presence or absence of a penis. His penis is infinitely precious to a little boy, but he also tends to be afraid of losing it, which is what, despite explanations, he believes must have happened to girls. A little girl tends to feel that she lacks a penis; an almost invisible vagina seems no alternative. Despite explanations, she often worries that her body has been damaged by having its penis removed. (Leach 2000, 477)

These sources sometimes discussed the role of social learning and (less frequently) biology in the development of gender, but they emphasized identification with the same-sex parent as the premiere mode through which children established a gender identity.

In sum, the data on theories point in two interesting directions. First, the role that socialization plays in the construction of gender is acknowledged in virtually all the sources that attempt to explain gender development. It is widely accepted by the advisors that parents, schools, and the media shape gendered behavior to some degree.

Second, many advisors, as will be evident below, entangle the development of sexual identity with the development of gender identity. Many make the assumption of this link, and most assume the development of heterosexuality. . . .

Often, especially from a psychoanalytic perspective, the development of a "normal" sexuality coincides with the development of a "normal" gender identity.

GENDER-NEUTRAL CHILD REARING

How do these child care advisors view gender-neutral or nonsexist child rearing? Twenty-five sources directly address this issue, and 16 at least minimally advocate for gender-neutral child rearing. Theory of gender development rather than credential or profession seems to predict an advisor's view of gender-neutral parenting. . . . [T]hose who advocate gender-neutral parenting are primarily those advisors who have a social learning or psychoanalytic theory of gender development.

Advocating gender-neutral parenting is different from saying that it is okay for a boy to play with a doll if he wants to. By "advocating," I mean that these advisors say that parents should not only permit but encourage children to move beyond gender stereotypes for their own good and/or the good of society. . . .

Eleven sources provide negative commentary about gender-neutral parenting. Those with a theoretical orientation that is primarily biological and those that review all theories tend to hold more negative views of gender-neutral child rearing. These advisors provide a range of negative commentaries from "it won't work" to

"it could be harmful." "Nowadays some feminists insist that there are no innate sexual differences and that boys and girls would behave alike if we treated them alike. Common sense, and most parents' observations, as well as our own, tell us that the two sexes tend to be worlds apart in their behavior" (Ames and Haber 1989, 46–47). Three of these negative commentaries also address some positive aspects of gender-neutral child rearing, but they are often undermined by suggestions that the effort is futile or potentially harmful to a child's development. . . .

It is not surprising to find that those who believe that gender differences are biological think there is little chance of gender-neutral parenting's having much effect on children's gender. However, it is interesting that these same theorists find such parenting potentially harmful. If gender is fixed by biology, gender-neutral parenting should matter little either way.

Thus far, we have seen that feminist ideas are embodied in contemporary parenting advice and seem to have had some effect on how gender is theorized. Furthermore, a fair number of advisors advocate some degree of gender-neutral parenting, in theory. In the next section, I examine the advice experts give to parents who are faced with a child whose behavior is gender nonconforming. As we will see, boys playing with dolls and girls roughhousing with boys become a bit more problematic as advisors navigate their way through sexuality issues.

CAN WILLIAM HAVE A DOLL?
ADVICE ABOUT GENDER NONCONFORMITY

Most of the advice about gender management is framed by real or hypothetical questions from parents who are concerned about their boys' doing "girl" things (wearing a dress, lipstick, or jewelry or playing with dolls or girls) or about girls' doing "boy" things (going without a shirt, playing with boys). There is, however, a gender difference even in the posing of the problem. These questions are much more frequently posed about boys.

Advice about managing gender is usually in answer to the question, "Is it a problem that my child is doing something gender deviant? And what should I do about it?" At first glance, it appears that these advisors answer "No, this is not a problem." . . . However, that advisors usually say it is not a problem does not mean that they have fully embraced the feminist position on gender socialization. Only two sources give feminist answers to this question (although these give other answers as well). I categorize these answers as feminist because they say explicitly that boys' playing with dolls and girls' playing with trucks or some other version of gender nonconformity are good for children and society. Spock and Parker (1998, 656) gave the quintessential feminist answer: "When individuals feel obliged to conform to a conventional male or female sex stereotype, they are all cramped to a degree, depending on how much each has to deny and suppress their natural inclinations. Thus, valuable traits are lost to the society. And they are all made to feel inadequate to the degree that they fail to conform to the supposed ideal." Surprising some, Leach (2000, 530) wrote, "If you try to make a boy stick to the 'right' gender, however good your reasons, you deprive him of exploring the potential of half the world, and if you are happy to let a girl switch over but not a boy, you inevitably contribute to the basic gender inequalities that still bedevil us all."

While these sources explicitly offer a feminist argument for why gender nonconformity is beneficial to children and the social world, a few sources present an argument that finds this behavior acceptable, essentially saying "There's no harm in that" without elaborating on its benefit (Barnes and York 2001, 53–54).

Finally, most advisors offer some acceptance of gender nonconformity in children, and they advise parents not to worry. However, their advice simultaneously emphasizes that gender nonconformity is problematic. These advisors give qualified and tenuous answers to parents' questions about gender nonconformity. About 60 percent of the sources can be described as giving (at least) one of three types of advice. Two of these types have long been stereotypic responses to homosexuality: (1) Don't make it worse and (2) recode the behavior. The third response explicitly addresses the link between gender and sexuality: (3) Don't worry; it doesn't lead to homosexuality.

First, advisors tell parents not to worry about their child's gender-deviant behavior as it is not a problem or it is only a phase, and their worrying about it will create a problem. They suggest that "we may inadvertently cause the very thing we fear if we react [to a boy wanting a dress] with anxiety, however understandable that may be" (naturalchild.com). Advisors suggest that parents' discomfort with a child's gender nonconformity creates "the problem." Or, for instance, in responding to a letter from a mother whose nine-year-old played with his sister's dolls, John Rosemond (1990, 151–52) responded,

> Your son's preference for dolls and "girl" toys is unusual, but *not* necessarily abnormal. There is no law which says that boys must play with trucks and

trains and sports equipment, or that girls must play with dolls and wear pink. . . . The problem does not lie with your son's preference for his sister's things. The problem is that you have made his choice of toys into a major issue, at the crux of which is the question of his autonomy. As long as you fight with him over whether he has a right to like dolls, he has no choice but to fight back. In the process of defending his "turf," he builds walls around it which not only keep you out ("Eventually, I always give in") but keep him in. *He won't have the freedom to expand his range of interests until you put an end to the battle.* (emphasis added)

Rosemond suggested more father involvement and recommended that the family seek counseling. . . .

Second, some advisors tell parents not to worry about gender nonconformity because the behavior is not really what it appears. They offer parents new ways to interpret their child's behavior so that it does not look like a problem of gender deviance. In essence, they recode the behavior or give parents the tools to recode it to make gender nonconformity acceptable gender behavior. Perhaps the best example of this can be seen in an advice column from naturalchild.com. A parent wrote that her "soon to be 4" son "is obsessed with wearing dresses" and that she does not "want to hurt, or interfere with [her] son's true identity. Please help." After some discussion of "sexual aberrations," the advisor wrote,

> Instead of demonstrating anything to do with sexuality or gender roles, your son may have something much more simple in mind. He may find dresses more comfortable than the pants he has worn. Perhaps his pants are too tight? Is the fabric uncomfortable? Does he get a skin rash when wearing certain fabrics? Does he find it easier to use the potty when wearing a dress? And so on. Or his behavior may have more to do with expressing resistance in general. Has the family gone through some stressful times recently, that he had no control over? . . . If he could have more time with his father or another male, he may begin to recognize why he is being asked to dress differently from you and his sister. I asked a colleague, Denise Green, for suggestions, and she asked if you might find a compromise, such as a kilt or other ethnic type of dress. She makes an interesting point here, because skirts and robes are worn by men in many different world cultures. It's the culture that is strange, after all: girls

can wear pants but boys can't wear dresses. Perhaps your son is ahead of his time, or perhaps like other children he likes wearing costumes as a way to understand what it's like to be a different person. Have you looked into acting classes, where he could wear many types of clothing in an acceptable way?

In this short piece of advice, the expert gives the mother many options for transforming her boy's dress wearing from a sexual aberration into a normal, sensible desire and behavior. In just a few sentences, the boy's dress wearing is recoded as an issue of comfort, an issue of toilet training, an issue of resistance or stress, an issue of time with his father, a form of ethnic dress, and a costume. All of these are implicitly more acceptable than his simply being a "soon to be 4"-year-old boy who likes to wear dresses. This nonconforming behavior would "worry any parent" because of its implication of "sexual aberration." I return to the issue of sexuality below but here emphasize that by offering all these interpretations, the advisor signals that this behavior needs to be interpreted, explained, and transformed into gender-normative behavior. . . .

Finally, despite the fact that gender nonconformity is rarely posed as a question about a child's (adult) sexual preference, and despite much debate among scholars about whether there is any connection between gender uonconformity and homosexuality, more than half of the advisors remark on the connection or lack thereof between gender deviance and homosexuality. The above advice, "don't make it worse" and "recode," is likely founded on this assumed, sometimes unspoken connection between gender nonconformity and homosexuality. Frequently, advisors suggest that gender deviance is not a sign of homosexuality and that homosexuality is a problem while gender deviance is not, at least in early childhood. "Relax. There isn't one shred of evidence that play that crosses typical sex-role boundaries is bad in any way unless it's the *only* sort of play your child engages in. It doesn't make boys sissies or girls tomboys. It doesn't lead to homosexuality. All it does is give children a wider range of fun things to do, and parents more options for presents to buy" (Needlman, drspock.com).

The advisors view homosexuality in a nearly uniformly problematic and negative manner. They often sympathize with parents, describing the prospect of homosexuality as understandably "alarming" to parents. For example, "Any parent in this situation would be alarmed. You are probably worrying that your child is a transvestite-in-training or gay" (parentsoup.com). Only Spock (and Dr. Needlman of drspock.com) connects this

"alarm" that parents feel to social prejudice. "When parents think that their little boy is effeminate or their little girl is too masculine, they may wonder whether the child will grow up to be gay or lesbian. Because of prevailing prejudices against homosexuality this can create worry and anxiety in parents" (drspock.com). All other advisors leave open the question of whether alarm about having a gay child is warranted. In fact, most leave the impression that this is something parents should be concerned about, while assuring parents that gender nonconformity is not (necessarily) linked to homosexuality. "Many parents who see their little boy straddling gender lines immediately jump to the conclusion that he may be showing homosexual tendencies. But it is too early for such a conclusion. It's not until around age three that gender-based behavior becomes more entrenched and even at that point, a child's choice of play things is in no way a sure predictor of future sexual orientation" (Eisenberg, Murkoff, and Hathaway 1996, 222). This advice suggests that gender nonconformity (until age three in this case) is nothing to worry about because of the absence of any link to homosexuality; thus, it implies that such a link would warrant concern about gender behavior. This stigmatizes homosexuality.

After sympathizing with parents, some advisors proceeded to describe homosexuality as an abnormal, problematic sexual orientation. They described homosexuality variously as "skewed" (Leach) and a less "appropriate sexual orientation" that comes with "warning signs" (Rosemond), implied it is in a category with "unhealthy sexual identities" (Sears, askdrsears.com) and "sexual aberration" (naturalchild.com), and suggested that such "eccentric" behavior will "alienate or draw fire from others" and thus warrants parental intervention (Reisser 1997, 352).

Similarly, some advisors suggest that parents play a role in whether gender-"deviant" behavior becomes linked to homosexuality. Rosemond explicitly blamed parental dynamics for homosexuality. In response to a letter from a teacher about a boy who likes makeup and women's clothing, he wrote,

The more rejecting and verbally aggressive the father is toward his son, the more the mother acts protective. This not only serves to strengthen the boy's identification with his mother, but further alienates him from his father as well. The closer the boy gets to his mother, the angrier the father gets and the more he blames his wife for the problems. The end result of all this mess is that the feminine side of the boy's nature comes to increasingly dominate. What the boy needs more than anything else is an open, accepting relationship with his father. Therein lies whatever possibility still exists of helping the boy develop better self-esteem and a more appropriate sexual orientation. (1990, 153–54)

According to Rosemond, the parents are to blame, and the father must be responsible for helping the boy to develop a "more appropriate" (read heterosexual) sexual orientation. The American Academy of Pediatrics (1999, 140), however, blames the mother: "Family studies indicate that effeminate boys often have unusually close relationships with their mothers and especially distant relationships with their fathers. Research suggests that the mothers of some effeminate boys actually encourage and support 'female' activities in their sons."

Many advisors tell parents to seek professional help for gender "deviance," especially when there is the implication that it is linked to homosexuality. For example, in a footnote to a sentence about what is not "a predictor of sexual orientation," Eisenberg, Murkoff, and Hathaway (1996, 222) wrote, if "a three-year-old plays only with dolls, shuns male playmates, and/or regularly wants to dress in girls' clothing, a discussion with his doctor may be helpful." . . .

Discussion and Conclusion

Child care advice today embodies liberal feminists' understandings of gender socialization. Contemporary child care advisors, even some of those who purport biological theories, describe how gender is socially constructed and emphasize to parents that their treatment of girls and boys is often different and produces gender differences. Furthermore, some advisors give their seal of approval to gender-neutral parenting, even if they are unconvinced about whether it will work. Finally, most advisors approve of behaviors that were nearly taboo 50 years ago—preschool boys' playing with dolls, girls' and boys' playing together, girls' playing sports, and the like. In many ways, the call of second-wave feminists, especially as it concerns girls, has been heard.

However, these data also suggest that the success of a gender revolution may require a sexual revolution, which is still missing. Experts do not fully advocate for gender-neutral parenting, for "bringing up" boys and girls "to

think of themselves as similar" (Spock 1974), because in doing so they run up against the prospect of "advocating" for homosexuality. While there has been and continues to be debate about the relationship between gender nonconformity and homosexuality, in popular consciousness, the homosexual as gender "invert" remains a formidable stereotype (Meyerowitz 2002).

Furthermore, homosexuality in the United States remains stigmatized. While many people and institutions "have a strong interest in the dignified treatment of any gay people who may happen already to exist" (Kosofsky Sedgwick 1993, 161), there are few, if any, institutions, including feminist or lesbian, gay, bisexual, transgender ones, that offer suggestions on how to raise people to be gay. "The presiding asymmetry of value assignment between hetero and homo goes unchallenged everywhere. . . . On the other hand, the scope of institutions whose programmatic undertaking is to prevent the development of gay people is unimaginably large" (Kosofsky Sedgwick 1993, 161). Child care experts advise parents from within these institutions. . . .

Finally, the gendered socialization of children seems only to have mildly waned since the height of the second wave. The data from these child care manuals provide insight into this wider cultural trend and suggest that there may well be rich research territory in the area of gender socialization that has been abandoned by many feminist researchers. At the very least, as gays and lesbians become more visible socially, politically, and in popular culture, how parents imagine and treat signs of homosexuality in children are important political and intellectual questions, as are questions of how and if parents try to ensure heterosexuality in their children. While the data presented here have begun to address these issues, the projects of feminist and queer sociology will benefit from more research about the hetero-normative socialization of children—in its most interactive and agentic-child modes.

Discussion Questions

1. According to Martin, how do most advocates of gender-neutral parenting handle parents' concerns about gender norms and sexuality?

2. Would you let your little boy play with dolls? Why or why not?

Source: "William Wants a Doll. Can He Have One? Feminists, Child Care Advisors, and Gender-Neutral Child Rearing" by Karin A. Martin, excerpted and with notes & references omitted from *Gender & Society*, Vol. 19, No. 4, August 2005, pp. 456–479. Reprinted by permission of Sage Publications.

----------------))))) ----------------

PART VII

GLOBAL ISSUES

The corporate domination of the globalization process has sparked a wide variety of global social problems. This chapter examines some of the current key globalization issues, such as terrorism, global climate change, McDonaldization, and the HIV/AIDS epidemic. It also looks at how social movements have addressed these issues.

In "Sociology of Terrorism," Austin Turk makes the case that terrorism had been largely under-studied in sociology up until September 11, 2001. He also points out the great need for sociologists to conduct studies on terrorism to look at such issues as the social construction of terrorism, the socialization of terrorists, the social control of terrorism, and theorizing terrorism. In doing so, Turk provides background on what we know now about these topics and asks questions that still need research.

In "Free-Market Ideology and Environmental Degradation: The Case of Belief in Global Climate Change," Yuko Heath and Robert Gifford find a relationship between support for free-market ideology and beliefs about global climate change. Their results indicate that those who support free-market beliefs are less likely to be aware of and/or care about global climate change. Heath and Gifford also show that those who believe in a free-market ideology are also more likely to have greater environmental apathy and are less likely to believe that organized groups can influence society.

In "Glocommodification: How the Global Consumes the Local—McDonald's in Israel." Uri Ram shows that corporate globalization does not simply destroy all local culture and customs. Instead it holds up symbols of the local while producing global homogenization at the structural level. For example, the Israeli falafels have been revived as a symbol of Israeli food but are now mass-produced in a McDonaldized manner.

In the last article in this section, "'In the Court of Public Opinion': Transnational Problem Construction in the HIV/AIDS Medicine Access Campaign, 1998–2001," Thomas Olesen describes the successful campaign to make HIV/AIDS medicine accessible to more poor victims of this global epidemic. He looks, specifically, at the organized efforts to stop the world's largest pharmaceutical companies from preventing governments from making cheaper antiviral drugs available to their citizens. In doing so, he describes the emotional and strategic elements necessary to create a successful global campaign.

As you read the articles in this section, keep in mind the following points:

- People's belief in and efforts to combat global climate change are related to their support for free-market ideology.

- Corporate globalization tends to result in structural domination but preservation of symbolic elements of local culture.
- HIV/AIDS is a global pandemic.
- Millions of poor people with HIV/AIDS cannot afford the medicine they need to stay alive.
- In order to understand terrorism, we must study its demographic, economic, and political determinants.

CHAPTER 26

Sociology of Terrorism

Austin T. Turk

The article provides a summary of current knowledge and defines research issues for each of the major foci of sociological studies of terrorism. These are (a) the social construction of terrorism, (b) terrorism as political violence, (c) terrorism as communication, (d) organizing terrorism, (e) socializing terrorists, (f) social control of terrorism, and (g) theorizing terrorism.

Introduction

Sociologists had until September 11, 2001, shown little interest in terrorism. Although conflict analysis, in one form or another, is a long established approach in the field, researchers have focused mostly on class and labor struggles, race relations, criminalization and other deviance-labeling, and the collective violence of riots and revolutions. Nonetheless, sociological concepts and methods have been fruitfully applied (albeit mostly by nonsociologists) in efforts to understand and counter terrorism. The aim of this review is to note what has been learned in order to suggest agendas for future research on the dynamics through which terrorism becomes a social phenomenon.

The Social Construction of Terrorism

Probably the most significant contribution of sociological thinking to our understanding of terrorism is the realization that it is a social construction (Ben-Yehuda 1993, Turk 2002a). Contrary to the impression fostered by official incidence counts and media reports, terrorism is not a given in the real world but is instead an interpretation of events and their presumed causes. And these interpretations are not unbiased attempts to depict truth but rather conscious efforts to manipulate perceptions to promote certain interests at the expense of others. When people and events come to be regularly described in public as terrorists and terrorism, some governmental or other entity is succeeding in a war of words in which the opponent is promoting alternative designations such as "martyr" and "liberation struggle."

More powerful conflict parties, especially governments, generally succeed in labeling their more threatening (i.e., violent) opponents as terrorists, whereas attempts by opponents to label officially sanctioned violence as "state terrorism" have little chance of success unless supported by powerful third parties (e.g., the United Nations). Superpowers such as the United States, of course, are highly selective and influential in determining which parties and their activities in violent struggles will be labeled. Lists of terrorist organizations and individuals, supporters, and sponsors are the results of policy decisions regarding the potential costs and benefits of including or excluding specific parties on such lists. Pronouncements by the U.S. State Department, for example, reflect assessments not only of objective threat but also of the political, economic, and military implications of naming particular entities as terrorist.

During the last decade of the cold war, the concept of "state-sponsored terrorism" was given full credence. Bulgaria, East Germany, Libya, North Korea, and Syria were named as Soviet-controlled sponsors of anti-American terrorism (Livingston & Terrell 1986, pp. 1–10). However, adequate evidence was never presented to support the listing of these nations as sponsors, much less under Soviet direction (Adams 1986). . . .

The United States has a long history of violence associated with political, labor, racial, religious, and other social and cultural conflicts (Gurr 1989). Assassinations, bombings, massacres, and other secretive deadly attacks have caused many thousands of casualties. Yet, few incidents have been defined as terrorism or the perpetrators as terrorists. Instead, authorities have typically ignored or downplayed the political significance of such violence, opting to portray and treat the violence as apolitical criminal acts by deranged or evil individuals, outlaws or gangsters, or "imported" agitators such as the radical Molly Maguires of Pennsylvania's coal miners' struggles. . . .

In sum, to study terrorism presupposes investigating the ways in which parties in conflict are trying to stigmatize one another. The construction and selective application of definitions of terrorism are embedded in the dynamics of political conflicts, where ideological warfare to cast the enemy as an evildoer is a dimension of the struggle to win support for one's own cause.

Terrorism as Political Violence

. . . It is increasingly clear that terrorism is most usefully defined, for empirical—research purposes, as the deliberate targeting of more or less randomly selected victims whose deaths and injuries are expected to weaken the opponent's will to persist in a political conflict (Turk 2002b). Terrorist acts are political, rarely involving psychopathology or material deprivation. Indeed, the evidence is mounting that terrorism is associated with relative affluence and social advantage rather than poverty, lack of education, or other indicators of deprivation. The typical terrorist comes from a relatively well-off part of the world, and appears to be motivated by political-ideological resentments rather than economic distress. Suicide bombers, for instance, appear increasingly likely to be respected individuals from advantaged classes, with stable family and community ties. Although their violent deaths may surprise relatives and friends, they are far more likely to be honored than to be condemned or stigmatized as somehow deviant.

Krueger & Maleckova (2003) have usefully summarized the results of recent studies on hate crimes and terrorism. Hate crime research shows that the presence of hate groups is unrelated to county unemployment rates in the United States, and positively related to education level. Similar county-level research in Germany found average education level and average wage were not related to the incidence of attacks on foreigners. Perceived threat associated with the presence of minorities or foreigners appears to be more important than are objective measures of material need or loss. . . .

Terrorism as Communication

The considerable and growing literature on the role of the media in framing images of criminality readily extends to terrorism (Jenkins 2003). Since the nineteenth century caricatures of anarchists in newspapers (deranged, bearded bombers), the established media have encouraged the belief that political violence in opposition to authority is both criminal and crazy. Assassins are widely portrayed as lone disturbed persons whose murderous acts are attributable to their individual pathologies, the consequences of loveless lives and frustrated ambitious (see Turk 2002a). Suicidal attacks are similarly pictured as the irrational or obviously misguided acts of uninformed people driven by despair or fanaticism.

Even when some recognition is given to the possibility that grievances may arise from real injustices, reportage in mainstream outlets tends to accentuate the theme that grievances never justify violence. The consistent message is that violence expresses hate, which only leads to reciprocal violence in destructive escalations of hostilities. Who is blamed for ongoing terrorist violence depends on which media one examines. For example, Western, especially American, media reports generally blame Palestinians and their supporters for the ongoing violence between Arabs and Israelis, whereas non-Western media reports in outlets such as al Jazeera generally blame Israel and supporters—especially the United States. . . .

Governmental and other organizational authorities are predisposed to minimize the risks of either public sympathy for terrorists or public fear of terrorism. Accordingly, the inclination in counterterrorism policy-making is to deny legitimacy to oppositional violence and to discourage the media from granting too public a voice to those who resort to or sympathize with terrorism. A complicating factor is that a satiation effect has been noted as a contributor to terrorism, in that acts of terrorism must be ever more horrendous in order to overcome the tendency for newsmakers and their publics to become inured to "ordinary" violence. . . .

Organizing Terrorism

. . . The classic model of the terrorist organization is a tightly organized hierarchy comprised of small, isolated cells whose members have little if any knowledge of planning and organization above and outside their cell.

They are disciplined by a blend of social isolation from all outsiders (especially family and former friends), blackmail after crimes demonstrating their commitment, physical threat, and indoctrination without access to other sources of ideas and information. The aims of such organizations have historically been relatively simple: to overthrow an oppressive regime or system or to drive an alien force from their land. The financial resources needed to sustain terrorist organizations were obtained from donations by sympathizers and sometimes supplemented by criminal acts (e.g., kidnapping for ransom, bank robbery, or protection racketeering).

As the last century ran its course, the motives and organization of terrorism became less simple and local. Nationalist and material concerns receded (though still significant in particular times and places, as in the Balkan conflicts ignited by Serbian ethnic cleansing), while ideological, especially religious, and wider geopolitical concerns were in the ascendant (e.g., the India-Pakistan conflict over Kashmir). Most recently, religious fundamentalism (Juergensmeyer 2000) has propelled the recruitment and organization of multitudes into loose networks of terrorist groups acting more or less on their own with encouragement and logistical assistance from facilitators with resources (on the global level most notably Osama bin Laden and al Qaeda, along with various Middle Eastern entities). Funds are increasingly provided by a wide range of legitimate business operations and donations to "independent" charitable organizations, and channeled through legitimate financial institutions. . . .

A corollary to the international trend has been the transformation of racist and xenophobic groups from easily identifiable secret societies such as the Ku Klux Klan to congeries of individuals (e.g., Timothy McVeigh, Terry Nichols, and sundry antigovernment rightists responsible for the 1995 Oklahoma City bombing) sharing Christian identity or some other extremist worldview. Adapting to governmental repression through civil and criminal procedures, such groups have moved from explicit organizations to movements of like-minded people willing to encourage and support terrorists such as Eric Robert Rudolph (the racist Atlanta Olympics and antiabortion bomber), even if they themselves do not commit violent acts. . . .

Socializing Terrorists

High on the research agenda is understanding why and how individuals become terrorists. Although some earlier commentators argued that political criminals were either deranged or lacking proper "moral socialization," it is now well established that opposition to authority or a particular social order is more likely to stem from a reasoned position than from pathology or deficient socialization. As indicated above, reasoning in cosmological, religious terms is increasingly characteristic of the rationales by which terrorists justify their acts to themselves and others.

People learn to accept terrorism as a political option when their experiences lead them to see truth in messages that defending their way and kind cannot be accomplished by nonviolent means. In democratic societies political radicals usually come from relatively advantaged sectors and go through a sequence beginning with conventional political activism (Turk 1982, pp. 81–108). The more educated and affluent their backgrounds, the more impatient they are likely to be with the inevitable disappointments of political life—where one rarely gets all that is envisioned. Socialized to be knowledgeable about the gaps between ideals and realities and to see themselves as significant participants in political struggles, higher class young people (especially from liberal or otherwise contrarian families and communities) are more likely than their less advantaged counterparts to become involved in a process of radicalization moving toward violence. Although social banditry and peasant uprisings may challenge social orders, organized terrorism is by far most likely to originate in the alienation and analytics of higher status younger people. Whether the Weather Underground of Vietnam-era America or the al Qaeda network of today, initiating and committing terrorist acts is nearly always the work of radicalized younger persons with the intellectual and financial resources, and the ideological drive, to justify (at least to themselves) and enable adopting the violence option.

However, although liberal family and educational backgrounds may encourage an openness to violence as a political option, few even of the most militant radicals become terrorists. Those who do appear to have undergone something of a conversion experience in making the transition from a willingness to "trash" public property and fight riot police, to a readiness to murder specific politically significant persons (e.g., governmental or corporate leaders, police officers, or soldiers), and then to the random targeting of populations including noncombatants as well as combatants. . . .

Once underway, campaigns of terrorism and related political violence tend to gain momentum. Inspired by the ideological messages, the charisma of leaders, the potential for material or status gains, or whatever else attracts them, others are likely to join. Particularly in nondemocratic societies, conflicts are likely to proceed along fault lines reflecting class, ethnic, racial, or religious divisions. If such conflicts persist, years of reciprocal violence tend to result in its institutionalization, so that individuals caught up in the conflict may have no real comprehension of why they go on attacking one another—the classic feud. The bloody years-long slaughter of whole villages of "conservatives" by "liberals," and vice versa, in Colombia's *la violencia* is a chilling historic example (Fals Borda 1969). In such contexts, explaining why people become terrorists is relatively straightforward: They see themselves as having to fight for "us" against "them."

The key to explaining the socialization of terrorists is understanding how specific individuals are brought to the point where they see themselves as bearers of the responsibility for violent actions. Education, training, socialization—deliberate or not—may encourage the development of a self-concept as one who must fight against the threat to "us." However, little has been learned so far about how eventual terrorists are selected in the course of their political socialization. It is woefully unhelpful merely to point to religious schools as "factories" producing terrorists, or to assume that only the foolish or aberrant become terrorists, or to blame terrorists as evil souls or acclaim them as heroic fighters. Researchers have to be much more aware of the impact of media and political-ideological influences on the definition and characterization of terrorists if their life courses are to be understood.

Social Control of Terrorism

Efforts to understand terrorism have generally been incidental or secondary to efforts to control it. By definition, the goal of operational studies is to provide authorities with information needed to prevent terrorist attacks and to neutralize terrorists. Operational research necessarily, then, prioritizes immediately applicable results rather than theoretical knowledge whose applicability is problematic. . . .

Nationally and internationally, legal systems and procedures have been developed without anticipating the contingencies involved in dealing with modern terrorism. For the first time in history, terrorists are gaining access to weapons of mass destruction. Credible threats of worldwide terrorist campaigns are now regularly documented, attacks and attempts in various countries are frequently reported, and multination cooperation in countering terrorism is a growing reality. Political pressures to lessen legal restraints on police, and military responses to terrorism have resulted in the, possibly temporary, erosion in the United States and elsewhere of legal protections against intrusive and secret surveillance, arbitrary detention, and hurtful interrogation methods, as well as assassination and extralegal executions.

When President George W. Bush declared a war on terrorism immediately following the catastrophic attack of September 11, 2001, not only most Americans but also governments and millions of people throughout the world agreed that international terrorism had to be stopped. But it has become obvious that "the devil is in the details." The extraordinary threat of modern terrorism has been mirrored by extraordinary counter measures. For example, the U.S. government adopted two fateful policies. The first was the decision to dilute or abrogate established legal restraints on governmental power. The second was the decision to invade Iraq without United Nations legitimation.

A series of initiatives testing and extending the limits of authority have been undertaken, routinely invoking the USA PATRIOT Act of 2001 (Uniting and Strengthening America by Providing Appropriate Tools Required to Intercept and Obstruct Terrorism). Among the departures from previously assumed legal norms are (*a*) indefinite detention of citizens along with the suspension of habeas corpus; (*b*) increased monitoring of electronic communications, financial transactions, educational and immigration status, and library records; (*c*) secret taping of attorney-client exchanges; (*d*) creation of military tribunals with the authority to try and sentence (including to capital punishment) both foreign nationals and American citizens defined as enemy combatants; (*e*) relaxing the prohibition of assassination to permit the extralegal killing of suspected terrorists, whether foreigners or citizens; (*f*) eliminating the barrier to information exchanges between national intelligence agencies and local law enforcement agencies; and (*g*) pressing for unlimited access to all datafiles on targeted individuals and groups, as well as the creation of a technologically sophisticated (e.g., including DNA code) identification card that would facilitate surveillance.

Critical reactions (Leone & Anrig 2002, Turley 2003) to these developments and proposals, coming mainly from liberals but increasingly also from conservative lawmakers and spokespersons, reflect concern that counterterrorism policies are eroding the freedoms being defended in the war against terrorism. Proponents (most notably President Bush and Attorney General Ashcroft) respond that the USA PATRIOT Act and related legislation and executive decisions have not eliminated legal procedures but merely adapted them to deal with the new conditions of extraordinary threat. Indeed, it is argued, further legal innovations are needed. . . .

The decision to launch an essentially unilateral invasion of Iraq was a huge departure from generally and increasingly accepted (outside the United States) international norms for reviewing interstate grievances and providing for a collective (Security Council) decision authorizing military action against a sovereign government. The long effort to subject national sovereignties to international legal restrictions (Jones 2002) has surely been set back by the globalization of terrorist and counterterrorist operations. With a war proclaimed, the military option is being emphasized over the legal option in attempting to control terrorism (Smith et al. 2002, Turk 2002c)....

Even though "control" is the originating and arguably the central concept of sociology (Gibbs 1989b), a pervasive bias favoring theory-driven versus policy-relevant inquiries has contributed to the dearth of explicitly sociological studies of terrorism. Still, what has been gleaned from sociological research on control offers many promising leads. For example, analyses of successes and failures of counterrevolutionary strategies suggest that maintaining the will to repress oppositional violence may be more effective than limited and erratic appeasement tactics. Alternatively, harsh repression without significant concessions in the face of widespread grievances seems in the long run to lead to cataclysms instead of social stability. Studies considering these propositions together could pay dividends in generating predictively useful theories bearing on policy decisions on when and how to use sticks and carrots. Too often such decisions depend mainly on ideological predilections instead of defensible theoretical predictions.

Theorizing Terrorism

Developing a sociological explanation of terrorism is apolitically and intellectually formidable task. Political obstacles abound: Officials are inclined to be wary of outsiders with independent agendas and resources. Policymakers and control agencies prefer operational findings clearly applicable to targeting and neutralizing defined enemies. Funding priorities are affected by rivalries within and among intelligence and enforcement agencies, as well as competition for budgetary influence among politicians, lobbyists, and other interested parties such as grant applicants, whose concerns seldom include basic research. The organizational penchant for keeping records confidential is heightened in agencies charged with controlling terrorism. Such political constraints exacerbate the intellectual problems encountered in terrorism research.

Gurr (1985) is one of the first to have explicated methodological options in studying terrorism and indicated which kinds of research questions are appropriate to each method. Theoretically significant levels of analysis are posited: global, national, group, incident, and individual. Gurr argues cogently for "question first" (i.e., theory-driven) research that treats terrorist groups and incidents, for example, as "independent" rather than "dependent" variables, focusing on their causation rather than their traits and consequences. The crucial need for relevant datasets is emphasized, as is the necessity for their availability to researchers "insulated from direct involvement in policy-making or operations" (Gurr 1985, p. 34).

Regardless of whether official or independent datasets are constructed, transforming information about terrorism into measures of conceptually meaningful variables is clearly a daunting task. For instance, decisions have to be made about what level of modeling is most appropriate for sorting out information about temporal and organizational processes in the formation of terrorist networks....

Complementing Gurr's (1985) assessment of methodological problems and strategies, Gibbs (1989a) provides a characteristically rigorous analysis of issues and problems in conceptualizing terrorism. Rejecting Laqueur's (1977, p. 3; see also 1999, p. 6) view that terrorism can be studied without defining it, Gibbs argues that productive research necessitates defining the research object to include elements of both theoretical significance and empirical applicability—which involves some regard for the essentially atheoretical definitions used in the nonscientific sources on which researchers frequently rely: the reports of government officials, journalists, and historians. He identifies five questions reflecting the issues that must be dealt with in defining terrorism. Is terrorism necessarily criminal? Is it necessarily undertaken to achieve a particular kind of goal? How does terrorism differ from conventional, civil, or guerrilla war? Can only opponents of government engage in terrorism? Is terrorism a distinctive strategy in the use of violence? His finely crafted (complex and lengthy) definition of terrorism constitutes his answers and may be paraphrased in summary form as follows: Terrorism is threatening, perhaps illegal, clandestine (avoiding conventional warfare) violence against human or nonhuman objects that is intended to change or maintain some belief, law, institution, or other social "norm" by inculcating fear in persons other than the immediate targets. To facilitate the recognition of logical connections and possible empirical associations among the components of the definition, an integrating and causally impressive notion is needed. He argues strongly that "attempted social control" is the most promising base on which to build an explanatory theory. . . .

Adding to the complexities of theorizing and researching terrorism, Black (2002) has proposed looking at terrorism as social control. Instead of delimiting the research object to resistance to political authority, or expanding it to include state terrorism, he defines terrorism "in its purest form" as "unilateral self-help by organized civilians who covertly inflict mass violence on other civilians" (Black 2002, Spring, p. 3). Although more akin to guerrilla warfare than to conventional military operations, terrorism is distinctive in that it targets civilians—although guerrillas may engage in terrorism and terrorists may engage in guerrilla war, depending on the nature of the target. Terrorism differs from ordinary crime in that it targets a population, applying a standard of collective liability for perceived violations of normative expectations. . . .

However one approaches the sociological study of terrorism, the distinctive objective is to develop an explanation of its causation, the dynamics of its escalation and de-escalation in relation to other forms of political violence, and its impact on the stability and change of social orders. Turk (2002d) has outlined a scheme for analyzing the social dynamics involved in the progression from coercive, to injurious, to destructive violence—the most extreme of which is terrorism. The main hypothesis is that terrorism is the culmination of a conflict process that predictably, having reached this extreme, ends in either the annihilation of one party or mutual exhaustion. Assuming that they must somehow continue to live in proximity and interdependence, survivors have to begin anew the search for a viable relationship. Whether "cosmic wars" can stop short of the extermination of one or both sides, and be ended by acceptance of the need to recognize one another's right to exist, has still to be determined.

Discussion Questions

1. What does Turk mean when he says that terrorism is a "social construction"?

2. According to Turk, what motivates people to commit terrorist acts? How can knowing the answer to this question help us to fight terrorist activities?

Source: "Sociology of Terrorism" by Austin T. Turk, excerpted and with notes & references omitted from *Annual Review of Sociology*, 2004, 30:271–86. Used by permission of Annual Reviews and the author.

CHAPTER 27

Free-Market Ideology and Environmental Degradation

The Case of Belief in Global Climate Change

Yuko Heath and Robert Gifford

The effects of support for free-market ideology and environmental apathy were investigated to identify some bases for not believing in global climate change. The beliefs that global climate change is not occurring, is mainly not human caused, and will also have positive consequences and weaker intentions to undertake ameliorative actions were significantly associated with greater support for free-market ideology, greater environmental apathy, less ecocentrism, and less self-efficacy. The results suggest that the relation between support for free-market ideology and the beliefs about global climate change is mediated by environmental apathy.

Global climate change is one of the most significant environmental issues in recent years (National Research Council, 1999). Natural scientists report many possible negative environmental changes as a consequence of global climate change, such as increases in the global sea level, more frequent droughts, and the destruction of ecosystems on a global level. Despite these serious potential effects, beliefs about global climate change by members of the general public are not well understood, and certainly one encounters some members of the public who express skepticism that change is occurring. . . .

Among the few studies that have examined lay beliefs about global climate change, Weber (1999) investigated the relations between expectations, beliefs, and adaptive responses to global climate change in a sample of Illinois cash-crop farmers. Just more than one half of the sample did not expect that climate change would happen in the next 20 or 30 years. Weber also found that farmers who believed in climate change were more likely to distort their memories about past weather in the direction predicted by climate change models and

tended to take some adaptive measures to reduce the negative consequences of climate change.

The results from a 1992 Gallup survey conducted in six countries (Canada, United States, Mexico, Brazil, Portugal, and Russia) portray another picture of public beliefs about global climate change (Dunlap, 1998). Although the majority in four of the six countries rated global climate change as a very serious problem, they tended to rate it as less serious than ozone depletion, rainforest destruction, and water and air pollution. Most participants did not believe that they understood global climate change very well; however, unlike Weber's (1999) participants, they also believed that it had already begun to happen or would begin happening within a few years. Although this survey provided a good picture of the general public's perception of global climate change, it included only demographic variables (age, gender, education, and the residency) and did not investigate other possible factors that may influence the perception.

Unlike the above two studies, O'Connor, Bord, and Fisher (1999) investigated the relations among risk perception of global climate change, environmental attitude, and the willingness to address global climate change (in terms of five different voluntary actions, such as carpooling, and voting intentions for relevant regulatory policies). Environmental attitude was measured using the New Environmental Paradigm scale (Dunlap & Van Liere, 1978), and risk perception was measured in terms of the expectation that the problem is occurring, the expectation that the consequences are negative, and knowledge of the causes. Their regression analysis of willingness to address global climate change on environmental attitude, three risk perception measures, and demographics (age, gender, and education) showed that five of the seven predictors, except for age and education, were statistically significant, although collectively they explained a relatively small amount (17%) of the variance in willingness to address the problem. They also concluded that knowledge about the causes of the global climate change would foster behavioral intentions to take action on these causes.

The current study extends this research by addressing three issues. First, using measures of climate change perceptions similar to those used by O'Connor et al. (1999), it explored the factors that affect beliefs about global climate change. O'Connor et al. used the three risk perceptions described above as independent variables to predict behavioral intentions but did not explore the factors that affect them. We examined three beliefs concerned with global climate change: the likelihood that it exists, whether it has human or natural causes, and whether its consequences are negative or positive.

Second, most investigations of the perceived risks associated with global climate change have been framed in a way that assumes the phenomenon will bring about serious negative consequences and that it is largely a result of human activities (e.g., Bostrom, Morgan, Fischhoff, & Read, 1994; Read, Bostrom, Morgan, Fischhoff, & Smuts, 1994). This may overlook the fact that not all laypersons believe that global climate change is under way, or that its consequences are always negative. We suggest that research should be framed in a way that avoids prejudging the existence and outcomes of climate change; such prejudging on researchers' part may alienate laypersons who do not subscribe to the majority assessment of global warming and its effects and may cause others to respond in socially desirable ways. By framing the question neutrally, it should be possible to identify factors that contribute to disbelief. Specifically, we proposed two constructs to explain the lack of belief in global climate change: support for free-market ideology and environmental apathy. These factors are discussed in more detail below.

Finally, in attempting to explain the willingness to act against global climate change, it is important to consider self-efficacy (Bandura, 1977, 1982). Specifically, we use the concept of self-efficacy of cooperation (Kerr, 1992), which we describe below. By including this concept, we expected that willingness to act will be better explained.

SUPPORT FOR THE FREE-MARKET SYSTEM

Some have suggested that the free-market ideology is one of the culprits of environmental degradation. For example, Gladwin, Newburry, and Reiskin (1997) claimed that "northern elites" (i.e., Europe, North America, and Japan) have an "unsustainable mind" (p. 238) that contributes to environmental problems such as air pollution. Gladwin et al. claimed that one source of unsustainable thinking is "an addicted contemporary mind" (p. 240) that has been powerfully programmed to believe in efficiency, economic growth, and techno-optimism. They further argued that this "contemporary mind" is programmed to favor market efficiency over social justice and quantitative growth over qualitative growth.

Shrivastava (1995) suggested a similar hypothesis: "Free markets are responsible for . . . all environmental problems. The basic assumptions are that negative consequences of economic production are not very severe. They believe all ecological impacts can be reduced to economic measures of costs and benefits" (p. 214). . . .

Concerning the attributed causes of global climate change, we hypothesized that those who support free-market ideology are more likely to believe that the causes are not human but natural. This hypothesis is based on the optimism described above and also on the notion of egocentric bias (e.g., Kunda, 1990; Wade-Benzoni et al., 2002); individuals tend to interpret information in a self-serving manner. Those who subscribe to the free-market ideology often assume that the market should be left alone and that government interference is undesirable. From this perspective, it is more self-serving to believe that human actions are not the causes of global climate change, and therefore government regulation of industry is unnecessary. . . .

SELF-EFFICACY

Facing a diffuse and seemingly distant environmental problem such as global climate change, from which a diverse range of consequences can occur, some individuals may believe that their own efforts will not significantly ameliorate the negative consequences, whereas others may think that their efforts will make a difference. The belief that the things one can do will make a significant difference should be a prerequisite for the willingness to make any personal effort, in this case to combat global climate change.

The type of efficacy used here is the equivalent of what has been called "self-efficacy of cooperation" (Kerr, 1992, p. 60) in the social dilemma literature, which reflects the belief that one's cooperative behavior has a significant effect on the outcome of a large group. This kind of self-efficacy may be distinguished from Bandura's (1977, 1982) original concept of self-efficacy, which refers to "beliefs in one's capabilities to execute the competencies needed to exercise control over events that affect one's welfare" (Bandura, 1986, p. 1), that is, the belief that one is able to perform a certain behavior. Kerr (1992) proposed that the self-efficacy of cooperation is positively and causally related to the rate or probability of cooperation in social dilemmas and called this proposition the "efficacy-cooperation hypothesis" (p. 60). This efficacy-cooperation hypothesis suggests that cooperation tends to decrease especially in large-scale social dilemmas because the individual's perception that one's cooperation will make a difference (self-efficacy of cooperation) decreases in a large group (Kerr, 1992).

We proposed that greater self-efficacy of cooperation will be associated with the tendency to take more concrete steps toward ameliorating the negative effects of global climate change.

Overview of the Analyses and Hypotheses

The major goals of the study are twofold: First, we investigated whether and how the proposed predictors explain the three beliefs about global climate change. Second, we investigated whether those three beliefs about global climate change, which represent the perception of risk, predict the intention to act against global climate change. In predicting this intention, we also investigated the effect of self-efficacy.

A set of hypotheses that are discussed above are summarized below:

> *Hypothesis 1:* Environmental apathy and the support for the free-market ideology will be negatively associated with the three beliefs of global climate change. More specifically, those who are environmentally apathetic and subscribe to the free-market ideology tend to believe that (a) global climate change is not occurring, (b) its causes are natural, and (c) its consequences are not all negative.

> *Hypothesis 2:* Ecocentrism will be positively associated with the three beliefs about global climate change described above.

> *Hypothesis 3:* Environmental apathy and the support for the free-market ideology will be negatively associated with the intention to act.

> *Hypothesis 4:* In predicting the intention to act against global climate change, ecocentrism will predict the intention better than anthropocentrism.

> *Hypothesis 5:* Self-efficacy will explain unique variance over and above the other variables in predicting behavioral intention.

> *Hypothesis 6:* Based on O'Connor et al.'s (1999) results, we also hypothesized that knowledge about global climate change will be associated with the belief in global climate change and the intention to take ameliorative action.

Method

Participants and Procedures

Six hundred questionnaires were delivered to houses on randomly selected streets in a western Canadian city. Each questionnaire package included a preaddressed and prestamped return envelope. We requested any person in the household older than age 18 years to complete the questionnaire and mail it back. . . .

Materials

Beliefs about global climate change. These were measured in terms of three conceptually different beliefs: (a) the belief that global climate change is occurring, (b) the beliefs about its possible causes, and (c) the beliefs of its possible consequences. The response format ranged from 1 (*strongly disagree* or *very unlikely,* depending on the wording of the question) to 5 (*strongly agree* or *very likely)* for all questions.

The belief that climate change is occurring was measured with a set of six items, including "How likely do you think it is that global climate change is occurring now?" Beliefs about the causes and consequences of global climate change were assessed with a set of four items each. Unlike previous studies, the questionnaire included items representing natural causes and positive consequences as well as human causes and negative consequences, to avoid predisposing participants toward any particular view of global climate change.

Behavioral intention. The intention to take action to address negative effects of global climate change was measured using four items. An example of the intention scale is "I intend to take concrete steps to do something to mitigate the negative effects of global climate change."

Other variables. Perceived knowledge about the causes of global climate change was queried by asking the following question: "I would say my technical knowledge about global climate change is" minimal, limited, moderate, extensive, and professional, coded from 1 to 5. Support for free-market ideology was measured with six items, such as "Free and unregulated markets pose important threats to sustainable development" (reversed item). Thompson and Barton's (1994) scales were used in their original form to measure environmental attitudes. Examples of the original items for each orientation are "I can enjoy spending time in natural settings just for the sake of being out in nature" (ecocentric); "The most important reason for conservation is human survival" (anthropocentric); and "I don't care about environmental problems" (environmental apathy). Self-efficacy of cooperation was measured using four items. An example of the self-efficacy scale is "There are simple things that I can do that will have a meaningful effect to alleviate the negative effects of global climate change."

Demographic information, including age, gender, education, and income, was also sought.

Results

DESCRIPTIVE STATISTICS

Demographics. Of the 600 questionnaires delivered, 190 were returned, a return rate of 31.6%. Five of the 190 were not completed and, thus, were excluded from the analysis, resulting in 185 completed questionnaires. Participants' ages ranged from 18 to 88 years, with average age of 51.4 (50.5% females, excluding 2 respondents who failed to report their gender). Reported income level ranged from CAN $ 16,000 to $ 175,000, with an average of $68,000. About 73% answered that they had completed a university or college education. . . .

Belief levels. The average level of beliefs that global climate change is occurring ($M = 3.94$), is mainly human caused ($M = 3.78$), and will have negative consequences ($M = 3.83$) was relatively high, as was the intention to engage in ameliorative actions ($M = 3.33$), all on 5-point scales. Nonetheless, not all respondents believed in global climate change. For example, 15.1% either disagreed or strongly disagreed with the item "I am quite sure that global warming is occurring now," and 14.1% either disagreed or strongly disagreed with the item "The main causes of global warming are human activities."

CORRELATIONS

. . . Most of the hypothesized associations were confirmed. Support for free-market ideology was negatively associated with ecocentrism, all three beliefs about global climate change, and behavioral intention. Environmental apathy was also negatively correlated with the three beliefs, behavioral intention, and self-efficacy, whereas ecocentrism was positively correlated with the same variables.

Perceived knowledge was positively associated with two of the three beliefs about global climate change and negatively correlated with anthropocentrism and environmental apathy, whereas it was not significantly correlated with ecocentrism or behavioral intention.

Among demographic variables, only age and gender were significantly associated with other variables. For example, older people tended to believe that the causes of global climate change are natural, that the consequences are not all negative, and were more apathetic about environmental issues. Gender was significantly associated only with self-efficacy. Females tended to report more self-efficacy than males.

PREDICTING BELIEFS ABOUT CLIMATE CHANGE

Next, regression analyses were performed for each of the three beliefs about global climate change. . . .

The following variables were entered to predict these beliefs: (a) age as a covariate, (b) perceived knowledge about global climate change, (c) support for free-market ideology, and (d) the three environmental attitudes: ecocentrism, anthropocentrism, and environmental apathy. . . .

MEDIATION: A POST HOC ANALYSIS

Although the zero-order correlations between the beliefs about global climate change and support for free-market ideology were as hypothesized, when all the predictors were entered in the regression simultaneously, support for free-market ideology was no longer a significant predictor of any global climate change beliefs. From the nature of the zero-order correlations and the results of the regression analyses, we suspected a mediated relationship involving support for free-market ideology and environmental apathy. Thus, we performed mediation analysis (Baron & Kenny, 1986) to investigate the underlying relationships.

The results of these analyses revealed that the effect of support for free-market ideology on each of the three beliefs was mediated by environmental apathy. This result may be interpreted as follows: Those who subscribe to the free-market ideology tend to be optimistic that an uninterrupted free-market system will lead to beneficial outcomes for all, which leads to apathetic, unconcerned attitudes toward environmental problems. These apathetic attitudes, in turn, influence beliefs about global climate change, in the direction that global climate change is not occurring, humans are not responsible for it, and its consequences will not be negative.

PREDICTING THE INTENTION TO ACT

Finally, we investigated whether these beliefs about global climate change contribute to the prediction of the willingness to act against global climate change. We used a two-step hierarchical multiple regression to examine whether self-efficacy would add unique variance over and above the other variables. . . .

Discussion

The current study investigated the bases of lay beliefs about global climate change. Regression analyses explained considerable variance in lay beliefs about global climate change (approximately 40% for all three beliefs) and the intention to take ameliorative actions (57%). Support for free-market ideology indirectly influences disbelief in global climate change, by fostering environmental apathy. Because relatively few studies have investigated a limited number of factors associated with risk perception of or beliefs about global climate change, these results further the understanding of laypersons' beliefs about global climate change. The specific findings are elaborated next.

ENVIRONMENTAL ATTITUDES

Rather than employing a unidimensional approach to environmental attitudes, the current study used a multidimensional measure: Thompson and Barton's (1994) ecocentric, anthropocentric, and environmental apathy constructs. This proved to be useful because the different dimensions of environmental attitudes influenced beliefs differently. For example, anthropocentrism and ecocentrism had different patterns of correlation with other variables, as hypothesized. Ecocentrism was positively correlated with beliefs about causes and consequences, behavioral intention, and self-efficacy and negatively correlated with support for the free-market ideology and environmental apathy, whereas anthropocentrism was not significantly correlated with any of these variables.

The third construct in Thompson and Barton's (1994) scale, environmental apathy, was most strongly (negatively) correlated with beliefs about the causes and

consequences of global climate change, and the intention to act. As seen in the regression analyses of the beliefs, the effect of environmental apathy overpowers that of other predictors, including support for free-market ideology and ecocentric orientation. Although this construct has been often neglected when researchers use Thompton and Barton's scales with the focus on eco- versus anthropocentrism dimension, our results suggest that environmental apathy may be the most fruitful predictor of global climate change beliefs and related behavioral intentions. . . .

PERCEIVED KNOWLEDGE ABOUT GLOBAL CLIMATE CHANGE

Perceived knowledge about global climate change was a significant predictor for two of the three beliefs about global climate change (i.e., that it is occurring, and that its consequences are negative). However, in the current study, it was not a significant predictor of behavioral intention, nor was it significantly associated with the behavioral intention at zero order. This suggests that the intention to take ameliorative action does not necessarily arise from greater perceived knowledge about global climate change. Rather, one's value orientations, such as ecocentrism, support for free-market ideology, and the belief in self-efficacy of cooperation, may be more important factors that promote the intention.

It is also interesting that perceived level of knowledge about global climate change had almost zero correlation with ecocentrism. This implies that having an ecocentric orientation and believing that one is knowledgeable about environmental issues are relatively independent. Further study is needed to confirm these points.

THE INTENTION TO ACT

Self-efficacy explained most of the variance in behavioral intention, followed by ecocentrism, and support for the free-market system. The importance of self-efficacy in behavioral intention found in the current study corroborates previous studies' findings (e.g., Geller, 1995).

This finding has important, if understandable, implications for understanding behavioral intention in this area. It appears that before individuals are ready to act against climate change, they must believe that even a small thing one individual can do will make a meaningful difference. For example, a number of successful letter-writing campaigns to protect the environment have been reported (e.g., see Web site: www.globalresponse.org/camphist.php). Thus, it will be fruitful to promote the sense of self-efficacy.

Second, the results of the regression analyses suggest that belief that global climate change is actually occurring is an important prerequisite to be willing to take action. This result corroborates the argument advanced by O'Connor et al. (1999), that "risk perceptions matter in predicting behavioral intentions. Risk perceptions are not a surrogate for general environmental beliefs, but have their own power to account for behavioral intentions" (p. 469). Our findings underscore this point.

Support for Free-Market Ideology

Free-market ideology has been pointed out as a culprit of various forms of environmental degradation (e.g., Gladwin et al., 1997). However, the current study is the first to our knowledge to empirically demonstrate the association between the construct and the perception of environmental problems. With respect to beliefs about global climate change, results from a correlational analysis indicate that those who value the free market system over environmental quality tend to believe that global climate change is not occurring, that the causes of global climate change are more natural than human caused, and that its consequences will not be negative. It was also a significant predictor of not taking action to address the negative effects of global climate change. . . .

Our study finding also suggests a new relationship that has not been discussed in previous literature: the mediated relationship between support for free-market ideology, environmental apathy, and beliefs about global climate change. The effect of support for free-market ideology on the beliefs appears to be indirect, mediated by apathetic orientation toward the environment. This finding corroborates Bjerke and Kaltenborn's (1999) results, in which environmental attitudes as expressed on Thompson and Barton's (1994) scales mediated between general values and more specific attitudes or beliefs toward large carnivores. This relationship makes sense from the cognitive hierarchy perspective (Homer & Kahle, 1988; Vaske, Donnelly, Williams, & Joker, 2001), which postulates the flow of influence from the most abstract values, to general attitudes, to beliefs about more specific objects and situations, to behavioral intentions. Support for free-market ideology, as a value that an individual holds, brings about optimistic and apathetic

attitudes toward the environment, and this attitude, in turn, influences the individual's specific beliefs about global climate change.

Having said that, it is of note that support for free-market ideology directly influenced behavioral intention to ameliorate the effect of global climate change, whereas environmental apathy did not. One way to understand this result is that beliefs about global climate change and behavioral intention are different constructs in nature. For example, it takes a sense of self-efficacy to be willing to take actions but believing whether global climate change is occurring. It can be that such beliefs are more influenced by apathetic orientation toward the environment than behavioral intention is. And these beliefs, in turn, influence the willingness to take actions directly. Nonetheless, further studies are required to establish more firmly this mediation relationship between support for free-market ideology, environmental apathy, and specific beliefs. . . .

Conclusion

The current study sheds light on the psychological mechanisms related to lay beliefs and intentions associated with global climate change. If climate change is indeed occurring, importantly caused by human actions, and will have negative consequences, then these results will help point the way toward changing behavior. Takala (1991) stated that the first necessary step to tackle the problems of global climate change is to systematically describe how people perceive environmental problems and how they become aware of risks. The current study is one step toward this endeavor.

Discussion Questions

1. What is the "self-efficacy for cooperation"? How is it important for large group efforts, such as combating global climate change?

2. Based on the findings in this article, what do you think is the best way to convince people to actively combat global climate change?

Source: "Free-Market Ideology and Environmental Degradation: The Case of Belief in Global Climate Change" by Yuko Heath and Robert Gifford, excerpted and with notes & references omitted from *Environment and Behavior*, Vol. 38, No. 1, January 2006, pp. 48–71. Reprinted by permission of Sage Publications.

CHAPTER 28

Glocommodification

How the Global Consumes the Local—
McDonald's in Israel

Uri Ram

McDonald's in Israel is used as an example of the author's belief that global technological, organizational and commercial flows need not destroy local habits and customs but may actually preserve or even revive them. However, the global does tend to subsume and appropriate the local, sometimes to the extent that the seemingly local, symbolically, becomes a specimen of the global, structurally.

One of the more controversial aspects of globalization is its cultural implications: does globalization lead to universal cultural uniformity, or does it leave room for particularism and cultural diversity? The global–local encounter has spawned a complex polemic between 'homogenizers' and 'heterogenizers.' This article proposes to shift the ground of the debate from the homogeneous–heterogeneous dichotomy to a structural-symbolic construct. It is argued here that while both homogenization and heterogenization are dimensions of globalization, they take place at different societal levels: homogenization occurs at the structural-institutional level; heterogenization, at the expressive-symbolic. The proposed structural-symbolic model facilitates a realistic assessment of global–local relations. In this view, while global technological, organizational and commercial flows need not destroy local habits and customs, but, indeed, may preserve or even revive them, the global does tend to subsume and appropriate the local, or to consume it, so to say, sometimes to the extent that the seemingly local, symbolically, becomes a specimen of the global, structurally.

The starting point for this analysis is the McDonaldization of Israeli culture. McDonald's opened its first outlet in Israel in 1993. Since then, it has been involved

in a variety of symbolic encounters, of which two are examined here: (1) the encounter between McDonald's, as the epitome of global fast food, and the local version of fast food, namely the falafel; and (2) the encounter between McDonald's, as a symbol of global-American consumer culture, and local culture, national identity and ideology, as it evolved around the branch location of Golani Junction. It is argued that, in both cases, local idioms have thrived, though only symbolically. On the structural level, they have been subsumed and appropriated by global social relationships.

In this study, McDonald's is considered a commodity in the Marxian sense; that is, a manufactured object embodying social and cultural relations (Marx, 1967: 71–83). Like Rick Fantasia, a student of fast food in France, we argue here that fast food '[has] less to do with food than . . . with the cultural representations of Americanism embodied within it' (Fantasia, 1995: 229). Since cultural representation does not relate merely to the expressive-symbolic level, but, concretely, also to the structure of institutional patterns and organizational practices, attention must be paid to the embeddedness of social relations and cultural representations in the commodities. Thus, it is argued that, behind the McDonald's commodity as an object, one should look for the societal intersubjective relations of production and consumption.

Global Commerce Encounters the Local Eating Habitus: McDonald's and the Falafel

The industrialized hamburger first arrived on Israel's shores back in the late 1960s, although the chains involved at the time did not make much of an impression. In 1972, Burger Ranch (BR) opened a local hamburger joint that expanded into a chain only in the 1980s. It took the advent of McDonald's, however, for the 'great gluttony' of the fast hamburger to begin. McDonald's opened its first branch in October 1993. It was followed by Burger King (BK), the world's second largest hamburger chain, which opened its first branch in Israel in early 1994. Between McDonald's arrival and the year 2000, sales in the hamburger industry soared by 600 percent. By 2000, annual revenues from fast-food chains in Israel reached NIS 1 billion (about US$200 million according to the 2002 exchange rate) (Barabash, 2000). McDonald's is the leading chain in the industry, with 50 percent of the sales, followed by BR with 32 percent, and BK with 18 percent. In 2002 the three chains had a total of 250 branches in place: McDonald's, 100; BR, 94 and BK, 56 (Zoref, 2003).

McDonald's, like Coca-Cola—both flagship American brands—conquered front-line positions in the war over the Israeli consumer. The same is true of many other American styles and brands, such as jeans, T-shirts, Nike and Reebok footwear, as well as mega-stores, such as Home Center, Office Depot, Super-Pharm, etc. Israel's globalization, as measured by the development of high-tech industry, and the spread of personal computers and Internet links, ranks high on the world scale (Ram, 2000). As for eating habits, apart from the spread of fast-food chains, other Americanisms have found a growing niche in the Israeli market: frozen 'TV dinners,' whether in family or individual packs, and an upsurge in fast-food deliveries (Barabash, 2000). These developments stem from the transformation of the familial lifestyle as an increasing number of women are no longer (or not only) housewives, the growth of singles households, and the rise in family incomes. All this, along with accelerated economic activity, has raised the demand for fast or easy-to-prepare foods. As has happened elsewhere, technological advancements and business interests have set the stage for changes in Israeli eating habits. Another typical

development has been the mirror process that accompanies the expansion of standardized fast foods, namely, the proliferation of particularist cuisines and ethnic foods as evinced by the sprouting of restaurants that cater to the culinary curiosity and open purses of a new Yuppie class in Tel Aviv, Herzliya and elsewhere.

As in other countries, the 'arrival' of McDonald's in Israel raised questions and even concern about the survival of the local national culture. A common complaint against McDonald's is that it impinges on local cultures, as manifested primarily in the local eating habitus both actual and symbolic. If Israel ever had a distinct national equivalent to fast food, it was unquestionably the falafel—fried chick-pea balls served in a 'pocket' of pita bread with vegetable salad and tahini (sesame) sauce (Chen, 1998). The falafel, a Mediterranean delicacy of Egyptian origin, was adopted in Israel as its 'national food.' Although in the 1930s and 1940s the falafel was primarily eaten by the young and impecunious, in the 1950s and 1960s a family visit to the falafel stand for a fast, hot bite became common practice, much like the visit paid nowadays to McDonald's. The falafel even became an Israeli tourist symbol, served as a national dish at formal receptions of the Ministry of Foreign Affairs (Zach, 2000: D1). Indeed, one kiosk in Tel Aviv advertises itself as a 'mighty falafel for a mighty people.'

Despite the falafel's fall from glory in the 1970s and 1980s vis-a-vis other fast foods, such as *shawarma* (lamb or turkey pieces on a spit), pizza and the early hamburger stands, and notwithstanding the unwholesome reputation it developed, an estimated 1200 falafel eateries currently operate in Israel. Altogether, they dish up about 200,000 portions a day to the 62 percent of Israelis who are self-confessed falafel eaters. The annual industry turnover is some NIS 600 million (US$120 million)—not that far short of the hamburger industry (Kotan, 2000; Zach, 2000). Thus, surprisingly enough, in the late 1990s, McDonald's presence, or rather the general McDonaldization of Israeli food habits, led to the falafel's renaissance, rather than to its demise.

The falafel's comeback, vintage 2000, is available in two forms: gourmet and fast-food. The clean, refined, gourmet Tel-Avivian specimen targets mainly yuppies and was launched in 1999—five years after McDonald's landed in the country—in a prestigious restaurant owned by two women, famed as Orna and Ella. Located in the financial district, which is swiftly being gentrified, it is known as 'The Falafel Queens'—a hip, ironic feminist version of the well-known 'Falafel King'—one of the most popular designations for Israeli falafel joints, which always take the masculine form. The new, 'improved' gourmet model comes in a variety of flavors. Apart from the traditional 'brown' variety, the Queens offer an original 'red' falafel, based on roasted peppers, as well as a 'green' falafel, based on olive paste. . . .

Apart from its 'gourmetization,' the falafel has simultaneously undergone 'McDonaldized' standardization. The Israeli franchise of Domino's Pizza inaugurated a new falafel chain, setting itself a nationwide target of 60 branches. Furthermore, its reported intention is to 'take the tidings of Israeli fast-food abroad' (Kotan, 2000). The falafel has thus been rescued from parochialism and upgraded to a world standard-bearer of 'Israeli fast food,' or, as one observer put it, it has been transformed from 'grub' into 'brand' (Zach, 2000: D1). In fact, the Ma'oz chain already operates 12 falafel eateries in Amsterdam, Paris and Barcelona and, lately, also in Israel. The new chains have developed a 'concept' of 'clean, fresh, and healthy,' with global implications, because: 'if you are handed an inferior product at "Ma'oz" in Amsterdam, you won't set foot in the Paris branch' either. In contrast to the traditional falafel stand, which stands in the street and absorbs street fumes and filth, the new falafel is served indoors, at spruce, air-conditioned outlets, where portions are wrapped in designer bags and sauces flow out of stylized fountains (Kotan, 2000). At Falafels, the balls are not moulded manually, but dispensed by a mechanical implement at the rate of 80 balls/minute. There are two kinds—the Syrian Zafur and the Turkish Baladi. And as befits an industrial commodity, the new falafel is 'engineered' by food technicians and subjected to tastings by focus groups (Zach, 2000: D1). . . .

One major change in Israel's culinary habitus as a result of its McDonaldization, therefore, is the demise of the old 'authentic' falafel and the appearance of the new commodified 'falafel 2000.'

But McDonald's had to surmount another—no less challenging—culinary hurdle: the Israeli carnivorous palate. The rise in the country's meat consumption is an indicator of its economic growth. Between 1960 and 1970 there was an almost 100 percent jump in meat consumption, the portion on the Israeli plate taking up an ever growing share. In 1999 Israelis consumed on an average more than twice the meat downed 30 years earlier, an increase unmatched by any other food staple. Given this hankering for meat, especially of the grilled variety, the McDonald's hamburger appeared rather puny, and the Israeli consumer tended to favour the Burger King broiled product. In 1998, McDonald's bowed to the Israeli appetite, changing both the preparation and size of its hamburger. It shifted to a combined technique of fire and charcoal, and increased portion size by 25 percent. The Israeli customer now has the distinction of being served the largest hamburger (120 grams) marketed by McDonald's worldwide. . . .

It may thus be concluded that the interrelations of McDonald's and the falafel are not simply a contrast between local decline and global rise. Rather, they are a complex mix, though certainly under the banner of the global. Indeed, the global (McDonald's) contributed somewhat to the revival of the local (the falafel). In the process, however, the global also transformed the nature and meaning of the local. The local, in turn, caused a slight modification in the taste and size of the global, while leaving its basic institutional patterns and organizational practices intact. The 'new falafel' is a component of both a mass-standardized consumer market, on the one hand, and a post-modern consumer market niche, on the other. This sort of relationship between McDonald's and the falafel, in which the global does not eliminate the local symbolically but rather restructures or appropriates it structurally, is typical of the global—local interrelations epitomized by McDonald's. So much emerges also in yet another encounter between McDonald's and Israeli culture, to which we turn next.

Global Commerce Encounters Local National Ideology: McDonald's and Golani

Golani Junction, a major intersection in northern Israel, named after an infantry brigade, was the arena of another encounter between McDonald's and Israeli culture. In this instance, Israeli national ideology fought against the spirit of American consumerism, and Golani—its reputation for toughness notwithstanding—lost the battle. The junction was named in the wake of the Israeli war of independence in 1948, Golani having been the military unit in charge of combat in the area. Its casualties were commemorated by a temporary monument, which in the late 1950s was replaced by a permanent one. During the next couple of decades, it became the memorial for all Golani soldiers lost in battle and a museum dedicated to the brigade was erected there. In December 1994, McDonald's opened its doors at Golani Junction, instantly raising a public outcry that the restaurant was diminishing the site.

What is the legacy of the Golani memorial and museum, and why is the mere presence of a McDonald's branch perceived as a threat? The venue is part of a dense network of hundreds of memorial sites on various scales scattered all over the country, whose aim, like elsewhere, is twofold: first, to consecrate former soldiers who died in battle and thereby motivate new soldiers going into battle; and second, to inscribe in 'blood' the affiliation of 'the people' and 'the land,' the two arches of the 'nation' (Mosse, 1990; Almog, 1991). The Golani site hosts annual memorials, inauguration parades for conscripts, and educational activities for soldiers, youth groups and visitors from abroad.

McDonald's large 'M' towering above the junction was perceived by some as belittling the site, and, indeed, as the desecration of a national shrine. D. Y., the father of a fallen soldier and one of the leaders of the campaign against McDonald's, put it eloquently:

> Golani devotees regard the site as a place to commemorate and commune with the dead, on both the personal and collective levels, as well as a place to perpetuate the glorious combat legacy of the Golani unit for generations to come. . . . McDonald's restaurant brims with tacky, flashy and vulgar American trappings incongruent with the nature of the site and offensive to our sensibilities, the sensibilities of Golani's retired and current soldiers, and some of the Israeli public.' (D. Y., 1998)

After their request to relocate the restaurant was turned down, the Friends of the Golani Site demanded that its appearance be modified, focusing on 'downplaying . . . showy, American hallmarks,' according to the same letter. For example, they asked that the golden 'M' atop the tall pole be removed. This specific demand was granted; not only was the 'M' removed, but it was replaced with the olive-tree insignia of the Golani brigade.

The basic dissonance between Golani and McDonald's is described further by the bereaved father:

> The encroachment by private business interests on public-national sites, such as the memorial site at Golani Junction, should sound an alert, especially at a time of concern about waning motivation for military service. We deem the coarse intrusion [of such interests] into the memorial site an assault on the fundamental national and social values fostered in the past and still fostered by the Golani brigade. . . . Our son's generation internalized a heroic legacy founded on commitment to and self-sacrifice for lofty causes. And what will the next generation inherit? McDonald's and cheeseburgers? (D. Y., 1998)

. . . Furthermore, to the chagrin of the bereaved, the army actually invited McDonald's and other fast-food chains onto its bases located in urban areas. Soldiers are provided with magnetic cards crediting them with a daily meal of their choice from a 'food court.' The convenience is aimed at discouraging them from wandering about street-side food stands or shopping malls just outside the bases, but it obviously dovetails the wholesale privatization policy spreading through Israel.

The army's outsourcing of catering services has an obvious post-Fordist effect—causing the layoff of hundreds of military employees in the service sector. This example of McDonaldization, however, was dressed in exalted social justification: officers declared that it alleviates the socioeconomic gaps evinced by the habit of soldiers from better-off families to circumvent the military kitchen and dine off base (Barzilai, 2000). And so, in an ironic twist, the flagship of American fast food was summoned to the rescue of the Israeli army's egalitarian ethos. Thus, it seems, even when the 'receiving culture' endeavours to resuscitate what is perceived as its own original social values, in the context of globalization the practice is imputed to the medium of the 'transmitting culture.' . . .

Discussion I: 'One-Way' or 'Two-Way'?

Based on this case analysis, how, then, are we to conceive the relations between global commerce and local idioms?

The literature on relations between the global and the local presents a myriad of cases. Heuristically, the lessons from these may be condensed into two competing—contrasting, almost—approaches: the one gives more weight to globalization, which it regards as fostering cultural uniformity (or homogeneity); the other gives more weight to localization, which it regards as preserving cultural plurality, or cultural 'differences' (or heterogeneity). The former generally predicts the Americanization of the various cultures; the latter predicts the resilience of local cultures and a variety of fusions between the global and the local. . . . For the sake of simplicity we shall call the former the 'one-way' approach, i.e. seeing the effect as emanating from the global to the local; and the latter, as the 'two-way' approach, i.e. seeing the effect as an interchange between the global and the local. Ostensibly, the question of which is the more valid can and should be answered by recourse to empirical evidence. The problem, however, appears to lodge elsewhere and therefore calls for a different form of reasoning. Shrouded in conceptual fog, it should be cleared up by theoretical elucidation. We begin by outlining the theoretical debate this article seeks to resolve.

The most prominent exponent of the one-way approach is George Ritzer, in his book *The McDonaldization of Society* (Ritzer, 1995). Ritzer, more than anyone else, is responsible for the term that describes the social process of McDonaldization. Ritzer sees globalization as sweeping and unequivocal homogenization, based on technological efficiency or what Max Weber defined as instrumental rationalization. He considers McDonald's the epitome of modernity in its Weberian sense: 'McDonald's and McDonaldization do not represent something new, but rather the culmination of a series of rationalization processes that had been occurring throughout the twentieth century' (Ritzer, 1995: 31). The principles of McDonaldization are efficiency, calculability, predictability and control. McDonaldization, for Ritzer, is analogous to previous manifestations of a similar tendency, such as Taylorism and Fordism, along with their standardization, routinization, deskilling and homogenization of production and consumption (Ritzer, 1995: 24–7). From this perspective, McDonaldization is an upgraded version of the prevalent rationalization of the 'lifeworld,' a process destined to annul all sorts of 'local' or premodern cultures. It is not difficult to discern here the footprints of both liberal and Marxist theories of modernization.

Implicit in this analytical approach to McDonaldization is a humanistic critique: it rejects the sacrifice of the unique, the personal, the communal, the spontaneous and the free dimensions of human life. Ritzer's Weberian approach has been taken to task for what was perceived as an overemphasis on rationalization, and a consequent lack of attention to both material commodification (a Marxian critique) and symbolic reification (a postmodern critique) (see Kellner, 1999). But all in all, whether McDonaldization is conceptualized primarily in Weberian (rationalization), Marxian (commodification), or Baudrillardian (consumerization) terms, it is perceived as an expression of sweeping and overwhelming globalization that undermines local cultures. In a more dialectical version of the one-sided view, Benjamin Barber captured the dualistic nature of globalization in his depiction of *Jihad vs. McWorld* (Barber, 1995).

. . . Contrary to this one-way approach to globalization and McDonaldization, the literature offers another view, which we call here the two-way approach. This view considers globalization only a single vector in two-way traffic, the other vector being localization. The latter suspends, refines, or diffuses the intakes from the former, so that traditional and local cultures do not dissolve; they rather ingest global flows and reshape them in the digestion.

Arjun Appadurai, for one, asserts that it is impossible to think of the processes of cultural globalization in terms of mechanical flow from center to periphery. Their complexity and disjunctures allow for a chaotic contest between the global and the local that is never resolved. To his mind,

> . . . the central feature of global culture today is the politics of the mutual effort of sameness and difference to cannibalize one another and thus to proclaim their successful hijacking of the twin Enlightenment ideas of the triumphantly universal and the resiliently particular . . . both sides of the coin of global cultural processes today are products of the infinitely varied mutual contest of sameness and difference on a stage characterized by radical disjunctures between different sorts of global flows and the uncertain landscape created in and through these disjunctures. (Appadurai, 1996: 34)

Ulf Hannertz estimates that in the course of time, the process of absorption of the global by the local, with the local domesticating the global—what he calls 'maturation'—would override what looks at first glance like 'saturation' of the local culture by the global (Hannertz, 2000). . . .

The two-way approach to the global–local encounter is usually portrayed as critical and espoused by radical social scientists, because it 'empowers' the sustainability of local cultures and fosters local identities. Yet, it too appears in a conservative variant. Its paradigmatic manifestation is that proposed by Samuel Huntington in his *Clash of Civilizations* thesis (Huntington, 1996). According to Huntington, the post-Cold War world is characterized by a lack of ideological conflicts, on the one hand, but a rise of cultural conflicts, on the other. The fault lines between groups are identity boundaries over which struggles are waged. Huntington assumes the existence of relatively fixed historical 'civilizations,' thereby rejecting the postmodern conception of fluid identities. Nevertheless, he shares its position as to the significance of cultural identity as the most important structural characteristic of any given society. Furthermore, despite the apparent contrast with the two-way approach, he endorses one of its basic assumptions—the fundamental distinction between, on the one hand, the economic and technological influences of globalization and, on the other, the western historical values that define its distinctive cultural identity. Different societies can, therefore, adopt certain components of the global effect and reject others.

Discussion II: 'Both Ways'

To return to the question of homogenization vs heterogenization in global–local relationships, we suggest here the following resolution: (1) both perspectives are valid; (2) yet they apply to discrete societal levels; and (3) the one-way approach is restricted to one level of social reality, the structural-institutional level, i.e. patterns and practices which are inscribed into institutions and organizations; the two-way approach is restricted to the symbolic-expressive level of social reality, i.e. the level of explicit symbolization. Finally, (4) we suggest a global–local structural-symbolic model, in which the one-way structural homogenization process and the two-way symbolic heterogenization process are combined. Thus, heuristically speaking, our theoretical resolution is predicated on the distinction between two different levels, the structural-institutional level and the expressive-symbolic level.

While each of the rival perspectives on the global–local encounter is attuned to only one of these levels, we propose that globalization be seen as a process that is simultaneously one-sided and two-sided but in two distinct societal levels. In other words, on the structural level, globalization is a one-way street; but on the symbolic level, it is a two-way street. In Israel's case, for instance, this would mean that, symbolically, the falafel and McDonald's coexist side by side; structurally, however, the falafel is produced and consumed as if it were an industrialized-standardized (McDonaldized) hamburger, or as its artisan-made 'gourmet' counterpart. Or, in the affair of the Golani Junction, McDonald's 'M' was substituted by the brigade olive-tree insignia, yet military bases and public lands were partially 'McDonaldized.'

The two-way approach to globalization, which highlights the persistence of cultural 'difference', contains more than a grain of empirical truth. On the symbolic level, it accounts for the diversity that does not succumb to homogeneity—in our case, the falafel once again steams from the pita; the Israeli hamburger is larger than other national McDonald's specimens (and kosher for Passover; on this see Ram, 2003); at Golani Junction, the brigade banner rather than the logo of a fast-food chain graces the flagpole; and Israelis have their choice of a culturally satisfying combo-'combina' (just as Egyptians are offered McFalafel). On the symbolic level, the 'difference' that renders the local distinctive has managed to linger on. At the same time, on the structural level, that great leveller of 'sameness' at all locales prevails: the falafel has become McDonaldized; the military has privatized food

provisioning; and Air Force 'Ms' can hardly be told apart from McDonald's' 'M.' . . .

A strong structuralist argument sees symbolic 'differences' not merely as tolerated but indeed as functional to structural 'sameness', in that they are purported to conceal the structure's underlying uniformity and to promote niches of consumer identity. In other words, the variety of local cultural identities 'licensed' under global capitalist commercial expansion disguises the unified formula of capital, thereby fostering legitimacy and even sales. It is in this vein that Fredric Jameson contends that the kaleidoscope of identities and styles that characterizes postmodern culture is, in fact, an expression of the new—post-Fordist—production system. The oft-changing, oft-fragmenting cycles of postmodern consumption well suit the technologically driven cycles of production, constantly creating new markets and constantly marketing inventions. Postmodernity, therefore, divulges the cultural logic of post-Fordist capitalism (Jameson, 1998). . . .

The case study presented here has shown a number of instances of the process whereby global commodities appropriate local traditions. To recap with the example of the 'new falafel', McDonaldization did not bring about its demise, but, indeed, contributed to its revival, vindicating, as it were, the two-way perspective. The falafel's new lease on life, however, is modelled after McDonald's, that is, a standardized, mechanical, mass-commodified product, on the one hand; or responds to it in a commercial 'gourmetized' and 'ethnicitized' product, on the other hand. In both cases, global McDonaldization prevails structurally, while it may give a symbolic leeway to the local. The Egyptian McFalafel is an exemplary point in case.

Thus, the question of global homogenization vs local heterogenization cannot be exhausted by invoking symbolic differences, as is attempted by the two-way approach. 'McDonaldization' is not merely or mainly about the manufactured objects—the hamburgers—but first and foremost about the deep-seated social relationships involved in their production and consumption—i.e. it is about commodification and instrumentalization. In its broadest sense here, McDonaldization represents a robust commodification and instumentalization of social relations, production and consumption, and therefore an appropriation of local cultures by global flows. Jürgen Habermas regards the major tension in contemporary society to be between 'systems' and the 'lifeworld' (Habermas, 1984, 1987). Likewise, Manuel Castells regards the major tension in the contemporary world to be between the 'net'—global sociotechnical flows, and the 'self'—local idiomatic and communal cultures (Castells, 1997). This study has illustrated these tensions, and proposes looking at the relations between the global and the local as a composite of the structural and symbolic levels, a composite in which the structural inherently appropriates the symbolic but without explicitly suppressing it.

Karl Marx defined the fetishism of commodities as the process in which human societal productive relations are concealed behind associations between produced objects. Intersubjective relations are thus objectified, whereas associations between commodities are expressed as relations between subjects; that is, human relations become limited to an abstract monetary exchange, whereas commodities come to serve as representations of identities (Marx, 1967: 71–83). Such fetishism of commodities is epitomized by the example of McDonald's in Israel—just one more case in the general drift towards planetary commodification and instrumentalization,

accompanied by a proliferation of symbolic identities and by cultural fragmentation, in the structurally post-Fordist and symbolically postmodern era of global capitalism. This is what is meant by glocommodification—global commodification combining structural uniformity with symbolic diversity.

Discussion Questions

1. How does Ram illustrate that globalization has "McDonalized" the world structurally while letting symbolic elements of local culture remain in place?

2. What are some examples that you can think of that illustrate how "homogenization" has occurred at the structural level? (The examples can be at either the national or international level.)

Source: "Glocommodification: How the Global Consumes the Local—McDonald's in Israel" by Uri Ram, excerpted and with notes & references omitted from *Current Sociology*, January 2004, Vol. *52*(1): 11–31. Reprinted by permission of Sage Publications.

CHAPTER 29

'In the Court of Public Opinion'

Transnational Problem Construction in the HIV/AIDS Medicine Access Campaign, 1998–2001

Thomas Olesen

The HIV/AIDS medicine access campaign, 1998–2001, began when some of the world's largest pharmaceutical companies initiated a court case again South Africa for violating the companies' patent rights. It ended with the withdrawal of the case. The objective of this chapter is to provide insight into the way campaign activists sought to make the issue of HIV/AIDS medicine access of concern and intelligible to audiences not directly affected by it. The campaign combined emotional and strategic elements and sought to bridge distance by connecting the universal and the particular.

Introduction

19 April 2001: people are dancing and cheering in a South African courtroom. In the following hours and days, the image circulates the globe. Large organizations such as OXFAM and MSF (Médecins Sans Frontières) (OXFAM et al., 2001) issue joint press releases speaking of 'a rare and very meaningful victory' and *The Guardian*'s (2001) leader chimes in, declaring '[a] victory for the poor' and for 'human rights activists round the globe.' What is all the fuss about? Three years earlier, on 18 February 1998, 39 of the world's largest pharmaceutical companies had filed a court case against the South African government. The disagreement concerned a constitutional amendment allowing South Africa to circumvent patent rights of HIV/AIDS drugs. On 19 April 2001, the companies withdrew the case. In the meantime, a transnational campaign had been orchestrated to support the right of South Africa (and other countries with severe HIV/AIDS problems) to make this move.

Since 1996, treatment of HIV/AIDS has improved with the introduction of anti-retroviral (ARV) drugs. But the benefits have been restricted mainly to citizens in Western Europe and the USA. The patents held by pharmaceutical companies let them charge a price that keeps anti-retro-virals beyond the reach of most people in the Third World (where the large majority of affected people reside). Today, and to the dismay of the companies, Third World governments are confronting this problem with parallel import or production/import of generic drugs. The steps taken by South Africa were not, therefore, unique, but it was the first time companies decided to form a united front and pursue a legal strategy in a national court. This immediately turned South Africa into a focal point for a transnational campaign confronting the moral and legal foundations of the companies' drug price policies and, in the larger picture, the global inequalities they cause.

Whether campaign activities were decisive in the companies' eventual decision to withdraw the case is difficult to establish. What is beyond doubt is that they played some role. The campaign especially had effect, as one activist put it (Elliott, 2003), by forcing the issue into 'the court of public opinion.' According to Richard Elliott (2003) of the Canadian HIV/AIDS Legal Network, the campaign thus started a spiral of negative publicity in which the pharmaceutical companies 'faced mounting global criticism and were stuck in the role of greedy global villains standing in the way of a developing country government trying to get medicines to millions of poor Africans needing medicines.' The pharmaceutical companies increasingly faced a deteriorating public image that could only be restored by withdrawing the case. The day after the withdrawal, J. P. Garnier, chief executive of one of the companies, GlaxoSmithKline, acknowledged the power of negative public opinion: 'We don't exist in a vacuum, [w]e're a very major corporation. We're not insensitive to public opinion. That is a factor in our decision-making' (Swarns, 2001).

Public opinion in this case was not so much expressed through large-scale demonstrations, but via claims made by central campaign actors; these were, in particular, media, civil society organizations and politicians. In the article, however, I focus on the activities of organizations. Organizations were among the first to mobilize critical opinion and had a strong effect on the way media and politicians responded to the situation. I do not mean to suggest a simple causality here. Still, it is also clear that many organizations were already deeply involved in the problematic of HIV/AIDS medicine access when the court case in South Africa began and therefore one step ahead of media and politicians in interpreting the situation.

What is interesting about this case is that 'the court of public opinion' was transnationally constituted. Or perhaps more precisely, it was made up by sentiments in several national public spheres in Western Europe and North America. Public opinion expressed indignation over the apparent greed of pharmaceutical companies in a situation where millions of lives could be saved. But why did people here care at all? As just mentioned, the publics most adamant in their criticism were Western European and North American. Since HIV/AIDS patients in these countries have access to anti-retroviral drugs, people there are not directly affected by the companies' drug policies. And further, critical sentiments were not mainly voiced by people suffering from HIV/AIDS themselves. They came, as indicated earlier, from a broad range of social and political actors such as media, civil society organizations and politicians.

When local or national problems are pushed into a court of transnational public opinion and become themes in settings not directly affected by them, it is the result of transnational problem construction. Constructing

transnational problems is a complex process of making issues and problems in one locality intelligible and concerning for people in other and distant localities. The complexity derives from the fact that in a transnational context distance has many more facets than in a local or national context. The transnational problem construction of organizations requires them to bridge physical, social and cultural distances. The article's main purpose is to analyse how civil society organizations in the HIV/AIDS medicine access campaign sought to accomplish this. As such it provides insight into a little studied case of transnational activism, but on a more general plane it also enquires into current processes of globalization. This is so because, essentially, globalization is about the reduction of distance. When local, national or regional problems become constructed as *transnational* problems, it is precisely the result of distance bridging activities by the actors involved. Analysing distance bridging is therefore a sine qua non if we are to further improve our knowledge of globalization. . . .

Theoretical Framework

In the theoretical jargon of social movement scholars, problem construction is a framing process (Snow et al., 1986; Snow and Benford, 1988, 1992). Frames are activist interpretations of reality, leaving some things out and zooming in on others. Sometimes frames attempt to turn a non-problem into a problem, while in other cases they give a new angle to an already recognized problem. Frames and the campaigns that construct them are thus engaged in contests over meaning, interpretation and definition. But what is the objective of frames? It is, in the language of Schattschneider (1960), to enlarge the scope of conflict. Enlarging the scope of conflict means to mobilize the support of the 'audience,' which I define as the media and public opinion. Mobilization of the audience changes the dynamics of the conflict, often to the advantage of the weaker parties in a conflict (Gamson, 2004: 242). Since campaign activities seek to pressure authorities such as states, institutions and companies to meet demands, and since campaigns typically possess fewer resources than authorities, scope enlargement is their most viable strategy. . . .

Frames intend to produce what McAdam et al. (2001: 331) call scale shift. Scale shift is a form of scope enlargement as it implies an increase in the number of actors in a campaign and a bridging of their claims. In a transnational perspective, scale shift occurs when a local or national problem becomes a transnational problem. In fact, transnational campaign success hinges on whether they can produce such scale shifts. Scale shift, according to McAdam et al. (2001: 333), occurs through two main mechanisms: brokerage (linking of two or more currently unconnected sites) and diffusion (transfer of information along established lines of interaction). Transnational scale shift may be divided into two phases that correspond roughly with diffusion and brokerage.

Campaigns are initiated by a small core of large and professional organizations. In the first phase, diffusion, organizations that are already part of the transnational activist community are mobilized. These may be smaller organizations within the issue area that do not possess the resources to initiate campaigns on their own, or organizations peripherally related to the issue area. This type of mobilization takes place through already existing networks. It thus corresponds well with one of the most consistent findings in the social movement literature; the importance of social networks in explaining mobilization (Tilly, 1978; Snow et al., 1980; McAdam, 1982).

In the second phase, brokerage, campaigns seek to enlarge and intensify the sentiment pool (McCarthy and Zald, 2001: 536) in national public spheres. The sentiment pool is the number of people with a preference for change along the lines demanded by the campaign, but I find it useful to also include the media in the sentiment pool. Since this process is directed to a broad and undefined public, activists cannot rely on already existing ties and networks as in the first phase (Jasper and Poulsen, 1995). This kind of mobilization requires brokerage. Brokerage is more complex than diffusion. Its challenge lies in connecting hitherto unconnected social sites, or, to use the conceptual vocabulary of this article, in constructing and framing problems in such a way that they become relevant and intelligible for individuals and organizations not directly affected by them. In the remainder of the section I therefore focus on brokerage in transnational campaigns.

In order to generate public and media interest in campaign claims, campaign framing and brokerage must bridge the universal and the particular. A call for action that involves distant events cannot base itself on generalities. It has to demonstrate to others the suffering of particular people in a particular place. By holding up this particularity, campaigns attempt to elicit an emotional and indignant reaction from the audience they are targeting. At the same time, however, they anchor this indignation in a universal understanding of the situation (Boltanski, 1999). The particular instance of suffering is for example interpreted as an affront to (universal) human dignity or rights. This linkage is necessary to overcome the distance between the situation of suffering and its spectators. I have argued elsewhere (Olesen, 2005) how campaigns often seek to establish this connection between the particular and universal through *democratic* framing. Democracy builds on a conception of universality. Democratic frames portray local and particular problems as democratic (and hence universal) problems. If this link is successfully constructed, campaigns can have it both ways, so to speak: they can expect the (undemocratic) suffering of particular people to create indignation, while at the same time drawing on the social and political legitimacy that world society today bestows on democratic norms.

Campaign frames intended to bridge the universal and the particular often employ what Jasper and Poulsen (1995) call moral shocks. Moral shocks are induced by information and symbols that create indignation and outrage and motivate public and media to support campaign claims. In their work on human rights campaigns, Sikkink and her colleagues for example demonstrate how activists attempt to 'shame' opponents by framing issues in emotional and moral terms (Keck and Sikkink, 1998; Risse and Sikkink, 1999). . . .

Best (1987: 110) has shown how success in turning missing children into a social problem in the USA was facilitated by the ease with which children were portrayed as blameless victims. This is not unlike transnational campaigns. Emotional framing require campaigns to portray recipients of support as blameless victims, either of uncontrollable natural disasters or repression by governments or other actors. The 'blameless victims' frame also makes the situation more interesting for the media. Most studies of movement–media relations conclude that drama and conflict are what attract the media (e.g. Oliver and Myers, 1999: 65–8). The blameless victims frame is relatively black and white. This absence of nuances and the presence of an unequivocal wrong make the human drama or conflict in the situation appear with greater clarity.

. . . As we have already discussed, campaign frames are structured around emotions and indignation. Emotion and indignation, however, cannot stand alone. They must be rooted in objective facts and in a disinterested position (Boltanski, 1999: 65). This may include empirical proofs of wrongdoing, and, following Best (1987: 106–7), estimation of the size of the problem and evidence that the problem will get worse if nothing is done. Similarly, campaigns have to make it clear for their audiences that their accusations are not dictated by narrow self-interests vis-a-vis the accused (Boltanski, 1999: 58). The challenge for campaigns, then, is to find and walk the balance between objectivity and subjectivity. Too much focus on the objective side leaves out the emotional and indignant elements crucial in arousing the interest of the media, the public and authorities. Too much emphasis on the subjective component, in contrast, leaves campaigns open to charges of manipulation, overreaction and soft-heartedness.

The emphasis on framing should not lead us to believe that a good frame that combines the factors discussed above is all it takes to generate transnational resonance. Let me propose two reservations. First, and drawing on the resource mobilization approach in social movement studies (McCarthy and Zald, 1977, 2001), it should be observed that frame success depends on other activist resources such as money, skills, organizational capacity, legitimacy and status. A frame usually fares better when it is backed up by economic and organizational resources that enable the 'marketing' of the frame, and when the organization(s) behind it have some legitimacy in the public sphere (Bob, 2003) and standing in the media (Ferree et al., 2002). Second, and drawing on the political opportunities approach to social movements (Tilly, 1978; McAdam, 1982, 1996; Tarrow, 1998), it is suggested that frames that are directly or indirectly backed by strong allies such as states and institutions have a better chance of making the desired impact. . . .

Analysis

In this section I offer an account of how the HIV/AIDS medicine access campaign was able to put pressure on the pharmaceutical companies by forcing the issue of medicine access into 'the court of public opinion.' To repeat what I said in the introduction, the argument is not that campaign activities necessarily determined the companies' decision to withdraw the case. Yet it is clear that they did play a role. How they played that role is what I discuss in this section. . . .

OBJECTIVITY AND SUBJECTIVITY

The resonance of campaign frames depends on the extent to which they successfully integrate and develop elements of diagnosis, prognosis and motivation (Snow and Benford, 1988). Diagnosis refers to the recognition and definition of a problem, prognosis to the formulation of solutions, and motivation to arguments that activism can help solve the problem. These elements were well developed and integrated in the HIV/AIDS medicine access campaign. Snow and Benford's scheme focuses on strategy and pays scant attention to the role of emotionality in the framing process (Goodwin and Jasper, 1999). However, as discussed in the theoretical section, emotions are an important part of campaign frames, including that of the HIV/AIDS medicine access campaign. In the following analysis of diagnosis, prognosis and motivation I therefore attempt to show how emotionality and strategy, subjectivity and objectivity, were combined in the campaign frame.

Diagnosis. This consisted of two levels: on one level, there was the extremely high number of HIV/AIDS sufferers in South Africa and many other poor countries and, on the other, the fact that the large majority of these did not have access to effective treatment, not because it did not exist, but simply because it was too expensive. In the theoretical section, I argued that campaigns dealing with distant suffering need to combine objective facts regarding the scope and severity of the problem with moral and emotional indignation. This combination was evident in the way the HIV/AIDS medicine access campaign frame diagnosed the problem.

Campaign activists recurrently pointed to the sufferings of ordinary people in South Africa, where numbers more or less speak for themselves. South Africa has more than 4.3 million people living with HIV, 'more than any other country in the world. In 2000 alone, 250,000 people died of HIV/AIDS' (MSF, 2001b). In the same press statement, Eric Goemare, head of MSF's HIV/AIDS programme in South Africa, described the consequences of the high cost of medicine and the failure of drug companies to address this problem in indignant terms: 'Everyday, dozens of people with HIV/AIDS come to our clinics in a poor township outside Cape Town looking for affordable medicine, but the high price of drugs means that we are only able to offer treatment to a limited number of people.' According to Goemare, people are 'dying because drug prices are too high as a result of patent protection. I find it appalling that the pharmaceutical industry is ignoring this and instead is trying to block the government's efforts to improve access to medicines' (MSF, 2001b). Activist frames continuously highlighted this discrepancy and 'shamed' companies for ignoring it. . . .

It was discussed in the theoretical section how resonance is facilitated if victims can be portrayed as blameless. While it could be argued that people with HIV/AIDS are not blameless because they engage in risky sexual behaviours, it is also clear how people in poor countries like South Africa (in contrast to the rich parts of the world) often get the disease because they lack the necessary knowledge and information to avoid it. At the same time, many poor countries are characterized by a very high number of women and children with HIV/AIDS. These are 'innocent' victims in the sense that most have been infected through their husbands or mothers.

Prognosis. Campaign frames appear more credible when they are able to offer plausible solutions to the problems they protest. Formulating solutions is a strategic exercise, but one that is anchored in the moral and emotional claims of the diagnosis.

In the case of the HIV/AIDS medicine access campaign, there was a relatively straightforward solution to be found. The solution suggested by campaign activists required the pharmaceutical companies to look at the issue in moral and not just economic terms. While it would not make HIV/AIDS problems go away antiretroviral treatments could significantly reduce the number of deaths caused by HIV/AIDS. The solution, in short, was to make treatment affordable for people and governments in poor countries. This could be obtained in various ways. According to OXFAM (2001b), pharmaceutical companies 'should exercise social responsibility with respect to their patent claims. They should not seek to enforce patent claims in the poorest countries on drugs essential to public health.' Further, they 'should reduce the price of key medicines in developing countries so that they are affordable to the poor.' A more sustainable way of solving the problem of medicine, according to OXFAM, would be to allow poor countries to 'produce, market, import and export affordable generic medicines.'

Motivation. The court case between the South African government and the pharmaceutical companies provided campaign activists with rare opportunities to motivate people to engage in different forms of critical action towards the companies. Transnational problems are often difficult to frame because their causes are structural and cannot be attributed to specific actors (for example, ozone depletion). This is a major challenge for activists. The question of medicine access and prices is no exception. It reflects structural inequalities at a global level and the 'guilty' (drug companies) are scattered around the world. The court case in South Africa, however, became a very visible symbol of what was framed and 'shamed' as the greed of pharmaceutical companies. Usually, medicine access activists need to target individual companies in various countries. By staging the court case in South Africa, the companies in a sense did an

unintended favour to activists by providing them with a transnationally visible 'all-in-one' focal point. The obvious drama of a court case where two opponents meet face to face in a legal boxing ring also made the issue more appealing to the media, who, as discussed in the theoretical section, favour stories that can be portrayed as relatively black and white conflicts between clearly identifiable opponents.

UNIVERSALITY AND PARTICULARITY

Transnational campaign frames are simultaneously communicated to actors at local, national and transnational levels. To gain resonance, frames therefore must bridge the physical, social and cultural distances that separate these actors. Put differently, and as argued in the theoretical section, frames need to combine the universal and the particular, the general and the personal. To forge this combination campaigns make use of democratic framing. Problems framed in democratic terms are concrete problems for someone in particular and in a specific place, but because democracy, at least in its theoretical core, has strong elements of universality, these problems attain a universal character.

Campaign activists tried to establish this connection by making use of personal and emotional stories told by HIV/AIDS sufferers in South Africa. . . . In general, bodily harm or gross legal and political inequalities tend to be the best motivators for emotionally driven transnational activism (Keck and Sikkink, 1998: 27), but especially, we may add, if those suffering can be portrayed as blameless victims. This argument was, as discussed earlier, easy to make in relation to HIV/AIDS suffering in South Africa and other poor countries.

At the same time, these 'individual' problems were portrayed by campaign activists as part of a bigger picture of global inequality and lack of democracy, or in the words of Booker and Minter (2001), of a global apartheid: 'To date, access to lifesaving medicines and care for people living with HIV and AIDS have been largely determined by race, class, gender and geography.' For Booker and Minter, the case of HIV/AIDS medicine was thus illustrative of strong global inequalities: 'Indeed, today's international political economy, in which undemocratic institutions systematically generate economic inequality, should be described as "global apartheid."' Although South Africa was not framed as the 'culprit' in this case, the reference to apartheid nevertheless had a strong emotional appeal in a case involving South Africa. Just as the 'original' apartheid, global apartheid denies basic rights to a large group of people. Global apartheid does not so much reflect racial differences, but rather global economic inequalities. For campaign activists, however, the consequences are the same. The democratic and human rights of people with HIV/AIDS in the poor countries are violated. The lack of access to life-saving drugs for poor South Africans, despite their availability in the rich part of the world, is a global democratic problem. . . .

RESOURCES AND ALLIES

Transnational problems construction is not just about formulating convincing frames. Generating transnational resonance is significantly aided by economic and skill resources and the presence of allies. Understanding resonance thus requires us to look at the resources commanded by campaigns and the support they receive from powerful actors such as states and institutions. This argument draws on the resource mobilization (e.g. McCarthy and Zald, 1977, 2001) and political opportunities (e.g. Tilly 1978; McAdam, 1982, 1996; Tarrow, 1998) strands in social movement theory.

Resources. Resources and their acquisition matter for all types of social movement activity. This is perhaps even more apparent in a transnational setting where potential audiences are larger and several media and public spheres have to be approached. The HIV/AIDS medicine access campaign was spearheaded by a number of large and resourceful organizations such as the Consumer Project on Technology, MSF, Health GAP, OXFAM and ACT UP. These are organizations with a well-developed and long-standing experience in disseminating their views to the public, the media, politicians and companies. They all have regular staff that are recruited and trained with informational activities in mind. Framing activities in the campaign were not, however, the sole responsibility of these organizations. As mentioned elsewhere, TAC [Treatment Action Campaign] in South Africa was a central actor in the campaign. Made up mostly by people with HIV/AIDS and rooted in South African civil society, it had a credibility none of the other aforementioned organizations could muster. For non-South African activists, TAC provided a focal point that made it easier to arouse the interest of the media and the public. What might have seemed an anonymous and technical legal dispute was given a human face with the presence of TAC and its leaders. Zackie Achmat, chairperson of TAC, for example, made headlines in the foreign media in October 2000

when he publicly 'smuggled' 5000 generic HIV/AIDS drug pills from Thailand to South Africa to demonstrate the enormous price differences. Before and during the court case, this story was widely circulated in the media (e.g. Mathiason, 2001).

Yet on its own, TAC did not have the experience or resources to make a transnational impact. During the campaign a close relationship evolved between TAC and the large American and European organizations mentioned earlier. The latter understood the importance of the legitimacy provided by the presence of TAC in the campaign. TAC in turn drew considerable support from foreign organizations in the time leading up to and during the court case. . . .

Allies. The direct or indirect involvement of states, international institutions and politicians in the HIV/AIDS medicine access campaign was crucial for its success. Transnational campaigns, as mentioned earlier, are not made up only of civil society organizations. When institutional actors intervene to support campaign claims they become part of it, albeit often only temporarily. In some cases, allies intervene by themselves, but in the majority of cases they do so only when campaigns have already generated some attention in the media and the public sphere. Politicians and governments have a large range of problems to attend to and are therefore rather selective. Campaign activism combined with media and public interest is often necessary to make them intervene (Schmitz and Sikkink, 2002: 531). Intervention can be both direct and indirect. Direct intervention occurs when an ally supports a campaign through official statements or concrete actions. Indirect intervention occurs when institutional actors who have hitherto supported campaign opponents withdraw this support. The HIV/AIDS medicine access campaign, as I show, provides examples of both types of support.

The US government initially backed the pharmaceutical companies' lawsuit. In 1999, the US Trade Representative (1999a) placed South Africa on its Special 301 list of countries in violation of WTO agreements. The concern was that 'South Africa's Medicines Act appears to grant the Health Minister ill defined authority to issue compulsory licenses, authorize parallel imports, and potentially otherwise abrogate patent rights.' But support for the law suit soon created domestic problems for the Clinton administration. Protestors from various organizations in the US (including ACT UP and Health GAP) turned up on Al Gore's presidential campaign trail, demanding a stop to US support of the pharmaceutical companies. In December 1999, the protests delivered the desired result: South Africa was taken off the Special 301 watch list (US Trade Representative, 1999c). The change in US policy was reflected in the pharmaceutical companies' decision to suspend the litigation in September 1999, a move publicly applauded by the US Trade Representative (1999b). While the US government did not actively support the claims of the campaign, its 'defection' from the companies' camp was nevertheless an important moment. The US withdrawal of support weakened the companies' case considerably. This suggests that just as strong allies are important for campaigns, so is the vulnerability of the target (Risse, 2002: 268). The vulnerability of the companies increased as state support began to erode.

This erosion also took place at the European level, where support for the campaign was in some cases more direct. In March 2001, EU trade commissioner Pascal Lamy (2001) responded to an open letter from MSF (2001a) by supporting countries' right to overrule patent rights under certain conditions. While this letter formulated its support rather vaguely and declined to make any statement on the court case, the European Parliament issued a more outspoken resolution, which directly called on the pharmaceutical companies 'to withdraw from the case' (European Parliament, 2001). . . .

The campaign could also count on at least the indirect support of countries facing the same kind of problems as South Africa in regard to HIV/AIDS and medicine access. These were, most notably, developing countries such as India and Brazil. In the months of the South African court case, Brazil was involved in a dispute with the US over HIV/AIDS drugs policies. In June, the US Trade Representative (2001) gave up on attempts to try the case before a WTO panel, effectively allowing Brazil to continue its strategy of generic drugs production. The united stance of developing countries on the issue was also instrumental in obtaining the concessions won at the WTO meeting in Doha in 2001 (see the history section).

Conclusion

The article has analysed how the HIV/AIDS medicine access campaign framed and constructed the problem of medicine access during the pharmaceutical companies' case against South Africa. The main objective of the article has been to provide insight into the way distant problems are made relevant and intelligible to audiences not directly affected by them. Although the aim of the article

has therefore not been to explain the successful outcome of the campaign, the analysis nevertheless allows us to make some observations that have relevance beyond the case studied in this article. In general terms, three sets of factors contributed to the successful outcome: (1) a frame that combined objectivity and subjectivity and universality and particularity; (2) the campaign's possession of significant organizational resources; and (3) the presence of direct and indirect allies in the form of states, institutions and politicians. What this suggests on a more general explanatory plane is that campaign framing activities cannot, theoretically or analytically, be separated from the resources and political opportunities with which they always interact. Analyses of transnational campaign success, in other words, need to combine constructionist and structural elements of explanations.

While the case studied in this article is thus an example of how civil society organizations can play a role in world political issues, it should not lead us to exaggerate the potential of such activities. Campaigns generally are carriers of humanistic ideals based in a global consciousness. Yet world political structures may impede their further development, just as their actions sometimes create effects that are contrary to their ideals. These arguments raise important questions regarding the future direction of globalization and the prospective role of civil society organizations in it.

. . . If we accept the view that the end of Cold War conflict made democratic and human rights norms more central in world politics, it is also plausible to speculate that the events of September 11 may have had an adverse effect. World politics once more gravitate around security and conflicts considered resolvable mainly through military means. For civil society activists, this has led to a world political environment where activism is becoming increasingly constrained and where the interest of the public and media in distant events is harder to attract as new problems that seem to have a more direct effect on people's everyday lives take centre stage. More importantly, perhaps, it has allowed the USA to take on a much stronger and hegemonic role at the global level. With the current conservative and strongly pro-capitalist administration at the helm, the prospects for any fundamental change in global inequalities in the area of medicine access (and other socioeconomic areas for that matter) appear to be dim indeed. However, the Live 8 concerts in July 2005 also show that there are other forces to be reckoned with, but whether they can gather momentum and effect real structural changes remains to be seen.

Discussion Questions

1. According to Olesen, why is it particularly difficult to frame a problem as a *transnational* problem?

2. According to Olesen's history of the case, what led the pharmaceutical companies to withdraw their case against the South African government? Do you think this was a good business decision on their part? Why or why not?

Source: "'In the Court of Public Opinion': Transnational Problem Construction in the HIV/AIDS Medicine Access Campaign, 1998–2001" by Thomas Olesen, excerpted and with notes & references omitted from *International Sociology*, January 2006, Vol. 21(1): 5–30. Reprinted by permission of Sage Publications.

---⦚---

PART VIII

SOCIAL MOVEMENTS AND SOCIAL CHANGE

The last section of the book looks at how change takes place and the role of social movements in creating social change. It considers the influence of different theologies on the role of believers in public life, the need for citizens to organize to counter the growing power of corporations in a globalized world, how culture jamming is used by social activists, and the need for social activists to remember that enacting national legislation is useful only when the legislation is carried out in local communities throughout the United States.

In "Making Theological Sense of the Migration Journey From Latin American: Catholic, Protestant, and Interfaith Perspectives" Jacqueline Hagan looks at how members of different religions have reacted to the issue of illegal immigration from Latin America. In doing so, she reveals that whether the churches have a communitarian (like the Catholic Church and "mainline" Protestant denominations) or an individualistic social theology (like Pentecostal and Evangelical churches) influences their reactions to undocumented immigrants. The churches with communitarian theological perspectives are much more likely to fight for the rights of immigrants than are those with individualistic theological outlooks.

In "Hate Crime Reporting as a Successful Social Movement Outcome," Rory McVeigh and his co-authors examine the degree to which hate crimes are reported in different areas of the nation. Their results indicate that reporting is largely dependent upon the will and interest of local law enforcement agencies and varies widely across the nation. Using these findings, they make a convincing case that the reporting of hate crimes is the true indicator of the success of the movement behind the creation of hate crime legislation.

Vince Carducci's "Culture Jamming: A Sociological Perspective" provides vivid examples of organized efforts to offer resistance against a consumerized culture. Carducci shows how culture jammers try to expose corporate efforts to influence the thoughts, tastes, and beliefs of consumers. He also points out that, ironically, culture jammers, in carrying out their efforts to expose the workings of corporations, often create alternative consumer cultures and unintentionally support the market culture.

In the last article, "Corporate Citizenship and Social Responsibility in a Globalized World," Juan José Palacios also addresses the rise in power of corporations in our globalized world. He argues that corporations cannot, by their very nature as profit-seeking organizations, be good citizens of the world without rules and regulations enacted and enforced to make them so. Palacios maintains that an organized global civil society must emerge in order to establish a transnational governing framework that can hold global corporations in check and promote good citizenship among them.

As you read the articles in this section, keep in mind the following points:

- The religions with the most communitarian social theology are those most likely to try to assist undocumented workers.
- Culture jamming is a political activity used in efforts to disrupt consumerism and promote anti-consumerism.
- Legislation can only be effective if it is enforced on the local, as well as the state and federal levels.
- Business corporations are legally treated as individual citizens in the United States. However, many social scientists argue that current laws do not have the power to ensure that global corporations act like good citizens.

CHAPTER 30

Making Theological Sense of the Migration Journey From Latin America

Catholic, Protestant, and Interfaith Perspectives

Jacqueline Hagan

The theological bases for pastoral care and social justice actions for migrants from Central America and Mexico are examined in the context of current immigration law and policy. The Catholic church and mainline Protestant churches embrace a communitarian social theology that translates into social justice activities. Pentecostal and Evangelical workers shy away from immigration politics, focusing instead of the needs and salvation of individual members of their ministries.

In recent years, the United States and Mexico have embraced their sovereign rights as nation-states and taken unparalleled steps to restrict the entry of unauthorized migrants by increasing enforcement efforts along their borders—strategic policies that pose huge human costs for journeying migrants. To be sure, the unauthorized migrant journey from Latin America to the United States has always posed danger. The harsh heat of the southwest desert and the unpredictable currents of the Rio Grande have long claimed numerous lives (Annerino, 1999; Chavez, 1992). But the dangers associated with crossing the southern U.S. border have escalated dramatically since the early 1990s, with the onset of "prevention through deterrence," a U.S. border enforcement campaign initiated in 1993 to stem the tide of unauthorized migration from Latin America, especially Mexico. Under this new campaign, the enforcement budget tripled between 1995 and 2001. In 2002, it exceeded US$2.5 billion (Reyes, Johnson, & Swearingen, 2002). Armed with these new funds, resources funneled to the border increased dramatically and new technology such as sensors, night vision, and lighting equipment; new

patrol vehicles; and more agents (10,000 by 2004) were deployed along well-established historical crossing corridors, including El Paso, Texas; San Diego, California; Brownsville, Texas; and Nogales and Douglas, Arizona.

Although there is no indication that the recent militarization of the southwest border has achieved its goals of slowing the tide of undocumented migration and the unauthorized labor supply (Hanson & Spilimbergo, 1999; Reyes et al., 2002; Massey, 2005; Massey, Durand, & Malone, 2002; U.S. General Accounting Office, 1997, 1999, 2001), tragically, these intensified enforcement efforts have made the U.S.-Mexico border a more dangerous area to cross (Eschbach, Hagan, & Rodriguez, 2003; Eschbach, Hagan, Rodriguez, Hernandez-Leon, & Bailey, 1999). In their attempts to cross the border surreptitiously, requiring travel away from urban areas of beefed-up enforcement and through more remote mountainous and desert terrain, migrants are often exposed to extreme environmental conditions that can prove fatal. It is not surprising that the increase in risk factors—especially exposure to harsh physical elements for longer periods of time—has elevated the death rate among undocumented migrants trying to enter the United States. Since 1992, more than 3,000 migrants have died trying to cross the U.S.-Mexico border, which translates into a tripling of their death rate (Eschbach et al., 2003; Eschbach et al., 1999; Massey et al., 2002).

Under pressure from the U.S. government to push the border farther south—and partially in expectation of gaining expanded residency rights for Mexican workers in the United States—in 2001, the Mexican government launched its border campaign, Plan Sur, to curb and regulate migration from Central America and to monitor escalating human rights abuses along the 600-mile border it shares with its southern neighbor, Guatemala. The enforcement arm of Plan Sur involved deploying government troops to the southern states of Chiapas and Oaxaca to install checkpoints along well-established crossing corridors. The consequences of the enforcement component of Plan Sur are greater risks and abuses to the journeying migrants—not that surprising given that the Mexican enforcement strategy is largely based on the U.S. prevention-through-deterrence model. To cross into Mexico, migrants are often pressed to pay *mordidas* (bribes) to officials. To circumvent checkpoints, which are located in or near towns, migrants traveling without authorization take riskier routes in remote and inaccessible areas, where they fall prey to vigilante gangs, such as the infamous Mara Salvatrucha.

To avoid checkpoints along train routes, migrants continue to risk injury and death as they jump off and later attempt to remount moving trains. In addition to the myriad physical dangers Central Americans face as they travel through the harsh jungle of southern Mexico, many are forced to overcome a host of social dangers, including rape, theft, and mistreatment by government officials. Crossing two borders results in a more dangerous journey for many Central Americans compared to the journey taken by their Mexican counterparts (Menjívar, 2000; Rodriguez, 2002). Despite efforts by the Mexican government to deploy migrant-protection officials—Beta Groups—along the border, deaths resulting from exposure to multiple social and physical dangers appear to be increasing. According to Grayson (2002, 2003), in 2000, 120 migrants in the area along the Mexico-Guatemala border died. By 2002, the mortality bill had increased threefold to 355. The number of migrant lives lost climbed further in 2003, peaking at 371. . . .

These enforcement policies by the U.S. and Mexican governments have come under fire by religious workers in Central America, Mexico, and the U.S. border areas—the corridors through which many poor Latin American migrants make their way to the United States. In contrast to the governments of Mexico and the United States, which claim their sovereign rights to protect and seal borders in the name of national security, many religious institutions, organizations, and workers argue that when the poor in their communities cannot find work to support themselves and their families—a situation in which many Mexican and Central Americans now find themselves—they have a right to cross borders to find work elsewhere. Although not explicitly challenging the right of sovereign nations to control their borders, as was the case during the heyday of the Sanctuary movement (a religious-based political movement founded in the 1980s in response to growing numbers of Central Americans fleeing political turmoil in their homelands and seeking political asylum in the United States; Coutin, 1993), religious actors and agents—Catholics and Protestants alike—are increasingly critical of current U.S. and Mexico border and interior enforcement policies because they violate the human rights and human dignity of migrants. Calling for immigration reform and social justice, a growing number of local, regional, national, and binational religious workers and coalitions explicitly seek policies that do not exploit migrants, place them in danger, violate their due process, or detain them indefinitely. To shield migrants from violations of their human and statutory rights, religious leaders urge their clergy to provide pastoral and humanitarian care for migrants during the entirety of the migration process, from departure, through the journey, to arrival.

Although largely unsuccessful in their attempts to reform U.S. and Mexican border policies, religious leaders have been quite effective in delivering their plea to local clergy, lay workers, and parishioners who counsel and provide for the poor and potential migrant. Drawing on several years of field observations, along with interviews with religious workers in Mexico, Central America, and along the U.S.-Mexico border, this article focuses on how religious workers make theological sense of contemporary Latin American immigration to the United States and apply these interpretations to pastoral activities for migrants and social justice actions vis-à-vis the state. . . .

The Catholic Church, the State, and Undocumented Migration From Latin America

Catholic social teaching has a long tradition in defending the right to migrate. This tradition is based on principles of Catholic social theology that emphasize the causes of migration, which are usually rooted in structural injustices that must be addressed—poverty, religious intolerance, and conflicts. Moreover, although the Catholic church recognizes the state's right to control immigration, it rejects such control when it is used for purposes of the accumulation of wealth or when it fails to respect the human dignity of the migrant (U.S. Conference of Catholic Bishops [USCCB], 2003). In modern times, as levels of international migration have gained considerable momentum, the church has increasingly incorporated into social teachings and pastoral work the concept of the right to migrate as a fundamental human right. . . .

Because most nations—including the United States—have rejected the right to immigrate, historical tension exists between nation-states and the Catholic church. . . .

In more recent years, and in direct response to the escalation of border enforcement activities along the Mexico-U.S. border, the Catholic church in Mexico and in the United States has reached across the shared border to publicly voice unified (a) support of the rights of individuals and their families to migrate and (b) opposition to governmental immigration policies that deny this right and border enforcement efforts that place journeying migrants in physical danger. In 2003, the Catholic bishops of Mexico and the United States, who collectively shepherd more than 150 million Catholics, published the first-ever joint pastoral letter on migration, *Stranger No Longer: Together on the Journey of Hope* (USCCB, 2003). Recognizing that contemporary Latin American immigration to the United States is both a necessity and a consequence of the social inequalities associated with the globalization of labor, the pastoral letter's overall message is that the current U.S. immigration system is broken and in need of reform. The bishops argued that the consequences of the current system—family separation, exploitation of migrant labor, and danger for journeying migrants—are objectionable to Catholic social teaching because they threaten the basic human dignity and human rights of migrants. . . .

Although the pastoral letter (USCCB, 2003)—and the global Catholic church more generally—recognizes that sovereign nations have the right to control their borders, it does not condone such a right when it violates the human rights and human dignity of a migrant, regardless of legal status. Thus, key to the social theology of the Catholic church is the belief that migrants must be treated with the respect due the dignity of every human person. Protection of this dignity for migrants—a communitarian

position—is fundamental to the political agenda of a Catholic social doctrine of migration (Blume, 2003). Indeed, the scriptural verse "Love the stranger then, for you were strangers in the land of Egypt" (Deuteronomy 10:18–19) embodies the moral principle of welcome, care, and solidarity toward the migrant. The links between theology and matters of migrant well-being are firmly carved into Catholic social theology and are manifest today in cross-border religious practices that directly challenge nation-state enforcement strategies.

The Catholic group of Mexican and U.S. bishops— the senior Catholic religious body involved in Mexican-U.S. migration concerns—practices a theology of migration at three levels: solidarity, advocacy, and hospitality. At the level of solidarity, the Tex-Mex Bishops—as they refer to themselves—support numerous nonprofit national and international organizations (e.g., Catholic Charities, Catholic Legal Immigration Network, Catholic Relief Services) that are active in providing an array of humanitarian, hospitality, social, and legal services for migrants. At the advocacy level, the binational conference issues public statements, such as the Mexico-U.S. joint pastoral letter (USCCB, 2003), and supports efforts that promote a more humane and just immigration policy. In the joint pastoral letter, in particular, the bishops called for the U.S. and Mexican enforcement authorities to abandon strategies that give rise to smuggling operations and push migrants to routes that place their lives in danger. . . .

The Scalabrini Perspective on Migration and Contemporary Pastoral Responses by St. Charles Missionaries

. . . Scalabrinians are well known by undocumented migrants from Central American and Mexico who rely on their safe houses for shelter and assistance during their journey north (Hagan, in press). Since its creation in 1886, this Italian Catholic congregation remains the only transnational religious group with the sole mission of pastoral care for migrants. In most of the 25 countries where it has a presence, including the United States, the charge of the St. Charles missionaries is to assist in the settlement of migrants and their families, and services are largely legal and educational. In Central America and Mexico, however, its mission is unique. It provides pastoral and humanitarian care for departing and journeying migrants, along with resettlement provisions for the returned migrant who has been deported home.

The theological basis for the pastoral work of Scalabrinians in Central America and Mexico is best understood by examining the social teachings of Bishop John Baptiste Scalabrini, the founder of the congregation According to Birollo (2003), the superior general of the missionaries of St. Charles, Bishop Scalabrini identified emigration as a natural and human right, one that should be free to those in need and seeking well-being and opportunity. Alarmed by the rise in emigration from Italy and the conditions of the migrants, and as a man of social action, his primary pastoral concern was migration intervention at all stages of the process, from decision making to arrival. Bishop Scalabrini also believed in immigration reform; he was vehemently critical of immigration laws because he believed that although they could never eliminate emigration, they had the adverse effect of placing migrants more at the mercy of unscrupulous persons who try to manage it, which he referred to as "merchants of human flesh" (Birollo, 2003, p. 13).

To this end, Bishop Scalabrini founded the congregation of the missionary priests and brothers; later, he founded a lay society and religious congregation of sisters. The first mission of these religious groups was to maintain Catholic faith and practice among Italian emigrants in the new areas of settlement and to ensure their moral, civil, and economical welfare. The congregation established itself in churches, hospitals, and other institutions to assist in the settlement of Italian migrants in various established destinations throughout the globe, from New York to Brazil. The second mission was to oversee the migration process. Recognizing that emigration was an inevitable social question that with time, would incorporate persons of various cultures, he called on his missionaries to counsel the departing migrants and if all else failed, to direct migrants toward a safe and promising passage. He also asked his congregation to monitor closely those officials who regulate the process to ensure that they do not violate law or exploit migrants.

It is this second pastoral challenge—the care of the journeying migrants—that occupies the work of the Scalabrinians in Mexico and Central America today. Since 1987, the Scalabrini missionaries have established a network of migrant shelters, called Casas del Migrante (migrant homes or safe houses), located adjacent to the most dangerous crossing corridors along the Guatemala-Mexico and Mexico-U.S. borders. The transit shelters provide humanitarian, educational, and psychological support. In addition to giving food, shelter, and clothing, the missionaries provide instruction on the dangers awaiting migrants on their journey north and their rights as undocumented migrants. If requested, religious counsel or a blessing is provided. Religious services are held, but migrants are not required to attend. The first Casa del Migrante in the region was established in 1987 in Tijuana, at that time a major crossing location for Mexican migrants. As flows have been redirected to other areas of the border, the Scalabrini missionaries have responded by erecting shelters in these more dangerous crossing locations along the Guatemala-Mexico and U.S.-Mexico border areas. . . .

The Casa del Migrante in Tapachula, Mexico, is a welcome resting point to the hundreds of undocumented Central American migrants that cross the treacherous Guatemala-Mexico corridor each day. In Father Maria Rigoni's eyes, these migrants represent the wandering Jesus who is forced to walk uphill on his journey north (personal communication, September 19, 2004). To care for the humanitarian needs of the migrant, Rigoni provides food, beds, and health and educational services. To welcome the migrant and provide for his or her spiritual needs, Rigoni erected a simple thatched-roof chapel made of palms, which he calls the Chapel of Emmaus, symbolically named for the town where Jesus, after having risen from the dead, is welcomed by his disciples not for who he is but as an unknown stranger (Luke 24:13–25). In this sense, the migrant, according to Rigoni, challenges us to see the face of Jesus. . . .

Opposing Views on the Right to Emigrate: Pentecostal and Catholic Clergy in Communities of Origin

Pastoral care for migrants often begins in their home communities. As spiritual anchors in their communities, many clergy—Protestant and Catholic alike—provide counsel to prospective migrants before departure. For many considering the journey north, turning to their trusted clerics helps them cope spiritually and psychologically with the inevitability of leaving all they hold dear and embarking on the dangerous journey north to the United States. At the individual level of migrant decision making, local clergy provide religious and moral sanction for the migration, a type of "spiritual travel permit" that in many poor and marginalized communities has enormous symbolic value.

Most clergy I interviewed agreed that in a perfect world, they would probably discourage the flight of their parishioners because of the devastating effects it can have on family. This is especially true of the religious leaders of small, independent Pentecostal ministries who depend on every individual for survival and who place such strong emphasis on family unity. But in the present-day context of declining economic opportunities in Mexico and Central America, Catholic clergy of the poor are sympathetic to the economic plight within their communities. People need jobs to feed their families. Yet priests and ministers are also troubled by the dangers of the trip and the consequences for the migrant's family left behind. More than simply a spiritual leader for their constituents, they understand that their advice may have vast repercussions for not only the migrants but also their families.

Father Quintero (personal communication, June 13, 2003), a soft-spoken Catholic priest who counsels prospective and journeying migrants at the pilgrimage site of Basilica de El Senor de Esquipulas in Esquipulas, Guatemala, which is located along the northbound migrant trail near the Honduras-Guatemala border, summed up the quandary that many clergy, especially Catholic priests who were trained in the tradition of liberation theology, face when advising migrants about their decision:

Migration is a fundamental part of the way of life here and the motivations behind the decision to migrate are always economic. Today the economic rationale is the declining price of coffee in Honduras and Guatemala, which makes the need for the American Dream stronger than ever before.

. . . Moreover, Father Quintero remarked that

it is not the Catholic way to tell them not to go. We support migration as a human right. We can't stand in their way. These are not young men; some are forty or fifty years of age. They have established families here. They own land, cars.

. . . The response by Protestant clergy to contemporary immigration issues and politics is more mixed. In general, Protestants are divided into two camps. One camp has a strong sense of social theology and in matters of migration, has institutionalized this into everyday advocacy, much like some Catholic groups. Most notable among this Protestant group are what many refer to as liberal Protestants, including Presbyterians, Methodists, Lutherans, and Episcopals. They do not have a strong presence among the poor in Latin America. The other camp, which has been far less politically active in immigration issues—both in the United States and Latin America—includes Southern Baptists, Pentecostals, and

Fundamentalists. This group of ministers generally eschews social issues and subscribes to what most would consider conservative theologies that emphasize conversion and personal experience with God. Evangelization, not social action, tends to be the priority of these churches (Hoover, 1998) . . .

Protestant ministers in migrant-sending communities in Guatemala and Mexico—the lion's share of whom identify themselves as Pentecostal, Evangelical, or Fundamentalist—are much less likely than their Catholic counterparts to support migration. Although some Pentecostal ministers have had no choice but to respond to the needs of their followers—many of whom are migrants or family members of migrants—and incorporate migration counseling into their ministries (Hagan, in press; Hagan & Ebaugh, 2003), most Pentecostal ministers interviewed for this study voiced opposition to emigration. Recognizing the devastating effects migration can have on family left behind, and also the financial loss to an independent church itself, Evangelical pastors often counsel their members against migration. Only when the suffering is too great do they sanction the migration. . . .

Church Versus State: Interfaith Protest Along the U.S.-Mexico Border

. . . Increasing deaths along the Tucson sector of the U.S.-Mexico border have galvanized a series of interfaith groups into action in opposition to U.S. government border enforcement policies. The membership size and goals of these faith-based organizations have grown in scope with the passage of years, and it is not surprising that some of the movers and shakers in these organizations can trace their roots to the Sanctuary movement, which was founded and then flourished in the Tucson area of Arizona in the 1980s (Coutin, 1993). Initially organized to provide humanitarian assistance to journeying migrants, these present-day interfaith efforts have mushroomed in number, culminating most recently in the collective, broad-based social movement geared at providing humanitarian assistance to journeying migrants, educating the larger U.S. population about the human consequences of U.S. border enforcement policies, and ultimately, reforming U.S. immigration policy.

The first religious organization to systematically challenge current U.S. border policy was a peace church that established its presence along the border in the late 1980s when the Quaker organization American Friends

Service Committee (2005) founded the Immigration Law Enforcement Monitoring Project. The program—implemented shortly after the Immigration Reform and Control Act of 1986, which beefed up enforcement efforts along the southern border—was charged with monitoring the civil rights and human rights consequences of U.S. border enforcement policy from 1987 through 2003, when the program was closed. With their funding, the first systematic study of death at the border was conducted and the problem was introduced to the larger American public (Eschbach et al., 1999). The presence of Quakers along the border is consistent with their position that all people have a bit of the divine in them and, therefore, are equal and entitled to dignity and respect regardless of nationality or legal status. Implicit in this position is the notion of a global community in which persons are free to choose where they live and work (American Friends Service Committee, 2005).

By 2000, a number of other local faith-based groups were responding and monitoring U.S. border enforcement efforts. As death rates continued to soar, Rev. Robin Hoover—a cowboy clergyman—of Tucson's First Christian Church, founded Humane Borders Inc., a binational interfaith organization established to "create a just and more humane border environment" (personal communication, June 12, 2002). To this end, Humane Borders has placed more than 50 water tanks marked with 30-foot flagpoles along well-traveled migrant paths across the southern Arizona desert. Dispensing more than 500 gallons of water a week, the tanks are located on private, county, and federal lands. Humane Borders's members are a very diverse group, including 70 Catholic and Protestant churches from Mexico and the United States, along with U.S.-based human rights organizations, corporate sponsors, and legal advocacy groups. Although initially established to provide temporary humanitarian relief, Humane Borders's mission statement has since expanded to call for a more equitable immigration policy that would provide legalization and temporary work opportunities for migrants living and working in the United States. Humane Borders's border ministry work is well within the limits of the law; a path Rev. Robin Hoover believes is essential if the organization is to continue its border ministry work. . . .

In 2003, Rev. Robin Hoover and others, including Rev. John Fife of the Southside Presbyterian church in Tucson and one of the founders of the Sanctuary movement, took things one step further and founded the Good Samaritan, a coalition of Quakers, Jews, Disciples of Christ, Methodists, Catholics, and Presbyterians that

makes regular trips to the deadly desert in all-terrain vehicles equipped with food, water, a medical team, and first-aid supplies. According to Fife (personal communication, June 13, 2002), the group was founded on the principle that it is the "right and responsibility" of civil organizations to aid victims of human rights violations. When migrants in distress are found, the group either calls on the U.S. Border Patrol for helicopter assistance or transports them to a local hospital.

Increasingly, faith-based organizations are less concerned with openly challenging laws they see as unjust and immoral. In the spring of 2004—with no hint of a slowdown in migrant deaths in the area—a broader effort developed to work for justice along the border and provide sustained 24/7 humanitarian relief for journeying migrants. The campaign is titled No More Deaths, and its members include a diverse binominal coalition of individuals, faith communities, and human rights grassroots organizers. Its members refer to No More Deaths as a *movement* rather than as an *organization*. They engage in direct and indirect action to limit deaths, challenge U.S. immigration policy, and raise public awareness.

The movement has developed a campaign to limit further deaths and challenge U.S. border enforcement policy (No More Deaths, 2005). Critical in the movement is the biblically inspired "ark of the covenant" effort, which involves placing moveable camps in the desert. The camps are named for a wooden Ark of the Covenant box in the Old Testament that symbolized the presence of God guiding the people of Israel when they were wandering the desert. . . . The desert camps provide water, food, clothing, and medical assistance for journeying migrants. If a serious medical problem arises, volunteers are instructed to transport the distressed migrant to a hospital or call the U.S. Border Patrol's Search, Trauma and Rescue unit. In a lesser case of dehydration, exhaustion, or minor injuries, volunteers can arrange for the person to be transported to either a Tucson church or clinic. In the month of June 2005 alone, the No More Deaths campaign rescued 175 migrants in distress in the Arizona desert. . . .

Conclusion

The mounting death toll associated with expanded enforcement efforts along the U.S-Mexico and Guatemala-Mexico borders has prompted a diverse set of religious groups to engage in various levels of political protest. Although the Catholic church has long been a spokesperson for the right to emigrate, it has become more vocal in its opposition to these new enforcement policies. Increasingly, therefore, the Catholic church expresses a communitarian worldview geared toward reforming political entities, in this case U.S. government policies. Most recent, leaders from the cross-border group of U.S. and Mexican Catholic bishops have called for a humane response to the migrant—and for public policies and pastoral work that "welcome the stranger among us." Churches and activists have responded to this call, most notably the Scalabrini congregation, which practices a pastoral theology of intervention in matters of migration. Taking their work to the field—where the migrants are— the Scalabrini in Mexico and Central America implement a pastoral response that emphasizes migrant hospitality and accompaniment in the journey north.

When it comes to immigration matters, the Protestant church remains divided; the Fundamentalist religious grouping, both in Central America and the United States, has largely shied away from taking a direct position on the right to migrate, even in light of increased dangers for journeying migrants. Lacking the communitarian worldview of Catholics or mainline Protestants, their concern is strictly with social change and reform as it applies to their own congregation. Pentecostal pastors who have migrants in their ministries, however, are aware of the implications of Latin American migration. Pastors in home communities recognize the devastating loss migration has on the ministries and the hardship it presents for family members left behind. In contrast, U.S. Pentecostal pastors are beginning to see immigration as an opportunity for the church to spread the gospel. Recognizing that Jesus and Abraham were both immigrants, Jesse Miranda, the commissioner on ethnicity for the Assemblies of God, claimed, "The Church had a mandate through scripture to embrace the stranger" (as quoted in Olivarez, 2004). In contrast to their Catholic or more liberal protestant counterparts, however, U.S. Pentecostal and Evangelical leaders are unwilling to challenge government policy and extend the welcome to the undocumented migrant in the form of humanitarian assistance. By contrast, the mainline Protestant churches—concerned with changing the system as opposed to the individual—have possibly been the most active in their opposition to state immigration policy, but primarily at the local level and along the U.S. Arizona border where Sanctuary activists from the 1980s have resurrected to form interfaith coalitions in defense of the right to migrate.

Discussion Questions

1. According to Hagan, what is Catholic social teaching on migration and how does it clash with the views of the US and other nation-states?

2. Are you religious? If so, what are your religion's teachings about immigration? If your religion and your government were at odds, whose rules would you follow? Why?

Source: "Making Theological Sense of the Migration Journey From Latin America: Catholic, Protestant, and Interfaith Perspectives" by Jacqueline Hagan, excerpted and with notes & references omitted from *American Behavioral Scientist*, Vol. 49, No. 11, July 2006, pp. 1554–1573. Reprinted by permission of Sage Publications.

CHAPTER 31

Hate Crime Reporting as a Successful Social Movement Outcome

Rory McVeigh, Michael R. Welch, and Thoroddur Bjarnason

Variation in compliance with public policies across local settings is examined through an analysis of the number of reported hate crime incidents in U.S. counties. Each hate crime reported to the federal government is conceptualized as a successful outcome of social movement mobilization. The presence of resourceful civil rights organizations in a county can lead to higher numbers of reported hate crimes, but the influence of civil right organizations is contingent upon the political context and upon objective conditions that lend credibility to civil rights framing.

Over the past several decades, a growing number of researchers have studied ways in which public policy formation is influenced by socially constructed definitions of public problems (Burstein 1991; Burstein and Bricher 1997; Jenness and Grattet 2001). A core insight advanced by this research is that development of new public policy often has little to do with a change in objective circumstances that renders existing policies ineffective. Additionally, some conditions that cause pain and suffering for large numbers of people may never be defined as public problems and are therefore unlikely to be addressed by new policy initiatives (Edelman 1988). Within policy domains, public problems are defined by political representatives, government officials, interest groups, and social movement organizations as part of a broader process of generating support for a particular political agenda (Burstein 1991).

To influence public policy, political actors must not only define a particular problem, but they must also offer a diagnosis of the problem and make a convincing case that the policy they are advocating will serve as an effective remedy (Cress and Snow 2000; Stone 1989). Stone (1989) argues that "problem definition is a process of image making, where the images have to do fundamentally

with attributing cause, blame, and responsibility" (p. 282). Political actors develop causal arguments as a means of demonstrating the merits of their proposed policies (Burstein 1991; Stone 1989). Public policy emerges through a competitive process in which various political contenders attempt to generate interest in their particular problem and to persuade others that their proposed policy represents the optimal solution (Burstein and Bricher 1997; Gamson and Modligliani 1989; Laumann and Knoke 1987; Weiss 1989). Those who possess ample material resources or who hold institutionally based power have a distinct advantage in this competition because these resources can be used to formulate a persuasive causal argument and to ensure that the argument captures the attention of lawmakers and the general public (Burstein 1991; Jacob 1988; Lauman and Knoke 1987). Like any causal argument, arguments advanced on behalf of a public policy can potentially be falsified by empirical observations (Babb 1996; Dobbin 1993). To be effective, the arguments should appear plausible to targeted audiences (Best 1999; Gamson 1992a; Snow et al. 1986).

Although there has been an abundance of research on the social construction of public problems in policy formation, less attention has been given to what happens after policies are enacted. Does the enactment of a public policy represent the end of the contest, or is it merely the opening stage of an ongoing battle? We address two general questions: First, what determines compliance with a public policy once it is put into place? Second, what factors explain variation in compliance with public policy across local settings? We propose that the enactment of public policy represents merely one phase in an ongoing process of defining public problems. We are particularly interested in the role that activist organizations play in promoting, or impeding, compliance with public policies.

We address these general questions through an analysis of reported hate crime incidents in the United States. As previous research indicates, civil rights activist organizations played a vital role in promoting hate crime legislation at the state level and also in promoting federal legislation that requires the government to collect data on hate crime incidents (Jenness and Broad 1997; Jenness and Grattet 2001). At the present time, however, hate crime laws are enforced much more diligently in some locales than in others (Boyd, Berk, and Hamner 1996; Franklin 2002; Nolan and Akiyama 1999). We develop a theoretical framework that allows us to identify several features of local contexts that contribute to higher numbers of reported hate crime incidents. We believe that the implications of our research extend beyond hate crime reporting, and we discuss these broader implications in the concluding section of the paper.

Federal Hate Crime Legislation

The Hate Crime Statistics Act (HCSA) became law in 1990 after receiving broad bipartisan support in the United States House of Representatives and Senate and a ringing endorsement from President George H. Bush (Levin and McDevitt 1993:199). The President described the act as a "significant step to help guarantee civil rights for every American" (*Washington Post,* April 24, 1990, Section 1, page A6). The law requires the Attorney General to collect data "about crimes that manifest evidence of prejudice based on race, religion, sexual orientation, or ethnicity, including where appropriate the crimes of murder, non-negligent manslaughter, forcible rape, aggravated assault, simple assault, intimidation, arson, and destruction, damage, or vandalism of property" (U.S. Department of Justice 1997:2). In 1994, the HCSA was amended to include crimes motivated by bias against individuals with physical or mental disabilities.

Thirteen years after passage of the HCSA, it remains unclear how effective the law has been. Supporters of the

bill believed it would provide a mechanism for gathering data that could be used to develop policy and provide information that could help law enforcement agents prevent, combat, and prosecute crimes of bias (Fernandez 1991; Jenness and Broad 1997: 38). Prior to 1990, many states collected data on hate crimes, but state-level differences in defining and reporting hate crimes made it difficult to compare the data and form a comprehensive understanding of the problem (Grattet, Jenness, and Curry 1998; Jenness and Grattet 2001). Yet even with a federal mandate for collecting hate crime data, comparisons across geographic boundaries remain problematic. For instance, a total of 1,943 hate crimes were reported to the federal government for the state of California in the year 2000, while not a single hate crime was reported for the state of Alabama, despite the fact that advocacy organizations identified several criminal acts of bias that occurred within that state (Southern Poverty Law Center 2001). Alabama, however, is only one example of a more widespread problem. A major study undertaken by researchers at the Center for Criminal Justice Policy Research (CCJPR) at Northeastern University has identified serious problems in the quality and accuracy of the hate crimes data (McDevitt et al. 2000).

Part of the problem stems from the fact that the HCSA requires the federal government to collect data on hate crimes, but it does not require local law enforcement agencies to participate. In addition, the act does not allocate any federal money to local agencies that could be directed toward enforcement of hate crime legislation or toward keeping records of hate crime incidents. And, the HCSA does not specify the mechanism for collecting hate crime data. . . .

Perhaps the most formidable barriers to effective hate crime enforcement and reporting are the difficulties that law enforcement agents face in determining whether an event qualifies as a hate crime incident. As Bell (2002) describes it, "Bias crimes require police officers to examine not only what happened, but also why it happened. Furthermore, the search for what happened is complicated by contested stories and by victims who are sometimes afraid to acknowledge the bias nature of the crime for fear of revictimization" (p. 13). The FBI does offer guidelines to local agencies on how to identify hate crime incidents. It advises agencies to adopt a two-tier approach in which the police officer on the scene makes an initial determination as to whether bias motivation is suspected. A second officer, or a special unit that has more expertise on hate crimes, then evaluates the case to determine whether it qualifies as a hate crime. If the case is determined to be a hate crime, information about the incident is included in Hate Crime Reports that are sub-mitted to the FBI's Uniform Crime Report program (U.S. Department of Justice 1997). The UCR then publishes a complete summary of reported hate crime incidents for each year. These incidents may or may not involve arrests or convictions. It is important to keep in mind that the FBI suggests, rather than mandates, the two-tiered process. Most police departments do not have specialized units for enforcing hate crime laws or for collecting hate crime statistics (Bell 2002: 28; Jenness and Grattet 2001).

The FBI also offers general guidelines for making decisions at both levels of the two-tiered process. Most of these guidelines require police officers to consider the broader context in which the incident took place in an effort to ascertain the offender's motive. For example, the training guide (U.S. Department of Justice 1997) instructs officers to consider questions such as the following:

Does a substantial proportion of the community where the crime occurred perceive that the incident was motivated by bias?

Were there indications that a hate group was involved?

Does a historically established animosity exist between the victim's and the offender's group? (P. 20)

Identification of hate crime incidents is heavily dependent on the way in which law enforcement agents interpret the event, and many law enforcement agents are less than enthusiastic about hate crime legislation (Bell 2002; Boyd et al. 1996). . . .

Political considerations weigh heavily on decisions about hate crime enforcement and reporting. As Bell (2002: 3) notes, there is a strong disincentive for police to identify crimes as bias-motivated because a high number of reported incidents can tarnish the image of the com-munity. Enforcing hate crime laws can also produce a political backlash in some locales because voters may per-ceive that government authorities are choosing sides in episodes of intergroup conflict (Bell 2002). Yet in other cir-cumstances, failure to report hate crime incidents can be politically perilous. For example, the recent response of Los Angeles District Attorney Steve Cooley to a near-fatal beating of a gay man in West Hollywood sparked consid-erable controversy. The perpetrators were charged with attempted robbery, assault with a deadly weapon, and conspiracy to commit robbery, but were not charged with a hate crime. Cooley's decision not to pursue hate crime charges outraged many residents of West Hollywood. At a protest rally, West Hollywood City Manager Paul Arevalo vowed that the city of West Hollywood would call on

"Governor Gray Davis and the State Attorney General's office to step in and lead in the prosecution of this hate crime" (CNN 2002).

Hate Crime as a Successful Social Movement Outcome

It is clear that differences in the number of hate crimes reported in various regions do not simply reflect differ-ences in the number of criminal acts motivated by bias. They may instead reflect different incentives to call acts of bias to the attention of local authorities, as well as dif-ferent incentives that influence law enforcement agents to respond to, and to report, hate crimes. In our analysis, we treat a reported hate crime as a measure of a success-ful social movement outcome rather than as a valid mea-sure of a particular type of crime.

Recent research on hate crimes in the United States has drawn attention to the important role that civil rights and other advocacy organizations have played in the development of hate crime legislation (Grattet, Jenness, and Curry 1998; Jenness and Broad 1997; Jenness and Grattet 2001). Social movement organizations acting on behalf of racial, ethnic, and religious minorities, women, gays and lesbians, and other constituencies actively pro-moted hate crime legislation at the state and national level (Jenness and Broad 1997). These organizations were able to influence policy not only by applying direct pres-sure on legislators, but also by framing discussion about the issue. Interpretive frameworks offered by these social movement organizations (see Snow et al. 1986) were ulti-mately endorsed by politicians and law enforcement agents (Grattet et al. 1998; Jenness and Grattet 2001). The frames developed by these organizations not only influ-enced the debate about what constitutes a hate crime, but also helped to create a sense of urgency by promoting the view that crimes of bias are on the rise and reaching "epi-demic proportions" (Jenness and Grattet 2001: 124). While researchers disagree on whether such an increase has actually taken place (see Jacobs and Henry 1996; Jenness and Broad 1997; Levin and McDevitt 1993), law-makers and judges have largely accepted the claims made by advocacy organizations and have used them to justify action based on the state's compelling interest in dealing with the problem (Jenness and Grattet 2001: 124).

DEFINING SOCIAL MOVEMENT SUCCESS

In one of the first major studies of social movement consequences, Gamson (1975) operationalized movement success in two ways. A movement was considered to have been successful if it (1) gained acceptance and recognition from the state and/or (2) secured new advantages for constituents. More recent research on social movement outcomes has focused primarily on new advantages resulting from social movement efforts (Amenta, Carruthers, and Zylan 1992; McCammon et al. 2001). As Amenta et al. (1992) point out, acceptance and recognition by the state can be unsatisfying if not accompanied by new advantages. In fact, recognition can be used as a tactic to avoid making real concessions to a movement. For example, recognition may be used as a way of persuading a movement to abandon militant tactics when militant tactics provide the primary source of leverage that the movement holds against the state.

It is clear that the social movement organizations promoting hate crime legislation successfully gained recognition and acceptance by the state. Yet proponents of hate crime legislation are concerned about more than gaining a symbolic victory (Gusfield 1963) and would also like to secure greater benefits for constituents—namely, real protection from violence and other crimes of bias. Problems in the enforcement and reporting of hate crimes pose a serious threat to the perceived legitimacy of the legislation and can limit the protection individuals receive. Each hate crime reported to the federal government, therefore, can be viewed as a successful social movement outcome. . . .

The Data

Our central goal is to account for variation in hate crime reporting across counties and county equivalents within the United States. While the choice of any ecological unit of analysis is open to valid criticism, there are several reasons why we have chosen to examine hate crime reporting at the county level. First, we see this approach as providing an improvement over state-level analyses because such analyses overlook substantial intrastate variation in features that are conducive to hate crime reporting. Because hate crimes occur in small towns as well as in large cities, we cannot restrict our analysis to Standard Metropolitan Statistical Areas. Comparable data appropriate for testing our arguments are available for almost all counties and county equivalents in the United States. We lose some of these cases to missing data, however, by including a measure of the crime rate. Even so, our analysis examines variation in hate crime reporting across 2,740 cases.

THE DEPENDENT VARIABLE

We analyze the total number of hate crime incidents reported in the Uniform Crime Report data for the year 2000. Hate crime incidents are reported for various types of locales, including towns or cities, counties, police precincts, and colleges and universities. In almost all cases, we were able to place the reported hate crimes in a specific county. Some cases were problematic, however, because they were reported as having occurred within a particular city that crosses the boundaries of two or more counties. For some of these cases, we determined the precise county in which the hate crimes occurred by calling the local authorities who are responsible for collecting hate crime data and forwarding the information to the FBI. In several cases, however, the local authorities were either unable to help us place the crimes within a specific county or failed to return phone calls after numerous attempts to reach them.

Rather than drop these problematic cases from our analysis, we utilize a strategy developed by Tolnay, Deane, and Beck (1996: 799) in their study of lynching rates in southern counties. In their analysis they had to contend with the problem of changes in county boundary lines that occur over time. To deal with this problem, they aggregated the data for counties that experienced a boundary change and created new geographic units that they called "county clusters." We use the same strategy in dealing with cases in which hate crimes are reported for cities that spill across county boundaries. In all, we constructed 32 of these county clusters.

According to the FBI's figures, a total of 8,063 hate crime incidents were reported for the year 2000. Eight of these are reported as multiple-bias incidents (e.g., motivated by both racial bias and sexual orientation bias). Of the 8,055 single-bias incidents, 53.8 percent were motivated by racial bias, 18.3 percent by religious bias, 16.1 percent by sexual orientation bias, 11.3 percent by ethnic bias, and .5 percent by a bias against the disabled. The majority of hate crime offenses were crimes against persons (65 percent), with 34.4 percent being crimes against property. The most frequently reported offense is categorized as intimidation (34.4 percent), closely followed by destruction of property (29.3 percent). There were 19 reported homicides: 10 were motivated by racial bias, 6 by ethnic bias, 2 by sexual orientation bias, and 1 by religious bias (FBI 2000: 5).

. . . [H]ate crime reporting is not distributed uniformly across counties. It is notable, for example, that hate crime reporting is concentrated heavily in far-western states and in the Northeast, while few hate crimes are reported in mid western states and in southern states such as Alabama, Mississippi, Louisiana, and South Carolina. It is also worth noting that the vast majority of counties did not report the occurrence of a single hate crime (76.4 percent). The variable has a range of 0 to 826 and a mean value of 2.62.

CIVIL RIGHTS ORGANIZATIONS

Data were obtained from the National Center for Charitable Statistics (NCCS) to construct two measures of civil rights activism in the counties. We used the NCCS 1999 Core Files data set in which Internal Revenue Service records are used to compile information on all nonprofit organizations that apply for tax exempt status each year. The nonprofit organizations are categorized by the NCCS according to the National Taxonomy of Exempt Entities classification scheme. To construct measures of civil rights activism, we first identified all organizations in the NCCS data file that are categorized from R20 to R30. The general category "R" includes nonprofit organizations involved in civil rights, social action, and advocacy. We include only those categorized from R20 to R30 because these organizations are most directly involved in activities that promote the objectives of hate crime legislation. As one measure of civil rights activism, we use the total number of these civil rights organizations located in the county. Higher numbers of organizations in a county indicate that more constituencies are represented, making it possible for civil rights organizations to exert influence on multiple fronts. We also expect that organizational resources should play an important role in determining the influence wielded by civil rights organizations. We calculated a measure of civil rights resources by summing the annual revenue reported by the civil rights organizations in each county and dividing that figure by the total population in the county. We calculate the variable in this manner because resourceful organizations should have greater influence on hate crime enforcement and reporting than would less resourceful organizations, and larger supplies of resources are typically required to exert influence on greater numbers of county residents.

POLITICAL INCENTIVES

Based on the logic of political mediation theory, we expect that political and legal authorities are more vulnerable to pressure from civil rights organizations when voters in the county tend to support the Democratic Party. Because members and adherents of civil rights organizations are considerably more likely to support Democrats than Republicans, local authorities in Democratic strongholds should be more responsive to the civil rights agenda. Withdrawal of political support from civil rights organizations could potentially result in electoral defeats.

Republicans, on the other hand, are less vulnerable to such pressure because, in many cases, they cannot count on support from civil rights groups and their adherents. In addition, proactive support for the civil rights agenda could potentially alienate traditional Republican voters. We measure Democratic voting as the percentage of votes cast for Democrat Bill Clinton in the 1996 presidential election (the election immediately prior to the year in which our dependent variable is measured).

Political mediation theory also suggests that political representatives are particularly vulnerable to pressure in competitive political environments. We expect, therefore, that local political and legal authorities tend to enforce hate crime legislation more diligently in politically competitive environments. To measure political competitiveness, we calculated the mean of the absolute difference between the percentage of voters voting Republican and the percentage voting Democratic for presidential elections held in 1992, 1996, and 2000. We multiplied this value by −1 so that higher scores indicate a more competitive environment.

CREDIBILITY OF HATE CRIME FRAMING

Hate crime reporting, as argued above, should be higher in counties in which objective conditions add credibility to claims that emphasize the importance of enforcing hate crime legislation. Racial and ethnic heterogeneity is one such factor. Acts of racial bias, for example, would be unlikely to occur in counties in which all residents belong to a single racial or ethnic group. There would also be a relatively large base of support for hate crime legislation in heterogeneous counties. . . .

We use the Supplemental Homicide Reports to construct measures of interracial homicide. Although not all interracial homicides are motivated by racial bias, the number of white-on-black homicides committed in local communities should add to the credibility of claims made by those who advocate hate crime enforcement. Homicides tend to capture substantial coverage from local media outlets and can, therefore, shape public perceptions about the nature of crime and the nature of race relations within the community. We calculate a measure of the average number of homicides that involve a white perpetrator and a black victim (white-on-black homicides) for the years 1997 through 1999. We also calculate the average number of homicides in a county during the same time period that involved a black perpetrator and a white victim (black-on-white homicides). We suspect that white-on-black homicides can add credibility to civil rights activists' claims. Black-on-white homicides, however, could conceivably have the opposite effect. These homicides could generate fear and suspicion of minority group members as perpetrators of violence rather than engender the support and sympathy that would be directed toward minority group members as victims of violence.

The presence of racist hate groups can also add credibility to claims made by advocates of hate crime legislation. As a measure of hate group activism we use data compiled by the Southern Poverty Law Center's (SPLC) "Intelligence Project." The SPLC compiles annual lists of hate groups known by the organization to have been active during a given year. . . . According to the SPLC, 602 hate groups were active in the year 2000.

CONTROL VARIABLES

We control for several features of counties that could be related to hate crime reporting or that generally tend to be associated with crime. First, we include the county rate of serious criminal offenses using the annual county-level Uniform Crime Report data collected by the Interuniversity Consortium for Political and Social Research (ICPSR). The Uniform Crime Report index consists of the total number of reports of the following crimes: murder, forcible rape, robbery, aggravated assault, burglary, larceny, and motor vehicle theft. A crime rate is calculated as the number of index crimes per 100 people in the county. . . . We also control for the percentage of people in the county who were 18 to 24 years old in the year 2000 because this age group commits a disproportionate share of various crimes (see Felson 1994).

We include a measure of per capita income in 1989 because relatively prosperous counties may have more resources that could be directed toward the enforcement of hate crime laws (Franklin 2002; Haider-Markel 2002; Nolan and Akiyama 1999; Walker and Katz 1995). We also control for the percentage of the population age 25 years old or older that has completed at least 16 years of schooling. Previous research demonstrates that individuals in the United States with high levels of education are less likely to express attitudes reflecting racial prejudice or anti-Semitism (see Bobo and Kluegel 1993; Weil 1985). Because higher numbers of hate crimes should be explained in part by population size, we also control for the population in the county in the year 2000. Additionally, we control for the percentage of the population in rural locations. Predominantly rural counties are likely to have fewer incidents that could be defined as hate crimes, and rural communities typically have fewer resources available that can be directed toward hate crime enforcement and recordkeeping. . . .

INTERACTION EFFECTS

We give special attention to interactions among our key variables. As our theoretical argument suggests, we expect to find that the impact civil rights organizations have on hate crime enforcement and reporting is contingent on several factors. In accord with political mediation theory, the positive influence of civil rights organizations should be strongest in counties where political incentives exist that would lead local authorities to be responsive to the civil rights agenda. As we argued above, civil rights organizations should have greater political leverage in Democratic strongholds. This is not to say that Republican politicians are necessarily unsupportive of hate crime laws. However, because members and adherents of civil rights organizations are more likely to support Democrats than Republicans, Republicans tend to have less incentive to be responsive to these groups, especially if doing so entails the risk of alienating traditional Republican voters. To test this argument, we examine interactions between our measures of civil rights activism and our measure of Democratic voting.

Based on our discussion of the model of discursive rivalry, we also expect to find that higher rates of hate crime reporting require a combination of resourceful civil rights organizations and objective circumstances in the county that lend credence to claims about the importance of hate crime enforcement. Therefore, we examine interactions of our measure of civil rights resources with our measures of ethnic heterogeneity, interracial homicide, and racist hate groups. . . .

Data Analysis

The nature of our dependent variable poses estimation problems. First, the majority of counties (76.5 percent) reported zero hate crime incidents. In some of these counties, it could be the case that no criminal acts of bias occurred during the year. Yet previous research . . . indicates that there are good reasons to believe that in many instances the absence of reported hate crimes tells us as much about local authorities' willingness and capacity to enforce hate crime legislation as it does about the actual number of bias incidents that occurred in the county. Second, the dependent variable is severely skewed. Among those counties reporting at least one incident, 51.3 percent reported 1 to 2 incidents, 28.6 percent reported 3 to 10 incidents, 16 percent reported 11 to 50 incidents, and 4.1 percent reported more than 50 incidents. Los Angeles County is an extreme outlier, with 826 reported hate crimes.

Our dependent variable is a cumulative total of the number of discrete events (reported hate crimes) that took place in each county over the course of one year. We strongly suspect that the likelihood of any one of these events being reported depends heavily on the number of prior events that had taken place within the county. For example, if 20 hate crime incidents had already been recorded in a county by June of 2000, the odds should be relatively high that at least one more hate crime incident would occur and be reported by the end of the year. In such a case, law enforcement agents had already defined several incidents as hate crimes, and they had already demonstrated a willingness and capacity to report the incidents to the federal government. If, on the other hand, no hate crimes had been reported by June of 2000, the odds of a hate crime incident being reported by the end of the year would be considerably lower. Either because few acts of bias occurred in the county before June, or because law enforcement agents had been unwilling or unable to act upon them, it would be a good bet that similar conditions would prevail in the second half of the year. . . .

Results

. . . [W]e find that population, per capita income, and percent age 18 to 24 have a positive effect on hate crime reporting, and percent rural has a negative effect. The crime rate has the expected curvilinear relationship with hate crime reporting. Although the zero-order correlation between percent college-educated and hate crime reporting is positive, percent college does not have a statistically significant impact on hate crime reporting when other variables are held constant. The results also show that the coefficient for racist hate groups is positive and statistically significant, while the coefficient for ethnic heterogeneity falls just short of statistical significance ($p = .053$). It is important to keep in mind, however, that our theoretical argument stresses the importance of interactions between civil rights activism and objective features of local contexts in producing higher numbers of reported hate crime incidents. The estimates of the effects of interracial homicide are particularly interesting. White-on-black homicides have a positive, statistically significant effect on hate crime reporting, but black-on-white homicides have a highly significant negative impact on the dependent variable. These findings are consistent with our argument that white-on-black homicides can add credibility to claims about the need for hate crime enforcement and reporting, while black-on-white homicides can generate fear and suspicion of African Americans, thereby diminishing support for hate crime enforcement and reporting.

We also find that Democratic voting does not have a significant effect on hate crime reporting. As expected, though, after controlling for the other variables, more hate crimes are reported in politically competitive counties than in noncompetitive counties. Finally, we see that the number of civil rights organizations in a county has a positive effect on hate crime reporting. Our measure of civil rights resources is not statistically significant. As we specified in our theoretical discussion, however, the effect of civil rights resources on hate crime reporting should be contingent upon political incentives and upon objective features of local contexts that add credibility to movement framing.

. . . As expected, the influence of civil rights organizations on hate crime reporting is heavily dependent on the level of support for the Democratic Party. Democratic voting has little influence on hate crime reporting in counties that do not have a civil rights organization. The main effect of civil rights organizations is negative, indicating that civil rights organizations are ineffective in Republican strongholds. To gain a better sense of how this interaction operates, we calculated the predicted probability of an additional reported hate crime at varying levels of Democratic voting and varying numbers of civil rights organizations, when all other variables are set at their mean values. We find that the effect of civil rights organizations is negative when Democratic voting is less that 47 percent. The effect of civil rights organizations on hate crime reporting is positive when Democratic voting is 47 percent or higher, with that positive effect growing increasingly strong at higher levels of Democratic voting. . . .

Our results are consistent with our claim that local authorities are more responsive to civil rights organizations in Democratic strongholds. In noncompetitive Republican counties, civil rights organizations actually have a negative effect on reported hate crimes. It is worth noting, however, that hate crime reporting tends to be quite high in noncompetitive Democratic counties. We believe that this is because local authorities in these counties have little to lose by enforcing hate crime laws when Democrats face little opposition, and much to gain by being responsive to civil rights organizations when adherents of these organizations are an important source of political support.

Next, we examine interactions between our measure of civil rights resources and variables reflecting objective conditions that should add credence to civil rights framing. . . . [T]he effect of civil rights resources on hate crime reporting is contingent upon the level of heterogeneity within the county. Ethnic heterogeneity has little impact on hate crime reporting in counties lacking civil rights resources. The positive effect of heterogeneity on hate crime reporting grows stronger, however, with increasing levels of civil rights resources. Civil rights resources tend to be ineffective in homogeneous counties.

The interaction between civil rights resources and racist hate groups is also positive and statistically significant. The presence of racist hate groups in a county has little effect on hate crime reporting in counties that lack civil rights resources. Similarly, civil rights resources have little effect on hate crime reporting in counties that do not have a racist hate group. The combination of civil rights resources and racist hate groups, however, results in higher numbers of reported hate crime incidents. . . . [T]he interaction between civil rights resources and white-on-black homicides is also positive and statistically significant. White-on-black homicides have little impact on hate crime reporting when civil rights resources are lacking, but the positive impact of these homicides on hate crime reporting grows stronger with increasing levels of civil rights resources. The coefficient for the interaction between civil rights resources and black-on-white homicides is also positive, suggesting that resourceful civil rights organizations can help counter negative public perceptions that can result from this type of interracial violence. When civil rights resources are lacking in a county, black-on-white homicides have a strong negative impact on hate crime reporting. . . .

Discussion and Conclusion

When a new social policy is enacted, there is no guarantee that the policy will be enforced effectively, or enforced uniformly, across geographic and political boundaries. Enforcement of hate crime legislation has been particularly problematic. However, hate crime legislation represents only a recent example of the difficulties involved in gaining compliance with laws that are designed to protect individuals who experience discrimination, or who are at risk for violent attack, because of an ascribed status. For example, in 1870 and 1871, the United States Congress passed the Enforcement Acts in response to a rising tide of violence and oppression directed toward African Americans in southern states. The federal laws were designed to deal with discriminatory practices used against African Americans, particularly in terms of electoral participation, and to protect African Americans from violence instigated by the Ku Klux Klan and by other groups. From 1871 to 1884, the courts handled 5,386 Enforcement Act cases, but only 28 percent of these resulted in convictions and a majority of cases were

dropped before any verdict was reached (Cresswell 1987: 422).

Northern Republicans and federal officials quickly learned that passing legislation to protect the rights of African Americans in the South would be easier than gaining compliance with the legislation. As one historian describes it, "White Southern Democrats insisted from the outset that the enforcement laws were unconstitutional, oppressive, and not worthy of respect. . . . With such a view widely held it was extremely difficult to gather evidence. Native whites were usually uncooperative, and Negroes were often reluctant to testify in the face of white hostility" (Swinney 1962: 209). For a number of reasons, northern Republicans eventually lost interest in protecting the rights of southern blacks. As a result, African Americans faced extreme oppression and were, for many years, frequently victimized by mob violence (McAdam 1982; Tolnay and Beck 1995).

Tolnay and Beck (1995) note that during the lynching era civil rights organizations were unable to gain sufficient strength in southern states to exert influence on local authorities. Because African Americans were disfranchised, legal and political authorities had little incentive to act on their behalf (also see McAdam 1982). It is worth noting, however, that even in such an oppressive environment, southern whites constructed images of black men as violent sexual predators in an effort to justify their own brutal acts of violence against them (Wells-Barnett [1894] 1969). The lynching rate eventually declined, but only after lynching became detrimental to the economic interests of the southern elite (Tolnay and Beck 1995: 202–43).

Contemporary proponents of hate crime legislation face a political environment that is considerably more open than that which confronted southern blacks in the early 1900s. Yet there is substantial variation across local contexts in terms of the strength and influence of civil rights organizations, political incentives to grant concessions to civil rights organizations, and public perceptions of the validity and the necessity of hate crime laws. In some locales, resistance to laws offering protection from crimes based on sexual orientation bias has been particularly strong. As Green, McFalls, and Smith (2001) note, "legislators are frequently unsympathetic to laws designed to help gay men and lesbians or in any way 'legitimate their lifestyles'" (p. 481). Processes of meaning construction are important not only in the development of public policy, but also in gaining compliance with public policy. We have focused attention on the role that civil rights organizations play in promoting compliance. We proposed that civil rights organizations can play an important role, but only under certain conditions. The effectiveness of civil rights organizations depends upon the availability of resources, a favorable political context, and objective features of local communities that lend credibility to civil rights framing. The results of our statistical analyses support this argument. We have shown that the presence of civil rights organizations and the resources of civil rights organizations can contribute to higher numbers of reported hate crimes in counties, but only in counties with relatively high levels of Democratic voting. The effectiveness of resourceful civil rights organizations is also conditioned by the degree of ethnic heterogeneity that exists in the county, levels of interracial homicide, and the number of racist hate groups that are located in the county. We also find that hate crime reporting tends to be higher in politically competitive counties.

Rather than treating reported hate crime incidents as valid measures of bias crimes, we conceptualized each reported hate crime as a successful social movement outcome. We then assessed the extent that civil rights organizations operating in local contexts contribute to those outcomes. We believe that the theoretical approach developed here should be useful in studying the unintended as well as the intended consequences of actions taken by social movement organizations and other community-based organizations. . . .

We believe that our theoretical approach applies to a wide variety of cases in which full compliance with public policy does not directly follow the enactment of the policy. More than 40 years ago, Kitsuse and Cicourel (1963) argued that sociologists should not avoid using official statistics (including those reported in the Uniform Crime Report) in their analyses because of the unreliability of such data. Instead, they suggested that it is precisely the unreliability of the data that make them valuable and interesting for sociological research.

The theoretical conception which guides us is that the rates of deviant behavior are produced by the actions taken by persons in the social system which define, classify, and record certain behaviors as deviant. If a given form of behavior is not interpreted as deviant by such persons it would not appear as a unit in whatever set of rates we may attempt to explain (Kitsuse and Cicourel (1963: 135).

Over the past 40 years, few criminologists have heeded Kitsuse and Cicourel's call. Instead, they have analyzed official crime data while acknowledging some data limitations, or they have abandoned the use of official crime reports, relying instead upon self-report and victimization surveys. Studies utilizing victim surveys and self-reports have generated many important insights, yet reliance on these data sources has not come without cost. Many serious crimes are of great concern to citizens, yet they cannot be studied effectively with survey data because the crimes may be committed infrequently, the types of individuals who commit these offenses are unlikely to be included in the sample under study, or because victims and perpetrators may be unwilling to acknowledge the criminal act (Hagan 1992). With this in mind, we conclude by identifying several topics that could be studied using an approach similar to the one we have undertaken here. These include studies of domestic violence, sexual assault, sexual harassment, discrimination in the workplace, tax fraud, white-collar crime, drunk driving, discrimination in housing, the use of illegal drugs, and the implementation of affirmative action. As is true of hate crime reporting, variation in compliance with public policy in each of these cases may depend on variation in local configurations of institutional resources, motivations, and credible narratives.

Discussion Questions

1. According to McVeigh et al., what is probably the greatest impediment to effective hate crime enforcement and reporting?

2. If you were an elected local public official, what would guide your efforts to comply with federal laws? What would you do if the majority of your constituents did not agree with a federal law?

Source: "Hate Crime Reporting as a Successful Social Movement Outcome" by Rory McVeigh, Michael R. Welch, and Thoroddur Bjarnason, excerpted and with notes & references omitted from *American Sociological Review*, 2003, Vol. 68, December: 843–867. Reprinted by permission of American Sociological Association.

CHAPTER 32

Culture Jamming

A Sociological Perspective

Vince Carducci

> Culture jamming is defined as "an organized, social activist effort that aims to counter the bombardment of consumption-oriented messages in the mass media." It is seen as an investigation into the apparatus or representation in late modernity, as it relates to both images and discourses of the media and commodity system and the expression of political will. By providing an incentive for producers to respond to consumer demands for environmental sustainability and an end to labor exploitation, culture jamming may ironically help rehabilitate the market system it often portends to transcend.

Introduction

Fieldnote, Monday, 10 May 2004, 11:54 a.m.

I'm walking down Fifth Avenue from the New York Public Library on my way back to the New School. Ahead, I see a guy standing in front of the Duane Reade drugstore on the northeast corner of 34th Street, across from the Empire State Building. He's handing out plastic bags to passersby who mechanically grab them as they hurry to make the light before it changes. From a distance, I notice the familiar red and blue interlocking 'DR' of the pharmacy chain's logo, and presume the store has a street promotion going on.

I come up to the corner, take my bag, and keep walking across the street, not making eye contact with the person handing it to me. I look down at my hand and notice that the 'DR' isn't a 'DR' at all, but a 'DG.' Underneath the letters, it reads not 'Duane Reade' but 'Dwayne Greed.' And underneath that it reads 'New York's Greediest Employer.'

It turns out the action on the street is a 'culture jam,' the appropriation of a brand identity or advertising for subversive, often political, intent. In this case, the 'jamming' is being done by the Retail, Wholesale, & Chain Store/Food Employees Union (RWCSFEU) Local 338. Inside the bag is information about how Duane Reade exploits its employees, overcharges its customers, and otherwise acts disreputably.

Inspired by the technique of electronically interfering with broadcast signals for military or political purposes, the term 'culture jamming' is believed to have been coined in 1984 by the West Coast-based performance/activist group Negativland to describe a variety of activities (Dery, 1993; Klein, 2000; Morris, 2001). These include such tactics as the alteration of corporate advertisements by the Billboard Liberation Front, the parody of corporate and nongovernmental organization (NGO) websites by the Yes Men, and the appropriation of consumer goods through shoplifting and rebranding by Yomango. Much of this activity is chronicled in the magazine *Adbusters,* published in Vancouver, British Columbia, and on various websites such as the Culture Jamming Encyclopedia at Sniggle.net. The ability of culture jammers to imitate and satirize commercial messages is facilitated in part by the desktop publishing hardware and software readily available to consumers at relatively modest prices when compared to the capital-intensive technologies of other forms of media production, such as print and broadcast. The internet is another important digital tool for sharing images and information, and it should come as no surprise then that culture jamming, properly named, first emerged in San Francisco, near Silicon Valley, and the Pacific Northwest, home of Microsoft.

. . . [A] number of commentators see culture jamming's attempt to contest consumer society as ironically offering new sources of distinction for stoking the fires of consumer desire (Heath and Potter, 2004; Holt, 2002; Kozinets, 2002; Morris, 2001, see also Klein, 2000: 422–37). Yet by providing an incentive for producers to respond to socially responsible demands for sustainability of the environment through 'green' products and an end to labor exploitation through fair trade and anti-sweatshop production and distribution, culture jammers may in fact be performing a beneficial and some might even say necessary function as a consumer avant-garde (Klein, 2000; Lasn, 1999). From this perspective, culture jamming is an ad hoc form of social marketing (Kotler and Roberto, 1989); a way of advocating for change in mindset and behavior.

The Culture in Culture Jamming

. . . The dichotomy between culture and civilization has run through social theory (indeed much of Western thought) for some two-and-a-half centuries (Taylor, 1989). It echoes in the early libertarian and abolitionist movements and in the writings of Ralph Waldo Emerson, Henry David Thoreau, and Walt Whitman (Goffman and Joy, 2005). . . . Yet as Kroeber and Kluckhohn note, the social interaction of humans with one another, in other words, civilization, is always already a prerequisite of culture (1952: 155). In addition, more recent theoretical perspectives on the heterogeneity of the 'imagined worlds' of various global cultures (Appadurai, 1993) and the idea of simultaneously operative 'multiple modernities' (Eisenstadt, 2002) suggest the dialectic is overly reductive from an empirical standpoint. Nevertheless, the dichotomy, a bequest of the expressivist turn, is embedded in the concept of culture that culture jamming portends to jam, especially as it relates to the question of 'authenticity.'

What might be termed 'bad' culture, i.e., culture industry, system, spectacle, commodity-signs, and other progeny of *civilisé,* is artificial, manipulative, 'engineered' (Holt, 2002). 'Good' culture, the province of *kultur,* on the other hand, is authentic, truthful and natural. Bad culture is managed from the top down; good culture is autochthonous, literally springing up from the earth itself. Earth-friendly and ergonomically designed products, organic foods and handcrafting all bear the mark of good culture authenticity. For example, the taste for natural fiber clothing that emerged in the early 1970s has been interpreted as a response to the perceived failure of social engineering represented by mass-produced synthetic fabrics (Schneider, 1994). The expressivist notion of good culture is apparent in the pronouncement by the founder and publisher of the culture jamming journal *Adbusters,* Kalle Lasn, that: 'Culture isn't created from the bottom up by the people anymore–it's fed to us top-down by corporations' (Lasn, 1999: 189). . . .

According to Holt, 'Postmodern consumer culture was born, paradoxically, in the 1960s counterculture that opposed corporatism of all stripes' (Holt, 2002: 82). This was when consumers began to embrace consumption as an activity through which identity could be constructed autonomously, and therefore authentically. They began to reject brands that appeared too inflected with the coercive, manipulative attributes of cultural engineering (Holt, 2002: 87). On the other hand, brands that were perceived as more 'authentic' began to prevail. In the 1970s, for example, Nike captured the running shoe market by embracing a brand positioning of 'authentic athletic performance,' gaining legitimacy first and foremost by the fact that all of the company's principals were runners, including one who had coached the 1964 USA Olympics men's track team (Carducci, 2003). The company also embraced a marketing strategy of selling rebellious self-reliance in the American transcendentalist tradition at a time when the cultural contradictions of mass-produced consumption and rationally administered institutional bureaucracies seemed to be most clearly revealed in rising indicators of social and economic upheaval (Carducci, 2004; Goldman and Papson, 1998). The authenticity claims of producers in the postmodern consumer paradigm have in some measure provoked culture jamming as well as other forms of consumer resistance. The 'trouble' between consumers and brands, of which culture jamming is a manifestation, is in essence a renewal of the conflict between good and bad culture, *kultur* and *civilisé:* as consumers become more reflexive as to how bra nding, marketing, and advertising work from the top down in the consumption process, they are prompted to question the authenticity of producers' claims.

One of the conflicts in the postmodern consumer paradigm results from 'peeling away the brand veneer' (Holt, 2002: 86), an activity perhaps most effectively exploited by culture jammers and for which they are most well known. This refers to exposing the 'backstage' of the brand, i.e. examining production practices, environmental impacts, competitive strategies etc. to hold corporations accountable to their authenticity claims by measuring what they do against what they say For example, through their seamless mirroring of the Dow Chemical Corporation website (at www.dowethics.com), the Yes Men gained worldwide attention for successfully mounting the 'Bhopal Hoax,' in which representatives of the culture jamming group were inadvertently invited by the BBC to speak on air in the capacity of Dow spokespersons on the anniversary of the chemical disaster in Bhopal, India. They used the occasion to announce that Dow was accepting responsibility on behalf of Union Carbide, now a subsidiary, and promising to make full restitution amounting to billions of US dollars (Deutsch, 2004). The point of this exercise was to highlight the alleged disparity between actual environmental responsibility performance and credit often taken by the company in presenting a favorable image to its various publics.

. . . By exposing the inconsistencies on the producer side of the ledger, culture jammers may in fact be the avant-garde of the evolution of consumer society, encouraging producers to conform to new consumer expectations in order to garner sales, and thereby continuing the development of socially conscious production in Western capitalism, which has included the abolition of slavery beginning in the early 19th century in the British Empire and the introduction of the high wage/high output model of Fordism in America at the dawn of the 20th century. In this environment, commodity-signs attract consumers into forms of community not bounded by geography but by the social relationships they are able to sustain. Muniz and O'Guinn (2001) term this relationship 'brand community.'

While brand communities are not bound by geographic constraints, they do exhibit other aspects of traditional community. According to Muniz and O'Guinn, these include: 'shared consciousness, rituals and traditions, and a sense of moral responsibility' (2001: 412). The first entails 'consciousness of kind,' that is, the shared perception of belonging to a particular group united by certain common attributes. The second encompasses formal and informal social practices and customs that embody and propagate meaning, value and solidarity as well as a sense of history among the group's current members and successors. The third entails the sense of obligation and duty individuals feel toward one another and the community as a whole, although such sense is admittedly more specialized and narrowly defined than the moral reciprocity of traditional community (Muniz and O'Guinn, 2001: 426). Muniz and O'Guinn also note that while members of a brand community by definition feel a connection with the particular brand that unites them, their sense of connection with one another is even stronger (2001: 418). That the hypothetically anti-consumerist cadre of culture jammers can constitute a brand community is a plausible if seemingly paradoxical contention. In this regard, the readers of the culture jammers' journal *Adbusters* are a relevant case study.

The self-proclaimed 'Journal of the Mental Environment,' *Adbusters* magazine does not accept paid advertising, exhibiting a sense of moral responsibility to its anti-corporatist constituency. Instead, the magazine's pages are filled with articles, artwork, and 'subvertising' (parodies of the ads of global brands such as Nike, Calvin Klein and Marlboro). *Adbusters* magazine and Media Foundation also promote ritual activities, like the annual worldwide 'Buy Nothing Day,' and the organization of local culture jamming networks around the globe. The magazine's editorial position is anti-consumerist and earth-friendly; deliberate articulations of its readers' sense of shared consciousness. . . .

Yet a study of *Adbusters* magazine by Rumbo draws an important conclusion about the publication and the culture jamming phenomenon—the difficulty of mounting an entirely successful challenge to consumerism per se (1999: 124). *Adbusters* promotion of 'green' consumption and the simplicity or 'downshifting' movement have emerged as market segments in their own right as Heath and Potter (2004), Holt (2002), Kozinets (2002) and Muniz and O'Guinn (2001) observe. These new market segments have attracted commercial interests to serve their wants and needs, making emancipation from the system of consumption elusive. *Adbusters'* own marketing efforts and product tie-ins for its 'Buy Nothing Day' anti-consumption event are themselves prodigious (Klein, 2000: 297). . . .

Culture Jamming as Remediation

A related term for what is meant by the expressivist concept of *civilisé*, or bad culture, is ideology. Culture jamming as a media practice directly confronts the authority of corporate representation, which takes the form of certain words and images and their meanings circulating in the consumer marketplace and in society in general. Based on the Habermasian (1984) theory of communicative action, the Handleman and Kozinets definition of culture jamming cited in the abstract of this article presumes that distorted communication can be 'clarified,' that the process of communication between sender and receiver can be rendered sufficiently transparent to enable the 'true' message to be revealed. The concepts of transparency and its opposite, distortion, are central to media theory. The functionalist model, for example, sees media as a neutral instrument for transmitting information (Crane, 1992). In Laswell's functionalist construct of media communications, 'Who says what to whom in what channel to what effect?' (cited in Tuchman, 1988: 606), distortion is the signal degradation that occurs as messages travel through an intervening mechanism (i.e. a medium) from point of origin to point of reception, a problem that can ostensibly be corrected by fine tuning on either end. . . .

Goods have always had cultural significance beyond being simply tools of exploitation whose meanings are distorted by media (Douglas and Isherwood, 1979[1991]). They are themselves communications media in the sense that people consume to express themselves as well as to fulfill their needs (indeed, Douglas and Isherwood argue that expression, in the form of display, *is* one of the needs goods satisfy). Brands are overt parts of the sign system of consumer culture. In postmodern consumer society, brands are said to represent a kind of authenticity; they are part of a consumer's self-identity, indications of a self-appointed claim (sometimes valid, sometimes not) to a certain position in the social system (Belk, 1988; Carducci, 2003; Fournier, 1998; Holt, 2002). Brands reveal the dual nature of goods as bearers of commercial ideology, agents of social control, and as autonomous forms of expression, things used to construct personal and social meaning (Lee, 1993: 39). In as much as branded goods fail to represent the truth, culture jamming provides feedback, which as certain studies assert, effectively remediates the system of consumption and the communications mechanism through which it operates (Frank, 1999; Holt, 2002; Kozinets, 2002).

Culture jamming is thus in some sense related to the hacker ethos, the value system of computer programmers, under the influence of dot-com libertarianism, that calls for ensuring the smooth and efficient operation of processing code through a procedure open for all to see and participate in. The affinity between media transparency in the theory of communicative action and

'open-source' computer programming ultimately stems from the subjective authority embodied in the expressivist tradition, that meaning and the means through which it is conveyed are distinct and that the former constitutes the 'real' message. In the case of culture jamming, exposing the 'source code' of commodity aesthetics, what Holt means by 'peeling away the brand veneer' (2002: 86), is an attempt to get at the authentic nature of goods in order to pass sovereign judgment over them. This transcends traditional advertising media, which have been adapted to the new consumer environment.

In fact, one of the recuperations undertaken as part of postmodern consumer culture's rejection of cultural engineering is the assimilation of skepticism toward advertising not just in terms of content but in terms of its very form. Word-of-mouth (Rosen, 2000), viral, one-to-one, and 'gonzo' (Locke, 2001) are just a few of the names given to new marketing practices that seek to ostensibly disintermediate the relationship between consumers and products. All recognize the suspension of disbelief among consumers as to the authenticity of commercial messages delivered via the mass media. One of the more recent influential theories of branding (Reis and Reis, 2002) is based on the thesis that advertising is no longer capable of establishing brand equity in the marketplace, a function now best achieved by the more 'believable' medium of public relations. More radical forms (Locke, 2001) portray the only viable marketing solutions as being essentially forms of social marketing (Kotler and Roberto, 1989), ways of promoting 'the good' by promoting the right goods to the right people in the right way. These efforts strive for the 'authentic voice' of the product or company to be heard (Locke, 2001: 198). And as for its part in that conversation, culture jamming attempts a kind of discourse analysis of just exactly who is speaking.

In an often-cited passage from *The World of Goods,* Douglas and Isherwood assert: 'Goods are neutral, their uses are social' (1979[1991]: 12). . . .

The World of Goods was first published in 1979, in the rising tide of informational society. This was the time when brands started moving from inside clothes to the outside, when the semiotic function of consumer goods came to more blatantly represent commercial interests. It was also when the disaggregation of mass-industrial production, particularly in the apparel industry, started ramping up (Gereffi et al., 1994). One of the roles of branding in this moment was to direct attention onto the consuming self through expressions of individual sovereignty in the display of distinctive goods (Holt, 2002: 87). The paradoxes of production and consumption are apparent in one of the emblematic products of the period, designer jeans, which responded to the countercultural desire for natural fibers, distinctive ornamentation, and form-fitting tailoring, all of which marked the consumer as an 'authentic' individual (Schneider, 1994). Yet behind this lay a production process, the regime of batch production, that mobilized vast new pools of low-wage labor in lesser-developed countries, exploited the natural resources of those countries, and helped to undermine the social democratic welfare state in the West through deindustrialization and the erosion of union power in such sectors as the American apparel industry (Gereffi et al., 1994). That the product was inextricably bound up in this process is undeniable. And it is at this level–i.e in revealing relationships of production and consumption–that the potentially most effective forms of culture jamming appear to lie....

Culture Jamming as Social Practice

... It may be best to understand culture jamming as an expressive outlet, a social practice that has affinities with contemporary social movements, such as feminism and environmentalism, surveyed by McAdams et al. in their review essay on the subject for Smelser's (ed.) *Handbook of Sociology* (1988). Like the other movements and activities they discuss, culture jamming is 'politics carried on by other means' (McAdams et al., 1988: 699), a claim of sovereignty for under-represented groups in the democratic political process.

That political engagement should find expression in unofficial channels such as culture and media has many precedents. Miller (in press) argues that popular culture, and consumption in particular, is where discontent has long been expressed in American society because 'ordinary Americans have few authorized political outlets for expressing their actual interests, for articulating their desires and aspirations.' In China, songs and ballads appeared during the Han Dynasty (202 BCE–220 CE) as forms of protest against the abusive practices of Imperial government (Innis, 1950: 151). Pamphleteering and newsletters arose in the 1600s for distribution in the coffeehouses and salons of Europe as a counterpoint to the official *communiqués* of government, providing a check on state power and a voice in the public sphere for the rising bourgeoisie (Habermas, 1962[1989]; Innis, 1950). From the time of the Reformation to the present, visual-culture producers have used parody and satire as weapons of propaganda in the form of political cartoons.

Culture jamming reflects a theory of culture as a site of political action, seeing consumer culture as a viable path to social change....

Culture jamming promotes anti-consumerism as one of its main agenda items (Lasn, 1999). By calling for active resistance to certain forms of consumption, culture jamming can be seen as a form of consumer boycott. The most dramatic is *Adbusters'* previously discussed annual worldwide 'Buy Nothing Day.' In another example, activists in early 2005 circulated an email over the internet encouraging consumers to boycott the entire economy of the USA on 20 January 2005, the day of the presidential inauguration, in protest of the Iraq war through 'Not One Damn Dime Day' (*AlterNet,* 2005). Other boycott targets include Nike, Coca-Cola, Nestlé, and Starbucks.

Consumer boycotts are among the most frequently, if not *the* most frequently, used organizing techniques for those outside the conventional power structure (Friedman, 1999: 3). Their use as an alternate means of politics has historically been to achieve either economic or social justice, following in the expressivist tradition of the call for universal human rights. Economic boycotts are typically the concern of consumers, and social boycotts often the concern of minorities. Examples of economic justice boycotts include the protests against high meat prices during the Great Depression and coffee in the 1970s. The Depression also saw the 'Don't Buy from Where You Can't Work' social boycotts for equal employment opportunity for African-Americans. The celebrated bus boycotts of the 1950s were instrumental to the civil rights movement.

Most consumer boycotts have historically been directed against commodities, such as meat, grapes and coffee, and not specific brands (Friedman, 1999: 66). They have also tended to be more market-oriented, that is, directed to effecting change by attacking a target's sales revenues, giving economic leverage to those mounting the action. Contemporary consumer boycotts, on the other hand, tend to be more media-oriented, seeking to have an effect by damaging the target's reputation (Friedman, 1999: 216)....

Parodies of brand names and marketing slogans are among the primary and more effective tools used in organizing contemporary consumer boycotts (Friedman, 1999: 221). This semiotic jujitsu is the culture jammer's stock in trade and its efficacy can sometimes be striking. For example, CNN reported that the Yes Men's mounting of the Bhopal Hoax sent Dow Chemical's stock price down 4.24 percent in 23 minutes on the Frankfurt Exchange, causing the company to temporarily lose US$2 billion in market value (CNN, 2004). (It recovered as news of the hoax became known and its stock price was relatively unaffected in other financial markets, but the negative publicity from the incident continues to circulate, especially over the internet.) Edward Herman asserts in a letter to the editor of *Adbusters* (cited in Morris, 2001: 27) that culture jamming is really only a tactic, not an end in itself for effecting social change, especially in terms of ameliorating the dilemmas of late-modern capitalism. And there is unquestionably a need to distinguish between culture jamming as an organized action perceived as an end in itself, and as an instrument of political action used by more conventionally defined social movements, such as labor and animal rights activists.

McAdams et al. define social movements broadly as having members, a network of communications, and leaders (1988: 715). Additional factors in understanding social movements include the mobilization of resources and the implementation of political processes, in other words, how well constituencies and capabilities are activated and associations created as mechanisms for taking action (McAdams et al., 1988: 697). Social movements at their highest organizational level claim to speak on behalf of constituencies and seek to influence policy (McAdams et al., 1988: 717). Their process is one of 'frame alignment' (McAdams et al., 1988: 713), bringing social action and worldview together to ameliorate relative deprivation and institutionalize a new paradigm. Social movements, if they persist over time, can evolve into enterprises, like the NAACP or the ACLU. By all of these measures, the community of culture jammers around *Adusters* magazine and Media Foundation can be considered at least a faction of a social movement, if perhaps not always an ultimately effective one in and of itself.

Adbusters' subscriber base, regular newsstand purchasers, and online communities constitute a membership of a kind. The magazine itself and the extended media of websites, listservs, discussion groups, and the like is a multidimensional communications network. Leadership is exhibited (for better or worse) by Lasn and other paid staff. Other less commercially visible groups also appear to meet the criteria, such as the bloggers who maintain the Culture Jamming Encyclopedia on Sniggle.net and the contributors to such alternative news and information portals as IndyMedia.org. Not unlike other consumer groups and special-interest organizations, *Adbusters* claims to speak for the consuming public at large. Besides seeking to affect corporate policies through negative publicity and product boycotts (as well as their opposite action, 'buycotts,' i.e., the patronizing of

approved products), *Adbusters* magazine and Media Foundation have sought to influence public policy through legal action and other advocacies against American and Canadian regulatory agencies and for-profit companies on freedom of speech issues, in particular those related to the placement of anti-advertising messages (Lasn, 1999: 192–9).

Social movements are traditionally perceived to respond to situations of relative deprivation; however, McAdams et al. note that a general condition of prosperity seems to be connected to a rise in social-movement activity (1988: 702). According to their analysis, some level of wealth provides favorable conditions for collective activity, including the ability to raise funds to support communications and community building, thereby creating opportunities for 'entrepreneurs of grievances' (McAdams et al., 1988:702). . . .

Social movements are not simply aggregations of individuals but 'collectivities' (McAdams et al., 1988: 709). They constitute an intermediate level of organization between individuals and the macrosocial contexts within which they live. Among the macrolevel factors culture jamming attempts to remediate are the plethora of commercial identities inserted into contemporary life, the pervasiveness of the culture industry, the seemingly all-encompassing spectacle of the commodity-sign (Baudrillard, 1981; Holt, 2002; Rumbo, 2002).

Conclusion

An analysis of culture jamming needs to supplement sociological examination with a consideration of its political and economic effects. To be truly effective as a cultural, media, and social practice, it appears that culture jamming must be tied to a larger purpose and not be taken as an end in itself. The most effective tendencies seem to be those that link with broader social concerns about global ecology and human rights. As a result of consumer activism, Nike, to take one example, now offers PVC-free products packaged in recycled boxes and has established a code of ethics for offshore suppliers. (Whether these initiatives are sincere, much less sufficient, is still open to debate.) But . . . affecting change on the consumer side of the market equation often has limited effect. Some producers have adapted and new producers have arisen to respond to postacute-postmodern consumer demands for environmentally sustainable, socially responsible goods. Sales of certified fair trade chocolate are growing, for instance, but remain trifling compared to total world consumption (Anti-Slavery International, 2004: 45).

Duane Reade still refuses to acknowledge its employees' desire to affiliate with RWCSFEU Local 338 and engage in collective bargaining, although the National Labor Relations Board has ordered the company to remedy its unfair labor practices and make full restitution to all employees and the union. The New York State Supreme Court in October 2004 also upheld the union's right to continue the 'Dwayne Greed' culture jam, noting that its factual allegations against the company were credible, not to mention protected as free speech under the First Amendment. Thus on the streets of New York City the jamming of culture continues, and every now and then flashes of the red-and-blue 'DG' logo can be seen on white plastic bags in the hands of rushing passersby.

Discussion Questions

1. What is culture jamming? Have you ever practiced culture jamming? If so, how and why?

2. Do you agree with Carducci that, to be truly effective, "culture jamming must be tied to a larger purpose and not be taken as an end in itself"? Why or why not?

Source: "Culture Jamming: A Sociological Perspective," by Vince Carducci, excerpted and with notes & references omitted from *Journal of Consumer Culture*, 2006, Vol. *6* (1): 116–138. Reprinted by permission of Sage Publications.

CHAPTER 33

Corporate Citizenship and Social Responsibility in a Globalized World

Juan José Palacios

By virtue of their very nature, transnational corporations (TNCs) cannot become fully responsible and accountable. Nonetheless, they can be induced to transform themselves in ways that may be compatible with socially and environmentally desirable objectives. The article explores paths for action and the potential of non-governmental organizations and anti-globalization social movements to become civil regulators able to push for the introduction of binding rules and regulations and the construction of a governance framework capable of restraining and harnessing the power of TNCs.

Introduction

The concept of citizenship ultimately evokes the idea of belonging to some sort of community or socio-political entity. More specifically, it suggests a status that has been historically linked to nationality. Having as a remote antecedent the figure of the citizen that emerged in the city-states of ancient Greece, the underlying concept of citizenship took final form in Europe with the birth of the nation-state between the seventeenth and nineteenth centuries.

The concept and its legal and political correlates have evolved significantly since then, particularly in the last decades, because of transcendental changes that have taken place in the international scene under globalization. New figures have emerged such as the long-distance nationalist as well as the global, the cosmopolitan and the virtual citizens. Relatedly, as transnational corporations (TNCs) grew and matured, another significant figure, the corporate citizen, took shape and with it a new kind of citizenship. As the counterpart of a status traditionally granted to members of a national community, corporate citizenship has received less attention and study compared to the citizenship of individuals. Nonetheless, the

spectacular spread and increased mobility and power of TNCs around the globe have led a growing number of scholars and analysts to put corporate citizenship at the centre of their intellectual inquiries in recent years. The purpose of this article is then to continue these efforts by assessing the limits to corporate social responsibility and exploring ways for making TNCs embrace sustainable development goals and aspirations in the context of an unprecedented transnationalization of capital and the rise of the Internet.

The Diversification of Citizenship and the Rise of Non-Territorial Identities

. . . The mobility of people across national borders has further increased over the last century and a half due to the technological advances and the intensification of capital and trade flows that the world has witnessed in those decades. As a result, the terms 'citizen' and 'citizenship' have gradually lost their rigid reference to a single, territorially defined nation-state, and have accordingly acquired new meanings. The world has thus seen the emergence of such unorthodox phenomena as multiple citizenships (Shafir and Peled, 2002) and new figures like the long-distance nationalist (Anderson, 1992), the cosmopolitan citizen (Norris, 2000), and the virtual citizen, as it is discussed below.

Long held notions of the state, the citizen, and citizenship have thus changed significantly, in particular with the advent of the Internet. This epoch-making innovation has even led to the creation of virtual national communities dubbed 'cyber-nations' that only exist in the imaginary realm of cyberspace. Nonetheless, these communities are proving to exert a strong appeal for a growing number of individuals who are seeking alternative affiliations, new forms of social identity, and a more satisfying sense of belonging in their daily lives. A new figure, of the virtual or cyber-citizen, is a result. . . .

Jane Jacobs (1984) argued earlier for the need to 'unbundle' nation-states in order to separate 'nation' from 'state,' and David Elkins advocated the formation of non-territorial entities like *La Francophonie*, which would comprise 'all francophones in Canada living outside of Quebec' (Elkins, 1995, p. 149). Drawing on Hobsbawn (1993) and Anderson (1991), Elkins further argued that 'nationalism no longer satisfies many people, perhaps because of its prior excesses, and religious or spiritual experiences of non-national-sorts seem more promising as motives and structures beyond nations' (Elkins, 1995, p. 250). This formulation corresponds with the rationale for the creation of cyber-nations.

Traditional notions of citizenship, thus, are coming into question, as new ways of conceiving of the role and place of individuals in society are emerging. They point to new forms of identity and new ways of experiencing a sense of belonging. This also occurs as a result of the ongoing unbundling of the nation-state and the loosening up of the once rigid and monolithic structures of the territorial state. All this has enhanced communication among citizens of different latitudes and increased mobility across national borders, thus helping to construct cross-border citizen networks. In this way, the dissemination of ideas and the sharing of common concerns and preoccupations about social equity, human rights and environmental preservation also are intensifying, thus contributing as well to the globalization of civil society itself.

Global Civil Society and the Birth of the Global Citizen

The above developments are favouring the intensification of the activities of groups, organizations and individuals

that promote sustainable development goals and principles, and in general the growth of transnational social movements of opposition and resistance to globalization. As a result, many scholars and observers in different latitudes are envisaging the emergence of a global civil society. . . .

With the emergence of a global civil society, a concomitant figure and its related noun have also come to the fore—the global citizen and global citizenship. . . .

[G]lobal citizens are activists that contest the social and environmental costs of globalization thus forming a movement that constitutes a decisive moment in the evolution of citizenship and democratic institutions. In a similar vein, Dower and Williams (2002a) contend that a global citizen is ultimately a member of a community wider than that of a nation-state, and that global citizenship embraces the ideals of achieving global responsibility and the creation of institutional structures through which this responsibility can be exercised. In sum, the intensification in the movement of people across the globe and the resulting cross-fertilization of cultures and identities are transforming both the figure of the citizen and the meaning of citizenship to give rise to new concepts that take account of contemporary realities. The appearance of the global or cosmopolitan citizen, who is mobile by nature and bears multiple citizenships, is in turn giving way to the emergence of a global civil society, which is facilitating the creation of rules and structures for regulating and restraining the power of global corporate citizens, making them more accountable and responsible in their operations.

Global Governance under Globalism

The global citizen comes into existence in and is a product of the present historical conjuncture, which has been moulded, in large part, by the unprecedented advances in transportation, information and communication technologies, especially the creation of the Internet, that have taken place in the past few decades. These factors have led to a dramatic shortening of geographic distances that is making national borders increasingly irrelevant, thus opening the way for what is now termed as 'globalization.' The other main drivers of this overarching phenomenon are the extension of the geographic reach and the maturation of the organizational structures and management philosophy of TNCs, as will be discussed later on.

For Robert Keohane and Joseph Nye Jr. (2000), globalization boils down to the shrinkage of distance on a large scale and the extension of networks of relationships on a regional and global scale. Coinciding with Flores and Marina's (1999) previous formulation, they also distinguish globalization from globalism, which they define as 'a state of the world involving networks of interdependence at multi-continental distances' (2000, p. 2), and distinguish four main dimensions of globalism: economic, military, environmental, and socio-cultural. Keohane and Nye further argue that globalization is best conceived as the increase of globalism, or, more significantly, as 'the process by which globalism becomes increasingly thick' (2000, p. 7). The point to note here is that thickness refers to the increase in the density of networks of interdependence that occurs under globalism, so that events in one place have major effects in other very distant ones and in different dimensions. . . .

This architecture rests on a complex, amorphous assemblage of nation-states, TNCs, multilateral economic institutions, regional development banks, United Nations agencies, international banks, and all sorts of civil and non-governmental organizations. . . .

Despite of the weakening, unbundling and hollowing out processes it is subject to these days, the nation-state continues to be the most powerful and influential player in this scenario. Other major players, especially TNCs, nongovernmental organizations (NGOs), and other non-profit entities are undermining and challenging such predominance. The point is, therefore, that the prevailing global governance structure consists of a multi-stakeholder system in which a governance order somehow prevails but without a permanent governing structure. . . .

The Global Corporate Community and the Emergence of the Corporate Citizen

As the carriers *par excellence* of private capital, technical know-how, management knowledge and technological innovation, TNCs became the top players in the world economic scene from the late twentieth century onwards. Together with the world's most industrialized nation-states, they are the dominant protagonists in the global governance stage at the dawn of the twenty-first century. Their power is unprecedented and growing. At least 65,000 TNCs operate globally through over 850,000 affiliates located in 122 countries. The stock of these affiliates, that is, foreign direct investment, was worth $7 trillion and accounted for 11% of world gross domestic product in 2001. The value added by all TNCs totalled $3.5 trillion and total sales $18.5 trillion, while world

exports only reached $7.4 trillion in 2001 (UNCTAD, 2002, p. 14). By the mid 1990s, almost one-half of the top 100 economies in the world were TNCs, 500 of them controlled 70% of global trade, and as few as 1% owned half the total stock of foreign direct investment in the world (Clarke, 1996, p. 298). . . .

Such a strong footing around the world notwithstanding, TNCs need to abide by the rules and legislation in force in the countries that play host to their affiliates and partners. In this sense, they have come to acquire a particular form of citizenship in each national setting. It is actually a multiple citizenship for TNCs operate under many national statutory frameworks. Therefore, it is no wonder that TNCs embody the figure of the corporate citizen as a natural counterpart of the cosmopolitan and the global citizen born by individuals. . . .

It is important to point out, however, that TNCs are no longer the monolithic, vertically organized entities they were in most of the twentieth century. They have undergone fundamental changes in the last decades, facilitating the horizontalization of their corporate structures and the flexibilization of their production processes. As competition has intensified in international markets, the largest TNCs headquartered in industrialized countries have found it both necessary and profitable to move from the old strategy of corporate expansion through the deployment of stand-alone affiliates in several host countries, to others that promote the segmentation of production processes and their assignment to multifunctional units in locations around the world.

Originally, stand-alone affiliates were capable of performing just about all of the parent firm's main operations as actual replicas of the latter. Then, from the 1980s on, TNCs began to adopt so-called complex integration strategies whereby any affiliate is able to perform any corporate-wide function either by itself, in association with other affiliates, or else in combination with the lead firm (UNCTAD, 1993). This requires that all operations be located wherever they can be performed most efficiently so as to best contribute to achieving the firm's overall objectives (Palacios, 2001a). Under this more integrated production scheme, and due to the pressures of competition, TNCs began to subcontract—outsource—key operations from other companies. Thus more extensive and sophisticated functional linkages began to be established along the parent firm's core value chain (UNCTAD, 1993). Outsourcing has led to a further flexibilization of their production schemes and the 'de-verticalization' and flattening out of their corporate structures from the 1980s on (Palacios, 2001b).

Complex integration strategies involve both a generalization of outsourcing practices and a deeper integration between firms and affiliates across both functions and national boundaries. The result is what Ernst (1997) terms as systemic globalization under which companies organize their operations within transnational production networks along an integrated supply chain, thus overcoming the limitations of rigid, hierarchical and centralized governance structures. Under systemic globalization, outsourcing has become an increasingly common practice that has helped large companies to solve the old 'buy-or-make' dilemma first posed by Ronald Coase in the late 1930s (Coase, 1937).

All these strategies have led to the breaking down of walls between the company and its key partners in the value chain, including suppliers, customers, distributors, and carriers. . . .

The erosion of their outer boundaries and the related integration and overlapping of their functions and processes with those of their partners pose the question about where the social responsibility of a company ends and where that of its suppliers, partners and subcontractors begins. As will be discussed in the following section, this leads to a more fundamental question about the extent to which corporations can become accountable and responsible citizens in the countries where they have presence and operations.

Corporate Citizenship and Social Responsibility

Corporate citizenship and corporate social responsibility are the foci of growing interest among sociologists, international political economists and other students of international issues nowadays. Traditionally, corporate citizenship has been analysed in terms of moral values and ethical arguments, but being a good corporate citizen is increasingly viewed as a good business practice. This belief is based on the so-called social responsibility thesis, which is a central element of what can be termed as the 'caring capitalism' doctrine. This thesis holds that it pays for firms to be credible and responsible because business is no longer a zero-sum game, so it is profitable to enact workers' benefits and environmental protection policies by conviction as well as by the need to abide by laws and rules (Makower, 1995). These views are based on the observation that companies that have failed to behave responsibly have seen their brand image deteriorate and their markets shrink in places where they have offended

public opinion. Moreover, according to McIntosh *et al.* (1998), it is imperative for corporations to behave responsibly because it is increasingly difficult for them to evade social and public scrutiny in the contemporary information age. Zadek (2001) also argues that TNCs face growing pressure to become good citizens in the countries where they operate and are thus encouraged to contribute to sustainable development by taking due account of their footprints in local and national environments. On this basis, corporate citizenship is defined as both a philosophy and a practice aimed at gaining public trust and legitimacy. Zadek holds that corporations should adopt the former and exercise the latter not for philanthropic reasons but because it can be in their benefit to promote sustainable development goals. . . .

Other analysts are less optimistic about the possibility for TNCs to be socially responsible. Ralph Estes (1996), for example, holds that TNCs are prisoners of what he refers to as 'the tyranny of the bottom line,' which is to make profits for stockholders. He adds that TNCs are largely unaccountable to the public and avoid scrutiny by governments and stockholders. From a similar perspective, Jerry Mander (1998) bluntly points out that to 'ask corporations to behave better by making growth and profit a lower priority is like asking armies to give up their guns. Managers who might personally like to develop more pro-social or pro-environmental policies are constrained; they cannot give such factors higher priorities than the bottom line, or they may find themselves out of work' (Mander, 1998, p. 309). More generally, Mander argues that profit and growth constitute the corporations' instinct to live. . . .

In sum, corporate social responsibility goes beyond the simple observation of the laws and regulations in force in host countries. It encompasses the behaviour of TNCs as responsible citizens socially accountable for their deeds to a wider range of stakeholders, including their own employees, the communities where their plants are located, and the governments of the countries that play host to their operations. More generally, corporate citizenship is about business taking account of its impact on both society and the environment, and about their being committed to delivering on social and environmental goods. The question is whether 'business' is willing or able to actually meeting all these expectations, and, more specifically, whether large firms can profess moral or ethical values, as individuals do, and thus be part of the efforts at abating social ills and preventing environmental degradation. More generally, the question is whether capitalism can be 'caring.'

According to the social responsibility thesis, business can actually meet such expectations because this is necessary for corporations to make profits and maintain a positive brand reputation these days of increasing public scrutiny. By extension, then, capitalism can be 'caring' in that context. However, the fact is that a societal order cannot be 'caring' or 'uncaring,' for it simply exists and functions as an anonymous, blind system guided by its inner logic and immanent 'laws of motion.' Capitalism has undergone significant changes, especially during the past few decades, with the advent of the Internet and the growth of the so-called new economy. Thus, a 'meta-capitalism,' which is driven by the Internet, business webs and meta-markets, is said to have emerged as a result (Means and Schneider, 2000). However, the fact is that capitalism's innermost essence remains unchanged. As Professor Michael Lebowitz has recently reiterated, 'the characteristic of capitalism is not *simply* that the mass of people must be wage-laborers. It is also that those who are purchasing that capacity to perform labor have only one thing and only one thing that interests them—profits (and more profits)' (2004, p. 19). . . .

What Is to Be Done?

. . . As discussed above, being responsible has become increasingly necessary for companies to rebuild or preserve their brand image and corporate reputation. This has been the case, for example, with apparel giants like Levi Strauss in the United States and Marks & Spencer in the United Kingdom. Both companies had refused to join the Apparel Industry Partnership (later renamed as Fair Labor Association) and the Ethical Trading Initiative, respectively, until both saw their brand reputation deteriorate in the late 1990s. Ultimately, these corporate giants joined those bodies as a way to recover public trust and the credibility of key stakeholders, including their employees and trade unions (Zadek, 2001). . . .

The above may be seen as part of the process of corporate transformation that is underway, as demands for social responsibility and accountability increase on corporations and 'powerful values-driven movements are spinning a virtual cocoon of new laws, standards and expectations around the g lobe, spurring a process of corporate metamorphosis' (Elkington, 2001, p. 3). . . .

The materialization of such corporate metamorphosis in general requires corporations to engage in some type of partnership with other major players in the social and economic international scene. TNCs can exercise this practice by joining forces with individual NGOs, labour and environmental protection organizations, transnational social movements, or multilateral development agencies. One of the most significant cases is the creation of the so-called Global Compact, a corporate citizenship initiative called for by the UN Secretary General in January 1999 and formalized on 26 July 2000. Its members include top TNCs such as Ford, BP Amoco, Shell, and Unilever as well as hundreds of other companies from most countries, international business associations, and labour, social and pro-environmental organizations.

The problem with these kinds of partnerships, however, is that they are voluntary and thus have nor enforcement mechanisms. . . . In addition, partnerships make possible for TNCs to build or preserve a good reputation while performing poorly as corporate citizens. Another problem is that by way of partnerships they reduce the pressures for the introduction of legislation aimed at regulating their operations. Still another is that this kind of partnership tends to legitimize globalization by taking for granted that it can be compatible with equity and sustainability goals. What is required then is a legal framework with binding rules, for it is definitely uncertain that TNCs will abide by the principles of sustainable development by simply making a voluntary commitment. Nonetheless, as Zadek argues, voluntary partnerships may prepare the way for the later introduction of binding rules and regulations.

The ambitious goal of making TNCs become responsible and accountable citizens will thus require a sound and solid governance framework understood as a coherent and coordinated set of rules and institutions that provide the necessary mechanisms and structures to enforce those rules and achieve that goal. The task is huge for it is ultimately geared at restraining and harnessing the power of TNCs. A durable governance framework will necessarily involve all major players in the global scene because corporations cannot become civil by themselves. . . .

On that basis, the framework in question should be designed to replace the still prevailing hierarchical global governance architecture, which, as pointed out before, rests on a network of corporate states built upon a grand alliance between big business and national governments. It should also be informed by Clarke's proposals of a 'new nationalism' and a citizens' manifesto. By new nationalism, he refers to a new conception of the nation-state inspired in the idea of popular sovereignty under global interdependence. His citizens' manifesto in turn establishes the sovereign rights of people over TNCs and banks; the need for TNCs to meet certain basic social and environmental conditions; the enactment of regulatory measures for ensuring democratic control over TNCs; and the commitment by social movements to uphold people's rights and aspirations (1996).

In that context, anti-globalization social movements have the responsibility to become both catalysts and instruments of initiatives for building such a governance framework. In order to be able to do so, global social movements will have to evolve from the uncoordinated, piecemeal, amorphous force they have been up to now, and coalesce into a coherent, solid, and coordinated transnational advocacy network able to acquire sufficient political leverage to both influence and be part of the new global governance milieu. . . .

An effective and proven way for committed groups to fulfil such mission is to use pressure and persuasion on governments and corporations through media campaigns, scientific reports and authoritative open statements. These are the weapons used by, for example, the Union for Concerned Scientists: Citizens and Scientists for Environmental Solutions (UCS), which have actively promoted global environmental causes for decades. The UCS, founded in 1969 in the United States, is an independent non-profit alliance of more than 100,000 concerned citizens and scientists that combines the application of scientific knowledge with 'innovative thinking and committed citizen advocacy to build a cleaner, healthier environment and a safer world.' . . .

It should always be borne in mind, however, that social movements and transnational advocacy networks can only aspire to counterbalance and restrain the systemic power of TNCs. Critics like Tony Clarke (1996) complain that such power is rarely challenged because citizen movements often focus instead on changing government policies. TNCs and large banks, however, also affect the lives of the vast majority of people on Earth and a massive shift of power has taken place from governments to corporations. Barbara Epstein (2001), on the contrary, observes that the main target of anti-globalization movements is corporate power, not capitalism. These perspectives, she continues, do not necessarily exclude one another, for the regulation of corporations to comply with human and environmental rights and their ultimate abolishment are not necessarily incompatible and even the line between regulation and abolition can eventually disappear.

Anyway, anti-globalization and pro-environmental movements constitute the most tangible and potentially effective agents for promoting and materializing the

design and introduction of a set of binding rules and legislation to restrain the actions of TNCs and make them behave as reasonably responsible and accountable citizens. These kinds of civil actions have already proved their efficacy, as when a wide spectrum of NGOs, academics and pro-environmental and resistance groups levelled a strong opposition to the ambitious Multilateral Agreement on Investment (MAI) proposed by OECD members in the late 1990s, and succeeded in making them to drop the initiative.

Ultimately, the first step should be to find the way to turn present day's atomized and disorganized anti-globalization groups into a solid and coordinated transnational network of civil regulators with the political clout and lobbying capabilities required to carry out its mission. . . .

Conclusion

As shown in the preceding sections, the corporate citizen is the most significant of the new figures that have emerged out of the diversification that the concept of citizenship has undergone in the last few decades as a result of an intensified globalization of economic and social life. The crux of the matter is that no laws and no binding rules exist for regulating the behaviour and international mobility of corporate citizens similar to those in force for individual citizens, even though the former have rights and entitlements similar to the latter. In principle, TNCs, as the embodiment of the corporate citizen, are supposed to observe the relevant legislation in host countries, but in practice they have advantages and privileges stemming from the economic and political leverage they command in national settings, which by definition are not applicable to individual citizens. TNCs cannot become fully accountable and responsible citizens, the same way as capitalism cannot be 'caring,' although they can be induced to embrace socially and environmentally desirable objectives.

The possibility of accomplishing such a task will ultimately depend on the balance that can be reached between the factors that impede or facilitate it. The most visible roadblocks are multiple and powerful. About all is the condition of TNCs as entrepreneurial organizations whose *raison d'être* is to make profits for stockholders and the derived fact that their behaviour is inherently guided by a cold business logic that responds to market imperatives. Profit-making will always have priority over equity or environmental protection objectives. Likewise, corporations' ubiquitous presence and sheer economic power and the political muscle associated with both allow them to further their interests and achieve their goals. The ability of TNCs to strike alliances with host governments, especially in countries where they are a major and even a vital source of capital investment, reinforces those advantages. Another barrier is the ongoing transformation of corporations into networks and the resulting enhanced sharing of key functions and operations with their business partners, which is making it increasingly difficult to identify the respective responsibilities among all the firms participating in the production process. An additional barrier is the absence of a global governance framework that enforces and monitors the expected accountability and responsibility by TNCs. Still another is the lack of legal power of the United Nations to issue binding rules and regulations. Lastly, the lack of coherence and organization of anti-globalization and pro-environmental movements and the resulting weakness and atomization they present nowadays is perhaps the single most substantial obstacle to the efforts at making TNCs more accountable and responsible citizens.

Enabling and facilitating factors are, in turn, less forceful, although have the potential for counteracting, and eventually prevail, over the above barriers. Perhaps, the factor with the greatest potential for softening the tyranny of the bottom line of profit-making is advancing the idea that corporate responsibility is profitable. . . .

Another, particularly important, enabling factor is the emergence of a global civil society made up of cosmopolitan citizens who are mobile by nature and engage in diverse activities of transnational reach aimed at promoting social responsibility and accountability by TNCs. Related are the intensification in the exchange of ideas, information and knowledge, as more and more global citizens around the world have been connected through powerful means of telecommunication, above all the Internet, the increase in the mobility of people across national borders and the thickness of networks of collaboration among committed citizens. An associated enabling trend is the hollowing out and unbundling of nation-states and the concomitant emergence of non-territorial forms of identity and societal organization. What remains crucial for counterbalancing movements to succeed, however, is the emergence of a global leadership with sufficient strength and coherence to organize the dispersed anti-globalization and pro-environmental groups that have proliferated and in the last decades, a leadership that may already be hatching in the fledgling global civil society of the early the twenty-first century.

Discussion Questions

1. According to Palacios, can capitalism be "caring"? Why or why not?

2. Do you agree with Palacios's call for NGOs and anti-globalization social movements to organize and construct a governance framework that can effectively control the power of TNCs? Why or why not?

Source: "Corporate Citizenship and Social Responsibility in a Globalized World" by Juan José Palacios, excerpted and with notes & references omitted from *Citizenship Studies,* Vol. 8, No. 4, December 2004, pp. 383–402. Copyright © 2004 by Taylor & Francis Group.

INTERNET RESOURCES

Culture and Social Interaction

Straight Edge Online   http://toefur.com/straightedge

This website provides a forum for those interested in communicating about straightedge topics. It also contains answers to frequently asked questions about straightedge.

Bureau of Justice Statistics   http://www.ojp.usdoj.gov/bjs/welcome.html

On this website, you can find a plethora of statistics related to our criminal justice system. It includes information on drug and alcohol use among college students.

National Social Norms Resource Center   http://www.socialnorms.org/index.php

The focus of the National Social Norms Resource Center is to help those interested in using the "social norms approach" to promote efforts to curb dangerous behavior, such as drinking and drug use on college campuses. The Center's website provides results of the latest studies on efforts to promote healthy lifestyles by informing people about the real, rather than perceived, behaviors of their peers.

Social Structure, Social Institutions, and the Media

National Center for Health Statistics Faststats A to Z   http://www.cdc.gov/nchs/fastats/unmarry.htm

This website provides statistical data about the health of people living in the United States. Included in the "Faststats" are the latest figures for the percentage of children born in the United States to unmarried women.

National Review Online   http://www.nationalreview.com/ and **Alternet** http://alternet.org

The National Review Online is a source for conservative news and information. Check it out and then compare what you find there with what is on Alternet, a progressive news source.

Bill and Melinda Gates Foundation   http://www.gatesfoundation.org/default.htm

The Bill and Melinda Gates Foundation website provides information about various structural inequities, particularly those related to education and healthcare. It also contains descriptions of various programs designed to diminish these inequities.

Deviance and Crime

Death Penalty Information Center   http://www.deathpenaltyinfo.org

This website provides information about the death penalty, including which states have the death penalty. It is also a source for information about efforts to abolish it.

Office of Juvenile Justice and Delinquency Prevention   http://ojjdp.ncjrs.gov

The OJJDP website provides resources for those seeking to prevent juvenile delinquency and effective means for working with juvenile offenders. It also includes various fact sheets about rates of juvenile delinquency and the victimization of juveniles.

Center for Safe and Responsible Internet Use   http://www.cyberbully.org/cyberbully/

This website provides assistance for those pursued by cyberbullies. It describes what cyberbullying is and the steps you should take if you are a victim of such a bully.

Social Stratification and Power

United Nations Population Fund   http://www.unfpa.org/index.htm

The UNFPA website contains a wide variety of information about the socioeconomic conditions of the world population. It also provides a description of the United Nations' Millennium Development Goals to reduce global poverty.

America's Second Harvest Hunger Study 2006   http://www.hungerinamerica.org

This study describes the extent of hunger in the United States. It also measures how well hunger-relief agencies are doing in their efforts to assist hungry Americans.

"Recent Changes in U.S. Family Finances: Evidence from the 2001 and 2004 Survey of Consumer Finances" by Bucks, Brian K., Arthur B. Kennickell, and Kevin B. Moore (with Gerhard Fries and A. Michael Neal). 2006. Federal Reserve Board   http://www.federalreserve.gov/pubs/bulletin/2006/financesurvey.pdf

This Federal Reserve Board report describes recent changes in U.S. family finances. Between 2001 and 2004, the wealth of the bottom 40% of the population fell while the wealth of the top 10% increased.

U.S. Department of Labor Bureau Statistics   http://www.bls.gov

This website provides information about such labor and economic topics as wages, benefits, and unemployment rates. It is an excellent source of information for those interested in finding out about the state of the U.S. labor force.

Race and Ethnicity

Understanding Prejudice   http://www.understandingprejudice.org/iat

This website offers resources on prejudice. It also includes an Implicit Association Test that you can take to test your unconscious attitudes toward members of other racial groups.

Association of American Colleges and Universities *Diversity Digest*   http://www.diversityweb.org/digest/Sp.Sm00/contents.html

Diversity Digest provides research and news articles about diversity issues on college campuses. Several articles look at the debate about affirmative action in college admissions and the influence of diverse campuses on students.

Homeland Security Office of Immigration Statistics   http://www.uscis.gov/graphics/shared/statistics/index.htm

The OIS website provides government statistics concerning the immigrant population in the United States. It also provides information on Homeland Security efforts to curb illegal immigration.

Sex and Gender

United Nations Development Programme (UNDP) Women's Empowerment   http://www.undp.org/women

This website provides information about the United Nation's Millennium Development Goals and how they relate to the status of women. The website also features various UNDP development projects for women, in various areas of the globe.

U.S. Equal Employment Opportunity Commission (EEOC)   http://www.eeoc.gov

The EEOC website contains a plethora of information about discrimination in the workforce. Some of the links refer directly to discrimination based on sex and sexual harassment.

American Psychological Association's "Just the Facts about Sexual Orientation and Youth: A Primer for Principals, Educators, and School Personnel"   http://www.apa.org/pi/lgbc/publications/justthefacts.html

This Fact Sheet was developed by "a group of education, health, mental health, and religious organizations that all share a concern for the health and education of all students in schools, including lesbian, gay, and bisexual students." It provides background material on sexual orientation development.

Global Issues

Environmental Protection Agency Global Warming Site   http://yosemite.epa.gov/oar/globalwarming.nsf/content/index.html

The EPA website provides background on global climate change. It also includes suggestions on what you can do to help curb it.

RAND Corporation   http://www.rand.org

The RAND Corporation sponsors research on a wide variety of topics, including such global issues as terrorism, energy, and the environment. You can check out their latest findings by clicking on your topic of interest under "research areas" on the RAND homepage.

World Trade Organization's "The WTO"   http://www.wto.org/english/thewto_e/thewto_e.htm
and
Public Citizen's "World Trade Organization"   http://www.citizen.org/trade/wto

These two websites offer starkly different interpretations of the World Trade Organization and globalization. Look at them both and compare their perspectives.

A World Connected   http://www.aworldconnected.org

This website, a project of the Institute for Humane Studies at George Mason University, offers thoughtful analysis of the globalization process. It also provides articles and news about global events.

Social Movements and Social Change

United Students Against Sweatshops   http://www.studentsagainstsweatshops.org

The USAS website provides background information about the movement's fight for labor rights. It also provides information on how you can join other college students to fight for decent working conditions and compensation for workers.

Environmental Protection Agency's Green Chemistry Site   http://www.epa.gov/greenchemistry

This website offers background information on Green Chemistry and current efforts in the field.

Adbusters   http://www.adbusters.org/home

This website is the online home of "a global network of artists, activists, writers, pranksters, students, educators and entrepreneurs who want . . . to topple existing power structures and forge a major shift in the way we will live in the 21st century" through culture jamming.

Industrial Areas Foundation   http://www.industrialareasfoundation.org

This website describes this broad-based group of affiliated member-based organizations that uses the power of organized people to hold government and business leaders accountable to the needs of the public. The goal of the IAF is to "continue to practice what the Founding Fathers preached: the ongoing attempt to make life, liberty, and the pursuit of happiness everyday realities for more and more Americans."

INDEX